MPC INDEPENDENT TRAVELLERS

Provence, Languedoc & Côte d'Azur

John A

MPC

Jacket photographs:
Front: Palais des Papes on the banks of the Rhône at Avignon.
(*International Photobank*)
Back/Spine: A view of the hillside village of Gordes. (*International Photobank*)

Published by: Moorland Publishing Co Ltd,
Moor Farm Road West, Ashbourne, Derbyshire DE6 1HD, England

ISBN 0 86190 539 3

First published in English in 1990 by HarperCollins Publishers Ltd,
under the title *Collins Independent Travellers Guide: Provence, Languedoc & Côte d'Azur*
First revised edition 1994

British Library Cataloguing in Publication Data:
A catalogue record for this book is available from the British Library.

Typeset by Ace Filmsetting Ltd, Frome, Somerset.
Printed and bound in Great Britain by The Cromwell Press Ltd, Melksham, Wiltshire.

John Ardagh was born in Malawi, East Africa, in 1928, the son of a colonial civil servant. He was educated at Sherborne School and Worcester College, Oxford, where he took an honours degree in classics and philosophy. He joined *The Times* in 1953 and from 1955 to 1959 was a staff correspondent in Paris and Algeria. Returning to England, he worked in television news, then spent five years as a staff writer on the *Observer*.

In 1968 his first study of modern France, *The New Revolution*, was published. His later books about the country include *France Today*, *Rural France* and *Writers' France*. He has also published *A Tale of Five Cities* and *Germany and the Germans*.

Today John Ardagh is an author, freelance journalist and broadcaster. As well as being devoted to almost every aspect of French life, his other interests include the cinema and gastronomy. He lives in Kensington with his German wife and three Burmese cats; and has one grown-up son by a previous marriage.

Other Independent Travellers Guides include:

Brittany & Normandy by Rex Grizell
Greek Islands by Victor Walker
Morocco by Christine Osborne
Portugal by Martha de la Cal
Rome, Umbria & Tuscany by Derek Wilson
South-west France by Rex Grizell
Spain by Harry Debelius

Contents

Provence, Languedoc & the Côte d'Azur

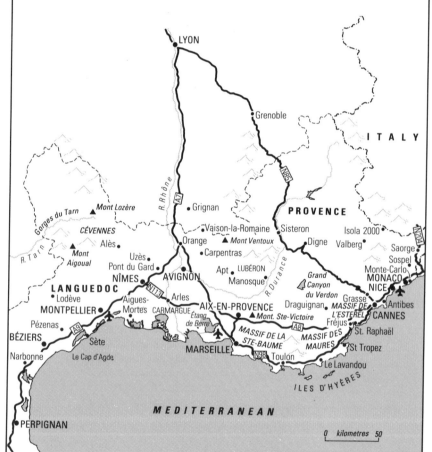

LYON

Grenoble

ITALY

R. Rhône

A7

PROVENCE

Gorges du Tarn   Mont Lozère   Grignan

CÉVENNES   Vaison-la-Romaine   Sisteron   Isola 2000

R. Tarn   Mont Aigoual   Alès   Orange   ▲ Mont Ventoux   Digne   Valberg   Saorge

Uzès   Carpentras   Sospel

Pont du Gard   Apt   LUBÉRON   Grand   Monte-Carlo

NÎMES   AVIGNON   Manosque   Canyon   MONACO

LANGUEDOC   Arles   du Verdon   Grasse   NICE

Lodève   Aigues-   AIX-EN-PROVENCE   Draguignan   MASSIF DE   Antibes

MONTPELLIER   Mortes   CARMARGUE   Mont. Ste-Victoire   L'ESTÉREL   CANNES

Pézenas   Étang   de Berre   Fréjus   St. Raphaël

BÉZIERS   A9   MASSIF DE LA   MASSIF DES   St Tropez

Sète   STE-BAUME   MAURES

Narbonne   Le Cap d'Agde   MARSEILLE   N98   Toulon   Le Lavandou

ILES D'HYÈRES

PERPIGNAN

MEDITERRANEAN

R. Durance

N85

N204

0   kilometres   50

Introduction

I have known the South of France for over forty years, since I first went on holiday in 1952 to Cassis. This was then just a quiet fishing village, still much as Dufy and Matisse had painted it a few decades earlier; few tourists or cars were around, our quayside hotel had no private bathrooms but it lavishly served splendid Provençal food at laughably low prices – and no one had yet heard of *nouvelle cuisine*. Today, huge blocks of holiday flats have been built on the hill behind the port, the snazzy new marble casino draws prosperous trippers by the thousand at weekends from nearby Marseille, and in summer the quayside is crammed with European visitors who would never dream of taking a room without a bath *en suite* and will cheerfully pay 200 francs for some *nouvelle* menu of tiny bits of fish and veg arranged daintily around the plate like Japanese flower patterns.

So has Provence been spoilt irretrievably, as some people assert? Not really. It's true that the glorious coast and some touristy places inland suffer cruelly from their over-popularity and especially from the excess of cars: many people who work there have grown irritable and blasé through too much hectic tourist pressure and are now almost Parisian in their brusqueness, not as relaxed and amenable as most other French provincials. But the wild and hilly hinterland, so vast, so beautiful, much of it still so empty, has not been spoilt: in fact, many of the old villages that were dying and depopulating have now been given a new lease of life by the arrival of artists and craftsmen, retired middle-class people, sophisticated summer residents, and other immigrants from northern towns. It's an artificial trend, maybe, and a blow to one's traditional view of quaint rural Provence, but better than letting these old places decay. And on the coast and in the towns, the concomitant of all the crowded bustle is an intense variety of exciting modern activity. Provence with its clear light, its bold sensuous colours, its strong tastes, still exerts a magic appeal; art and landscape, sunshine and wine, ancient history and up-to-date sophistication, blend into an alchemy that makes a heady impact on mind and senses alike. Provence, and Languedoc, remain my favourite parts of France – and of Europe.

These are the only French regions that are truly Mediterranean. And France is the only country of western Europe to belong both to its north and its south. If you drive down from northerly Paris into the Midi (as the French call the South of France), you will be made acutely aware of this: whether you come over the mountains or via the

Rhône Valley, you will at some point cross that mysterious cultural frontier that separates Europe's north from its south. Suddenly the light is clearer, the air drier, the sun beats stronger. The stone houses all have red-tiled roofs; lone cypresses stand by old barns; the air bears the scent of pines, or maybe a hint of wild thyme or lavender; hills terraced with vines and olives stretch to blue horizons. In village squares, under the plane trees, leather-jacketed youths parade with their *motos*, while old men play *boules* or drink *pastis* accompanied by black olives. And out in the fields the special white light of the Midi dazzles and reflects on the chalky hillsides, just as Cézanne and Van Gogh saw it.

The main subject of this book is Provence; but it deals also with Languedoc, which is fairly similar in history, architecture, life style, cuisine and landscape. These two regions in some ways contrast with the rest of France, but their own internal boundary, culturally at least, is not entirely fixed. In the Middle Ages, the old frontier between Languedoc and independent Provence was always the River Rhône; and today, likewise, that river marks the border between the modern political *région* of Provence-Côte-d'Azur and that of Languedoc-Roussillon. However, the Nîmes area, although in Languedoc, is in many ways more Provençal in character and tradition. And Languedoc as a whole is not a very clearly-defined entity. Historically it was the heartland of that area called Occitania where they spoke the *langue d'oc* ('yes' in the Occitan language was *oc*, as opposed to *oui* in northern French). The ancient province of Languedoc, ruled till the thirteenth century by the powerful Counts of Toulouse, used to cover a wide swathe of land from Rhône to Garonne, and its capital, Toulouse, lay on its western fringe, close to Gascony. Today – somewhat confusingly – the *région* of Languedoc–Roussillon comprises only eastern or 'lower' (*bas*) Languedoc along the coast, from Carcassone to Montpellier, plus Roussillon (French Catalonia) to the south, and some other areas to the east and north; Toulouse has been hived off as capital of the adjacent Midi-Pyrénées *région*. Blame all this on French administrative caprices, first Napoleonic, then post-1945. And blame me for the fact this book does not include Roussillon. However, it does cover the whole of Bas Languedoc, including the Gard (Nîmes area), also the Lozère department to the north (Cévennes and a part of the Massif Central) which is very different in character from the coastal belt.

For some twenty-five centuries Provence and Lower Languedoc have been a meeting-place of civilisations, each of which has left its powerful imprint, so that almost every bend in the road reveals something different and surprising – be it a Roman ruin, old abbey or modern art museum. In fact, I can think of no other part of Europe, nor perhaps of the world, that offers so dazzling a density and variety of interest in an area of comparable size. History here lies layer upon layer – the Roman legions, the troubadours and Cathars, the Popes at

Avignon, on until the heyday of the port of Marseille in the nineteenth century and the time when crowned heads came to gamble at Monte Carlo in the belle époque, today as much a part of history as Romans or Cathars. Provence and Languedoc remain a land of contrasts: remote medieval hill-villages; nuclear stations and oil refineries in the lower Rhône Valley; Cannes and Nice with their glittering promenades and traffic-jams; the modernistic architecture of La Grande-Motte.

The scenery, too, is extremely diverse. In Provence, the entire coast from Italy to Marseille is one of Europe's most beautiful, a succession of rocky headlands and wooded coves, covered with umbrella pines and sometimes with palms, cacti or bright flowers. Hills rise behind, in places steeply – notably along the mountainous eastern part of the Côte d'Azur, from Nice to Menton. Most of this coast today is heavily urbanised, a succession of resorts and camping sites. Yet nothing is more striking in Provence than the contrast between this busy coast and the silent hinterland, serene and unspoilt, that begins just a few kilometres inland. Just behind Nice and Menton are ancient hilltop villages, and just behind these rise the snowy Alps, good climbing and skiing country. The central hinterland of Provence is a series of limestone plateaus stretching westward from the Alps to reach their highest point at Mont Ventoux ('windy mount'). Here there are gorges, pine forests, rolling hills where sheep graze, and a wonderful sense of space and freedom. To the west is the Rhône Valley, leading down to the wide plain between Avignon and the Rhône delta. This is a very fertile land, covered with orchards and vineyards, olive groves and market gardens: but the plain is broken in places by ranges of barren limestone hills. In Languedoc, the coast is entirely flat, quite unlike that of Provence, with a long sandy beach backed by lagoons. Behind this coastal plain, covered with seemingly endless vineyards, the barren stubbly hills known as *garrigue* form the lower slopes of the wild Cévennes and Espinouse mountains, clothed with pines and chestnut trees. Beyond these ranges is the land of the *causses* – high limestone plateaus cut by the deep, spectacular gorges of the Tarn, Jonte and Doubie.

History

Provence

From earliest times, Provence has been a melting pot of different peoples. During the Bronze Age it was inhabited by primitive Ligurian tribes. Then around 600 BC the first Greek colonisers arrived, Phocaeans from Asia Minor: they founded Massilia (Marseille), and later Antipolis (Antibes) and Nikaia (Nice), as well as some places in the Rhône delta. At about the same time, large numbers of Celts were arriving from the north: they allied and intermarried with the Ligurians, and this union was to form the basis of Provence's population. Meanwhile Massilia under the Greeks became an important trading centre, in frequent conflict with the Celto-Ligurians, who helped Hannibal to cross the Alps in 218 BC.

The Roman period

The Greek Massiliots appealed to the Romans for help: so the Roman legions arrived, and in 125 BC under Sextius they inflicted a decisive defeat on the major Celto-Ligurian tribe, the Salyans, destroying their stronghold at Egremont, just north of Aix. This was an historic turning point, the beginning of the potent Roman colonisation of Provence that was to mark it so deeply. Sextius founded a thermal station, Aquae Sextiae, at what is now Aix. Then when Teuton invaders in turn emerged from the north, another Roman general, Marius, defeated them heavily in 102 BC in the hills east of Aix (he is still a local hero, which is why so many Provençaux have Marius as a first name). Next the Romans steadily consolidated the whole of coastal Provence and Languedoc as a *provincia* or permanent possession (hence the name Provence), calling it first Provincia Transalpina and then Gallia Narbonensis, after they had set up its capital at Narbonne to the west (see below). Meanwhile Julius Caesar conquered the rest of Gaul. In his civil war in 49 BC with Pompey, Massilia was unwise enough to side with the hapless Pompey and for this it was punished by losing its independence; the main Roman towns of the province now became Nîmes, Arles and Fréjus, as well as Narbonne. The ensuing Roman period was one of grandiose construction and intensive colonisation. The Pont du Gard viaduct was built in 19 BC; majestic arenas, theatres, baths and temples were erected at Nîmes, Arles and Orange, as well as Vaison, Glanum, Fréjus, Cimiez (Nice) and other places. Residential Roman towns such as Vaison grew luxurious by the standards of the time.

In the early fourth century the Emperor Constantine, converted to Christianity, chose Arles as his favourite town in the west and built a palace there. This marked the start of Arles' golden age as the leading town of Provence; in AD 400 it was made capital of the 'Three Gauls' (France, Spain and Britain) by the Emperor Honorius. Christianity now took root widely in Provence, as demonstrated by St Cassien's founding of the Abbey of St Victor in Marseille in 413. However, this was followed by the fall of the Roman Empire: Arles was seized by the Visigoths in 471, and soon Vandals, Franks, Ostrogoths and other Barbarian hordes were invading and devastating the area. On their heels in the seventh and eighth centuries came the Saracens (Moors) from North Africa, who made incessant destructive raids on the coastal towns. The Dark Ages, as in much of Europe, was a long period of confusion, decadence and shifting alliances, as one local ruler was ousted by another. The Merovingians, a Frankish dynasty, brought a certain brief stability, and so did the Frankish overlord Charlemagne, crowned Emperor of the West in Rome in 800. Later his empire was split between his three grandsons; Lothair, the eldest, received Provence and in 855 elevated it into a kingdom, with his son Charles as king.

The Middle Ages

After repeatedly changing hands, Provence in 1032 joined the Holy Roman Empire, and was now ruled by local counts who kept much autonomy. The area west of the Rhône was within the domain of the Counts of Toulouse; the lands east of the river belonged to the Counts of Provence who made Aix their capital in the twelfth century. The region had by now finally emerged from feudal anarchy and began to develop a new and fairly prosperous society: many fine Romanesque abbeys and churches were built, and towns such as Forcalquier emerged as powerful local entities. In the early thirteenth century, Provence was affected by the spread of the Cathar heresy (see below), but it did not suffer such severe retribution from Paris as Languedoc: while Languedoc was virtually annexed to the French crown, Provence remained autonomous. In 1307 the Papacy moved from Rome to Avignon and stayed there until 1377, protected and helped by the French kings and by the Counts of Provence.

The late fourteenth century was a difficult time for Provence, racked by famine and plague and by high-class brigandry, such as that of the terrible Viscount of Turenne, lord of Les Baux. Finally, the Dukes of Anjou took control of Provence, by marriage, and in 1434 René of Anjou, exiled King of Naples, became Count of Provence. 'Le bon roi René', as he is called, was a cultured and fun-loving man who also did much for the local economy. He is remembered affectionately to this day (see p. 215). However, his successor and nephew, Charles of Maine, then rashly bequeathed the countship to Louis XI of France – and so in 1481 Provence was at last incorporated into the French kingdom, thus ending its long and proud era of virtual independence. A Provençal parliament was set up in Aix, with some regional powers of autonomy: but in practice the French kings never allowed it to assert itself.

Wars of Religion

In the sixteenth century, after the Reformation had made its impact in France, the catastrophic Wars of Religion engulfed Provence. First an ancient Protestant sect in the Lubéron hills, the Vaudois, descendants of the Cathars, began to be persecuted, and hit back by attacking churches in the area. They were then brutally massacred on the orders of François I. But Protestantism continued to spread (see below), and from 1562 to 1598 there was continual fighting between Catholics and Huguenots. Richelieu finally repressed the Huguenots, destroying ramparts and castles at Les Baux, Uzès and other towns with Protestant sympathies. After this, Provence remained peaceful for a long time, and by the eighteenth century was quite prosperous. In 1746, in the War of the Austrian Succession, the Austro-Sardinian Army advanced as far as Antibes.

The Revolution and after

In May 1789 it was the Comte de Mirabeau's election as member for Aix of the French 'Etats-Généraux', a kind of parliament, that helped pave the way for the Revolution, for his radical ideas and oratorical powers had tremendous impact in Paris. In 1790 the Revolutionary Government stripped Provence of what autonomy it still retained and carved it up into three *départements* of the new centralised France: politically it no longer existed. However, it did play some incidental role during the Revolutionary and Napoleonic periods. In 1792, 500 volunteers from Marseille marched through Paris singing the newly-composed 'Battle Hymn of the Army of the Rhine', and so this song got the name of 'La Marseillaise'. In 1793, at the siege of Toulon, the young Napoleon Bonaparte first made his military reputation. And in March 1815, on his return from exile in Elba, he landed at Golfe-Juan near Cannes and then marched on Paris, along what is now called the Route Napoléon.

During the nineteenth century, although it had lost every trace of independence, Provence increased hugely in prosperity. The French conquest of North Africa, then the opening of the Suez Canal in 1869, both gave a mighty boost to the commerce of Marseille, which became one of the world's greatest ports. New industry developed in that area. However, the traditional world of agriculture, although benefiting in some ways from modernisation, also suffered from foreign competition and from the ravages of phylloxera in the vineyards. It was in the Nice/Cannes area, which the British dubbed the Riviera and the French came to know as the Côte d'Azur, that nineteenth-century changes were perhaps the greatest under the impact of a new phenomenon: tourism. In 1822 the growing British colony at Nice financed the building of the Promenade des Anglais, which was named after them; and in 1830 another Englishman, Lord Brougham, settled in

Cannes and initiated its rise as a resort. Then in the 1860s the Prince of Monaco built a casino at Monte Carlo. Soon the rich and titled of Europe were flocking to the Riviera every winter, to enjoy the mild sheltered climate as well as the gambling. The Nice area, which for centuries had belonged to the Italian House of Savoy, was integrated into France in 1860.

During the early part of the twentieth century, Provence's history was uneventful. In the Second World War, when France was divided in two after the German victory of June 1940, Provence and Languedoc both formed part of the Non-Occupied Zone ruled from Vichy. Then in November 1942, after the Allied occupation of North Africa, the Germans seized the entire Vichy Zone: but Vichy's fleet eluded them by scuttling itself at Toulon. By 1944 some active Resistance had developed in the hillier parts of Provence. On 15 August, the Allies landed on the coast around St Raphaël and St Tropez, and within two weeks they had liberated all of Provence.

Post-war Provence

After the end of the Second World War, Provençaux joined actively in the nationwide task of French renewal, and by the mid-1950s there were plenty of signs of new prosperity. As farming modernised, many thousands of people moved off the land to new jobs in the towns. For a time, this renewal was vitiated by the trauma of the Algerian War (1954-62) which especially affected Provence, directly across the sea from Algeria. Then, when Algeria won its independence in 1962, some 800,000 French *pieds noirs* (colonists) returned to France and many of them chose to settle in Provence, where the climate and life style were more familiar to them than those of the Paris area. At that time of fast economic growth, they easily found new jobs; and their entrepreneurial spirit brought new vigour and dynamism to the region.

In 1953 the Socialist leader Gaston Defferre was elected Mayor of Marseille, a post that he held until his death in 1986. He was the dominant figure in post-war Provençal politics. On a national level, he was also a prime architect of the decentralisation of the mid-1980s that has benefited all French regions. In 1964 the ninety French *départements* had been loosely grouped into twenty-one 'regions' for economic planning purposes, and six *départements* were put together to form the Provence-Côte-d'Azur region. In 1973 President Pompidou took this a timid stage further, by granting an indirectly elected council to each of the regions: but it had no real power. Then when the Socialists took office in 1981, President Mitterrand chose Defferre as Interior Minister, with the prime task of granting real devolution at last. Under his reforms, Provence, like the other regions, has since 1986 had a directly elected assembly with a proper budget and some degree of internal autonomy. But for the ageing Defferre, just two months before his death, it was ironic that these first elections threw up a Right-wing assembly, in a Provence where the Left had been dominant.

In the mid-1980s Provence also became the prime stronghold of the newly-emerged extreme-Right-wing Front National party, under Jean-Marie Le Pen: it won much of its local support from *pieds-noirs* with their racist dislike of Algerian Muslim immigrants. In Provence's regional elections of 1992, the Socialists' vote again fell, whereas the Front National made new advances, bringing its share of the vote up from 19 to 23 per cent, ahead of the Socialists. Le Pen himself was elected a councillor in Nice. In the new regional assembly, the FN had 34 seats, the older right-of-centre parties 43, the ecologists 6, the Socialists 30, the Communists 10. The centre-Right, under Jean-Claude Gaudin, held on to power, but had to rely on FN support.

Languedoc

The early history of Lower Languedoc was closely parallel to that of Provence. Here too the Celts arrived on the heels of the Greeks. The Greek impact was modest: their only major colony was Agathé (Agde), founded by Phocaeans in about 560 BC. Later the Romans moved in in large numbers, founding Narbonne in 118 BC, which in 27 BC Augustus made the capital of a vast province, Gallia Narbonensis, stretching from the Alps to the Pyrenees. Languedoc later fell victim in its turn to Visigoths and other barbarian invaders: the Saracens took Narbonne in 719, though in 759 it was recaptured by a Frankish leader, the charmingly named Pépin le Bref.

The Cathars   From the time of Charlemagne onwards, all Languedoc came under the sway of the powerful Counts of Toulouse, entirely independent of France. By the eleventh century it was developing a remarkable civilisation of its own, prosperous and cultivated, full of *joie de vivre*: its glories were the literature of the troubadours and their 'courts of love', fine Romanesque architecture and a thriving textile industry. Then in the twelfth century the Cathar heresy spread into Languedoc from the Balkans (it became known also as Albigensian, for Albi was one of its main centres). The true Cathars were anything but apostles of *joie de vivre*: they preached a doctrine of purity and asceticism, in reaction against the Church of Rome, which at that time was undeniably corrupt and widely despised. The Cathars were Manicheans, holding that the universe was made up of two contending forces of good and evil: all that was spiritual was good, but the world and the human race were in the hands of the powers of evil. Catharism was never a formal church but a loose network: it did, however, have its elite, the *parfaits* (perfect ones), ascetic celibates. Around them were the mass of ordinary lay believers who were tacitly permitted by the *parfaits* to lead normal earthy lives, so long as they turned to asceticism on their deathbeds (after all, not too hard). So Catharism, which to a modern reader may seem stunningly hypocritical, was an odd mixture of rigour and tolerance. This helps to explain the paradox of its flourishing in the heart of the sensuous Languedoc civilisation, alongside the romantic culture of the troubadours.

An infuriated Rome saw Catharism as a threat to its hegemony and a challenge to its own doctrines. In 1208 Pope Innocent III ordered a Crusade against the Cathars, finding willing allies in the Capetian rulers of France who gladly seized this chance to extend their domain into the Midi. After a papal envoy had been murdered at St Gilles, the Count of Toulouse was excommunicated and charged with conspiracy. Then, under the command of Simon de Montfort (whose son later played a key role in English history), a French army of 30,000 knights and infantry descended on the south – and the entire Languedoc rallied against them in the Cathars' defence. What had begun as a war of religion became mainly a colonial war. Moreover, the Languedoc ruling nobility had long been sympathetic to the Cathars: the Count's sister was herself a *parfaite*.

The Crusade was ferocious and merciless, as town after town fell to the invaders. At Béziers, 15,000 men, women and children were massacred. When one officer asked his superior how he could tell heretics from true Catholics he was told, 'Kill them all: God will then recognise His own.' Carcassonne too was besieged and captured; 180 *parfaits* were butchered at Minerve. Finally, in 1229, three years after Louis IX (Saint Louis) had assumed the throne in Paris, Count Raymond of Toulouse surrendered to him, and Lower Languedoc was formally annexed to France, soon followed by Toulouse itself: thus ended a glorious civilisation, which was now pulled back into the barbarism of much of the rest of Europe at that time. Little pockets of Cathars continued to hold out in the mountain fortresses to the south, and it was not until 1244 that the citadel of Montségur eventually yielded and 200 *parfaits* there were burned alive. After this, outward Cathar resistance ended, but its spirit and practice went on underground, like dissent in Stalinist Russia. As late as 1318, it was still so much alive in some Pyrenean villages that the Bishop of Pamiers staged an Inquisition to try to wipe it out. The verbatim transcript of his enquiries in one upland village, Montaillou, has survived to this day, and in 1978 the great social historian Emmanuel Le Roy Ladurie edited and reworked them into a fascinating and best-selling account of medieval rural life (both Montségur and Montaillou are just outside the area covered by this book).

Wars of Religion During the Middle Ages, some of Languedoc was under Spanish feudal domination: for example, from 1204 to 1349 Montpellier was a possession of the Kings of Aragon and Majorca. The English too were on the horizon, during the Hundred Years' War (1337-1453): but they never got closer to Languedoc than the Rouergue, north of Albi. In 1348 as much as a third of the population was killed by the Black Death. Then followed a long period of relative calm – until 1560, with the outbreak of the Wars of Religion, which continued on-and-off in eastern Languedoc for well over a century.

After the Reformation, Calvinism spread across Languedoc more strongly than in any other part of France, especially in the area around Nîmes and in the Cévennes behind it: by 1560 over half the population was Huguenot (as the French called the Calvinists). Sporadic fighting then broke out between Protestants and Catholics; and it continued until the Edict of Nantes (1598), whereby Henry IV granted religious tolerance to the Huguenots and allowed them eighteen 'places of safety' in the region. However, this truce eventually broke down, and after 1661 Louis XIV began systematic persecution of the 'heretics': dragoons were sent to try to convert them by force. In 1685 the king went so far as to revoke the Edict of Nantes, so that Calvinism was now outlawed. This led to a mass exodus from France of some 400,000 Huguenots, many of whom settled in Britain and Germany; and the commerce, industry, farming and intellectual life of Languedoc were left the poorer.

The king's dragoons now intensified their campaign against the remaining Protestants, many of whom fled for refuge into the wild Cévennes interior, which they called *'le désert'* (see p. 268). Here they continued to practise their faith in secret. The rebels acquired the nickname of *'Camisards'* from the white blouses they wore, *camiso* being an Occitan word for shirt. In 1702, in the Cévenol village of Pont-de-Montvert, some of them accidentally killed the Abbé du Chayla, the royal agent in charge of operations against them – and this marked the signal for a general uprising, led by the *Camisards'* hero, 'Rolland'. Their revolt was bloodily suppressed: and today the Protestants' sufferings are still honoured in the Cévennes, just as the martyrdom of the Cathars is honoured in the area further west. The persecutions continued until 1787, when Louis XVI finally granted freedom of worship to Protestants – a last noble act from a doomed regime.

Languedoc in modern times

After the Revolution, Languedoc lost its last shreds of regional autonomy and was split up into *départements*, like Provence. Little was heard of it during the nineteenth century, and it settled down quietly to the making of cheap table wine. However, the growers were badly hit by the phylloxera epidemic of the 1870s, and in 1907 a serious drop in wine prices provoked one of the sharpest of the violent revolts by *vignerons* that have characterised Languedoc in this century – some 500,000 people demonstrated at Montpellier.

In 1943 to 1944, the Aigoual massif of the Cévennes was an important centre of the Resistance. Then after the war, in the 1950s, when the great economic renewal of the French provinces gathered steam, Languedoc seemed ill-placed to share in this brave new world: it had virtually no industry, its economy was far too dependent on the growing of inferior wine, and its local leaders had little spirit of enterprise. So the Government decided to impose on this region some major schemes that might shake it out of its stupor. It dug a wide irrigation canal from the Rhône westwards, with the aim of inducing the *vignerons* to uproot their vines and switch to more useful produce. In the 1960s it began to build a chain of eight massive modernistic tourist resorts, with a planned total of 280,000 beds, along the coast from the Rhône delta to the Pyrenees.

The Paris technocrats implanted these projects with typical arrogance, hardly bothering to consult; and the local people, instead of being grateful for the help, reacted angrily at what they saw as Parisian 'neo-colonialism'. After all, tribal memories still ran deep in a region that had never forgiven Paris for the Cathar massacres and the annexation that followed. So the mass of little local vinegrowers, instead of welcoming the canal, at first rioted against it. Whenever a bumper harvest sent wine prices tumbling, they rioted again. And especially they rioted against the mass imports of Italian wine, after the coming of the EEC (now EU). Slowly, however, over the years, the vinegrowers have been persuaded to improve the quality of their wines, so as to reduce the problem of annual surpluses of unsaleable plonk: the worst vines have now been uprooted and better ones planted. The growers remain very fearful of Spanish competition within the EEC free market, but basically they accept that they have no choice but to adapt and to modernise. The new tourist resorts are now accepted, too, for the jobs that they bring. And a new and more realistic generation of Languedoc leaders has arisen.

In the 1960s and 1970s, when the government in Paris was Right-wing, Languedoc voted Left: four of the main towns had Communist mayors and some were Socialist. This seemed a typical expression of the region's atavistic hostility to Paris, stronger than in any other part of France. However, today matters have changed. Under the Defferre reforms, the region in 1986 was able at last to elect its own assembly, with real powers, and this produced a Centre-Right majority (although the mayor of Montpellier is Socialist). In fact, though they feud and bicker, Left and Right have always tended to get on quite cosily in Languedoc, in a Peppone/Don Camillo sort of way: insults are hurled flamboyantly in public, but there's also a certain mateyness *à l'italienne* between Languedociens of all colours. After all, this is the Midi, where ideology counts for less than human contact.

The essential issue is not one of Left v. Right, but of Languedoc v. Paris. At last, today, Languedoc is beginning to feel that it can take its destiny in its own hands. New dynamic, forward-looking local leaders have emerged, such as the mayors of Nîmes and Montpellier (see pp. 236 and 245); modern industry is arriving; the old stupor *has* been thrown off! And so the 750-year old complex about being 'colonised' by Paris is at last on the wane.

Architecture

Provence and Languedoc are treasure troves of many different styles from different periods, including the ultra-modern. The buildings, very often made of local limestone, harmonise with the landscape as well as with each other. These regions contain some of Europe's finest Roman monuments, such as the Pont du Gard and the theatre at Orange; also some of the grandest medieval ones, such as the Papal Palace at Avignon and the fortress of Carcassonne.

Roman (first century BC to third AD)

Western Provence and the Nîmes area contain the best-preserved range of Roman relics outside Italy. Not only are there grandiose buildings such as the arenas at Arles and Nîmes and the Pont du Gard, but also works that show the Romans capable of delicacy – the carvings on the triumphal arches at Orange and St Rémy, and the elegant proportions of the Maison Carrée at Nîmes. Roman villas and other domestic architecture can be studied at Vaison-la-Romaine.

Merovingian (fifth to eighth centuries)

Not much from the Merovingian period has survived, save the curious octagonal baptistries at Aix, Fréjus, Riez and Venasque. Merovingian art was a mixture of Roman Classical and Germanic-Frankish styles. The Merovingian kings helped to consolidate Christianity in France.

Romanesque (eleventh to twelfth centuries)

Provence in the twelfth century produced a golden age of Romanesque which is quite distinct from that of Normandy and can be seen at its purest in the Cistercian abbeys of Fontfroide, Sénanque and Thoronet. The carvings and the fine limestone masonry show the influence of Roman antiquity, while the churches are mostly in the form of a cross, with a semi-circular apse at the end of a broad nave, often without side-aisles. The tall pillars and barrel vaulting give a sense of spaciousness, but the smallness of the windows adds to the aura of austerity. West fronts can be richly sculpted; for example, St Sauveur at Aix and St Trophîme at Arles. Cloisters at Arles, Montmajour and St Rémy have fine carved capitals.

Gothic

The Gothic style stemmed from northern France and is marked by a more elaborate decoration and the use of ribbed vaulting, pointed arches and flying buttresses. These new techniques enabled space to be freed for larger windows (many with stained glass) and the thickness of the walls to be reduced. This produces a lighter, soaring, vertical effect, contrasting with the horizontal lines of Romanesque. Apart from the cloisters at Fréjus, the basilica at St Maximin, Béziers cathedral, and the newer part of Avignon's Papal Palace, the Gothic style is poorly represented in the south-east. Its final phase, exuberant and ornate, called 'Flamboyant Gothic' because of its flame-shaped columns and window tracery, can be seen in the facades of St Sauveur at Aix and St Siffrein at Carpentras.

Fortified architecture

Medieval kings and feudal lords built defensive castles to live in, often on hilltops (for example, Les Baux, Sisteron), but sometimes on the plain (for example, Tarascon). Such castles have a keep (*donjon*), turreted battlements (maybe with openings for dropping missiles or molten lead on attackers), and perhaps a moat if they are on a plain. Some early churches, too, have battlements and a fortified appearance (for example, at Les Stes-Maries, and St Victor at Marseille), for they were built partly as a refuge against Saracen and other marauders. The best examples of a medieval walled city are Aigues-Mortes and Carcassonne. The invention of heavy cannons in the fifteenth century then made this kind of defence obsolete; but in the seventeenth century Louis XIV's military architect, Vauban, built forts of a far more impregnable kind – such as those that ring Toulon.

Renaissance and Classical

Classical columns, pediments and balustrades marked the Renaissance style, which was much influenced by the Italian Renaissance. Despite the closeness of Italy, this style never caught on widely in Provence, but its influence can be observed in some facades, courtyards and stairways – in Pézenas and the old part of Nîmes, and in the ducal palace at Uzès. Then in the seventeenth and eighteenth centuries came Classicism, which left a more powerful mark, seen in the mansions in the heart of Aix, Avignon and Montpellier.

The nineteenth century

This opulent era, with its dubious taste, produced grandiose imitations of earlier styles – for example, in Marseille, the new cathedral and the basilica of Notre-Dame-de-la-Garde (both neo-Byzantine), and the Palais de Longchamp (neo-Baroque). On the Côte d'Azur, the growth of upper-class tourism in the decades before 1914 spawned such dazzling neo-Baroque marvels as the casino and Hôtel de Paris in Monte Carlo.

The post-war era

Le Corbusier designed one key building in Provence, the Unité d'Habitation in Marseille (1952), a big block of flats on supports: it had some influence at the time, but now looks dated. His ideas helped to generate the 'neo-gigantism' in vogue in France in the 1960s and early 1970s: witness the vast curling blocks of the Marina Baie-des-Anges near Antibes and, rather more attractive, the ziggurats of La Grande-Motte, near Montpellier. By contrast, some other recent tourist developments – notably Port-Grimaud, and Port-Galère on the Esterel coast – have cleverly used a pastiche vernacular style that blends with the landscape. J. L. Sert's design for the Fondation Maeght museum at St Paul-de-Vence shows an equal sense of harmony. But in the late 1980s his fellow Spaniard, Ricardo Bofill, returned to a new kind of monumentalism with his Antigone housing complex at Montpellier.

Artists and writers

Provence has produced a quantity of notable artists and writers through the centuries – Fragonard and Cézanne, Mistral and Giono, to name but a few. Avignon and Nice in early times were important centres of religious painting; and ever since Mistral's day, literature with a regional flavour has flourished more vigorously here (witness Daudet and Pagnol) than in any other part of France. Given the region's strong personality and traditions, this is not surprising. Nor is it strange that so many outsiders should have been drawn to live and work in Provence, attracted by its bold light and vivid colours, or by the people, climate and life style. Van Gogh came to Western Provence, and so more recently has Lawrence Durrell. However, the prime venue in this century has been the Côte d'Azur. The appeal that it has held for such an array of great painters – Renoir, Picasso, Matisse and Chagall, among many others – has left the coast with a marvellous heritage of modern art in its museums. Many writers have come also, often enticed by the glamour of the Riviera in what Scott Fitzgerald called 'the lost caviare days'. Over in the Cévennes, Stevenson hiked with a donkey in an utterly different spirit.

Art: the schools of Nice and Avignon

Two schools of religious painting were influenced by the Italian Renaissance. A school of 'primitives' flourished at Nice in the late fifteenth century, led by Louis Bréa, his brother and nephew. Their prolific works, mostly painted altarpieces, can be seen in the village churches of the Nice hinterland: perhaps the best is at Lucéram. In the same period, over at Avignon, Enguerrand Charenton (or Quarton) was producing such masterworks as his 'Coronation of the Virgin' (now at Villeneuve), while Nicolas Froment was court painter to 'King' René at Aix (his superb 'Burning Bush' is in the cathedral). These two painters helped to found the so-called Avignon School, which persisted in various forms until the nineteenth century. Its leaders in the seventeenth century were the Parrocel family and Nicolas Mignard, whose works now adorn many local churches.

In that century, artists began to turn also to secular subjects. For example, Greek classical themes were chosen by Pierre Puget of Marseille, Provence's greatest sculptor, who is often compared to Bernini: some of his works can be seen in Marseille and Toulon, though the best are in Paris and Italy. The Van Loos, a Dutch family of the eighteenth century who worked in Nice and Aix, produced some vivid portraits and *genre* paintings: some of the best are in the Musée Cheret at Nice. Provence's greatest eighteenth-century artist, Pierre Fragonard, was born at Grasse, but then moved to Paris and Italy, where he devoted himself to sensuous and frivolous subjects, well in tune with his age. The region contains few of his works.

From Impressionism to Picasso

The Impressionists, who revolutionised art in the 1870s, were always much concerned with the effects of light – and under the sun of the South they found an ideal clarity and luminosity. Paul Cézanne, initially an Impressionist though later diverging both in outlook and technique, was born in 1839 at Aix where he spent many of his later years, putting on to canvas the scenery that he loved – red-roofed farmhouses, lone cypresses, chalky hills. Fascinated by colour and tone, he painted repeatedly in different lights the stern pyramid of Mont Ste-Victoire. Van Gogh, too, found a fierce inspiration in the sun, sky and landscape around Arles and St-Rémy where, descending into madness, he spent his final years, 1888 to 1890. None of his work is in local museums; nor, more curiously, is there much by Cézanne either.

Towards the end of the century painters began to frequent the coast. In 1892 Paul Signac, a neo-Impressionist, settled in then little-known St Tropez and so set a trend: Matisse, Bonnard and others would pass the summer in this fishing village, whose museum now houses many of their vivid seascapes and landscapes. Nearer to Nice, at Cagnes-sur-Mer, Auguste Renoir spent his final years, painting exuberantly to the end, though crippled by arthritis. Then after 1918 the Côte became a veritable artists' colony. Matisse lived at Cimiez (Nice) and at Vence from 1917 until his death in 1954, painting the still-life subjects and odalisques that are among his most important work. Picasso did not come until 1945, but his short period at Antibes from 1946 to 1947 was one of the most fertile of his long career, and such works as 'La Joie de Vivre' were manifestly inspired by Provence. His move later to the nearby pottery town of Vallauris gave a fresh outlet to his many-sided genius, and much of his later life was devoted to ceramics.

Marc Chagall, too, moved to the Côte only late in life, but there found a new inspiration, evident from the sensuous southern colours of his 'Biblical Message', painted at Vence when he was over seventy, and now in his museum at Nice. Vlaminck, Braque and Dufy (he lived in Nice) are others who caught the colour and vivacity of the Côte – as did Jean Cocteau, whose romantic fascination with the life of local fisherfolk can be observed in his murals at Villefranche and Menton. Léger also lived and worked in Provence (his museum is at Biot), and so does Vasarély (unusual 'didactic' museums at Aix and Gordes): but the region's influence on them has not been so direct.

Provence's native writers

The earliest known writers of the region were the troubadours – lyric poets of the twelfth and thirteenth centuries who wrote and sang in Occitan. They were active all over southern France at the time, in Gascony and Languedoc more than in Provence where their leading centre was the feudal castle of Les Baux. These troubadours were court poets and musicians attached to noble families, and their theme was love – courtly and usually chaste love for ladies who were often their employers' wives. After their era ended, Provence then produced no really important writers, save for the physician and astrologer Nostradamus in the sixteenth century.

It was not until the 1850s that the literary life of the region was revitalised: in 1854 a group of writers in the Avignon area founded a movement that they called the Félibrige, after a Provençal folk tale. They were not nationalists in any political sense, but they resented the oppression of Provençal culture and tradition by the new centralised France, and so they embarked on a crusade to revive local interest in the region's history, customs and spirit – and above all in its language, which Paris had forbidden to be taught in schools. Their driving force was a young poet, then only twenty-four: Frédéric Mistral. Their success in promoting the Provençal language was only slight, but they did in a wider sense stimulate the region's culture and sense of identity. They caused some stir in French literary circles, for Mistral was a poet of undoubted genius. His *Mirèio* (*Mireille* in French), the tale of a girl's tragic love affair set on the Crau plain near the Camargue, is the best known of his epic poems of Provençal rural life, whose glories he sang so passionately. As he wrote only in Provençal, it is not easy to assess his true literary stature. But as a man he was handsome, romantic, full-blooded and charismatic, able to fire visitors with his own love for the land where he spent all his life (in the village of Maillane, south of Avignon). He won the Nobel Prize for Literature in 1904. In his lifetime a cult grew up around him, which remains alive today (although many people see him as a somewhat reactionary, sentimental figure).

While few of them also wrote in Provençal, many later writers were influenced by Mistral – and none more so than Alphonse Daudet. Born in Nîmes, he spent his adult life mainly in Paris, but he drew much inspiration from western Provence, as can be seen from his satirical trilogy *Tartarin de Tarascon*, and from *Lettres de mon Moulin*, sentimental sketches of rural life that centre on an old windmill at Fontvieille, near Arles. Closer to our own time, Marcel Pagnol made his name with the *Marius* trilogy of plays set in Marseille, and then made films and wrote stories, notably *Jean de Florette* and *Manon des Sources*, about the rural life of the city's hinterland, around Aubagne where he was born. More gifted as film-maker than as novelist, he nonetheless had a keen feeling for the peasant *mores* of his region. His contemporary Jean Giono, a more serious and philosophical writer, and one of the great French novelists of this century, spent all his life in the Manosque area where he was born, and there he set his lyrical studies of peasants living in close rapport with nature. Henri Bosco, from Avignon, wrote in a somewhat similar vein about the Durance Valley and the Lubéron hills where he lived. And the surrealist poet René Char expressed his feelings for the area around his home town of l'Isle-sur-la-Sorgue, also near Avignon.

Immigrant writers

The first of the many famous non-Provençal writers influenced by the region was the Italian poet Petrarch. As a child he moved with his parents in 1312 to the Papal court at Avignon: he came to hate that city and its corrupt court, where he worked, but he was inspired by the nearby Fontaine de Vaucluse where he later spent sixteen years, as well as by his chaste passion for Laura, an Avignonnaise. In our own time, Avignon has been extolled vividly (in his novel *Monsieur or the Prince of Darkness*) by Lawrence Durrell, who now lives at Sommières in the Gard.

Above all it is the Côte d'Azur that has lured outsiders. Mérimée and Maupassant came often to Cannes, Colette lived for a while at St Tropez, Sagan set *Bonjour Tristesse* on the Esterel coast, and J. M. G. Le Clézio today lives in Nice. But it is foreigners more than the French who have made the Côte their own, starting back in the eighteenth century when Tobias Smollett spent some months in Nice and wrote about it luridly. Then, when the Riviera became fashionable, it began to attract writers of all nations (even Nietzsche stayed often in Nice); and the giddy expatriate circles of Cannes, Nice and 'Monte' became settings for a spate of novels both good (for example, Michael Arlen's *The Green Hat*) and bad. Katherine Mansfield lived for a short while at Menton, Somerset Maugham a long time at Cap Ferrat, and both set some of their best stories in the area. In the 1920s, Scott Fitzgerald in *Tender is the Night* described the antics of the American socialite set on Cap d'Antibes, and in the 1930s Cyril Connolly stayed at Haut-de-Cagnes and there set his sardonic novel *The Rock Pool*. Today, Anthony Burgess lives in Monte Carlo and Graham Greene in Antibes, where in *J'Accuse* he has inveighed against corruption in Nice.

Languedoc and Cévennes

The foremost poet from Languedoc is Paul Valéry, who lies buried in his home town of Sète, in the cemetery by the sea that inspired one of his best poems. André Gide had Protestant family links with the Uzès area. The Huguenot milieu of the Cévennes has been sympathetically described by the Protestant novelist André Chamson, and more critically by the agnostic Jean Carrière, both of them from Nîmes. Lastly, a Protestant from Scotland memorably strode over the Cévennes with a donkey in 1878 – and got on rather well with the Catholic monks who sheltered him.

Modern Life and Old Traditions

The Breton philosopher Ernest Renan wrote in 1872: 'The similarity between England and Northern France appears increasingly clear to me every day. Our foolishness comes from the south, and if France had not drawn Languedoc and Provence into her sphere of activity, we would be a serious, active, Protestant and parliamentary people.'

That may be an extreme view: surely these two regions have contributed hugely to French civilisation? And yet, more than a century after Renan's day, there are still huge differences between northern and southern France. This may be in some ways a very centralised country, yet the regions each retain a strong individuality – and few of them more than Provence and Languedoc.

It is true that modern life has taken its toll of the old folk traditions: except at special festivals, and then somewhat artificially, people no longer wear the old local costumes or dance the *farandole* to the tune of a *galoubet*. And the old Provençal and Occitan languages have almost everywhere died out from local speech. However, the houses with their red-tiled roofs are totally different from those of the North. The twangy accent of the South endures, and with it the use of many local words. The cuisine, too, remains distinct, as do many customs and sports – you will not find bullfights in the North as you still do around Nîmes and Beziers, and no Alsatian would exchange his *Mirabelle* liqueur for the *pastis* of Provence.

Likewise, the essential temperament of these Mediterranean peoples has been little affected by the impact of television, or computers, or jet travel. They remain less reserved than northerners, more instinctive and in some ways more emotional. A Provençal has the quality called *bon enfant*, the easy-going ability to make rapid human contact; he enjoys scheming and feuding, yet he takes it all with a pinch of salt. He may fly into a sudden temper, but not with malice, and moments later he will offer to stand you a drink, with his arm round your shoulder. He works hard (some Languedociens may tend to be lazy, but Provençaux are less so), yet he is not obsessed with punctuality, and like so many French he is clever at the so-called *Système D*, the twisting or circumventing of bureaucratic rules. These traits may not be as pronounced as in Pagnol's day, but they still apply to many country people, and to the earthily humorous Marseillais. It is true that in the smarter resorts of the Côte d'Azur there is now such an influx of newcomers from the North that the local temperament is more varied. But a real Niçois is still typically Mediterranean. The people of the Midi are usually stockily built, dark-haired, sometimes swarthy. Among city folk, their sharp nasal accent (*byeng* for *bien*) tends to be harsh, but is more mellifluous among country people. In the old days their main language was Occitan or its variant, Provençal, the common tongue of the Midi in the Middle Ages. From the sixteenth century the Government in Paris began to impose the French language, but this made so little headway that Racine, visiting in the 1660s, found he could not understand what the locals were saying. By the 1850s, however, Provençal was no longer in daily use in the towns. Efforts to revive it were made by the Mistral and his Félibrige (see p. 22), but outside literary circles they made little impact.

Today, Government curbs on these languages have been removed. They used to be banned in schools, but are now options for the *bac*, and can be studied at some universities. A few books are published in them, and among local intellectuals there is quite a new vogue for their study. However, the general public responds very little. People find it far more practical to speak French, and more useful to learn Modern European languages such as English, which is compulsory in all schools. So the old languages are dying out in daily use, even in the villages, and their maintenance has become rather artificial, as with Latin. It is a pity, for you have only to read Mistral's poems aloud to realise how beautiful and melodious they are.

Rural architecture

Tradition here survives better. The farmsteads and villas that dot the countryside usually have stone walls and gently sloping roofs of terracotta tiles. Very often their north walls are blind, as a defence against the Mistral, the icy north wind that spasmodically sweeps through Provence in winter. The front doors and windows are on the south side; and for protection against summer heat these too can be quite small, making the interiors cool and dark, in contrast to the dazzle outside. A large farmhouse or mansion is known as a *mas* (from the same Latin root as *maison*); a smaller one is a *bastide*. The post-war tourist and residential boom has thrown up a mass of new rural building, but happily – with some sorry exceptions – this has disfigured the landscape less than it might, partly due to strict regulations whereby all building or alterations must conform to traditional styles: so new villas, too, have pale stone walls and red tiled roofs. But in some places they are in all styles, or huge modern buildings scar the hillsides. Often this is because some local mayors are lax in interpreting the rules, and permit this growth for the money it brings into their communes.

Social revolution in the hill villages

The kind of revolutiuon that took place on the Côte d'Azur a century or so ago is now, in a different way, hitting the hill villages of the interior. One of the most distinctive features of the Provençal landscape, and to an extent of Languedoc's too, is the hundreds of old fortified villages that are set on hilltops or terraced along mountainsides. Some lie very close to the big towns: Peillon, for instance, is within 20 kilometres of Nice, but seems a world away. Some are spectacularly sited, such as Eze, perched above the Côte d'Azur, or Saorge which clings to a cliff north of Menton, its houses rising one above the other. Most villages are made of local stone, so that some of them, such as Les Baux and Gordes, seem to merge into the rocks on which they have been built. Often they nestle beneath some half-ruined château or are girt by the remains of ancient ramparts. And their alleys are sometimes so narrow and steep that cars cannot enter. Inside is a labyrinth of vaulted archways and winding stone steps, of little squares and shady arcades where fountains plash.

They are all charming. Yet today not all of these places are lively communities of authentic local villagers. Some are derelict, silent, falling into ruin. Others are overlaid with a new chic, their alleys lined with boutiques and tourist bistros, their stone façades expensively restored – and the strollers in their alleys look less like local peasants than Parisians, Londoners or Hamburgers, which is probably what they are. In a word, dramatic change has recently hit the Provençal hill village, causing a kind of death, and a kind of rebirth.

The villages were built on high ground for security, first against Saracen pirates, then against the marauders of the Middle Ages. The peasants would go out by day to till their fields, then sleep within the ramparts. With the coming of settled conditions in the nineteenth century, many villagers began to live down in the valleys. More recently, the modernisation of farming has produced a mass exodus from the rural areas, as in the rest of France. As a result, many of the more remote villages have become partly or totally abandoned. Yet, at the same time, very different trends have been giving some of them a new lease of life. A few, such as Eze, Les Baux and St-Paul-de-Vence, have become major tourist centres, crammed with cafés and souvenir shops. Alleys, formerly of rough cobbles, have been neatly paved; old stone façades are embellished with fancy ironwork and tidy flowerpots. Hundreds of other villages – and this is the major trend – have been engulfed by the post-war vogue for buying country homesteads and converting them into weekend, summer or retirement homes. Middle-class Parisians and other city dwellers, as well as Britons,

Germans, Dutch and others, all eager for a place in the sun, have acquired hundreds of thousands of such places in Provence, so that land and house prices have rocketed. Some of these restored villages are now quite smart, haunts of the well-to-do intelligentsia – notably, places near the coast such as Mougins, Grimaud and Bormes-les-Mimosa, and others up in the hinterland east of Avignon, such as Gordes and the villages of the Lubéron hills, today very trendy. This artificial renaissance is surely better than letting the villages die. But it can lead to social tensions.

Take Bargemon, for example, a biggish village in the Var, 50 kilometres inland. Before 1914 it was a busy centre, with 3,000 people and small factories making shoes and pasta. Then the factories closed, killed by modern competition, the farm workers drifted away too in the 1950s, and by 1970 the population was down to 850. Since then it has risen again to 1,140, due to the influx of retired well-to-do people, and in summer it is much higher still; one alleyway is dubbed 'promenade des Anglais' because of the number of houses owned by English families. As elsewhere, the influx has revived local commerce: some food shops which had closed have reopened, and there is even a branch of Lloyd's insurance. So a former peasant/artisan economy is moving towards the suburban or resort model, full of service industries. However, the boom is a fragile one, for most of the newcomers are there only in summer, and in winter the shops can do little trade. And social integration is far from complete. Of the two cafés in the main square, one remains the preserve of the locals, mostly old men playing cards, while the other is used by the neo-residents and by tourists. In another village, an antique dealer from Paris told me that although he was on superficially friendly terms with the villagers, he had failed after ten years to enter into their social life and was still looked on as an outsider. All this is not very surprising. The Provençaux remain wary of those known in their *patois* as *'les estrangers'* (a term that includes all non-Provençaux) and there are many who feel that the influx has spoilt the true character of village life. Or they resent the new private swimming pools that use up the water so badly needed by the farms in high summer.

Over at Montpellier, I was given further insights by a university professor who for the past twenty years has lived in a tiny village 20 kilometres north of the city: 'The mutation here has been total. This place used to be a world apart, in the middle of nowhere: now, on the fringe of the city's commuter belt, it's been dragged into the modern world. It used to be a small enclosed society, bitchily gossipy yet protective, truly caring to its members. Now *"les estrangers"* (city commuters and weekenders) have moved in, estates of modern villas have been built, the farm population has dropped by two-thirds. Local people used to spend the warm evenings sitting outside their houses in the narrow streets, chatting: but television has killed that kind of social life. Farmers used to get up at 5 a.m. to look after the horses: now they have just cars and tractors. And they have bought machines for the grape-harvest, for it's cheaper than hiring pickers. So the old social ritual of the grape-harvest, which used to be a two-week fête, is now more like an impersonal factory procedure.'

Festivals and traditions

Inevitably, many of the old folk traditions have been disappearing from daily life – and how Mistral's ghost must grieve! No longer, except at special fêtes, do women wear the lovely old Provençal costumes and head-dresses. At a leading hotel in Arles, the waitresses until recently were expected to dress up in them daily, to please the tourists: but the process of doing the coiffure to put on the famous Arlesian bonnet takes over an hour, and the women no longer want to do it.

However, as in many other parts of France such as Brittany, since the 1960s efforts have been made locally to revive the old traditions, not for daily life but for festivals and special events. In the Var department alone there are now thirty-two federated folk groups, which perform at local fêtes or compete against each other at big galas. In most cases, the impetus for this revival has come less from the old villagers than from students, teachers and other intellectuals, or from the new non-Provençal residents. So it's less a spontaneous movement than a self-consciously 'cultural' one, but far better than letting the old traditions die. The groups have learned to dance the old Provençal *farandole*, and their musicians have taught themselves to play the *tambourin* (a narrow drum) and the *galoubet* (a three-holed flute). A few artisans still make these old instruments. For the fêtes, the old embroidered folk-costumes are taken out of mothballs; in some villages, new ones are again being made, for use by the groups or for sale to tourists.

Every village has its annual traditional fête, held often to mark some saint's day. Usually it's a two- or three-day affair, prepared weeks ahead. It will include contests and games of various kinds, and a big open-air communal feast known as an *aïoli* after its main dish (see p. 49). There may well be an afternoon folk-group display, but the music for the nightly dancing is far more likely to come from a modern rock band. The fête is still the high point of the village year, but it seldom excites the inhabitants as it used to when they had few other forms of distraction: the young now have cars and go to discos each weekend, so they tend to feel blasé about the fête, which attracts tourists as much as locals.

However, a few of these fêtes contain elaborate pageantry, dating back centuries, often religious in origin – and this is dutifully kept up, by an age that has largely lost touch with the original meaning. Among the best known are the fête of the Tarasque at Tarascon, fifteenth-century in origin, where a green papier-mâché monster is paraded round the town; the pageants at Roquebrune, also fifteenth-century, where villagers enact the Passion of Christ; the two *bravades* at St Tropez, where the bust of a local saint is escorted round the town by locals in eighteenth-century military uniform; the curious Fête de St Marcel at Barjols where people dance in the church and a cow is ritually sacrificed; the Nice carnival and flower battles (not exactly village affairs); and the gipsy pilgrimage in May at Les-Saintes-Maries in the Camargue. Over in Languedoc, fêtes can be very rumbustious. At Cournonterral, near Montpellier, men are rolled in pools of wine-lees at harvest time; in some villages, people are thrown into heaps of mud, or pelted with flour and eggs; or, as in the Basque country, wild bulls are let loose in the streets and people run for their lives. And in the Nîmes and Arles areas, festivals include bullfights and bull races (see p. 54). In many places there are also tournaments of *boules* (see p. 56), the local version of bowls that is played daily in village squares.

Cribs and santons

Boules is a rare example of a local daily tradition that survives strongly. So, you could say, is the drinking of *pastis* (see p. 53). And so, even in an age when religious practice has declined, is the Christmas crib and the making of *santons* for it. These clay costumed figurines, usually some 50 cm high, were invented in Marseille in the late eighteenth century. Initially they represented just the figures of the Nativity story, but the range was soon widened to include stock Provençal types such as the *gendarme*, the drunkard and the Camargue cowboy. Many families still have their *santon* collection, either for a crib at Christmas in the salon or purely as secular ornaments; and *santons* today are still made by craftsmen, for sale to local people as well as tourists. Marseille has a big *santon* fair in December. Many churches have prettily-lit cribs full of *santons* in the Christmas period. And there are fascinating historical displays of cribs and *santons* in the folk museums of Aix, Arles, Marseille and Monaco. What's more, in a few villages the tradition of the 'live crib' survives – a midnight Mass on Christmas Eve in the form of a Nativity pageant. The best known, and very popular, are at Les Baux and Séguret. Some villages also still keep up their annual pilgrimages in summer – a costumed procession to the local shrine of a saint.

Handicrafts

The making of *santons* is one of a number of traditional local crafts that have been revived since the war, along with the general folk renaissance. Others include olive-wood sculpture, ceramics, and the weaving of Provençal fabrics. These old activities were in decline not long ago, but have since been given a new lease of life in some places by the arrival of artists and artisans from Paris, keen to make a living in the sunny south if they can (Picasso, who spent six years, from 1947 to 1953, in the ceramics town of Vallauris, was the foremost setter of this trend). By the 1970s these immigrants had become as numerous as the indigenous craftsmen, especially in fashionable villages such as Tourrette-sur-Loup, St-Paul-de-Vence and Roussillon. Today many of these craftsmen have found the going hard, and have left. The

Provençal handicrafts revival, like the whole future of local folk tradition, remains precarious.

The economy

Agriculture used to be the mainstay of the economy, but has now been joined by mass tourism and modern industry, in what used not to be a very industrial part of France. It is true that Toulon, La Ciotat and Marseille have long been centres of shipbuilding and repairing, but their yards have now closed or are moribund. Marseille still has some engineering, chemicals and food-processing firms. However, since the 1950s the area's industrial centre of gravity has moved westward, to the lake of Berre and the new port of Fos: here are huge oil refineries, petro-chemical works and Europe's largest helicopter factory, as well as new steelworks which inevitably have been hit by the European steel crisis. In the Durance valley, and by the Rhône north of Avignon, there are big hydro-electric works and nuclear power stations, the latter a reminder that over 75 per cent of French electricity is nuclear-generated, the world's highest proportion by far.

The Côte d'Azur has found a surprising new vocation to supple ment tourism, for it is now marked out as a zone for high-technology research. A large 'international scientific park', Sophia-Antipolis, has been created since the 1970s near Antibes, where several firms have built laboratories and research units; and IBM has a big research centre nearby. Over in Lower Languedoc, where advanced industry is even more of a novelty, Montpellier has been attracting much new industry. There IBM has its largest factory in France, which today has been hit by recession. However, when companies have the jobs to offer, they do not find it at all hard to persuade executives and scientists to come and work in the sunny south! The Nîmes area continues to produce textiles, as it has for centuries. And some traditional Provençal industries are still active, based on use of local resources – ochre quarrying near Apt, bauxite mining near Brignoles, cork production in the Maures forests, salt-works at Hyères and near Aigues-Mortes. The last of the local coal-mines, at Alès on the edge of the Cévennes, closed a few years ago.

Agriculture is very varied. Thanks to sunshine, irrigation and a fertile soil, the lower Rhône Valley is the leading market garden of France, exporting its early fruit and vegetables – melons, asparagus, peaches, strawberries and much else – to many parts of Europe. In the Camargue, rice is cultivated. The chalky soil of the South is good terrain for both vine and olive: Provence is France's foremost producer of olives and olive oil, also of almonds, while lower Languedoc turns out 40 per cent of French table wine. Lavender grows on the plateaux of upper Provence. In the lush valleys behind Cannes, flowers are cultivated on a large scale (roses, jasmine, carnations, violets, mimosa), mainly for the cut-flower markets of Europe, and less now than in former times to make essences for the Grasse perfume factories. Silk-worm breeding, too, once a major industry, has died out. But lemons are still a speciality of the sheltered coast at Menton. And the fishermen remain active along the whole coast, charging high prices. Upland areas both of Provence and Languedoc are used for sheep grazing, and transhumance is still practised: the flocks are taken to browse on the high plateaus in summer, then are brought down to the lowlands for winter. Bulls are reared on the Camargue plain.

Tourism is increasingly important for the economy, and has become highly diversified. In the big resorts of the Côte d'Azur, the old elitist tourism now brings in far less money than the new 'business tourism' of the convention and incentive trades. Elsewhere, the hotels today cater for fewer visitors than the crowded camping sites, the rented villas and farmsteads (*gîtes*). Tourists come for a whole variety of reasons – to ski or water-ski, to walk, bathe or gamble, to look at museums and churches or to enjoy local cooking – or for all of these at once.

The Weather and When to Go

In summer the weather is pleasantly hot: the average temperature on the coast is then 24°C (75°F), and that of the sea is 19°C (66°F). Even in late October it can still be sun-bathing weather, but this may be punctuated by sudden storms. In winter the temperature on the coast averages 9°C (48°F), but this can vary between really warm periods and sudden chilly spells, while the hills of the hinterland will by then be cold and maybe snowy. In spring, short sharp showers help the flowers into bloom, and in winter there can be downpours. Generally, though, the rainfall level is low – above all in summer, as you can tell from the parched aspect of the vegetation by September, and from the frequent forest fires.

Provence and Languedoc can be visited and enjoyed in any season. May and June are ideal months, notably on the coast. The sun is pleasantly hot, and the sea is warm enough for bathing; the resorts are active, but not yet overcrowded; and the rural areas are full of flowers. What's more, continental summer time (April to September) means that in May to July it stays light till nearly 11 p.m. The French mostly take their holidays in late July and August, and if you go then it can have both advantages and drawbacks. The resorts are really swinging, many offering their full range of amenities, such as outdoor discos, only during that period. On the other hand, the crowds on the coast are dense, traffic jams are fearful, and hotel beds hard to find impromptu. September is maybe a better month, when the crowds are thinning out but the sun is still hot. However, while big places like Nice and Cannes stay open all year, the bathing resorts along the coast further west begin to close down in late September, and by mid-October even in St Tropez most hotels will have closed.

On the Riviera itself from Cannes to Menton, with its mild, sheltered climate, winter used to be the fashionable season until the 1930s. Today, when the summer mobs have gone, these older resorts still remain active in winter, thanks to the conference trade and a select tourist clientèle. This can be a good time for a visit, so long as you don't plan to sunbathe. There is the added bonus of skiing, two hours' drive away in the mountains; and the true local life of the towns, behind their tourist façade, is best revealed in winter. In the rest of

Provence and in Languedoc, spring or autumn can be good periods for cultural sightseeing: in winter many of the smaller museums will be closed, and in the more touristy villages it may be hard to find hotels still open. Bear in mind, too, that from September to March the chill north wind known as the Mistral, scourge of Provence, will be blowing intermittently but irritatingly. Its whirling nerve-fraying blasts continue for a few days, then suddenly stop. Only the Côte d'Azur resorts, protected by mountains on their north side, are at all immune.

Travelling Around

By car

Roads and traffic

There are several useful *autoroutes* (motorways) in the south of France, but their tolls are expensive: only *autoroutes* in urban areas, or between some big towns close together such as Marseille and Aix, are free of tolls. The other main roads, *routes nationales* (N), and the secondary *routes départementales* (D), are also toll-free, but are often heavy with traffic. Nearly all French roads today are well surfaced, and the touristic mountain routes are very well engineered. So driving in the south of France can be a pleasant experience: for example, note the brown signs along the *autoroutes* that keep you informed about the scenery and historic places you are passing. However, the dense traffic can be tedious, especially on or near the coast in summer, and on the approaches to towns. Road traffic in and out of Provence and Languedoc is especially heavy on the weekends when the French begin their annual holidays (from mid-July to early August) and end them (late August to early September).

Driving habits

Frenchmen who in private life may be considerate and courteous will tend to become savages at the wheel – impatient, egotistical and inconsiderate. They have fast reflexes, and are intolerant towards slow or clumsy drivers. So they may try to push ahead of you, or not wait to let you extricate your car from a parking space in a narrow street. And they drive on their brakes: at a zebra crossing, they will zoom up fast, then stop abruptly, which can be unnerving for a pedestrian. Pedestrians hit back by assiduous jay-walking, and by not observing their red lights at crossings, so the motorist too must keep his wits about him.

It is true that in all these matters Parisians are worst, followed by the crypto-Parisians of the Côte d'Azur, while people in rural areas are gentler: so beware of number plates ending in 75 or 92 (Paris and its suburbs) or 06 (Alpes-Maritimes). Lorry-drivers, by contrast, tend to be helpful in waving you on to overtake when they see that the road is clear. Incidentally, the law stipulates *priorité à droite*: that is, you should give way to a vehicle coming from the right, unless otherwise indicated.

Petrol

Petrol comes in two grades, *super* and *normal*. Lead-free petrol, in two or three grades, is now widely available, save in some remoter rural areas. Petrol stations mostly close at around 8 p.m., though you'll find all-night ones in big towns and on *autoroutes*.

Repairs and garages Most garages, especially smaller ones, tend to be efficient, swift and helpful, ready to come out to give assistance at awkward hours (but they do not often accept credit cards). Spare parts for the main European makes of car can usually be obtained rapidly, but this is less true of Japanese ones.

Car hire This is a bit more expensive than in Britain or the United States, and it may prove cheaper to make the reservation with a major international company before you leave home, rather than book with the same firm inside France. Some travel agents offer attractive fly-drive deals, and some rental firms allow you to return the car at a different town from where you picked it up.

Parking Parking can be a problem in the towns in summer, even though there are plenty of big paying car-parks, also meter parking (usually you buy a ticket from a machine and put it behind your windscreen). Beware of leaving the car on a street marked *stationnement génant* (obstructive parking), for it is liable to get towed away (not clamped): you must then enquire for the local *fourrière* (car pound) and pay a sizeable fine. Apart from this, a visitor with a foreign number-plate can afford to take a few chances, such as parking up on the pavement for a few minutes in a quiet street. The French themselves do this a lot, being undisciplined and inconsiderate when parking as when driving. Often they will double-park in the street, thus blocking your own exit: the best solution is then to enquire in nearby shops, where they may know where the culprit is. Or, if he's left his car unlocked, just get in and push.

In the centre of most bigger French towns, traffic is heavy, parking is hard, and some streets are now a pleasant pedestrian zone. So, having parked once, it's best to do central sightseeing on foot, or by taxi.

● Please note that car break-ins are common, so never leave anything visible in your car. Overnight it's advisable to empty the boot too, or at least to park in a well-lit main street.

Speed limits and fines The current speed limits, are 130 kph (81 mph) on toll *autoroutes*, 110 kph (69 mph) on free *autoroutes* and dual carriageways, 90 kph (56 mph) on other roads, and 60 kph (37 mph) in towns. In practice the police are tolerant of speeds of up to 10 or 15 kph in excess of these. However, they can, and often do, impose on-the-spot speeding fines, on a sliding scale according to the degree of excess speed. Often they lie in wait at danger points, for example at a warning sign to slow down before a curve or crossing. In serious cases, especially after an accident, they have the right to confiscate a driver's licence and impound his vehicle for a certain period.

Road safety The French do not drive carefully, and by 1972 the result was a toll of over 16,000 road deaths a year, twice the British figure. Nearly half of these accidents were caused by drink. Since then a strenuous road safety campaign, including stricter speed limits and tighter rules against drinking, has succeeded in reducing the fatalities to some 11,000 a year. The French do now drive a little more prudently than in the past, especially on main roads. Seat belts are compulsory. Breathalyser checks are usually made only when a driver has been stopped for speeding, or after an accident; but the on-the-spot fines can be severe.

If you are involved in an accident, do not admit liability or incriminate yourself, even if you feel you might have been partly to blame. Contact the police, try to get statements from witnesses, exchange insurance and details with other drivers involved. The French police tend to behave in a slow and bureaucratic manner after an accident, and the questioning may drag on endlessly; but generally the final results are fair.

By train

The French are proud of their rail technology, and their trains are among the fastest and most efficient in the world, as well as being well above average in comfort, cleanliness and punctuality. Kinds of train

Kinds of train

The famous *Train à Grande Vitesse* (TGV), one of the world's fastest trains, does the 450-km journey from Paris to Lyon in just two hours, on a specially-built line, then proceeds more slowly on an older line to Marseille, Nice and Narbonne (see under 'Getting there' in each of these towns). There are some other fast train services, notably the Corail and the Trans Europ Express (TEE). You need to reserve seats in advance both on the TGV and TEE, but this can often be done at the last moment. Local trains are a little less efficient, and many branch lines have closed in recent decades, especially in the Provençal hinterland: however, the State rail company, SNCF, now operates very good bus services which call at the disused stations on many of these lines, as well as linking up with the schedules of the main-line trains.

Tickets and cheap fares

The TEE trains carry a supplement, and so do TGV ones at certain peak hours. Before you board any train, be sure to validate your ticket in one of the orange automatic machines at the platform entrance, or you may have to pay a surcharge. The SNCF offers a range of cut-rate fares, varying with the time of travel: generally Sundays and around midday are cheapest. For the foreign tourist, the best deal is the *France Vacances* pass, available from many travel agents and main rail centres abroad: this allows unlimited rail travel over certain periods of time, and other bonuses.

You can travel to the South of France by overnight sleeper from Paris and other points north: the compartments are six-berth if you

Couchettes, Motorail and dining cars

travel second class, four-berth for first class (there's no sex segregation in either), or you can pay extra for a one- or two-berth sleeper. There are overnight Motorail services for motorists to a number of cities in the South.

Catering – oddly, for France of all countries – is now the weakest element in the French rail service. Only TEEs have a proper dining car, while on the TGV you are served an average quality meal at your seat, and many trains just have a bar serving indifferent snacks, or no refreshments at all. However, you can get excellent meals at many of the station brasseries.

By air

There are airports with regular direct scheduled flights to Paris at Montpellier, Nîmes, Avignon, Marseille, Toulon, St Raphaél and Nice; from Marseille and Nice you can also fly direct to London and many other foreign cities. The main domestic French airline is Air Inter, a subsidiary of Air France; some smaller private ones also operate scheduled flights, such as Air Littoral.

Fares and discounts

The normal APEX regulations apply on international flights. On domestic ones, you can get special cheap flights from Paris to Marseille or Nice if you are staying between seven and thirty-five days.

Airports

The larger airports, such as Marseille/Marignane and Nice-Côte d'Azur, are well equipped with shops, banks and restaurants. Smaller airports will have fewer facilities. All operate regular bus services to and from city centres.

By bus

This is the cheapest way of getting around, and can be pleasant if you are not in a hurry. The SNCF (see above) operates many local bus services that connect with its main-line trains, some of them following the routes of closed branch lines. Apart from this, regular local buses in rural areas tend to be infrequent and crowded, very often geared to market days and to getting children to and from school. In summer, a great many private companies run tourist excursions from the towns to places of interest. For details of all local bus services, it is best to go to the enquiry office of the local central bus station, Gare Routière.

By taxi

Taxis can be hailed in the street or found at ranks; in most towns you can also phone a central taxi pool to order one. Rates are reasonable, but they go up on Sundays and at night, and you will have to pay extra at a station or air terminal. Officially registered taxis have a 'taxi' sign on the roof and a meter and list of charges: beware of the pirate meterless cabs that prowl at airports and stations and can charge what they like. Most taxis are converted private cars, often a bit battered.

By other means

By boat

There are regular ferries from Corsica to Nice and Marseille; also passenger services to Marseille from North African ports, used mainly by Algerian and Tunisian workers and their families. Marseille is still a port of call for some passenger liners on Far Eastern and African routes. Within the region, you can take river cruises along the Rhône, or hire a boat along the Canal du Midi in western Languedoc.

Hitch-hiking

This is not permitted on *autoroutes* but is possible on other roads. The French do pick up hitch-hikers. Women are not advised to hitch on their own, but can more safely do so in pairs.

By bicycle

Owing to the heavy traffic, this is not recommended in the coastal areas, nor in or near big towns where lorries thunder. It is more feasible in country areas – so long as the hills are not too steep. Bicycles can usually be hired locally. Some tourist offices have mapped out possible bike routes; and some travel agencies in Britain specialise in French bicycling tours.

Departments and
Administrative
Regions

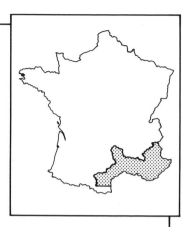

LOZÈRE

HAUTES-ALPES

GARD

VAUCLUSE

ALPES-DE-
HAUTE-PROVENCE

PROVENCE

ALPES-
MARITIMES

LANGUEDOC

BOUCHES DU RHÔNE

VAR

HÉRAULT

ROUSSILLON

AUDE

0   *kilometres*   100

Where to Stay

Hotels and inns

Good hotels in Provence and Languedoc are numerous, and in this book's gazetteer I give only the briefest personal selection, in the different price ranges. For a fuller choice, look at the red *Michelin* guide. Hotels in southern France are of all kinds, to suit all tastes and purses, ranging from the ultra-luxurious palaces along the Côte d'Azur, to smaller utility hotels in cities, useful as a base but lacking in ambience. In between are the old country auberges (inns), some simple, some smart, and the family-run seaside hotels. In smaller resorts, hotels catering mainly for tourists tend to be open only from about Easter to October.

Chains, groups and associations

Of the large modern city hotels used mostly by businessmen, many belong to the big French chains: the leading ones are **Meridien**, **Pullman**, **Sofitel** (part of the **Accor** group), and my own favourite, **Concorde**. Some Concorde hotels are modern, but more often they are classic hotels newly renovated, such as the Martinez at Cannes. **Altéa** hotels, variable in quality, are medium-price members of the Pullman group; **Novotel, Mercure** and the cheaper **Ibis**, all within the huge Accor group, are modern utility hotels, pleasant and reliable, often located on the edge of towns. I can also recommend **Campanile**, a new chain of superior motels found near main roads.

Many privately-owned hotels have grouped themselves into associations for joint marketing, but retain their individual character. **Relais et Châteaux**, well known internationally, are mostly converted manors or châteaus: they are luxurious, pricey and often pretentious. The **Relais du Silence**, mostly medium-priced, are noted for their quiet locations, as their name implies. Above all, I can recommend the **Logis de France** association, nearly all of them family-run two- or one-star hotels, quite small and cheap, usually found in small towns or villages. They tend to be reliable, friendly and unassuming – in short, very good value. Throughout France there are 4,015 of these Logis, plus 533 **Auberges de France** which belong to the Logis group but are even smaller and simpler. Quite a proportion of these Logis and Auberges are in south-east France, and you can buy their little green-and-yellow annual handbook at a tourist office or good bookshop. All the members of these various associations submit to annual inspections, which helps to keep up standards.

41

In addition, bed-and-breakfast places in private homes are beginning to become more numerous in France, though they are still much less so than in, say, Britain or Ireland. They are designated by the sign, *'Chambre d'hôte'*. There's an officially-sponsored network of approved bed-and-breakfast places, known as *'Café-couette'*, and a local tourist office should be able to give you a list of the addresses in its area.

Official gradings   The Ministry of Tourism inspects hotels annually and grades them, from ★★★★luxe down to ★, as plaques at their doorways indicate. These gradings are based on facilities and give little guide to real quality; the ratings in the French hotel guides are more helpful.

Prices   Room prices are low by British or American standards, and about average for the continent. Prices are highest in smart resorts such as Monte Carlo, lowest in the hinterland where value for money can be remarkable. In tourist hotels on the coast, rates are 30 to 40 per cent more expensive in summer than winter. A hotel's apparent price category may be deceptive, however, for although in a modern establishment the rooms tend to be fairly similar in style and price, in many older hotels they can vary hugely in size and comfort: under the same roof, you could pay three times as much for a big sea-facing room with balcony as for a pokey one at the back with no bath. So it's best when reserving to specify the kind of room needed, and to check the price. What's more, you are charged for the room rather than per head, so that two people sharing a room pay only slightly more than one – especially if it is double-bedded, as is usually the case (many newer hotels, however, are moving over to twin beds).

In this book, I give four price-brackets. These can only be a rough guide because – I repeat – *within the same hotel the price of rooms can vary enormously*, in a ratio of as much as 1:3. The cheaper rooms usually get booked up first, and in smarter hotels the most expensive ones will probably be suites. Bearing this in mind, these are my categories, based on 1994 prices, for an average room generally with bath or shower:

● **top price**: over about 750 francs for a room (in luxury palaces on the Côte d'Azur, the price will seldom be less than 1,000 francs, but elsewhere there are very few hotels charging more than about 800 francs).

● **upper-medium price**: about 550 to 750 francs;

● **medium price**: about 350 to 550 francs;

● **inexpensive**: below 350 francs.

Reservations   It is wise to book well in advance for visits in season (Easter, and mid-June to early September) to the better holiday hotels. If you tour impromptu during these periods, you will probably find somewhere to stay, but not of the best quality – at least not in coastal areas. When booking by letter, enclose a reply coupon.

Please note that the dates of annual closure given in this book, under each hotel, are approximate and can vary from year to year.

Comfort and equipment

Standards of comfort have improved greatly, and no longer is French plumbing a ghastly joke. Even the cheapest of my recommendations have at least a few rooms with bath or shower. And bedrooms in the upper-medium price categories will generally have colour televisions, electric hair-dryers, and so on. In less expensive hotels, you may well not relish the long, sausage-like bolster that serves for a pillow; but if you ask, you'll usually be given a softer cushion-type pillow.

Breakfasts

Breakfast is usually charged extra. And in a French hotel it still tends to be a frugal affair – coffee, rolls and croissants, small pre-packed portions of butter and jam. The lavish slab of butter or bowl of home-made jam are rarities in the cheaper hotel, as is fresh orange juice. Eggs or cereals will usually come if you ask, but are charged extra. A growing number of bigger hotels now offer a copious German-style help-yourself buffet.

Meals in hotels

In Britain, 'hotel food' is a term of disparagement, but in France, especially in the more traditional type of rural or small-town hostelry, the food – solid and unpretentious – tends to be every bit as good as in restaurants. In fact, the *patron* of an auberge will very often see himself as foremost a chef/restaurateur and only secondly a hotelier. However, in holiday hotels on the coast, open only for a few months, the chef may change frequently and standards thus be more variable. Though by law they cannot force their guests to do so, most such hotels in season expect you to take at least one main meal a day (*demi-pension*), if not both (*pension complète*), and it is wise to check on this when booking. The *menu pension* will probably be simpler, and with less choice, than the hotel's more elaborate menus, but you can take special dishes if you pay extra. The French expect to spend money on food, and in many hotels a dinner for two with wine will work out at much more than the cost of the bedroom.

Self-catering accommodation

It is not difficult to hire a holiday flat in a town on the coast, or a villa or *gîte* up in the hinterland. A *gîte* is generally a modernised farmhouse or farm building, or a small converted house in a village: often the owners will be living next door, so the experience enables you to share in village life and see something of the 'real' rural France. A *gîte* holiday can be the best way of getting beneath the surface of French life, and is much cheaper than a hotel. You bring your own sheets and towels, but other bedding and kitchen equipment are provided – and then there is the fun of going shopping for your meals in nearby markets, and trying out local recipes *in situ*. Of the organisations that arrange *gîte* holidays, I can recommend especially the British-based **Vacances**

Franco-Britanniques, Normandy House, High Street, Cheltenham, Gloucestershire GL50 3HW; tel. (0242) 235515. On their books they have a large selection of *gîtes* all over France, which they inspect regularly: I enjoyed three holidays recently in their attractive *gîtes*, both in Provence and Languedoc. *Gîte* holidays can also be arranged through **Brittany Ferries**, Wharf Road, Portsmouth PO2 8RU; enquiries and reservations tel. 0752 221321. They have a good selection. A third organisation, larger and officially-sponsored but a little less satisfactory than the other two, is **Gîtes de France**, 178 Piccadilly, London W1V DAL, tel. 01-493 3480, who have many hundreds of *gîtes* on their books and publish a guidebook to them. You can book a *gîte* holiday through that London address, or through the French Government Tourist Office in New York: 610 Fifth Ave, New York, NY 10020. It is wise to book early for high summer periods. You can also book a *gîte* at the last moment on the spot in France, by going to a local tourist office which will give a list of the addresses in its area. But in high summer, the choice is likely to have become extremely limited.

Camping

There are hundreds of organised camping sites in Provence and Languedoc, some on or close to the coast, some on the edge of towns such as Avignon, some up in the wilds of the hinterland. Recognised French campsites are graded by the Ministry of Tourism with one, two, three or four stars and are inspected. Those in the three- and four-star categories are within enclosed areas, marked off into pitches and guarded night and day; they are usually well equipped, with communal toilets and washing facilities that include hot showers. Most have shops and restaurants or bars serving hot food as well as drinks; many have plenty of sporting facilities, too, and swimming pools. Prices vary greatly, depending above all on proximity to the coast, and on the season. Just a few sites are open all year. The big ones near the coast can get unpleasantly crowded in high summer, when they come to seem more like superior refugee camps than holiday centres.

For most sites, you can make reservations in advance by writing to the site, but it is unwise to send money until the reservation has been confirmed. For further information, apply to any major French government tourist office, which will provide a list of recommended sites; or you can buy the green Michelin guide to camping and caravanning in France. Below I give a selected list of a few especially attractive camp sites, some of them open just to caravans, not to people with tents. All, unless otherwise specified, have hot showers, shops, a restaurant, kids' playground or playroom, are guarded night and day

Côte d'Azur

and will accept reservations. Nearly all are three- or four-star ones. **Castellane:** Camp du Verdon, Domaine de la Salaou, 04120 Castellane; tel. 92 83 63 64. A large, well-equipped camp, in a fine upland setting near the Gorges du Verdon, far from the coast. Two heated swimming pools; lake for boating and trout fishing. Open 15 May to 15 September.

Opio: Caravan-Inn, 06860 Opio; tel. 93 77 32 00. For caravans only, a small but nicely terraced and shady site, in the lovely hills east of Grasse. Tennis. Open March to October.

Vence: Domaine de la Bergerie, 06140 Vence; tel. 93 58 09 36. Some 14 km from the sea, just west of Vence, a large but fairly quiet camp suitable for families. Open March to early November.

The coast from Cannes to Marseille

Agay: Esterel Caravanning, 83700 St Raphaël; tel. 94 82 03 28. For caravans only, a small, quiet camp on the Esterel coast just east of St Raphaël. Tennis, two swimming pools. Open Easter to end September.

Cavalière: Les Mimosas, 83980 Le Lavandou; tel. 94 05 82 94. For caravans only, a quiet, shady camp near the beach in a small, busy resort. No shops; not guarded at night. Open mid-March to mid-October.

Grimaud: De la Plage, 83310 Saint Pons les Mûres; tel. 94 56 31 15. Near the sea, just outside Port Grimaud, a large, attractive camp with lots of amenities (swimming pool, tennis, etc). Open April to September.

Mandelieu-La Napoule: Les Cigales, Avenue de la Mer, 06210 Mandelieu; tel. 93 49 23 53. A pretty site about 2 km inland. No shops or restaurant. Open March to October.

St Raphaël: Douce Quiétude, Blvd. Jacques-Baudino, 83700 St Raphaël; tel. 94 95 55 50. Set quietly in a big wooded park, just back from the sea. A disco, live music and sports competitions add to the fun. Open Easter to end September.

The hinterland of Provence

Château-Arnoux: Les Salettes, 04160; tel. 92 64 02 40. In the Durance valley, a comfortable and well-equipped place, near a lake where you can fish or sail. No restaurant. Open all year.

Cucuron: Le Moulin à Vent, 84160 Cadenet; tel. 90 77 25 77 (90 77 21 64 out of season). Small and only modestly equipped, but beautiful, amid glorious Lubéron countryside. No restaurant, shops or kids' playground; not guarded at night. Open Easter to mid-September.

Nans-les-Pins: International de la Sainte-Baume, 83860; tel. 94 78 92 68. A very attractive camp near the foot of the Ste-Baume massif. No restaurant or kids' playground, but tennis, riding and swimming pool. Open Easter to September.

Villes-sur-Auzon: Les Verguettes, Route de Carpentras, 84570 Mormoiron; tel. 90 61 88 18. Well laid out, in a lovely open setting near the slopes of Mont Ventoux. No shops, restaurant, kids' playground;

Western Provence

but swimming pool and tennis. Open June to September.

Aix-en-Provence: Chantecler, Avenue du Val-St-André, 13100; tel. 42 26 12 98. Large and shady, 3 km south-east of Aix. Well equipped: there's even a library, as well as games room and swimming pool. Open all year.

Avignon: Pont St-Bénézet, Ile de la Barthelasse, 84000; tel. 90 82 63 50. On a flat island in the Rhône, with fine views of the Palais des Papes just opposite; large and well equipped. Bathing nearby. Open March to October.

Maussane-les-Alpilles: Les Romarins, 13520; tel. 90 54 33 60. A very attractive municipally-owned site, medium-sized, near the foot of the rocky Alpilles. No shop or restaurant. Bathing nearby. Open mid-March to mid-October.

St Rémy: Mas de Nicolas, 13210; tel. 90 92 27 05. Just outside St Rémy, another attractive municipal site. No shop or restaurant, but swimming pool. Open mid-March to November.

Languedoc and Cévennes

Anduze: Le Malhiver, route de Nîmes, 30140; tel. 66 61 76 04. Smallish, just outside the town, near a river; fishing, tennis, etc. Open May to September.

Crespian: Mas de Reilhe, 30260 Quissac; tel. 66 77 82 12. Outside a village west of Nîmes, in open country, a quiet, well-run site. No restaurant, but swimming pool. Open late May to early September.

La Grande-Motte: Lous Pibois, 34280; tel. 67 56 50 08. On the edge of the resort and close to a sandy beach, a biggish well-laid-out resort with good modern equipment. No reservations, so come early. Open mid-March to mid-October.

Le Grau-du-Roi: Elysée-Résidence, Route de l'Espiguette, 30240; tel. 66 51 98 88. A huge new site (1,800 pitches) with varied and excellent modern equipment, 2 km from the sea, inland from Port-Camargue. Olympic-size swimming pool; sports include windsurfing, canoeing, riding, tennis and archery. Outdoor theatre. Open Easter to mid-October.

Lézignan-Corbières: La Pinède, 11200; tel. 68 27 05 08. Attractively terraced on a hillside, near a swimming pool, and by the main road to Carcassonne. No restaurant, but bar food. Open April to mid-October.

Remoulins: La Soubeyranne, route de Beaucaire, 30210; tel. 66 37 03 21. A biggish camp not far from the Pont du Gard. Swimming pool, tennis. Open May to mid-September.

Vias: Californie Plage, 34450; tel. 67 21 64 69. Right by the sandy beach, just west of Agde, a quiet, well-kept and well-equipped site suitable for families. Open all year.

Eating and Drinking

French cuisine is the world's best, of course – but it's also easy to eat out badly in France. Quite apart from the new downtown fast-food horrors, or the excesses of over-priced *nouvelle cuisine*, today there are plenty of clip-joints along tourist routes to trap the unwary, while even the decent family bistro will sometimes cut unjustifiable corners and end up with mediocre results. Average standards are not as high as they used to be. So you need to select your restaurant with care, armed with a good guidebook and some local tip-offs – and with your own *nez*. One obvious point is to wait till 8.30 p.m. or so, then stroll through town to see which places are filling up with local-looking people guzzling eagerly. Those could be the ones to go for.

In Provence and Languedoc, the delights of eating out are as great as anywhere in France. In fine weather, there's all the variety of alfresco locations, from some vine-clad patio up in the hills to the dazzle of a coastal promenade. There are luxury palaces, busy brasseries, old rural inns, and the kind of small, plain downtown restaurant that may look nothing special but offers superb value for money – in France, more than anywhere, smartness of decor is little guide to quality of cooking. Most of the best places are family owned and run: the wife is front-of-house while her husband cooks, and will often emerge in his white jacket at the evening's end to chat with guests.

Choosing a menu

Usually it is much better value to choose a fixed-price menu than to eat from the *carte*, where the same three courses will cost about twice as much. Restaurants generally display their menus outside, and may well offer three or four *prix fixes* varying hugely in price, say, from 80 to 250 francs (but sometimes the cheapest one is served only on weekday lunchtimes). They won't mind if you order the cheapest menu: but the best specialities (notably fish) might only be on the dearer ones. In the provinces, more than in Paris, the French usually prefer to eat a set menu rather than *à la carte*: the exceptions are in modern downtown brasseries, pizzerias or steak-houses, or in some top luxury restaurants where star dishes often are only on the *carte*.

As a starter, soup is more usual in the evening and a salad-type dish at lunch, but many menus offer both. Meat is not smothered with several vegetables in the Anglo-Saxon manner, but usually is served with just one which the chef has chosen to give his dish the right balance. If you order another vegetable, it will come later as a separate dish. The French prefer to eat steaks and lamb chops rare (*saignant*) or semi-rare (*à point*), and a serious *patron/chef* might even refuse to serve someone who insults him by asking for it well done (*bien cuit*). The French always eat cheese before dessert, if they are taking both (this is mainly because the red wine served with the meat can then continue with the cheese).

Price categories

Since a restaurant will often have several set menus varying hugely in price (see above), it is not easy to give price categories, for much will depend on which menu you choose. A smart restaurant may have menus ranging from, say, 200 to 350 francs, plus a very simple cheaper one at 120 francs; conversely, quite a simple place may offer menus ranging from, say, 80 to 150 francs, plus a special 'gastronomic' menu at 250 francs. With this major proviso, my four categories (1994 prices) are based on the cost of a cheaper menu for one person, plus half a bottle of one of the cheaper wines on offer:

- **top price**: over 350 francs;
- **upper-medium price**: 200-350 francs;
- **medium price**: 100-200 francs;
- **inexpensive**: under 100 francs.

Snacks and light meals

For a light lunch, there are plenty of pizzerias and brasseries; or you can go into a simpler restaurant and order just a salad. Many cafés sell hot snacks such as *croque monsieur* (toasted cheese), or *un sandwich* (half a French loaf split down the middle, filled maybe with ham, cheese or pâté). *Pan bagnat* (*salade niçoise* inside a big bun) is a good filling snack.

Times of meals

Unlike Spaniards, their fellow southerners, the Provençaux tend to lunch early: service starts at noon and usually ends by 2 p.m. Dinner, on the other hand, rarely gets going before 8 p.m.: in the big resorts it's smart to dine late, almost *à l'espagnole*, and some places will stay open till midnight or later. But many rural restaurants stop serving as early as 9 p.m. The French do not eat in the afternoon, except the odd sticky cake, and nearly all eating-places are shut between 3 and 7 p.m.: you'll then have to make do with a café snack – or, in a town, with a fast-food delight.

- Please note that the weekly and annual closing times quoted in this book, for each restaurant, are very approximate and may vary slightly from year to year. It is wise to telephone in advance.

The cuisine of Provence

Don't think that in the South you will get nothing but local regional specialities: many of the dishes appearing on menus are common to France as a whole, not specifically *Provençal*, or they are the chef's own *nouvelle* inventions. However, in most good restaurants, especially rural ones, the cooking will at least have a regional bias: that is, it will be done in the manner of southern France, not of central or northern France. So what does this mean?

Provençal is, in my view, one of the great regional cuisines of France, and possibly the one with the strongest personality. Spicy and Mediterranean, it is a cuisine of clear, bold flavours, drawing heavily on garlic, on local herbs such as basil, thyme and fennel, and on olive oil which generally replaces the butter used in north French cooking; the garlic enhances the natural flavours, and is not used unsubtly. The cooking of Provence is marvellously varied, a mix of the traditions of mountain and fishing folks, as befits an area where high hills descend to the sea. This is a richly endowed region, the foremost market garden of France, with an abundance of fresh fruit and vegetables in season, as well as fish in staggering variety, and game from the hills in winter. The cuisine draws generously on all this local produce. Tomatoes, artichokes, asparagus and melons are especially succulent.

Provençal starters and soups

As appetisers, a meal might begin with *saucisson d'Arles*, a kind of salami made from donkey (!), or *tapenade*, a purée of crushed black olives and anchovies, delicious when made properly; some restaurants will bring a basket of crispy raw vegetables with mustard and vinaigrette dips. Starters include *tomates provençale* (grilled with oil, garlic and parsley) and a wide range of salads, much the commonest being *salade niçoise*, a rich mix of tomatoes, cucumber, hard-boiled eggs, plus either anchovies or tunny, or both. Some restaurants lay on a help-yourself lunchtime buffet of spicy hors-d'œuvres. The best soups are *pistou*, a thick vegetable broth with a paste of basil and garlic, and the ubiquitous *soupe de poissons*, made from a pungent stock of varied fish and shellfish, served with toast crusts, grated cheese and a reddish garlic sauce (*rouille*): it is often at its succulent best in some simple fishing-port bistro.

Fish dishes

For main dishes, fish reigns supreme, on or near the coast. That queen of Provençal cooking, *bouillabaisse*, is a garlicky, saffrony stew made from rockfish and shellfish, its crucial ingredient being *rascasse*, a spiky fish unique to this part of the Mediterranean. The taste is magically subtle, but the dish might *look* alarming to the novice, for the fish in their orange stew are weirdly cadaverous. *Bouillabaisse* is best in Marseille, but can be found elsewhere too. Often it needs to be ordered in advance: as it's time-consuming to prepare, few restaurants keep it in daily stock. And it's expensive – as are many of the other best fish dishes, such as *bourride*, a simpler garlic stew made of white fish, and *loup au fenouil*, grilled sea bass with fennel. Cheaper fish include grilled fresh sardines, *rouget* (red mullet), *daurade* (John Dory), often richly cooked with herbs and tomatoes, and the idiosyncratic *brandade de morue*, a creamy paste of salt cod, olive oil, milk and garlic. Inland you will find trout and *écrevisses* (crayfish), the latter often in a rich sauce. And do not fail to try *aïoli*, whose very name makes the Provençaux wax lyrical (Mistral even founded a magazine called *l'Aïoli*): it is a garlic mayonnaise served usually as a sauce with boiled cod and vegetables, and it often forms the main dish at village feasts.

Meat dishes

In inland areas, meat predominates. The beef, seldom of high quality, is often served grilled on a wood fire, with herbs on it: you might do better to take it stewed in red wine and herbs (*bœuf en daube* or, in the Camargue area, *bœuf gardianne*). The lamb can be excellent, notably *agneau de Sisteron*, whose aromatic flavour comes from grazing on wild herbs on upland pastures. Rabbit is frequent, cooked in a mustard sauce or else *à la provençale* (in a tomato and garlic sauce); chicken and frogs' legs are also done *à la provençale*. In winter, game is prepared in many ways – try roast wild boar (*sanglier*) or *civet de lièvre* (jugged hare). *Pieds et paquets*, a tripe dish from Marseille, is maybe an acquired taste.

Cheeses and desserts

Local cheeses are few, and not among France's greatest. Try the small round goats' cheeses, served with garlic and herbs; or *cachat*, a sheep's cheese often marinated in brandy and herbs; or *banon*, soaked in wine and wrapped in chestnut leaves. Desserts generally lack finesse, except in some smarter restaurants: but lemon pie (*tarte au citron*) can be good. Fresh fruit is plentiful in season – cherries, peaches and grapes, green figs from the Marseille area, and pink melons from Cavaillon.

The cuisine of Nice

The Nice area, Italian till 1860, has its own distinctive cooking, halfway between Provençal and Italian. It is mostly a simple cuisine of inexpensive ingredients, as witness its starters: *pissaladière* (a kind of pizza), *anchoïade* (anchovy tart), *tian* (a grill of vegetables, rice and grated cheese), *socca* (a pancake of ground chickpeas), and ravioli, subtler than the Italian kind. *Mesclun* is a dressed salad of dandelion and coarse lettuce. Of Niçois ways with fish, the most notable is *estocaficada* (stockfish stewed with vegetables in brandy and garlic; not to all foreign tastes). *Ratatouille* (an oily stew of aubergines, peppers, and so on) is a local dish that, like *salade niçoise* and *soupe au pistou*, has spread far outside the Nice area.

The cuisine of Languedoc

In the coastal areas, the starters and fish dishes are much the same as in Provence, plus a few local variations: the port of Sète, for instance, has its own specialities, notably *rouille de seiche* (cuttlefish in garlic sauce). Many meat dishes are similar too. But Languedoc also has its own skewered sausages (*saucisses*), sautéed in goose fat and served with spicy tomato purée. And in the west, around Carcassonne, you enter the country of *cassoulet*, a name that identifies Languedoc quite as much as Cathars or rugby football: this supreme dish is a white bean stew with *confit d'oie* (preserved goose), pork and mutton, spicy sausages and pork rind. Don't eat too much for lunch, if you want to stay awake. Up inland, the country people have some unusual soups, such as *ouillade* (cabbage, beans, mushrooms and salt pork) and *mourtaïrol* (chicken bouillon with saffron).

Cévennes and Lozère

The peasant cuisine of these uplands, unsophisticated but tasty, is quite similar to some other parts of the Massif Central, such as Auvergne. You will find rough, dark country ham (*jambon du pays*) and other charcuterie; and such main dishes as *choux farcies* (cabbage stuffed with mincemeat) and *tripoux* (tripe cooked in wine). One Lozère speciality is *aligot,* a purée of potatoes and cheese, served with meat. Local chestnuts and truffles enter into many dishes, and in winter there's wild boar and other game.

Nouvelle cuisine

Although the traditional dishes of Provence and Languedoc, and of France as a whole, still form the staple fare of most restaurants, a large number of the more expensive, ambitious and trendy ones are nowadays strongly influenced by the style of cooking that has swept France since the 1960s. This so-called *nouvelle cuisine* (or *cuisine inventive*) was conceived as a reaction, not against simple country cooking, but against the heavy sauces and high calories of grand-hotel *haute cuisine.* It has marked a return to a lighter, purer manner, using very fresh ingredients cooked rapidly in their own juices, to bring out their full flavours. The chef is expected to deviate from classic recipes and try out daring new blends.

In the hands of a master chef, the results can be wonderful – and several renowned exponents of the new style are today at work in Provence, such as Roger Vergé at Mougins, Dominique Le Stanc at Nice, Alain Ducasse at Monte Carlo. In their restaurants, you will sample inspired cooking, based on seasonal local produce. Unfortunately, a great many less talented or less scrupulous cooks have also succumbed to the trend: in their hands, minuscule portions are arranged over-decoratively around the plate, and the tastes are bland and chi-chi (for example, minced vegetables shaped like tiny cakes, or wafer-thin strips of meat with a dull spinach purée). No, give me a pungent *cassoulet* any day! And as this style is still *à la mode* with a moneyed clientéle, chefs can get away with fancy prices: many *nouvelle cuisine* places offer poor value for money. It's an expensive vogue, which you'll not find in a modest auberge.

Happily, the better *nouvelle* chefs are not so much turning their back on regional cuisine as seeking to re-explore it – and the style was never meant as a break with the classic tradition, more an adaptation of it to suit a calorie-conscious age. In Provence, many of the best chefs are using old local recipes as a basis for their innovations – and the results can be a subtle blend of the old and new. This fashion for presenting old homely traditional dishes in a new, lighter form – the rediscovery of *'la cuisine de gran'mere',* it's called – has gained ground in recent years. But chefs often give their dishes long and complex names, and are constantly changing their menu by adding different inventions. So how can a visitor tell whether a place is serving *nouvelle* or traditional food? Simply by seeing how the menu is written. And how can he differentiate in advance between good and bad *nouvelle cuisine*? Simply by reading the guidebooks or taking local advice. But a lover of French food, unless his purse is very fat, might be advised to stick to the traditional restaurants.

Foreign cuisines | There was a time when the French despised all foreign cuisines and outside Paris it was hard to find any but French. More recently, under the impact of immigrants, foreign holidays and the general opening of frontiers, things have changed. In southern France, the exotic restaurants that you will come across everywhere are Vietnamese and south Chinese; Italian (often run by Corsicans or Niçois); and to an extent North African (serving dishes such as *couscous* and *merguez*, and usually run by *pieds-noirs* repatriates). In the bigger towns, the range is wider. In Marseille, for instance, you can eat Armenian, Brazilian or Hungarian; in Nice, German, Irish or Moroccan. Flip through these pages, and you'll discover where to find Danish food near Vence, American in Cannes, or English puddings in Avignon and Menton – should you want to.

Wines of Provence and Languedoc

There is a massive variety, and most local wines are palatable, even if these two regions have few 'great' wines compared with Bordeaux or Burgundy. Some of the best, going from east to west, are given here.

The hills behind Nice produce Bellet, a rare, select wine that comes as red, rosé or white (this last, very dry, goes well with shellfish). The Côtes de Provence come from north of Toulon: Ott, Pierrefeu and Château Minuty are labels to look for. The area east of Marseille produces two fruity reds, Bandol and Château Simone, as well as the dry white wine of Cassis, ideal with shellfish or *bouillabaisse*. Of the Coteaux d'Aix-en-Provence, I can especially recommend the Château de Fonscolombe. In the Rhône Valley, the famous Châteauneuf-du-Pape, warm and full-bodied, tends to be a bit over-priced. Better bets are the fruity Côtes du Rhône, such as Gigondas (white as well as red). Cheaper but still very drinkable are the Côtes du Lubéron and Côtes du Ventoux, such as the Domaine des Anges, whose grower is English.

In Languedoc, the area just west of the Rhône produces Tavel, a strong, dry rosé, not cheap; also Listel gris-de-gris, a light and cloudy rosé from vines growing on sand near the sea south of Nîmes. The plain around Montpellier, Béziers and Narbonne produces a vast quantity of *vin ordinaire* that used to have a poor reputation. However, many of its vineyards have now been replanted and upgraded, and wines such as Coteaux du Languedoc are perfectly pleasant and still quite cheap. Further west is the country of Corbières and Minervois, two robust reds that are generally underrated and thus good value: Fitou is worth looking out for.

In the wine-producing areas, a great many wine-châteaux and other wine-farms will admit visitors who want to look round their premises and then do some tasting with a view to buying. Usually it is best to telephone in advance. You will probably be shown the *chais* (wine-making equipment and storerooms), and will be allowed to taste a few samples, then, if you wish, place an order, and maybe take some cases away with you in the car. But you won't be welcome if you try to do a lot of free drinking without buying any bottles! Inside most wine-marketing towns, such as Châteauneuf-du-Pape or Montpellier, there are also *caves* (wine-cellars), run by local firms or growers' cooperatives, where you can also taste and purchase, or just buy a drink as in a café. In the regional chapters of this book, I give a number of addresses of châteaus, wine-farms and *caves* that can be visited in this way.

Although in a shop you can buy reasonable wine for a few francs, restaurant mark-ups tend to be heavy. However, some places do offer a house wine in a carafe or jug, at a fair price. Bottled wines from a particular area are classified *appellation contrôlée* (or AOC for short), except for the very cheapest which are *vin de pays*. A *vin de table* is a simple blended wine from no special area, and in restaurants these often come in *pichets*.

The local beers are nothing special; Alsatian or imported ones are better, but pricier. If you want draught beer, ask for it *pression*; a half-pint glass is *un demi*. For non-alcohol drinkers, a good refreshing drink is *diabolo menthe* – fizzy lemonade with peppermint syrup. As for apéritifs, by far the most popular one locally is *pastis*, produced en masse in the Marseille area. Aniseed flavoured, not unlike Greek *ouzo*, it is drunk diluted with water and ice which make it go cloudy, and on a hot day it's most refreshing – but also heady stuff. Ricard and '51 are the drier brands; Pernod is sweeter.

Entertainment

Fêtes and festivals

Nearly every village has its annual local fête, while in many places you'll find more elaborate traditional events (see above, under folklore traditions, and under each town in the gazetteer). Summer arts festivals have also become very popular: among the best known are the theatre festival at Avignon, the music festival at Aix, the opera season at Orange, the modern dance festival at Montpellier and the Jazz Parade at Nice, which are all highly international. To get the best seats you need to book ahead. So much in vogue are events of this kind that many a small town or village now stages some music or drama festival each summer, such as concerts in an old church or château. The artistic quality may be uneven, but the ambience is generally sympathetic.

Opera, music and theatre

Year-round culture is also of variable quality. Monte Carlo, Nice, Marseille, Avignon and Montpellier all have opera houses with resident companies that mount their own productions, usually October to March: the sheer number of these companies compares well with the provincial opera scene in Britain, although standards may be low compared with Germany. The French have become a music-loving nation, and in many towns you'll find regular concerts of all kinds. As for theatre, the best state-backed repertory company is in Marseille; this city and Avignon both have a lively theatre scene, including a number of small fringe groups, whereas on the Côte d'Azur the picture is more bleak. In some bigger towns you'll find *café-théâtres* or satiric cabarets; but to understand these you need good French, and some knowledge of the local scene – often of the local patois too!

Cinemas

In bigger towns there are always one or two cinemas showing foreign films with the original soundtrack plus subtitles: these are marked 'vo' (*version originale*) in the newspaper listings. Most imported films are shown dubbed ('vf' or *version française*); and the same applies on television, except for films of some artistic quality. The French remain a cinemanic nation and the range of films on offer is usually very wide by Anglo-American standards; as well as the cinemas there are various small film clubs. Bigger towns publish a weekly or monthly listings magazine of the *What's On* type, useful for theatres and sport as well as for films.

Bullfights

Real Spanish-style bullfights, where the bulls are killed, take place in summer in the old Roman arenas at Nîmes and Arles, and in some other towns of western Provence and Languedoc. The bulls and matadors mostly come from Spain, but the toreadors are often local. Also popular are the much less lethal *courses à la cocarde*, when amateur toreadors compete to snatch rosettes from the bulls' horns.

Football As in so many countries, association football is one of the most popular of spectator sports, and there are matches at weekends in many bigger towns: Marseille has a notably good team. In Languedoc, rugby football is something of a cult pursuit, and Béziers has one of the best teams in France.

Motor racing Much the best racing track in the region is the Circuit Paul Ricard, near Bandol, with many big annual events (see p. 168).

Zoos and dolphinariums The nicest zoos are at Bandol and St Jean-Cap-Ferrat, preferred to those at Monaco, Toulon and Marseille. Best of the safari parks is the big one at Sigean near Narbonne, a cut above that at Fréjus. Up in the Lozère, at Marvejols, there is a park of tame wolves, while the Camargue has a huge bird sanctuary (you need special permission to visit). Marineland at Antibes puts on lively dolphin displays. For all these places, see the Gazetteer.

Casinos Under French law, casinos are allowed only in tourist resorts or spas, not in ordinary towns: so Marseillais must go out to Cassis for their gambling. American games are everywhere nearly as common today as continental ones, bringing a touch of Las Vegas, and the fine old *belle époque* casinos with their opulent decor are now full of people in casual clothes: the old 'sport of kings' has been cheerfully democratised. Monte Carlo remains much the liveliest gambling centre in the region, with four casinos; in France itself, the best are at Cannes, Cassis and Beaulieu. Casinos are open year round, except public holidays. They are obliged by law to supply general entertainment, too, so many of them have discos, dinner-dances, and so on. To gamble, you must be over twenty-one and show a passport or identity card.

Nightlife Discos are everywhere, even in villages, where they tend to operate just at the weekends. The smartest discos and nightclubs are in St Tropez, Cannes, Monte Carlo and one or two other such towns, where often they are attached to some smart hotel. Such nightspots are not private clubs requiring membership, nor are they truly public: they will let you in at their own whim, according to whether your face fits, and how full they are. The best tactic is to dress modishly and show some air of authority.

Sport

Boules

This is one of the great traditional games of France, above all in the South, and today it remains just as popular: everywhere you will see the locals playing it intently, not only in little village squares but also beside smart promenades. It's a kind of original version of bowls, played with small metal balls on an earth pitch; there are two teams, and as in bowls a team must roll its balls as close as possible to the jack without hitting it. If you are adept at bowls, you can always ask to join in – and might be accepted. With *pétanque*, a local variant of *boules*, the pitch is shorter and the players stand in a circle.

Fishing

In the open season, roughly March to September, there's plenty of scope for trout fishing, also carp and perch, in the many rivers and lakes of the wild hinterland. A permit is easy to obtain and not expensive: ask for details at a tourist office, or through your own local angling association.

Golf

This is becoming very popular in France and many new courses are being built. Temporary club membership is usually possible: ask at a tourist office. The best golf courses, with superior nineteenth holes, are near Monte Carlo, Cannes and St Raphaël: see the gazetteer.

Skiing

The south of France is not simply sun, sea and sand, but skiing too if you want it – and close at hand. There are some small ski resorts just behind Nice; better and bigger ones, Auron, Isola 2000 and Valberg (see pp. 101–2), are further up in the mountains but still within ninety minutes' drive of the coast. They have excellent pistes, lifts, ski schools and facilities for children. You can hire or buy skiing equipment on the spot.

Swimming and beaches

There are bathing beaches at frequent points along the coast. Most are sandy: but be warned that from Antibes to Italy the beach is shingle, save for some roughish imported sand at Monte Carlo and Menton. Beaches in or near towns get crowded in summer. Beaches are free, apart from the fee-paying 'smart' ones at St Tropez, Cannes, Nice and Monte Carlo: some of these belong to hotels and most are well equipped with beach-mattresses and parasols for hire, also changing rooms, bars, even restaurants. Many of the better hotels have swimming pools, while in almost any little town you can find a *piscine municipale*. Toplessness is now almost universally accepted, indeed is the norm; at some places on the coast – notably Cap d'Agde and Port Cros – there are nudist beaches.

Campaigns against pollution have been fairly effective. Only in the industrial sector west of Marseille, and in some places between Nice and Menton, do some beaches still tend to be dirty.

Tennis and squash

Some of the better hotels have their own tennis courts, but squash courts are rarer. In many towns you can join a tennis or squash club as a temporary member, or hire a public court by the hour. All courts are hard.

Watersports

All the main resorts offer sailing, windsurfing and water-skiing; in some you can also do water-parachuting, scuba-diving or underwater fishing. Ask at the local tourist office. Many resorts have big, well-equipped marinas full of sailing boats, but the hiring of moorings is expensive: best are Cap d'Agde, La Grande Motte, Port-Camargue, Embiez, Port-Grimaud, La Napoule, Cannes and Monte Carlo.

Shopping

A certain number of traditional, locally-made articles can be bought at boutiques in the cities or, a little more cheaply, in the villages where they are produced. Items that might be worth seeking out include: olive oil and olive-based products, such as soaps and olive-wood sculptures; Provençal ceramics, notably the white faience of Moustiers-Ste-Marie; glasswork, especially that from Biot, near Antibes; painting on silk; coloured fabrics and Provençal costumes (Souleiado and Les Olivades are well-known shops with branches in several towns); chocolates, sweets and biscuits (notably in Arles and Nice); and *santons*. Among the many villages (see the gazetteer for details) where local artists and craftsmen are at work in some numbers, or where their wares can be bought, are Biot, Cabris, Cogolin, Gordes, St-Paul-de-Vence, Salernes, Seillans, Tourette-sur-Loup and Vallauris.

Modern shops of all kinds are plentiful, including the giant new supermarkets (*hypermarchés*) on the edge of towns: these have their own car parks and often are open till 10 p.m. If you are on a self-catering holiday they can be convenient, for their range of fresh foods is huge and their prices are very competitive. But it can be more fun – after all, you're in France – to visit a traditional open-air market or the kind of covered market made up of a number of small foodstores. Almost every town has its outdoor market in some shady square or avenue, where farmers come to sell their produce. Some are open daily, some weekly (mostly Saturdays), and often mornings only. Their food tends to be fresher than in the shops, and slightly cheaper: the prices are marked, and little is gained by trying to haggle.

General Basics

Banks, currency

The French franc is divided into 100 centimes: there are coins for 5, 10, 20 and 50 centimes, and for 1, 2, 5 and 10 francs, and banknotes for 20, 50, 100, 200 and 500 francs. Shops and restaurants usually give change gladly, even for 500 francs on a modest purchase. All prices are written in new francs, but colloquially many people still talk with each other in old francs (100 new francs), even though the old franc officially ceased to exist over thirty years ago. This can be confusing.

Banks are generally open from 9 a.m. to 4 p.m. or 5 p.m., though nearly all close for an hour or more at lunchtime. They are closed at weekends, but in bigger towns you will find exchange bureaux open at main stations, airports and tourist offices, at least on Saturdays. Many hotels will change money, but you get a much better rate in a bank (and often better still in your own bank back home). Travellers' cheques issued by American Express, Thomas Cook and the better-known banks are widely accepted, but the commission on them tends to vary: it can be a good idea to shop around.

The French do not yet use credit cards as widely as the British or Americans, and many smaller hotels, restaurants and garages will not take them. The most widely accepted card is Visa (Carte Bleue), to which Eurocard/Access/Mastercard is now affiliated in France, so this should be equally valid. These cards also enable you to draw money from banks and main post offices that display the relevant sign. American Express, and to a lesser extent Diners' Club, tend to be accepted by larger establishments in tourist areas. For UK nationals, a useful alternative to travellers' cheques and credit cards is the Eurocheque system, now quite widely used in France: ask for details at your own bank.

Loss or theft of travellers' cheques or a credit card should be reported at once to the local police and by phone to your bank.

Clothing

If you want to look right in the smarter resorts on the Côte, dress informally and lightly but with style. The French are fashion-conscious and tend to judge people by their dress; and though for instance a man need seldom wear a tie, the quality and cut of his shirts, trousers and shoes will be noted. In country areas, it matters less what you wear. In spring and autumn, as well as winter, temperatures can vary rapidly, so it's best to bring some warm clothes as well as light ones.

Customs and courtesies

The French are still quite formal in their manners: they like to shake hands and often kiss on greeting and parting, they call each other 'Monsieur' and 'Madame' without surnames (except between friends). It is true that these formalities are now waning among a younger generation, who use titles less than their elders, and Christian names much more. But *vous* is used rather than the familiar *tu*, except between relations, close friends and some workmates, and when speaking to small children. Of course, friends conversing in a bistro will appear anything but formal, especially in the easy-going South: but a foreign visitor will rarely penetrate into these intimate circles, and you must expect to stay on *vous* terms with new acquaintances, except between students.

When invited for a meal in a French home, it is customary to bring a gift such as flowers or liqueur chocolates (but not a bottle of wine, which is such a routine object in France that it would be almost like bringing your hostess a cauliflower).

Documents needed for entering France

Nationals of thirty-eight countries no longer need a visa to visit France, but just a passport, for stays of up to three months. They include all EU countries, plus Canada, Japan, New Zealand, Switzerland and the USA. British and Irish citizens can obtain a visitor's passport at a post office, valid for a year. If you want to stay more than three months, EU nationals will need a *carte de séjour*, obtainable from a French consulate or from the police or *préfecture*, and non-EU nationals will require a *visa d'établissement*, for which you should apply to a French consulate before you leave for France.

If coming by car, you will need a full driving licence (but not an international one), as well as the car's registration logbook, a national identity sticker, and an insurance certificate proving that you are covered for third party. A 'green card' is no longer essential for EU nationals, but it is advisable to bring one, as the best means of proving that you have valid cover.

Electric current

The voltage nearly everywhere is 220 volts, save in a few rural areas where it may still be 110 volts. Most plugs are standard European two-pin, but some are three-pin (two 'female', one 'male'), so it's wise to bring an adaptor – and a non-electric razor too.

Embassies and consulates

Sixty-eight countries have consulates or consulates-general in Marseille, among them:

Germany, 338 Avenue du Prado, 13008; tel. 91 77 60 90.
United Kingdom, 24 Avenue du Prado, 13006; tel. 91 53 43 32.
United States, 13 Blvd. Paul-Peyral, 13286; tel. 91 54 92 00.

There are also nine consulates in Monaco, and sixteen in the Nice area, including:

United Kingdom: 2 Rue du Congrès, 06000 Nice; 93 82 32 04.
Eire, 152 Blvd. Kennedy, 06600 Cap d'Antibes; tel. 93 61 50 63.
United States, 31 Rue Maréchal-Joffre; tel. 93 88 89 55.

Australia and New Zealand are not represented in the South of France.

Health, insurance and chemists

British visitors can use the French health service on the same conditions as the French, but American and Commonwealth ones have to pay full medical costs. Under an EU reciprocal agreement, those entitled to full UK benefits can obtain the same reimbursements for medical care as the French, so long as they can produce form E111. You acquire this before you leave home by asking your local DHSS office for leaflet SA28/30, and filling in form CM1 on its back page: ask also for leaflet SA36, which will tell you how to use E111 in France.

This may sound fearfully bureaucratic, but it could save a lot of money and hassle, should you fall ill or have an accident. Non-EU citizens would be wise to take out medical insurance before they come to France. The French health service is not entirely free. Patients must pay their bills directly, then apply at a French social security office for a refund, which is usually around 70 to 75 per cent of the doctors' and hospitals' authorised charges; and this can take months. So even Britons might do well to take out some extra insurance. A GP will generally charge 70 to 80 francs for a consultation, a specialist much more. The brighter side of this picture is that public medical care is generally of a high standard, hospitals are well equipped and doctors excellent, though nursing can be a bit rough-and-ready. It is easy in larger towns to find English-speaking doctors.

Chemists in towns stay open on Sundays and late at night on a rota basis: the local paper or the window of any chemist will give details. In Marseille, chemists always open late are: Garbit et Michel, 166 La Canebière, and Brémond, 183 Rue de Rome; in Nice, Pharmacie Principale, 10 Rue Masséna.

Laundry and dry cleaning

Dry cleaning shops are numerous, rapid and efficient, and many will also launder shirts or advise you where to go. The larger hotels often have a laundry and valeting service, but it tends to be expensive.

Newspapers, radio, TV

There are several major daily papers in the region, though none is very inspired. They each tend to circulate widely outside the city where they are published. In Marseille, the main dailies are *Le Méridional*, rightwing, and *Le Provençal*, pro-Socialist, while *Le Soir* is the evening paper. In Nice the local daily is *Nice Matin*, and in Montpellier *Midi Libre*, both right-of-centre. These and some other towns also have weekly magazines of the *What's On* type that list cultural and sporting events and useful addresses. British papers and the *Herald Tribune* are widely available at kiosks, on the day of publication or the next day.

Now that radio in France has been freed from state control, a mass of little local radio stations have sprung up, even including one in English in the Nice area, *Riviera 104*, that has regular news bulletins. *Radio Monte Carlo* and the local stations of *Radio France* are good for local news. There are six regular French TV channels, including *TF1*,

France 2 and *Canal Plus*, a subscription service showing films and sport. *France 3* is regionally slanted and has evening regional news and magazine programmes. A few of the larger hotels offer some English-language channels by satellite.

Opening hours and dates

For banks and chemists, see above; for post offices, see below. In the French provinces nearly everyone still takes a long lunch break: most offices will close between 12 and 2 p.m., and food shops between 1 p.m. and 3 or 4 p.m., though larger stores may remain open. Most shops stay open till 7 p.m., and food shops till 8 p.m. or later: in resorts and larger towns, especially in season, you'll find quite a range of shops open very late. Many shops that stay open all Saturday will remain closed on Monday morning.

● Please note that all State museums and many others too are closed on Tuesdays; the remainder tend to have a weekly closing day which is often Monday. Many are closed on the main public holidays. Most museums close for at least a month in winter, often November, and in rural areas they are likely to close all winter. As these details change constantly, they are not given in the gazetteer, so you should enquire locally.

Police and the law

Should you be arrested, your rights as a detainee are not as clear-cut as, say, those in Britain. The police are allowed to hold a suspect for up to forty-eight hours without making a charge, and this period can sometimes be extended to ninety-six hours. If arrested, you should at once ask to telephone your consulate, and request that they send an official to advise you of your rights and help you find a lawyer. After a maximum of ninety-six hours, if you are not then released, the case will be handed over to a *juge d'instruction* (examining magistrate), and a lawyer will then be able to help you more fully. For what to do if involved in a car accident, see p. 37.

The French police – *les flics* in popular parlance – are of several kinds, and are very often armed. The Gendarmerie Nationale, formally part of the army, operates mainly in rural areas and deals with such matters as traffic accidents. The Police Nationale has a fairly similar role in towns. The famous Compagnies Républicaines de Sécurité, used mostly for crowd control and handling riots, today keep a fairly low profile. The French police used to have a reputation for roughness and rudeness, but recently they have been trying to improve their image, with some success, and are now quite often friendly and helpful to visitors.

Post and post offices

Post offices are marked with a yellow sign or with the letters PTT. The larger ones are open 8 a.m. to 7 p.m. on weekdays, 8 a.m. till noon on Saturdays, but in smaller places they tend to close much earlier, at 5 p.m. or even 4 p.m., or from 12 to 2 p.m. You can collect Poste Restante mail at any central post office, but must bring proof of identification and pay a small charge. Stamps can be bought from yellow vending machines or in cafés – much quicker than queuing in a post office where the staff are often disagreeable, especially in bigger towns. Letters within Europe go automatically by air; elsewhere they may go by sea unless you specify air mail. Letters sent from the South of France to Britain will take three or four days, and to North America by airmail up to ten days.

Postcodes It is important to put the right postcode on a letter to France. The postcode is always five numerals, placed before the name of the town or village, and the first two numerals are the number of the department (you will see those two numerals also at the end of car number plates, for example, 06 for the Alpes-Maritimes, 13 for the Bouches-du-Rhône whose capital is Marseille). The capital of the department will be those two numerals plus 000, while other towns will follow on: thus Marseille is 13000, Aix-en-Provence is 13100, and so on – it is all very Gallically logical. Further complications are that a big city such as Marseille will have *arrondissement* codes, for instance, 13001 etc, while many businesses now use a 'cédex' system which gives a more complicated coding. In short, it's best to try to find out the postcode before sending a letter. In the gazetteer we have given the postcode for each town, to help you when writing to a hotel. The departments in Provence and Languedoc, with the postcodes of their capital towns, are as follows:

Alpes-de-Haute-Provence	04000 Digne
Alpes-Maritimes	06000 Nice
Aude	11000 Carcassonne
Bouches-du-Rhône	13000 Marseille
Gard	30000 Nîmes
Hérault	34000 Montpellier
Lozère	48000 Mende
Var	83000 Toulon
Vaucluse	84000 Avignon

Public holidays

The national public holidays are: 1 January, New Year's Day; Easter Monday; 1 May, Labour Day; 8 May, VE Day; Ascension Day (sixth Thursday after Easter); Whit Monday (second Monday after Ascension); 14 July, Bastille Day; 15 August, Assumption; 1 November, All Saints' Day; 11 November, Remembrance Day; 25 December, Christmas Day. On most of these days, many shops, hotels and restaurants will remain open. But when the holiday falls on a Tuesday or Thursday, most people in offices and businesses will *faire le pont*, that is, give themselves a four-day weekend by taking the Monday or Friday off too. This can make tourist spots very crowded, even in November.

Religion

The vast majority of France's population is at least nominally Catholic; only about 3 per cent are Protestant, while some 700,000 are Jewish and 1.5 million are Muslim, nearly all North African immigrants. However, the influence of the Catholic church has been waning and average weekly attendance at Mass is no more than 14 per cent (higher in rural areas).

In the South of France, there are still a few Anglican churches with resident clergy that hold services in English for their communities. They include: St John's, Menton; Holy Trinity, Nice; St John's, St Raphaël; and All Saints', Marseille. There are many Protestant 'temples' (as they call their churches) in the Cévennes and the Nîmes area (see p. 16), but they are most unlike Anglican churches. Marseille, Nice and some other towns have synagogues.

Telephoning

The French telephone service, which used to be an appalling sick joke, has improved out of all recognition and is now very efficient. Over 90 per cent of homes have a telephone, and almost all new applicants get one installed within a fortnight. Modern high-tech gimmicks are all the rage: for example, the Minitel, a home videotex service used primarily as an electronic nationwide telephone directory. Several million homes, as well as offices, are now equipped with these computer screens, which are due to replace printed directories.

Street telephone cabins, which used to be rare, are now commonplace, though as in some other countries they tend to break down or get vandalised. They take 50c, 1- or 5-franc pieces. The cabins taking telephone cards (*télécartes*) are less often out of order, and are convenient when phoning long-distance; but though common in towns these are still rare in country areas. You can equally well ask for a booth in a post office and pay afterwards at the counter; or phone from a café. But beware of the high surcharges levied by most hotels on calls made from bedrooms. Anywhere, the cost of a call will vary with the time of day. For telephoning abroad, the cheap rates apply between 8 p.m. and 8 a.m., and on Saturday afternoons and Sunday. Within France, an elaborate scale applies: in short, it is cheaper to phone at lunchtime or after 6 p.m., and it becomes much cheaper after 9.30 pm and on Saturday afternoons and Sunday. All French telephone numbers have eight figures, and in the provinces you just dial these with no prefix: but if telephoning to Paris you must first dial 16-1. The prefix for calls abroad is 19, followed by the country code. The ringing tone in France is long regular bleeps, and the engaged signal is short sharp ones.

Time difference

French time is one hour ahead of British time, except for about three weeks in March/April and three weeks in September/October when it is the same (this varies annually). French time is six hours ahead of US and Canadian East Coast time.

Tipping

Extra service charges are now illegal in France, and all bills will automatically include service. However, if you are pleased with the service in a restaurant or café, it is usual to leave a small tip of some 2 or 3 per cent. Hotel porters and staff who carry luggage will also expect a few francs. Taxi drivers and hairdressers should be given 10 to 15 per cent.

Toilets

French toilets and plumbing, like the telephone service, have improved greatly in recent years. Gone from the pavements are the old public *vespasiennes*, satirised in *Clochemerle*, and in their place have come, in towns, smart high-tech contraptions called *sanisettes* for which you pay a franc or two. They are unisex. But beware of letting play around in them, for the powerful flushing can be dangerous. In cafés and restaurants, toilets are of variable quality, generally clean, but often still of the old-style hole-in-the-floor variety which are considered more hygienic than a sit-down seat. If you are cut short and want to use a café's toilet, it is polite at least to order a drink.

Vocabulary

The Provençal and Languedocien accent is harsh and nasal: many words ending in 'n' or 'nt', where in standard French these final consonants are not pronounced, acquire an ugly 'ng' sound in the south. Thus *'maison'* sounds like *'mesong'*, *'pain'* like *'pang'*, *'maintenant'* like *'mangtenang'*. People speak fast, and it may take time to get used to their accent.

Here's a short glossary of local words (for food terms, see pp. 49–51):

baou–high rock
bastide–large farmhouse or mansion
borie–primitive beehive-shaped stone hut
boules–early version of bowls
causse–limestone plateau
gardian–Camargue herdsman
garrigue–stony, shrub-covered foothills of the causses
manade–herd of bulls or horses (in the Camargue)
mas–mansion or large farmhouse
mistral–strong north wind, blowing mainly in winter
pastis–aniseed-flavoured apéritif
pic–conical-shaped hill or peak
santon–costumed figurine, made of clay or wood.

Gazetteer

Introduction

The gazetteer dealing with Provence is divided for convenience into four parts: the Côte d'Azur, that is, the coast from Menton to Cannes, and its sub-Alpine hinterland; the coast to the west, from the Esterel as far as Marseille; the central hilly hinterland of Provence, from the mountains behind Marseille up as far as Sisteron and across to Mont Ventoux; and the plain of western Provence. A fifth chapter deals with Languedoc.

The Côte d'Azur

The Côte d'Azur

Introduction

The English in the nineteenth century gave the name 'French Riviera' to the beautiful stretch of coast between Menton and Cannes that became the foremost playground of Europe. The French dubbed it 'Côte d'Azur', a term nowadays used also to embrace the resorts further west, notably St Tropez: but the true Côte d'Azur does not go beyond Cannes. This is now the Alpes-Maritimes department, still the leading tourist area of France; and its capital and biggest town is Nice (which until 1860 was under Italian rule).

Until the 1930s, tourism on '*la Côte*' (as the French always call it) was confined mainly to the winter months, when the leisured and wealthy from northern Europe would seek out its warm, sheltered climate. Today fashions have changed. Not only is summer now the main season, but also the old elitist visitors are vastly outnumbered by a new mass-market tourism. However, the Côte stays active in winter too, thanks in part to the booming new vogue for 'business tourism' (conventions and incentive trips). And the towns are big enough to have a busy all-year-round life of their own, irrespective of visitors. The four main resorts, in intense rivalry, are intriguingly different in personality. Flowery Menton, favoured by the elderly, has a cosy prettiness and a genteel, old-fashioned air. Monte Carlo, only 8 km away, is a total contrast: very up-to-date, brashly glamorous, more than a little Americanised, a town of skyscrapers and publicity-conscious jet-setters. Nice is a bustling metropolis. And Cannes, smaller than Nice but smarter, is an efficient, glittering showcase of modern high-quality tourism. This coast of a mere 100 km is very built-up, just one succession of towns, and new high-rise building has wrought some havoc on the landscape. However, just inland is a wild and lovely hinterland – medieval hill villages, Alpine peaks, even ski slopes within a few minutes' drive of Nice.

Nice

06000

The city extends for many kilometres along the curving silver shore of the Baie des Anges, and its new suburbs have pushed their way far up into the hills that rise steeply behind. Seen from any such vantage point, the Côte d'Azur's capital looks a big place, as indeed it is – not just a tourist resort but a busy and diverse commercial city, the fifth largest in France (all-year population 338,486).

It is a town of strong character – and of contrasts. The sophisticated seafront hotels along the Promenade des Anglais, and the expensive boutiques in the streets behind, seem a world away from the teeming medieval alleys of the Vieille Ville, where many poor people still live. And the tidy, smoothly-run façade of the city does not easily accord with its other image of gross civic corruption and Mafia-style crime, which is connived at in high places. How to explain these paradoxes? Are they something to do with the variety of the city's inhabitants? Some are true Niçois with deep local roots, others the descendants of immigrants from Italy or Russia, or retired people from northern towns, not to mention the constant ebb and flow of visitors. The Niçois are business-geared and hard-working: but like all southerners they relish the periodic release of exuberant entertainment – as in their famous Lenten carnival and flower battles.

Getting there and transport

With its huge tourist trade, Nice is well served by all kinds of transport. Nice-Côte d'Azur Airport, on the coast 7 km west of the town and recently much enlarged, is one of the four busiest in France, with direct flights to some eighty cities worldwide; there are over twenty daily flights to Paris (tel. 93 21 30 30). A bus runs every fifteen minutes to the town centre. The main station, quite central, has two TGVs to Paris a day (journey time seven hours) as well as good rail links with Marseille, Milan, and so on; in summer a fast and frequent local train service runs along the coast. A new *autoroute*, winding over the hills behind, is only 4 km from the city centre and will take you to Genoa, Marseille and Paris. Regular bus services operate to most nearby towns, while the city itself has a good bus network (infrequent after 9 p.m.). There are tourist offices at the station, tel. 93 87 07 07 and at 5 Avenue Gustave-V, tel. 97 87 60 60.

History

Nice was founded in c. 350 BC by Greeks from Marseille who gave it the name Nikêa after their defeat of local tribes (*Niké* was their goddess of victory). The Romans then chose the inland hill of Cimiez, in today's northern suburbs, as site for a major town that grew to some 20,000 population, but was later ruined by Saracen and Barbarian invasions. A town was rebuilt at Nikêa, and after the tenth century it flourished, first under the Counts of Provence, then after 1388 under the Italian Dukes of Savoy. From around 1450 to 1550 it was the centre of an important school of religious painting headed by the Bréa family, many of whose works can today be seen in churches and museums in the area. In 1631 Nice suffered fearfully from a plague. From 1793 to 1814 it switched allegiance to France, but was then taken back by Savoy, and was not finally unified with France until 1860. It still has a somewhat Italianate character.

By the 1860s Nice was already a busy winter resort, thanks mainly to the English who had started to come in the late eighteenth century, led by the writer Tobias Smollett in 1763. This truculent man came to ease his consumption, and startled the local doctors by taking up sea-bathing, which he found did him good. But he hated the cooking, notably the garlic, and thought the Niçois uncultured and inhospitable. 'Most of the females are pot-bellied,' he wrote, adding: 'The great poverty of the people here is owing to their religion. Half of their time is lost in observing the great number of festivals; and half of their substance is given to mendicant friars and parish priests.'

Nice as a resort pre-dates Cannes or Menton. In 1822 the sizeable English colony, annoyed by the difficulty of access to the shore, financed the building of a wide coastal path – and this became the promenade that still bears their name. In 1864 the arrival of the railway gave a new impetus to tourism, and British, Russian and other aristocrats were soon flooding in every winter, led by Queen Victoria. She came with her retinue to the palatial Hôtel Regina (see p. 77) which was built for her; she also enjoyed touring the countryside in a small donkey-drawn buggy, chatting with local peasants. For this she became very popular, and is still venerated in the area. Meanwhile the Russians built their splendid cathedral; and grand hotels with names like West End and Westminster sprang up along the front. Nietzsche and Oscar Wilde were among the visitors.

Nice today A mayor in any big French town wields immense personal power – and from 1928 to 1990 Nice was ruled by a kind of elective dynasty, the right-wing Médecin family. Jean Médecin, mayor from 1928 to 1965, played an equivocal wartime role. At first he backed Vichy, but then he quarrelled with the Italians when they occupied Nice, and moved to support the Resistance: for this he was rewarded by being permitted to remain in office after the Liberation. On his death in 1965 his son Jacques took his place, and was then re-elected for further six-year terms in 1971, 1977, 1983 and 1989. He was a charming, cultivated man with a rich American wife, and a fine administrator who ran his city with dynamic efficiency: he made it clean and well ordered, and gave it excellent amenities such as new roads and car parks, free museum entrance, free outdoor concerts and festivals, and so on. However, Médecin's authoritarian style, and above all his wheeler-dealing methods of rule, were constantly criticised. He practised what is known as *clientèlisme*: that is, he skilfully won over the various local interest groups, with promises and practical favours, and thus was able to infiltrate his own loyalists into most key positions, in the city itself and throughout the Alpes-Maritimes, of whose *conseil général* he became president. It was as if he virtually owned the department.

All this might be judged acceptable – even normal, in a Mediterranean town – were it not that Médecin was also known to have been friendly with those allegedly responsible for the major criminal scandals that have rocked Nice in recent years. Albert Spaggiari, charged with a massive burglary of the Société Générale Bank, and Jean-Dominique Fratoni, implicated in the corruption case that led to the closure of the famous Ruhl Casino, are both today sought by French justice, but have 'disappeared' to foreign hide-outs.

Then in 1982 none other than Graham Greene entered the fray (he lives in Antibes), encouraged by his Niçois friend Max Gallo, the Socialist politician who was Médecin's most potent adversary in the city. In his polemical pamphlet *J'Accuse: The Dark Side of Nice*, Greene described how the daughter of close friends of his had been viciously persecuted by her ex-husband, a member of the Nice Mafia, who appeared to be enjoying the protection of certain local officials and so could not easily be brought to justice. Greene began his book with a warning to those planning to settle on the Côte: 'Avoid the region of Nice, which is the preserve of some of the most criminal organisations in the South of France; they deal in drugs . . . they have close connections with the Italian Mafia.' Greene wrote also of 'the connivance of high authorities' – and indeed there have been many other instances of the Ministries of Justice or of the Interior in Paris not being able to exert their control over the Nice area's police or judiciary, who are either scared of the local Mafia or in some cases maybe in its pay. Not only does Nice have an above-average crime rate, but also stories of corruption are rife – and they did not stop at the *mairie*'s front door. Under Médecin's rule, Nice became a byword in France for civic corruption, and finally he met his nemesis. In 1990, facing charges of tax fraud and bribe-taking, he fled to Uruguay, where in 1993 he was arrested, to be extradited to France where he had already been sentenced to prison *in absentia*. Thus ended the rule of the Médecin dynasty in Nice.

And yet, despite his criminal behaviour, this mayor did much to spur on the city's economy. New high-tech industries arrived; research institutes were developed, notably in oceanography and astronomy (a large hilltop Observatory has recently been constructed); and the university, a post-war venture, now has 20,000 students. Tourism is the major earner: but the luxury elite tourism of the *belle époque* is no longer viable on its own, so this industry has broadened its appeal to cater for other needs. A huge new convention centre has been built, Acropolis, and the big hotels now depend much more on this trade, and on package tours, than on individual duchesses or film stars. Only the splendid Hôtel Negresco, popular with visiting royalty and heads of state, keeps up the old superior traditions. However, Cannes and

Monaco are both more successful than Nice with the lucrative new congress trade, and they are eyed jealously.

Amid so many immigrants, the true Niçois born-and-bred are in a minority, though they still control local government. Their older bourgeois families form something of a closed society, hard to penetrate; they entertain each other at home and do not go out much at night (the bars and restaurants are full mostly of visitors). Older Niçois will often converse in their own dialect, closer to Italian than to Provençal. Like most meridionals, they are at once easy-going and volatile, quick to pick a quarrel, but just as quick to patch it up over a drink. In the southern manner, they like to haggle, barter and intrigue. And they are cynical about their politicians – how could they not be?

Main areas The central district is in two contrasting parts, divided by the dried-up riverbed of the Paillon. To the east is the Vieille Ville (see p. 76), a compact area of old alleyways next to a grid of seventeenth-century streets that still contains many of the main public buildings; above looms the rocky hill where the castle once stood, and beyond is the port. By the sea at the mouth of the Paillon is the pleasant palm-shaded Jardin Albert Ier, used for open-air plays and concerts in summer; and just inland is the stately Place Masséna, true hub of the city, whose arcaded red-stucco houses were built in the 1830s, in Genoese style. West from it leads a network of little traffic-free streets around the Rue Masséna, popular with youthful evening strollers, but now lurching downmarket – as its fast-food bars, pizzerias and cheap boutiques indicate.

One small area between here and the sea, around the Rue Halévy, has become a sleazy Soho, full of tawdry sex shops and tacky *boîtes*. Yet it's right by the eastern end of the majestic promenade that Queen Victoria loved. This palmy Promenade des Anglais, still lined with big hotels, also with blocks of flats and some offices, attracts the strolling crowds when the weather is fine: but it is far less the focus of local life than is La Croisette at Cannes, and the smart shopping streets that run parallel to it tend to be dead at night. The vibrant centre of the town's business and entertainment life has been shifting eastwards, to the Place Masséna, to the Cours Saleya in the Old Town, and to the Paillon – partly because this riverbed, once empty and derelict, has now been redeveloped for commerce and pleasure, elegantly decked out with floodlit fountains and modern works of art. It makes the sea-walk that the English built seem old hat.

North-west of the Place Masséna, a grid of commercial streets stretches up to the station, either side of the Avenue Jean-Médecin. Beyond, to the north, is the hill of Cimiez, still a select residential area. Many well-to-do people live also on the hilly Mont-Boron/Mont-Alban headland, east of the port, where some fine ornate villas survive from the *belle époque*. New housing estates and high-rise flats stretch into the hills west of the city, around Magnan and La Madeleine. And further west, near the airport and by the Var estuary, the high swivelling cranes signal the rapid advance of factory and commercial growth.

A new series of flyovers and underpasses (*mini-tunnels*) makes it possible to transit through Nice fairly fast, but within the city traffic is often dense and street parking hard. You could use your car for visits to suburban places such as Cimiez; in the city centre it's best to look for a multi-storey car park and then go on foot, or by taxi. Theft from cars is rife: leave nothing visible.

What to see

Nice has several interesting museums and other sights: the list below follows a route from east to west, starting at the castle and old town, going up to Cimiez, then down towards the airport. Municipal museums are free; others demand an entrance fee.

Château

A high rocky promontory neatly rounds off the eastern end of the Baie des Anges, forming a backdrop to the Promenade des Anglais. Here the Greeks set their acropolis and the Dukes of Savoy built their castle, which in 1706 was destroyed on Louis XIV's orders by Marshal de Berwick, a British-born French general, bastard son of James II. Today, still known as 'le Château', this flat hilltop is a sizeable public park, containing a football field as well as some Greek and Roman vestiges and the ruins of the old cathedral. You can drive or walk up, or go by lift from the promenade – and it's worth it for the fine panoramic view of Nice from the *table d'orientation* by the old *donjon*: this is the Terrace F. Nietzsche, for when living in Nice he liked to wander and ponder there.

The **Naval Museum** in the Tour Bellanda, by the sea on the south-west side, has models of warships and other memorabilia. To the east of the harbour is the old port of Nice, full of fishing and pleasure boats, from where the ferries leave for Corsica.

Vielle Ville

This urban triangle between castle, sea and Paillon is much the most fascinating part of Nice, teeming with life and rich in Baroque churches and palaces, and it well repays a detailed stroll – especially by day, when its many little shops are open. The northern part is the oldest – a maze of dim alleys festooned with washing and lined with bars, bistros and stores. Despite the inflow of tourists, artists and bohemians, this is still old-style Nice. It's very Italian as you might expect from the town's history: you could be in the backstreets of Genoa. In the Rue Droite is the **Palais Lascaris**, an ornate seventeenth-century Genoese-style mansion, now a museum decked out with furniture and works of art of the period; it includes a charming eighteenth-century pharmacy. Nearby is a statue of Cathérine Ségurane, the local heroine who is said to have repulsed the Turkish besiegers, dagger in hand, in 1543. You should also look at the church of St Jacques, and that of St Martin-St Augustin where Garibaldi was baptised and Martin Luther is said to have celebrated mass in 1510.

The southern part of the Old Town is a grid of seventeenth- to eighteenth-century streets, containing the neo-Classical opera house. Here the now-fashionable Cours Saleya has a famous market, the church of St François-de-Paule is splendidly Baroque, and the Galérie de Malacologie contains a fine aquarium and collection of molluscs.

Cimiez This hill in the northern suburbs was formerly Nice's smartest residential district, as its big villas bear witness. At the top of the Boulevard de Cimiez towers the Hôtel Regina where Queen Victoria used to winter – a gigantic monstrosity in Victorian Rococo style. Today it's a block of flats, rather down-at-heel, but the Queen's statue still stands in front of its gates.

Just to the east is the newly-excavated Roman settlement of Cimiez, which includes the remains of third-century baths, a small amphitheatre, and a high hunk of masonry that was part of a Temple of Apollo. The site is now a public park, often used for festivals. Next to it is a sixteenth-century former monastic church: its *trompe l'œil* exterior is nineteenth-century Gothic, but inside are three fine paintings in wood by the Bréa family. In the adjacent cemetery Henri Matisse lies buried.

Musée Matisse lived and worked for much of his life in Nice and Cimiez,
Matisse where he died in 1954. Next to the Roman remains at Cimiez is this attractive museum, which is being refurbished and due to reopen in 1990. It contains some thirty of his paintings, ranging from his sober early period, through his Impressionist-influenced phase, to the clear shapes and colours of his maturity, as well as many of his drawings, engravings and sculptures, and some personal effects.

In a new nearby building, a small archaeological museum contains pottery, statues and other objects found on the Roman site.

Musée Marc Born in Russia in 1887, Chagall lived for many years at St-Paul-de-
Chagall Vence where he died in 1985, aged ninety-seven. This beautiful museum in the lower part of Cimiez, opened in 1973, houses the world's fullest collection of his work and will enthrall his admirers: it was specially built for the 'Biblical Message', a series of seventeen big canvases painted from 1954 to 1967 when he was already old. Twelve of these paintings, in one gallery, evoke the Garden of Eden, Moses, and other Old Testament themes. Other rooms contain drawings and sculptures by Chagall; the elegant music room (concerts are held here monthly in summer) is bathed in a marine light from his stained-glass windows depicting the Creation; outside is a Chagall mosaic of Elias rising to heaven. His bold, sensuous colours and his whimsical sense of fantasy convey a humanistic and spiritual force, allied to his strong Jewish faith.

Russian Street names such as 'Boulevard du Tzarewitch' are reminders that
Orthodox Nice's former large Russian colony used to live in this part of the
Cathedral western suburbs, where regular services are even now held in Russian in this fine cathedral, built in 1903 in the style of churches in Moscow: its sumptuous exterior, with six green-gold, onion-cupolas, is matched by the interior where icons adorn the altar. The colony may be dying

out, but you can still hear Russian voices here. Notices in the porch appeal for help for the Christian churches in mother Russia.

Musée Masséna

This imposing seafront palace was built in the 1890s by the great-grandson of Maréchal Masséna who, like Garibaldi, was a famous son of Nice. There are mementoes of them both in this museum, which has several fascinating rooms devoted to Nice's history, as well as Bréa primitives, items of local folklore, and oriental jewellery and pottery. The palace now belongs to the city council, which holds receptions in its fine Empire-style rooms.

Musée des Beaux-Arts

Up a hill in the western suburbs, this large and highly eclectic museum of art, formerly the Musée Chéret, is full of diverting surprises. Apart from Renoir's famous 'Les Grandes Baigneuses', its works by major painters such as Fragonard, Monet and Braque are not remarkable. However, it scores heavily with lesser-known artists closely connected with Nice – the intriguing Symbolist Gustave Mossa, Marie Bashkirtseff from Russia, Van Dongen (a room of naked figures) and Jules Chéret himself, whose wild fanciful canvases are very striking. Ziem, Van Loo and Dufy, all associated with Provence, are well represented too. But be prepared to be bored by whole galleries full of mediocre portraits, badly hung.

Musée d'Art Naif

A pink villa out towards the airport houses this remarkable collection (some 600 works) of what is aptly named 'naïve art', a specific genre of paintings mostly by self-taught artists who never learned perspective, but had a vivid if ingenuous vision of daily life. These lively, gaily coloured canvases may not be 'great art', though in their own way they are most endearing. The best here are by Yugoslavs, masters of the genre, notably Josip Generalic; twenty-six other countries are represented, including some works by Anatole Jakowsky, a Romanian, who bequeathed this collection to the city.

Musée d'Art Moderne et d'Art Contemporain

A new museum in Paillon riverbed with many interesting modern works.

What to do

Festivals and other annual events

The two weeks before Lent are taken up with the **Carnival**, one of the largest events of its kind in Europe (along with Cologne and Viareggio). A costumed pre-Lenten parade had been held in Nice since the Middle Ages, but the present Carnival dates from 1873. Much time and money is spent preparing the illuminations, the giant floats and grotesque figures; and the whole jamboree culminates in a big firework display on Shrove Tuesday, followed two days later on the Quai des Etats-Unis by the main **Battle of Flowers**, with throwing of tons of confetti (other flower battles take place during the summer). The best grandstand seats for these events are expensive, and need to be booked well in advance (ask at a tourist office). The carnival is mainly for Niçois, the flower battles more for tourists, although even the carnival is short on audience participation by joyous Cologne standards (let alone London's Notting Hill's): the townsfolk just stand and watch an event that, alas, has become increasingly professional and commercialised.

Other events: in February there's a festival of modern music, and in April a dog show, book fair, automobile rally and tennis tournament. In May the Fête des Mais, a folklore event, takes place every Sunday at Cimiez park. In July, Cimiez is the venue for the Grand Jazz Parade, Europe's leading jazz festival, attracting many top names; July also sees an international folklore festival in the Jardin Albert Ier. In August, Cimiez park is used for a wine fête. In October: another automobile rally, and the Nice Philharmonic Orchestra's autumn music festival. Something for everyone, indeed.

Year-round culture

The Opéra, and the Acropolis convention centre, are both used for productions (of average quality) by the town's opera and ballet companies, and for autumn concerts by the Nice Philharmonic; summer outdoor concerts are held in the Jardin Albert Ier. The theatre scene is rather poor: a state-backed company performs out-of-season in the ugly Nouveau Théâtre de Nice, in the Paillon (a new theatre is being built). Au Pizzaiolo, Rue du Pont-Vieux, is a bawdy, boisterous cabaret theatre where the waiters are the actors (they perform in local dialect). 'Art' cinemas with subtitled foreign films include Meliès and the Acropolis Cinémathique.

Sport and bathing

The beach at Nice is shingle, and not ideal for bathing. Much of the beach by the promenade is public, but there are some well-equipped private sections where you pay: best is Ruhl-Plage which offers water-skiing and water-parachuting with trained instructors.

For tennis, try the private Nice Lawn Tennis Club or the municipal Club Vauban which also has squash courts. There is ice-skating at the Palais des Sports; for golf you must go to the Cannes or Monaco areas (see pp. 119 and 90).

Shopping and markets

In the Old Town, there's a splendid outdoor flower, fruit and vegetable market every morning except Monday in the Cours Saleya. The nearby Rue St-François has a fish market of staggering variety. The best traditional shops for local produce are also in the Old Town: Alziari, 14 Rue St François de Paule, for olives and olive-based products; Henri Auer, almost opposite, for chocolates and crystallised fruit. At La Confiserie de Nice, Quai Papacino, you can watch the bright-coloured jams being cooked and prepared. The nearby Village Ségurane is a good, varied antique market.

In the newer town, the main shopping streets are Avenue J. Médecin, and in and around the pedestrian Rue Masséna where Galérie Soisson, at no. 4, sells lovely ivory and jewellery. La Boutique Provençale, 55 Rue de France, has locally-made clothes and fabrics.

Bars, cafés and nightlife

The best bars for a drink at any time are those of some of the big hotels – the Negresco (very select), La Pérouse, Westminster, and the Méridien and Beach Regency, both with piano-bars. In a more exuberant genre, try the Brasserie Pam-Pam, Place Masséna, popular with young Niçois: it has a loud Latin American orchestra, 'tropical' decor, 'exotic' cocktails and ices, and is rather expensive. The nightlife of Nice is not very exciting. Best of the discos is trendy and noisy La Camargue, Place Charles-Félix. The famous Casino Ruhl, reopened recently, has nightly gambling; also a dinner-dance with floor show and a disco, Le Jock Club. Up a sideroad in the western suburbs, La Madonette is a rather cramped cabin-like restaurant where the waiters wear roller-skates, and satiric songs and sketches begin at 10 p.m. If your French is not equal to this, it might be better to try La Folkothèque, 8 Rue Maréchal Joffre, a new tourist-geared venture with a folk spectacle of high quality and good local folk-dancing; the food is only average, however.

Where to stay

A city with over 350 hotels has very few of real character. The more expensive hotels are along the front or near the Place Masséna; cheaper but serviceable ones are in the streets behind.

Top price

Negresco, 37 Promenade des Anglais; tel. 93 88 39 51. This noble white palace built in 1912, one of the world's greatest hotels, is privately owned and still diligently maintains the grandest traditions of the *belle époque* (the bellboys wear red breeches and white gloves). It has been classified *monument historique*, and its sumptuous interior is worth a look, even if you don't plan to stay: Picassos and Légers adorn the walls, the huge Salon Royal has a chandelier that was made for the Tsar, the exquisite bedrooms are in various period styles. The perfect service has real warmth, and most guests are suitably distinguished. 150 rooms. The hotel's superb and famous Chantecler restaurant is now in the hands of Dominique Le Stanc, a highly reputed chef.

Beau Rivage, 24 Rue St François de Paule; tel. 93 80 80 70. Matisse lived for two years, and Chekhov wrote *The Seagull*, at this classic hotel, now newly modernised, on the edge of the Old Town. Lovely bedrooms (128), excellent food and service, private beach.

Upper-medium price

Grand Hôtel Aston, 12 Avenue Félix-Faure; tel. 93 80 62 52. Central, smart and well modernised. There's a roof-garden with a fine view, and an elegant restaurant, **Le Café de l'Horloge**. 160 rooms.

La Pérouse, 11 Quai Rauba-Capeu; tel. 93 62 34 63. Apart from the Negresco, the nicest hotel in Nice in my view, with a prime position up on the side of the castle hill (superb views from many of the 63 bedrooms). Friendly atmosphere, lovely swimming pool, solarium, and a pretty garden where light lunches are served in summer.

Medium price

Oasis, 23 Rue Gounod; tel. 93 88 12 29. In a quiet residential street between main station and seafront. Small garden. Good service.

Relais de Rimiez, 128 Avenue de Rimiez; tel. 93 81 18 65. Away from the centre, on a hill in the northern suburbs, a small modern hotel in local style, with a garden and views. 24 rooms. No restaurant.

Windsor, 11 Rue Dalpozzo; tel. 93 88 59 35. This unusual hotel near the front is remarkable value: odd oriental furnishings, small but comfortable rooms (63), small swimming pool. No restaurant.

Inexpensive

Les Orangers, 10 bis Avenue Durante; tel. 93 87 51 41. Near the station; rooms (12) clean and fair-sized. No restaurant. Closed November.

Regency, 2 Rue Saint-Siagre; tel. 93 62 17 44. Also near the station; pleasant owners and all basic comforts. 22 rooms; no restaurant.

Where to eat

The myriad eating places, many goodish, few excellent, tend to be grouped by area – roughly as follows, going from east to west: fish restaurants around the port; countless small bistros of all kinds (German, Dutch, Irish, American, Oriental, as well as French and Niçois) in the older part of the Old Town, frequented by locals as well as tourists; to the south, trendier medium-price places with fancy decor, popular with Nice's yuppies on their evenings out, on and near the Cours Saleya; modish brasseries and steak bars, some open all night, along the Avenue Félix-Faure and around the Place Masséna; pizzerias and fast-food bars in and near the Rue Masséna. Apart from the big hotels, there's not much on or near the promenade. Nice has its own distinctive cuisine (see p. 50), but it's not particularly easy to find – a few places specialising in it are listed below.

Top price

Chantecler: see Hôtel Negresco, p. 80.

Upper-medium price

L'Esquinade, 5 Quai des Deux-Emmanuel; tel. 93 89 59 36. By the port, and newly *à la mode* with showbiz and media people. Rustic decor, friendly service, excellent fish. Closed January, Sunday.

Palais Jamai, 3 Quai des Deux-Emmanuel; tel. 93 89 53 92. For a change, try this elegant Moroccan restaurant: pastilla, tajine, mechoui, couscous all commended. Closed July, Monday.

Barale, 39 Rue Beaumont; tel. 93 89 17 94. A renowned local institution, eccentric but endearing, and specialising in authentic Niçois cuisine. The elderly Hélène Barale and her family serve a gargantuan set menu, amid bizarre bygones including two vintage Citroëns and an old printing press, and then tell risqué stories, taunt their guests and get them to sing. Dinners only: booking obligatory. Closed Sunday, Monday.

La Mérenda, 4 Rue Terrasse; no telephone! In the Vieille Ville, an unusual and charming place serving excellent authentic Niçois dishes. No reservations – you just turn up. Closed February, August, weekends.

Medium price

Safari, 1 Cours Saleya; tel. 93 80 18 44. One of the better of many trendy youthful restaurants around the market. Closed Monday.

La Taca d'Oli, 35 Rue Pairolière; tel. 93 62 07 40. You'll find good local dishes at this friendly, studenty bistro in the old town; jokey owners.

Inexpensive

L'Escalinade, 22 Rue Pairolière; tel. 93 62 11 71. This simple, atmospheric bistro in the old town serves real Niçois dishes.

Farigoulo, 6 Rue de France; tel. 93 87 11 21. A pleasant, unassuming auberge-style place, with some local dishes.

Au Bon Coin Breton, 5 Rue Blacas; tel. 93 85 17 01. Sympathetic little Breton restaurant off the Avenue Jean-Médecin. Good value on the cheaper menus. Closed August, Monday.

The coast from Nice to Monaco

This renowned 30-km strip of coastline is as beautiful as any in Europe, even though its lower slopes are now heavily built-up. Rocky cliffs and wooded hillsides tower above the shimmering blue sea, as the coast forms a succession of deep bays and pine-clad promontories. Nice is linked to Monaco and Menton by four parallel corniche roads, all finely engineered: the Basse Corniche, winding along the coast, built in the nineteenth century; above it, the Moyenne Corniche, N7; higher up, the Grande Corniche, now a modern highway but first built by Napoleon on the path of the Romans' Via Aurelia; and yet higher, the A8 autoroute linking Nice with Italy. All the corniches are connected by steep zig-zagging minor roads.

Villefranche
06230

Considering that Nice and Monte Carlo are both so close, Villefranche (population 7,411) remains remarkably unspoilt. Founded in the fourteenth century as a customs-free port (hence its name), it lies in a beautiful, deep bay that gives shelter to shipping; it was an American naval base until France quit NATO, and is still visited by Allied warships whose sailors tumble into the quayside cafés. It's a fishing and pleasure port, too: its picturesque harbour is lined with tall Italianate eighteenth-century houses, red and orange, while behind there rises a maze of narrow alleys and stairways, some vaulted (for example, the aptly named Rue Obscure).

The tiny fourteenth-century chapel by the quay, where fishermen once stored their nets, was in 1957 decorated by Jean Cocteau with quaint but pallid frescoes of lay and religious scenes. The entrance fees go to a charity for retired fishermen.

There's an arts festival in the citadel in July and August.

Where to stay
Upper-medium price

Welcome, 1 Quai Courbet; tel. 93 76 76 93. A comfortable classic hotel by the quayside, newly modernised, usually true to its name. Of the 35 rooms, the upper ones are smallest but quietest. Closed late November to mid-December.

Medium price

Provençal, 4 Avenue Maréchal-Joffre; tel. 93 01 71 42. French families pack out this very central, friendly, unassuming place in a sidestreet. 45 rooms. Decent cooking.

Where to eat
Medium price
St Jean-Cap-Ferrat
06230

St-Pierre. The restaurant of the Hôtel Welcome (see above) has a fine terrace facing the harbour and is very good for fish.

With Cap d'Antibes, Cap Ferrat is the most beautiful of the Côte d'Azur's peninsulas, covered with palms, pines and wild flowers, amid rocky coves and headlands: but since Victorian days almost every corner of it has been bought up by the wealthy and famous for their majestic villas and gardens, so there are few public footpaths for scenic walks. However, one path leads from Paloma beach to the Pointe St-Hospice, and from here and the lighthouse at the south cape there are fine views of sea and hills. St Jean itself is a pleasant little fishing village. The few beaches are shingly; but at the Grand Hotel's private beach non-residents can hire mattresses at not too great a cost.

Two famous villas, neither open to visitors, are Les Cèdres, which belonged to King Leopold II of Belgium, and the Villa Mauresque near the south cape where Somerset Maugham lived for forty years until his death in 1965. Here he entertained many famous names in noble style, but could give short shrift to tourists who tried to visit him as a 'sight': to one gate-crasher he is said to have snarled, 'What d'you think I am, a monkey in a cage?'

What to see
Foundation
Ephrussi de
Rothschild

Baroness Ephrussi de Rothschild had this Italianate villa specially designed to house her works of art (for example, its ceilings were to be frames for her Tiepolos), and today its lavish collection bears witness to the Rothschilds' varied tastes: Louis XVI costumes, Aubusson tapestries, Renaissance and Victorian furniture, Sèvres and Dresden china, paintings by Fragonard, Monet, Renoir . . . and much else. After the guided tour, you can wander freely through the ornate gardens, past colonnades, lily ponds and exotic shrubs. In summer, concerts and plays are held in the villa.

What to do
Zoo

King Leopold's former estate now contains an attractive private zoo, with a good range of animals, birds and reptiles in spacious outdoor cages. Six times a day the clever chimpanzees hold a tea-party: this explains Maugham's remark (see above).

Where to stay
Top price

Voile d'Or, tel. 93 01 13 13. A glamorous luxury hotel on a headland by the harbour; lovely terrace-garden, two swimming pools by the sea, beautiful colour schemes; 50 rooms. Open March to October.

Brise Marine, Avenue Jean Mermoz; tel. 93 76 04 36. In the town, close to the sea, with sea views from many of the big bedrooms. Garden for drinks and breakfasts. Closed November to January.

Where to eat
Top price

Voile d'Or (see above). Splendid fish dishes in the classic mode, served in an elegant setting (in summer, on a canopied terrace or by the pools).

Beaulieu-
sur-Mer
06310

In pre-1914 days Beaulieu (population 4,302) was *the* most fashionable of Riviera resorts. Today with its floodlit palms it still retains a certain sedate chic, appealing to rich, elderly people who enjoy its sheltered climate. The beach is stony, but there's a big marina, and from the casino you can walk along the seafront to St Jean-Cap-Ferrat. The many stately *belle époque* villas include the Villa Léonine, former home of the Marquess of Salisbury, and the Villa Namouna, which belonged to Gordon Bennett, the *New York Herald* owner who sent Stanley to find Livingstone.

What to see
Villa Kérylos

Standing alone on a tiny headland, this sumptuous reconstruction of an ancient Greek villa was built c. 1902 by the archaeologist Théodore Reinach, and is one of the few great Riviera villas to be open to the public. The Greek vases, statuettes and mosaics are authentic, and the setting is sublime.

Nightlife

The casino, open daily, has regained its position as one of the three or four best on the Côte.

Where to stay
Top price

Métropole, 15 Blvd. du Maréchal Leclerc; tel. 93 01 00 08. A famous luxury hotel in its own elegant garden by the sea: pretty modern decor and perfect old-style service. Heated swimming pool; private rock beach. The 53 rooms vary greatly in price. Closed November to mid-December.

Réserve, 5 Blvd. Général-Leclerc; tel. 93 01 00 01. The Métropole's next-door rival, created by Gordon Bennett, is a classical pink palace of extreme refinement, still appealing to a discerning international clientèle. Sea views, elegant patio, private rock beach, superb service; 50 rooms. Closed December to early January.

Where to eat
Top price
Medium price

Métropole (see above). Classic cuisine of a high order, served in the gracious dining-room or on the terrace, with sea views.

African Queen; tel. 93 01 10 85. By the port, lively and popular, with a big terrace; straightforward cooking.

La Pignatelle, 10 Rue Quincenet; tel. 93 01 03 37. A sympathetic family-run auberge with good, copious Niçois cooking, and an outdoor terrace for summer. Closed Wednesday, mid-November to mid-December.

Eze
06360

Giddily perched on a rocky outcrop beside the Moyenne Corniche, 390 m almost sheer above the sea, this ancient fortified hill village (population 2,064) is inevitably overrun with tourists, more than any other on the Côte. However, its restoration has been tasteful, and the countless souvenir shops are not *too* vulgar: so, after parking at its entrance, it's worth making the climb through its narrow crowded alleys, to the summit where the ruins of a castle stand beside an exotic cacti-filled garden. The coast lies before you in all its grandeur. The path leading down to the lower corniche is named after Nietzsche, who loved to walk here.

Shopping

Among the many artists at work in Eze, with studios that sell their wares, you could try Aicardi for wrought-iron work or José Benito for jewellery and coloured glass.

Where to stay
Top price

Château de la Chèvre d'Or, Rue du Barri; tel. 93 41 12 12. A medieval castle in the old village, cleverly converted into a small (8 rooms) luxury hotel, run with style. To sip cocktails by the pool, as soft music plays and Cap-Ferrat lies far below, is a dazzling treat. If some bedrooms are cramped, blame the eleventh-century architect. Open March to November.

Where to eat
Top price

Chèvre d'Or (see p. 84). Famous people frequent this lovely panoramic restaurant, where hot oysters in champagne are typical of the light, elegant cooking. A romantic experience.

Medium price

Le Troubadour, Rue du Brec; tel. 93 41 19 03. For those who do not fancy Chèvre d'Or prices, here's a pleasant alternative. Closed December, two weeks in February, Sunday dinner, Wednesday.

La Turbie
06320

Beside this old village on the Grande Corniche above Monaco stands the famous **Trophée des Alpes**, the monument erected in 6 BC to celebrate Augustus' defeat of the local hill tribes who had been disrupting links between Rome and Gaul. Topped by a statue of the emperor, it stood 50 m high. Later it was partly dismantled, then blown up by the French in 1705. More recently, American funding has enabled it to be restored: the huge inscription of the names of the defeated tribes has been reconstructed, while the adjacent museum contains data about Roman Provence and a model of the Trophy in its original state.

Some 3 km north-west of La Turbie, at **Laghet**, is the seventeenth-century sanctuary of Notre-Dame, a pilgrimage centre full of curious ex-votos (votive offerings). To the east, on the plateau of **Mont Agel**, is a famous and excellent golf course, with marvellous views.

Monaco (and Monte Carlo)

Monaco is a Lilliputian sovereign state, wealthy, glamorous and dynamic, where 28,000 people live squeezed on to a 198-hectare strip of land between sea and mountains: there's no room to build except upwards (hence the tiers of skyscrapers) or outwards (31 hectares have just been reclaimed from the sea). Here, assisted by an elected council, Prince Rainier III rules like a Medici. As well as being the name of his principality, Monaco is also the 'Old Town' on its headland where his Royal Palace stands; beyond the port is the newer district, Monte Carlo, still casting its magic spell on tourists and business visitors alike.

I always find it an amazing, hypnotising place, surely unique in the world, almost frightening in its sheer streamlined efficiency. Here the aristocratic traditions of the old days, when queens and princes flocked to the casino, serve as background for a modern, ritzy style of glamour, fuelled and funded by a hard-headed business dynamism, for this today is a centre of banking and finance. Here the old world meets the new in high style – a union that was symbolised by the marriage of Prince Rainier, member of Europe's oldest ruling family, the Grimaldi, with the Hollywood film-star daughter of a Philadelphia industrialist. After Princess Grace's death in 1982, in a car accident on the heights behind the town, Monaco took some years to recover its panache.

Getting there

Monaco is 16 km from Nice Airport (see p. 72) and is linked to it by a regular helicopter service, running fourteen times a day. There are express trains to Paris (journey time about seven and a half hours) and to other cities; in summer fast trains go along the whole coast every thirty minutes. You can also go to Nice and other towns by bus. The quickest road to Nice is the Moyenne Corniche, which leads into Monaco, while good sideroads wind up to the Grande Corniche and the autoroute, high above the town. Tiny Monaco has its own internal bus network, frequent and efficient. Tourist office: 2a Blvd. des Moulins, tel. 93 30 87 01.

History

The Grimaldi ruling family, of Genoese origin, who in those days owned various lordships in the area, such as Cagnes and Antibes, purchased the rock of Monaco from Genoa in 1308. After this, Monaco had a turbulent history, being occupied at times by the French and Spanish. But in 1860, when the Dukes of Savoy ceded the rest of the Nice area to France, it managed to keep its independence. However, Prince Charles III was forced to sell Menton and Roquebrune to France, thus losing his income from the olive oil and lemon trades, and this threatened him with bankruptcy. So he decided to build a casino (these were still banned in France, but were becoming successful in Germany).

Opened in 1865, on a low rock that was named Monte Carlo after the Prince, the original casino experienced difficulties at first, but after the coming of the railway it soon began to attract the aristocracy of Europe: they stayed at the majestic new Hôtel de Paris, built specially for them, and threw themselves into the new pastime of gambling. Prince Charles had given the concession to a clever entrepreneur, François Blanc, who made a brilliant success of the operation: 1878 saw the opening of a stately new casino with an opera house, all designed by the great Paris architect Charles Garnier. And so Monaco rapidly became rich. Individual fortunes were made too: in 1887 an English confidence trickster, Charles Deville Wells, won $40,000 in three days to become 'the man who broke the bank at Monte Carlo'.

Monaco today

The principality has stayed rich, but only by again adapting to the times. When Rainier III came to the throne in 1949, aged only twenty-five, Monaco was in decline, for high-society gambling was no longer in itself a viable basis of income. However, the astute Prince has a strong business flair, and in the past decades he and his associates have boldly revitalised Monaco, transforming it into one of the world's most efficient, modern and high-powered centres of business-cum-pleasure. He has been called 'The Chairman of Monaco, Inc', for the style is somewhat American. The level of taxation is low, and this has attracted the world's banks, forty-five of which now have branches here, including Citycorp and Crédit Suisse; many other financial and service firms have also set up offices. And a number of well-to-do, well-known individuals, fleeing the high income tax in their own countries, have chosen to become residents. Among those with apartments here are Sophia Loren, Roger Moore and Ringo Starr, writers such as Anthony Burgess, financiers such as Adnan Kashoggi, and sporting stars such as Nicki Lauder and Bjorn Borg.

Today only 4 per cent of the state's revenue comes from gambling, and 25 per cent from tourism, while the rest is from business. Under an agreement with Paris that dates from de Gaulle's day, French residents and firms pay tax: but others are largely exempt. Of Monaco's 28,000 population, some 12,600 are French, 4,500 Italian, and 1,100 British. Only 4,500 have the privilege of being Monegasque, and citizenship is hard to acquire: natives do no military service and pay no income tax. Monaco depends on France for its defence and many public services, and the currency is the same; but it has its own police and postage stamps.

Except in high summer, the chief emphasis today is on 'business tourism' – conventions and incentive tours – and the giant hotels cater mostly for this, much more than for individuals. Just below the casino, a huge, ultra-modern convention centre has been built over the sea; and another is now planned. Monaco hosts over 600 conventions a year: your hotel is more than likely to be full, say, of groups of insurance agents from Norwich or doctors from Denver, all engaged in a non-stop round of seminars, cocktails, dinner-jacket galas, and dips in the pool. There's a busy calendar of special events – festivals, rallies, tournaments, charity dinners – and Monaco claims, perhaps fairly, that a greater diversity of activities and tourist attractions are crammed into one small space than in any comparable area of the globe: culture (the opera and a leading orchestra), science (the famous Oceanographic Museum), sport (the Grand Prix and Rally), and much else. The firm that helps to keep all this running smoothly is the same one that Blanc created in the 1860s, the mighty Société des Bains de Mer (SBM), of which the principality owns 69 per cent. Today the SBM owns or runs four of the leading hotels, three of the four casinos, many of the office blocks, and most of the beaches, sports clubs and nightspots, many of them recently created.

Outside the main Casino at night the scene is dazzling, like a film-set. There are immaculate formal gardens with palms and flowerbeds. Flags and banners. The imposing neo-Baroque façades of the Casino and Hôtel de Paris. Uniformed porters opening the doors of Rolls Royce and Mercedes for jewelled ladies to alight. And yet, isn't there just a touch of flamboyant vulgarity about the whole operation? And what are those pinball machines doing in the chic Café de Paris? What would the tsars and dowagers of yesterday have made of the Bermuda shorts in the Hôtel de Paris? Just as Monte in the grand old days had an English flavour, so today it's Americanised – *Las Vegas-plage* is a French sneer – and English is spoken widely. It's a place of many facets, some truly glamorous, some less so. But it's still a magnet for the world's diamond-studded jet setters, and its night-life is the smartest on the coast, in a less Bohemian style than St Tropez.

The Prince's three much-publicised children help to set the pace, when they're at home. The Prince also gives them special responsibilities – Caroline for culture, Albert for sport and the economy, Stéphanie (spasmodically) for youth and education. Rainier is no absolute monarch, but rules jointly with a directly-elected National Council, assisted by ministers and councillors. In practice, however, his word usually goes. And now in his early seventies, he shows little sign of wanting to hand over the reins to his son.

Main areas

The principality is in four main parts, strung along the coast. In the middle, there's the **Old Town** of Monaco, with the palace and museums. To its north, you'll find the commercial area of **La Condamine**, and north-east of that, **Monte Carlo** on its rock, with a long beach curving beyond.

Lastly, south-west of the Old Town is **Fontvieille**, a remarkable new 31-hectare zone of activities, on land recently reclaimed from the sea. It includes blocks of flats, some pollution-free light industry, a heliport, an ultra-modern circus arena used for various shows, and the Princess Grace memorial rose garden next to a park and a lake full of swans with white wings and black necks. Above all, there's a huge new multi-level sports stadium built on anti-seismic principles: the football stadium on the roof literally floats on top of the enormous swimming pool.

There are plenty of car parks, and street meter parking. And as there's virtually no crime in Monaco, risks can be taken when leaving your car.

What to see

Palais du Prince

Parts of the Prince's Palace are thirteenth to sixteenth century, but it was much rebuilt in the late nineteenth: hence the quaint mock- Moorish crenellated towers, popular at the time. The palace is closed from mid-October to early June when the Prince is in residence: visitors must then be content with watching the changing of the guard (daily just before noon), or with visiting the little Musée Napoléon in one wing, filled with historical souvenirs. When the palace is open, visitors are shown the sixteenth-century arcaded courtyard, the Throne Room and other state rooms, some decorated with seventeenth-century Italian frescoes or hung with pictures by Holbein, Brueghel and others. Nearby is a waxworks museum of the Grimaldi family, and the ostentatious neo-Romanesque cathedral, built from 1875 to 1903 from the

Casino's profits: its main interest today is that it contains the tomb of Princess Grace. On the other side of the palace is a rather cramped and crowded zoo, notable for its monkeys.

Musée Océano- graphique

This is one of Monaco's chief glories, and the world's finest museum of its kind. It exists thanks to Prince Albert I's passion for oceanography, which he financed with profits from the Casino. He was Monaco's ruler from 1889 to 1922, and in the late nineteenth century he made twenty-four voyages in his yachts, bringing back many rare ocean species: then in 1910 this stately museum was opened on the headland, and is directed today by Commander Jacques Cousteau, the underwater explorer. One hall contains the skeletons of whales and other sea mammals, while upstairs is a fine display of marine technology, old and new. There's a large array of seashells, some huge, and of artefacts made from sea produce, such as sharkskin bags. The big aquarium, probably Europe's best, contains a marvellous variety of fish of all sizes, colours and shapes, with labels giving their culinary uses – very French.

Jardin Exotique

This cliffside garden at the western entrance to Monaco provides good views over the town. It has about 1,000 kinds of cacti, mostly from America and Africa, some weirdly shaped: the ones that look like spiky footballs are known as 'mother-in-laws' pillows'. Also in the garden are the **Grottes de l'Observatoire**, caves with stalactites and stalagmites where Neolithic man lived, plus a museum with relics found in these caves and in others near Menton.

Casino

Charles Garnier, architect also of the Paris Opéra, designed this neo-Baroque extravaganza whose four towers point skywards, between a formal palm-laden garden and a terrace above the sea. Even if you hate gambling, you should go inside to admire the sumptuous gilded decor that recalls the grand old days.

Musée National

Garnier also designed this graceful little villa in the Avenue Princesse-Grace, now housing a superb collection of dolls and mechanical toys: the guides generally set these in motion only for groups or when the museum is full. Note the big eighteenth-century crib with some 300 figures.

What to do

The programme is intense, and there's nearly always something special going on. Among the main events: January, the big Monte Carlo automobile rally, and the festival of St Devoté, patron saint of the principality; February, international television festival; spring, Arts Festival; April, tennis championships; May, Monaco Grand Prix (car racing); July/August, international fireworks festival; September, Baroque Music Festival; 19 November, Monegasque National Fête; December, international circus festival.

Festivals and annual events

All-year culture

This is mostly of a high international standard, certainly the best on the Côte. The Prince has long been anxious to offset Monaco's image as a philistine centre of banking, sport and gambling, and has been making particular efforts to promote culture, helped by his daughter Caroline, with some success. The elegant opera house in the casino is used for winter and spring productions by its resident company, and by the newly recreated Monte Carlo Ballet. The Rainier III Hall in the convention centre hosts concerts by the Monte Carlo Philharmonic Orchestra, which performs also in the courtyard of the royal palace in summer. The Princess Grace Theatre is used for plays, and for concerts during the Spring Arts Festival.

Sport
The amenities are numerous and of a high standard. For tennis and squash, the best place is the Monte Carlo Country Club, while the golf club at La Turbie is one of Europe's best. The Yacht Club de Monaco runs sailing lessons and deep-sea fishing trips.

There are no free beaches and the sand is imported and rough, but better than shingle. If you want to bathe in the sea, try the Plage du Larvotto or the well-equipped Monte Carlo Beach which offers most watersports. Some of the big hotels open their pools to the public for a fee. Best of the various all-year heated pools is the California Terrace, which also has a health and fitness centre.

Shopping
There are many smart boutiques, even a branch of Sotheby's, but few supermarkets or small shops selling local produce.

Nightlife
Drawing its clientèle from far around, Monaco's nightlife is the most elaborate and intense on the Côte (this helps to explain why Nice's is so dull). The **Casino** is open for gambling from 4 p.m. to 4 a.m.: its *salles privées*, once so exclusive, are now hardly more private than the *salles publiques*, but they do demand that ties be worn. Some rooms have gaming using American rules. The Casino also puts on dinner-dances and cabarets from September to June: the atmosphere is decorous and the floor-show not outstanding.

Loews Hotel, too, has a casino, where the gaming rules are American, the entrance unrestricted, and the ambience a bit like Las Vegas. By contrast, Loews' renowned dinner-dance cabaret, La Folie Russe, is quite sophisticated and its floor-show brilliant.

The Société des Bains de Mer's misleadingly-named **Monte Carlo Sporting Club** has no sports but is a large and luxurious complex of five nightspots, on a stretch of land reclaimed from the sea. Here the Salle des Etoiles, a huge hall with a roll-back roof, is used for special galas, and in July/August for nightly dinner-dance/cabaret when the Casino's cabaret is closed. The Sporting Club's other ventures also tend to be for summer only. They include a casino with nautical decor, and Parady'z (sic), an outdoor disco where you dance by a lake; also the famous **Jimmy'z**, most fashionable disco on the Côte, haunt of celebrities and *le très beau monde* (dress chic if you want to be let in). September to June, Jimmy'z moves to simpler premises near the Casino. Other popular nightspots, open all year, are Tiffany's, L'X Club, and the stylish bar of the newly-reopened Café de Paris.

Where to stay

Monte Carlo has several well-known luxury hotels, some new, some dating from the grand old days – and I list them partly because they are so notable. They do their trade mainly with groups, who get special rates. The town has few good hotels in the medium and cheaper ranges. So, if you want to visit the principality without paying high prices, it is best to stay somewhere just outside, such as Menton (see p. 95).

Top price

Hermitage, Square Beaumarchais; tel. 93 50 67 31. A stunningly beautiful monument to the *belle époque*, once used by English and Russian royalty, now lovingly restored by SBM. The rear winter-garden foyer with its green decor and domed glass ceiling is exquisite, as are the spacious bedrooms (220). The wide terrace bar with its sea views is much used by Prince Albert, and the Rococo restaurant is excellent. Dignified service by well mannered staff.

Loews, Avenue des Spélugues; tel. 93 50 65 00. The Côte's largest hotel by far (641 rooms), this modern American titan seems typical of the new Monte Carlo – brash, efficient, airy and amusing. It's like a state-within-the-state, so wide is its range of amenities, including five restaurants, casino, cabaret, shops, health centre and rooftop swimming pool. Smallish but cheerful bedrooms.

Monte Carlo Beach, 06190 Roquebrune; tel. 93 78 21 40. Away from the downtown throng (in fact, inside France), an enchanting little luxury hotel with pretty rooms (46) including one where Eva Peron used to sleep, and a beach.

Hôtel de Paris, Place du Casino; tel. 93 50 80 80. The doyen of them all, opened in 1865 to house the aristocrats flocking to the Casino – and still incredibly grand, with its opulent neo-Baroque decor and staff in white tie and tails (but the guests have changed radically). Attractive bedrooms (246), but ambience a bit stiff.

Upper-medium price

Abela, 23 Avenue des Papalins; tel. 93 25 21 01. A brand-new three-star hotel at Fontvieille. Efficient, serviceable; 192 rooms.

Balmoral, 12 Avenue de la Costa; tel. 93 50 62 37. Modestly priced, a bit old-fashioned, but comfortable and friendly; 75 rooms.

Inexpensive

Cosmopolite, 19 Blvd. Général-Leclerc; tel. 93 78 36 00. Cheerful, newly renovated hotel in Beausoleil, run by a young couple. No restaurant; number of rooms unavailable.

Villa Boeri, 29 Blvd. Général-Leclerc; tel. 93 78 38 10. Almost next door, a friendly little place: some rooms have sea-facing balconies. No restaurant; 30 rooms.

Where to eat

The variety is enormous, from small bistros to the fancy cuisine of the big hotels – and from Argentinian food to English.

Top price

Louis XV (see Hôtel de Paris, above). The best in town. Renowned chef Alain Ducasse serves a brilliant and very personal Italo-Provençal cuisine amid elegant Louis XV decor. In summer it can be more fun to eat on the terrace of the ornate **Salle Empire**, whose cooking is more classical. The hotel's third restaurant, the rooftop **Grill**, is slightly cheaper, but equally in vogue with high society. Louis XV is closed first half of March, Tuesday, Wednesday.

La Coupole, 1 Avenue Princesse-Grace; tel. 93 25 45 45. The Hôtel Mirabeau's luxurious restaurant, newly redecorated. Superb cooking by Yves Garnier. Closed for lunch in summer.

Upper-medium price

Argentin (see Loews Hotel, p. 91). Excellent South American dishes, such as *ceviche* and spiced beef, served in style by a deft and friendly young staff, in a most civilised setting.

Café de Paris, Place du Casino; tel. 93 50 57 75. This large and famous brasserie has been newly redecorated in a dazzling style, using nineteenth-century stained-glass murals designed by Garnier: it's now much in vogue with the glossiest people and stays open till 2.30 a.m. Good food and a lovely terrace, although the gambling machines in the room next door strike a jarring note.

Le St-Benoît, 10 Avenue de la Costa; tel. 93 25 02 34. Good classic cooking, in an elegant setting with a wide terrace overlooking the harbour and sea. Highly thought of locally. Closed Monday, December.

Le Pinocchio, 30 Rue Comte F.-Gastaldi; tel. 93 30 96 20. Busy, crowded trattoria in Monaco's old town. Closed December, January.

Medium price

Flashman's, 7 Avenue Princesse-Alice; tel. 93 30 09 03. A cosy, slightly raffish English pub, serving so-so English food, popular with visiting Brits, especially for a late drink. Closed Sunday.

La Panthère Rose, 1 Rue des Roses; tel. 93 50 88 25. Up a side-street, an intimate 'in' place frequented by media and sporting stars, Prince Albert, and so forth. Classic dishes. Closed Sunday.

Polpetta, 6 Avenue Roqueville; tel. 93 50 67 84. Lively little Italian trattoria, up a small street just inland. Often crowded with the glamour set, but not pricey. Nice terrace. Closed two weeks October, three weeks February.

Inexpensive

L'Aurore, 8 Rue Princesse Marie de Lorraine; tel. 93 30 37 75. A simple, very busy little place up in Monaco town, where you eat at long tables. Lunch only.

Menton and Roquebrune

Roquebrune-Cap-Martin
06190

This commune (population 12,578) sprawls along the hilly coast between Monaco and Menton, and is in three parts: the old village high above the Grande Corniche; the modern resort; and the wooded peninsula of Cap-Martin, which is largely given over to big private villas with gardens and has long been a haunt of the famous and wealthy. In the nineteenth century it was first made fashionable by the Empress Elizabeth (Sissi) of Austria and the Empress Eugénie of France who used to stay here. Winston Churchill came often in his final years, and painted this coast; W. B. Yeats died here in 1939; and Le Corbusier, another regular visitor, was drowned while swimming off the cape in 1965. A scenic footpath leads round the bay from the Avenue Winston Churchill to Monte Carlo Beach – a lovely walk that is best done with the sun behind you.

The medieval hill village of Roquebrune has been studiously restored, perhaps too much so – I find it a bit artificial. The Rue Moncollet and other quaint alleys, neatly paved and lined with trendy boutiques and artists' workshops, curve up under Romanesque arches to the feudal hilltop castle (floodlit at night, and visible from afar), which was built as a defence against Saracens. Begun in the tenth century, the present structure dates mostly from the thirteenth and belonged to the Grimaldis from 1350 to 1848. Then in 1911 Sir William Ingram, an English resident, bought it and gave it to the town. It's an austere building with massively thick walls, but the rooms are small. Rather bare of furniture, they now contain old photos and documents on the history of Roquebrune. Above the roofless ceremonial hall is the guardroom with adjacent prison, and above that the seigneurs' pokey dwelling quarters with archaic kitchen. Living there cannot have been much fun – even with the stupendous view from the roof-terrace that today's visitors can also enjoy.

Gorbio and **Ste Agnes** are two attractive old hill villages behind Roquebrune, in wild and spectacular settings, with fine views.

Festivals On the evening of Good Friday and the afternoon of 5 August, two colourful processions fill the old streets – as they have for 500 years, in fulfilment of a vow that is said to have saved the village from the plague in 1467. Amid much pageantry, the costumed villagers enact scenes from the Passion of Christ.

Where to stay
Top price **Vista Palace**, Grande Corniche; tel. 93 35 01 50. More spectacularly sited than any hill village, this remarkable modern luxury hotel, German-owned and managed, clings giddily to a cliffside 300 m sheer above Monte Carlo. Glamorous decor is matched by extreme comfort; the leisure centre includes Turkish baths, squash and archery; five of the suites each have a private swimming pool. There are 71 rooms. Restaurant. Closed March, November, December.

Inexpensive **Westminster**, 14 Avenue Louis-Laurens; tel. 93 35 00 68. Far, far below the Vista, pricewise as well as geographically: near the shingly beach (there's a railway between, but trains are few at night), this efficient holiday hotel has a pretty garden facing the sea; 31 rooms. Restaurant. Closed mid-October to mid-February.

Where to eat
Upper-
medium price **Au Grand Inquisiteur**, 18 Rue du Château; tel. 93 35 05 37. Charming old farmstead with vaulted rustic dining-room, up in the old

village below a great rock. Good local cooking. Closed November, December.

Menton
06500

Menton (population 25,449) is set around a beautiful wide bay, backed by rocky heights. With its mellow old-fashioned charm, it is the prettiest and gentlest of the major resorts on the Côte, also the warmest in winter: hence the luxuriance of sub-tropical fruit and plants, and the acres of lemon groves for which it is famous. For centuries it was a modest fishing port in liege to the Grimaldis, until ceded to France in 1860. About the same time, an English doctor wrote a book praising its mild climate, and so the English gentry descended on the town, to retire or spend the winter, and they were followed by other European nobility. In 1900 its British population of 5,000 was the largest on the continent.

Today, two World Wars later, British residents are down to a mere 100 or so. The palace-hotels along the sea-front and just behind – the Balmoral, Bristol, Winter Palace and so on – have been torn down or turned into holiday flats. And yet, nostalgic traces of the old days remain, such as the grandiose foyer of the ex-Hôtel Imperial. Remarkably, the English church, St John's, opposite the casino, still has weekly services and runs an English lending library.

West of the port runs the graceful, palm-lined Promenade du Soleil, while to the east towards the Italian frontier are new beaches and marinas. The picturesque alleys of the *vieille ville* rise just behind the port, topped by the seventeenth-century church of **St Michel** and the chapel of **La Conception**, both fine examples of Baroque. The old cemetery near the church has the tombs of great European families who lived in Menton, many of them British.

The writer Katherine Mansfield was one of the many consumptives who came to Menton. From 1920 to 1921 she took a villa, the Isola Bella, on the east side of town, in a street that now bears her name. 'I love it as I've never loved any place but my home,' she wrote of the villa. But the warm climate failed to arrest her decline. The town council have now arranged one room as a memorial to her.

What to see

The main sights in town can be visited on foot, but it's best to drive by car up to the Jardin des Colombières. A miniature train will take you on a forty-minute trip round the town.

Musée du Palais Carnolès

This handsome eighteenth-century mansion in the western suburbs has an eclectic range of paintings from the thirteenth century to the present day: Henri Manguin, André Derain and Paul Delvaux are among the moderns.

Musée Cocteau

This small museum installed in the harbour bastion contains drawings, tapestries and stage sets by the ever versatile Jean Cocteau. Most striking are his bright-coloured harlequin paintings.

Hôtel de Ville: Sall des Mariages

The town hall's room used for marriages was decorated by Cocteau in 1957 with some charming and lively frescoes on classical and Provençal themes including Orpheus and Eurydice, a Menton fisherman and his bride in a Niçois hat.

Jardin des
Colombières

Ferdinand Bac, writer, humorist and alleged bastard son of Napoleon III, laid out this spacious Italianate garden, with its cypresses, pools, urns and statues, on a hillside in the suburb of Garavan. It must have been lovely in its heyday, but is now rather run-down. So is the curious villa in the grounds, designed by Bac in lavish Hellenic-cum-Roman style, with arches, statues, frescoes and a colonnaded atrium. Here you can take lemon tea, gazing over the coast below. There are also bedrooms to let, with Roman baths. Below the garden is a big olive grove, and below that the Jardin Botanique Exotique, which has a wide range of sub-tropical flora.

What to do
Festivals

The famous lemon festival, with floats of fruit and pretty girls, lasts for two weeks around Mardi Gras, in February. In August, a high-class festival of chamber music is held outside the church of St Michel, elegantly floodlit.

Shopping

Just inside Italy at **Ventimiglia**, only 11 km away, a marvellous Friday market draws crowds from kilometres around with its low prices and superb choice of leather goods, pottery and foods.

Nightlife

The casino, one of the more sedate on the Côte, has *thés-dansants* on Sunday afternoons, and a dinner-dance/cabaret in summer.

Where to stay

Unlike the other main resorts on this coast, Menton has no smart luxury hotels, but a wide choice of decent middle-range ones.

Medium price

Chambord, 6 Avenue Boyer; tel. 93 35 94 19. A sedate, comfortable modern hotel, just inland from the beach; 40 rooms. No restaurant.

L'Aiglon, 7 Avenue de la Madone; tel. 93 57 55 55. Near the beach, an Edwardian former private house in a garden with fruit trees; some of the 32 rooms have balconies. No restaurant, but snacks are served by the swimming pool at lunchtime. Closed November, December.

Inexpensive

Londres, 15 Avenue Carnot; tel. 93 35 74 62. A quiet and pleasant little modern hotel near the beach; dullish food; 26 rooms. Closed November, December.

Where to eat
Medium price
Inexpensive

Au Pistou, 2 Rue Fossan; tel. 93 57 45 89. A cosy, friendly place, very central; some local dishes. Closed Tuesday.

Les Arches: Chez Diana, 31 Quai Bonaparte; tel. 93 35 94 64. So the British regime in Menton lives on, in a new guise! This popular quayside bistro has for some years been owned and run with panache by Diana Archer ('Lady Di' to the local French), daughter of a Lancashire textile magnate. She'll gladly tell you the Grand Guignolesque life story that led her to Menton, and after dinner she delights her guests with her Piaf-like songs in many languages. The sound Provençal menu extends to sherry trifle and real lemon meringue tart. Closed November, Wednesday.

The hinterland behind Nice and Menton

One bonus of a beautiful mountainous coastline is that the hinterland is usually similar – and so it is here. Behind the crowded coast the pine-clad hills roll for a long way, empty and serene, and only a few minutes' drive from Nice or Menton you find ancient unspoilt hill villages, much less touristy than Eze or Roquebrune. Further inland, in the shadow of the high Alps along the Italian border, you will come to excellent hiking country, and to a few small ski resorts. You will also find some fascinating surprises, not to be missed – the dramatic hill village of Saorge, the frescoes in the chapel near La Brigue, and the mysterious rock carvings of the aptly-named Valley of Marvels.

Sospel
06380

The road from Menton winds up for 19 km to this summer resort in a verdant valley, an excellent hill-walking centre. It's a charming old town (population 2,278), whose fine medieval bridge has a tollgate halfway across. The church of **St Michel** is Baroque, while its tower is Romanesque.

Where to stay and eat
Inexpensive

Auberge Provençale, Route du Col de Castillon; tel. 93 04 00 31. Unassuming auberge on the Menton road. Meals served on the terrace. Closed mid-November to mid-December.

Saorge

One of the most startling hill villages in Provence. As the N204 main road emerges from the deep Gorges de Saorge, suddenly there you see it high above you, clinging precariously to the mountainside – a terraced crescent of fifteenth- to seventeenth-century houses in shades of yellow, pink and grey. It looks inaccessible, but in fact you can reach it by car from **Fontan** to the north, where you must park, then clamber through the maze of steep stepways. Do not miss the fifteenth-century church with its Baroque interior, nor the seventeenth-century Franciscan church on the outskirts whose terrace offers a fine view on to this still surprisingly unspoilt village.

The N204 continues up the Roya Valley through the wild Gorges de Bergue whose high red rocks have been eroded into bizarre shapes. Above the road are the many high viaducts of the Nice–Turin railway which was reopened only in 1980 after wartime destruction. Its building in the 1930s was an amazing feat of engineering, for such is the terrain that some of the tunnels are loops within the mountain: you can see a train enter the cliff at one point and then later emerge from it directly above!

La Brigue

The wild sub-Alpine area around the villages of La Brigue and **Tende** was once the private hunting ground of the kings of Italy (for wild boar and chamois) and was not ceded to France until 1947. La Brigue is a delightful unrestored village of cobbled streets, whose

Nice Hinterland

Romanesque church has a Lombard belfry and some fine sixteenth-century furnishings and primitive paintings. The ruined castle of the Lascaris, former local seigneurs, stands on a hill above.

Absolutely not to be missed is the lonely medieval chapel of **Notre-Dame-des-Fontaines** (ask any hotel in La Brigue to lend you its key), which stands 4 km to the east in a fertile upland valley, amid streams, orchards and grazing sheep. The outside is quite plain, but inside the rich decoration is exceptional. The walls are covered with fifteenth-century frescoes by two Piedmontese artists, depicting with powerful and poignant realism the life and Passion of Christ: note above all the anguish of Judas Iscariot. On 8 September there's a pilgrimage to the chapel, combined with a village fête.

Where to stay
and eat
Inexpensive

Mirval, 3 Rue St Viencent-Ferrier; tel. 93 04 63 71. On the edge of the village, a friendly country inn (18 rooms), simple but modernised, with sound local cooking (fresh trout, home-made pasta). Open April to October.

Vallée des Merveilles

This 'valley of the marvels' is indeed one of the strangest and most evocative places in all France. Out in the Alpine wilds to the west of La Brigue, accessible only on foot or by jeep, it consists of a rock- and lake-strewn landscape at the base of remote Mont Bégo and other peaks. As if this were not haunting enough, the rock faces are marked by some 30,000 mysterious carvings of daggers, bulls and totems, which were discovered by the English naturalist Clarence Bicknell in 1895 and are thought to be the work of Iron or Bronze Age tribesmen on pilgrimage to Mont Bégo.

The tourist office in Tende (tel. 93 04 60 91) will give details about access to the valley and where to stay. Jeep trips take a full day and are expensive, but the drivers will point out the carvings, which are not easy to find. You can also go on foot (June to September only), but for this you should allow two days (there are two Alpine hostels, often booked out in advance). Take warm weatherproof clothing, for storms can blow up fast.

From St Dalmas-de-Tende you can go by car for 14 km as far as Casterino, from where you can hike for about 8 km along either the Valmasque or the Fontanalbe path (both are clearly marked) to a string of Alpine lakes, each a different colour. This is the heart of the rock-carving area. The lakes can also be reached by a different path from the Lac des Meshes, where a former Renault worker runs a commune that gives craft courses and offers simple beds for the night.

Where to stay and eat
Inexpensive

Auberge Marie-Madeleine, Casterino; tel. 93 04 65 93. Popular with boisterous French families on hiking trips, this friendly mountain auberge (11 rooms), in a glorious open setting, offers good Alpine and Niçois cooking. Open May to October.

Col de Turini and **Peira-Cava**
06440
Escarène

Two small ski and summer resorts, popular with Niçois, north-west of Sospel in a wild Alpine setting – rock-strewn forests of tall pines, bracing air and majestic views. Peira-Cava is a bit dull; the Col de Turini is more fun, and from it you can drive through the lovely Turini pine forest to the **Pointe-des-Trois-Communes** where the views of the snowy Alps are magnificent.

Where to stay
Medium price

Trois Vallées, Col de Turini; tel. 93 91 57 21. For skiers and hikers, a big Alpine chalet near the ski lifts, with scenic views; 23 rooms. Simple, copious food. Closed mid-November to mid-December.

Lucéram

A fortified hill village less than 30 km from Nice, yet unspoilt (the only blight has come from a serious fire in 1986 which charred much of the forest around it). Above the jumble of tall, old houses and steep stepped alleys, some vaulted, stands the interesting fifteenth-century church with Italian Rococo decor: its six retables of the prolific Bréa School bear witness to Lucéram having been a key centre of painting in the fifteenth century. Its silver treasures include a curious statuette of Ste-Marguerite standing on a dragon.

Peillon
06440
Escarène

Perched on a rocky spur in a deep winding valley, this medieval hill village seems utterly remote, yet is only 19 km from Nice. Most of its old stone houses, nicely restored, now belong to Niçois who are commuters or weekenders. The chapel of the Pénitents Blancs has some fine fifteenth-century frescoes by Canavesio. Further down the valley, at La Grave, the Vicat cement works has torn vast gashes in the hillside, thus improving the local job situation but not the scenery. A road winds over the rugged hills to **Peille**, another pleasant *village perché*, with an old church (there's a quaint 'fête of the olive-sticks' on the first Sunday in September). The roads across the plateau from here to Monaco or Menton have fine views.

Where to stay and eat
Medium price

Auberge de la Madone; tel. 93 79 91 17. The Millo family create a warm, civilised atmosphere at their very popular auberge on the edge of Peillon village. There are 18 bedrooms, some with balconies. The regional cuisine can have its off-days. Closed mid-October to mid-December.

Coaraze
06930 Contes

Brightly enamelled sundials (Jean Cocteau designed the one by the town hall) embellish the square of this delightful hill village north of Nice. Its narrow alleys are arched and vaulted, and there's a good view from the terrace of its church. The sundials are made locally, and some craftsmen will sell them to visitors.

Where to stay and eat
Medium price
St Martin-du-Var

Auberge du Soleil; tel. 93 79 08 11. A friendly auberge in the village, sunny indeed with its terrace facing the lovely scenery. Eight comfortable rooms and excellent country cooking.

Broad, flat and partly industrialised, the ugly valley of the River Var contrasts strikingly with the rest of the Nice hinterland and has little to tempt the tourist as he drives up the N202 motorway towards Digne. Little, that is, save one superb but pricey restaurant, by the N202 at St Martin, 27 km north-west of Nice.

Where to eat
Top price

Issautier: Auberge de la Belle Route; tel. 93 08 10 65. A comfortable old inn, where Jean-François Issautier provides some of the best cooking in Provence, using the finest fresh ingredients, combining classic recipes and his own inventions. Closed early November, two weeks February, Sunday dinner, Monday.

Levens *06670*
St M-du-V
Where to stay
Inexpensive

This lively hill village 23 km north of Nice is close to some spectacular viewpoints down over the Vésubie Gorges.

La Vigneraie, Route Sainte Blaise; tel. 93 79 70 46. An ideal rural retreat from the busy coast: outside the village, a neat modern villa with a nice garden; friendly owners; 18 rooms. Closed October to January.

Where to eat
Medium price
Gorges de la Vésubie

La Vigneraie (see above). Good country cooking at fair prices, and a vine-clad patio for fine days. Very popular.

The River Vésubie winds through 10 km of deep gorges between St Jean-la-Rivière and Plan-du-Var. One road follows the riverbed, but the best views of the chasm are from the higher D19 from St Jean to Levens. Here one beauty spot, 300 m sheer above the valley, is the 'Saut des Français', so named because here in 1793 Republican soldiers were hurled into the depths by royalist rebels.

Utelle

From St Jean, a road winds up steeply to this mainly unspoilt old village whose large, handsome church has a Gothic vaulted roof and contains some fine works of art, mostly sixteenth-century. The views of the Vésubie Valley are good: but for a really sensational panoramic vista, possibly the best in the Alpes-Maritimes, you should zig-zag up to the remote hilltop sanctuary of the **Madone d'Utelle**, founded in 850 and rebuilt in 1806 (pilgrimages 15 August and 8 September).

St Martin-Vésubie

A big Alpine village in the verdant upper Vésubie Valley that has burgeoned into quite a chic modern summer resort, yet keeps its picturesque charm: the Rue du Dr-Cagnoli, in particular, is a steep, paved alley with elegant old houses and a rivulet flowing down its middle. Whether you are *sportif* or not, there's a lot to do and see in the area. For example, at the entrance to the little hill village of **Venanson**, on the heights south of St Martin, is the tiny chapel of Ste Claire whose inside walls and ceiling are covered with brightly-coloured fifteenth-century frescoes, remarkably well-preserved, depicting St Sebastien's life and martyrdom. And up a narrow road 12 km east of St Martin, remote and alone in the Alps, is the fourteenth-century sanctuary of the **Madone de Fenestre**: every 2 July, the thirteenth-century wooden statue of the Virgin in St Martin's church is taken up here in solemn procession.

Not far from this sanctuary is the mountain resort of **Le Boréon**, where you should park the car for hiking in the Alpine National Park of **Le Mercantour** that stretches from here to the Vallée des Merveilles and the Col de Turini. No cars, guns or dogs are allowed within this splendid wildlife reserve with its gorgeous scenery, where you may well spot marmots and chamois. Mountaineering courses are held here in summer.

Valdeblore

A scattering of hamlets on a bracing sub-Alpine plateau west of St Martin. The name comes from *val-des-pleurs* (vale of tears), for long ago a local lord locked up his wives here and let them starve to death, ignoring their cries. In today's happier times, the plateau is filling up with chalets, flats and hotels for holidaymakers. At La Colmiane, there are courses for skiing in winter, and for hang-gliding and rock-climbing in summer; the less energetic can take the funicular to the Pic de Colmiane for a great view.

Alpine ski-resorts and the Route Napoléon

The two leading ski resorts in Provence, Auron and Isola 2000, lie near the Italian border, above the Valley of the Tinée. To reach this remote Alpine valley you should turn off the N202 at Pont de la Mescla, and drive through the sombre Tinée and Valabres Gorges as far as the old village of Isola. Here turn right up a looping mountain road to Isola 2000.

Isola 2000
06420

So named because its altitude is 2,000 m, this big modern ski resort (8,000 beds) was created in the 1970s by British enterprise and British finance; and today the British are its most numerous visitors after the French. Its hideous brutalist architecture is nothing to wave the Union Jack about, but it does have high sunshine levels (you can even claim a refund if there are less than three days' sunshine in the week) and it offers good *pistes* for beginners and middle grades. The resort is closed in summer.

It is a serpentine complex of tall concrete blocks, comprising flats, hotels, restaurants, shops and cafés, connected by a series of zig-zag corridors with Métro-style signposting. Frankly it is tatty and weather-beaten, but there's fun for everyone, including discos, a cinema, a children's playground, a skating rink and a ski school. And the bustling skiers in their bright clothes do provide some relief from the bleak urban environment.

Where to stay
Top price

Diva; tel. 93 23 17 71. Opened in 1989, this chalet-style luxury hotel stands above the resort, aloof from its concrete jungle, and has fine views from the balconies of its 28 bedrooms. It has cheerful Art Nouveau decor, a sauna and piano-bar, and a sun-terrace where you can lunch outdoors even in winter. The Roux brothers of London's *Le Gavroche* have master-minded the cuisine, which is less *nouvelle* than classical and not *too* pricey. Open mid-December to mid-April.

Upper-
medium price

Le Chastillon; tel. 93 23 10 60. At one end of the resort's main building, near the ski lifts; Alpine wood decor and a breezy ambience. Outdoor buffet lunches. Open mid-December to mid-April.

Auron

Higher up the Tinée Valley and older than Isola 2000, this ski resort stands on a spacious plateau at 1,600 m, surrounded by high peaks. Tennis, swimming and cinema supplement the winter sports. Two goodish hotels that open in July and August as well as for the skiing season are the **Pilon** and **Las Donnas**. In the old village, the twelfth-century chapel of St Erige, scene of some medieval legends, has an apse covered with charming fifteenth-century frescoes.

St Etienne-
de-Tinée
06660

The beautiful broad valley of the upper Tinée has pretty foliage, wide panoramas, and Alpine air that is sharp and clear. Its main village, St Etienne, was once a religious centre – as witness its church with a fine Romanesque bell-tower, and three chapels covered with frescoes (ask for keys at the tourist office). There is an interesting market on Sundays.

Higher up the valley, a road to the left brings you to **St Dalmas-le-Selvage**, a remote upland village amid majestic scenery; its church has a notable sixteenth-century altarpiece. The main road along the valley finally loops giddily up to the **Cime de la Bonnette** (2,862 m), one of the highest Alpine passes, closed in winter. Here the suitably-named oratory of Notre-Dame-du-Très-Haut is the venue in August for a religious pilgrimage combined with a shepherd's fête and motor-rally – something for all tastes.

Valberg
06470

Valberg, third of the sizeable ski resorts in this area, lies in a remote setting 30 km west of the Tinée Valley. It has good skiing for beginners and intermediate grades, but is not for experts. In summer there is swimming, tennis, riding, shooting and excellent mountain hiking; or you can take a chair lift to the Croix de Valberg for amazing views in every direction. Amid Valberg's modern buildings is a tiny ancient church with a brightly-decorated interior.

There are some spectacular drives to be made in the Valberg area. You can go west to **Guillaumes**, a sleepy village with a ruined castle, and from here take the D2202 that offers dramatic views over the deep **Gorges du Daluis**, through which rushes the infant River Var. East from Valberg the hill-road zig-zags to Beuil, a pleasant village with an ornate church, and on to Roure, clinging giddily to its mountainside. At Beuil the D28 winds south through the narrow and majestic **Gorges du Cians**, noted for their unusual red rocks. Some parts of the road are one way, carved out of the rockface. At other points you get fabulous views of the jagged rocks high above, their redness contrasting with the greens of the bushes and lichen that cling to them, amid cascading waterfalls.

Where to stay
Medium price

Adrech de Lagas; tel. 93 02 51 64. A cheerful modern holiday hotel; 22 rooms, all with balconies. Reasonable food on the pension menu. Open July to mid-September, mid-December to mid-April.

Puget-Théniers

This pleasant little townlet where the Var meets the Roudoule is on the N202 Nice–Grenoble road. In the church, note the curious fifteenth-century woodcarvings of the Crucifixion and Resurrection, and the serene altarpiece that shows St James as a pilgrim to Santiago de Compostela, wearing a scallop shell.

Where to eat
Inexpensive

Auberge du Vieux Chêne, 1 Place Conil; tel. 93 05 00 14. In the northern outskirts, a friendly little place (12 rooms) where you can eat and drink on a vine-clad terrace.

Les Acacias; tel. 93 05 05 25. You'll find real local and Niçois cooking at this pleasant bistro by the main road. Closed January, Wednesday.

Entrevaux

One of the most interesting places in the region, this fortified village stands not on a hilltop but right by the River Var, across a bridge from the main N202. For centuries it was a border town between France and ducal Savoy: its ramparts, built by the military engineer Vauban in 1695, today survive intact, as do its moats and three gates, through one of which you pass to enter the sleepy village with its steep alleys. Zig-zag ramps lead up to Vauban's citadel, from which there are fine views. The former cathedral, seventeenth century, is part of the ramparts: the outside is plain and austere in the Provençal manner, but within, the paintings, silver ornaments and choir stalls are all decorative. The adjacent bell-tower dates back to the eleventh century.

There's a festival of Baroque music every August, and on the weekend nearest to 24 June a costumed religious procession.

Annot
04240

Where to stay
Inexpensive

St André-
les-Alpes
04170

Where to stay
Lower-medium
price
Castellane
04120

Where to stay
and eat
Medium price

Senez

A graceful village just off the N202, in a valley full of lime and lilac, lavender and chestnut. The old quarter is a maze of neatly-paved alleys, tall Renaissance houses, archways and running streams, and has often attracted painters. Nearby, easy to reach on foot, are sandstone hills eroded into strange shapes.

L'Avenue; tel. 92 83 22 07. Pleasant, newly redecorated and central, with tasty, copious food; 14 rooms. Open April to October.

Set among orchards and lavender fields in a wide upland valley, amid ideal hiking country, this village is a pleasing and popular summer resort. Just to its south, the River Verdon has been widened into an 11 km-long artificial lake, the **Lac de Castillon**, by the building of a hydro-electric dam. It is suitable for bathing.

Le Colombier, La Mûre, Route d'Allos; tel. 92 89 07 11. Up in the mountains, very quiet; some of the 24 rooms have balconies.

The N85 from Grasse to Digne is more or less the road that Bonaparte took on his historic journey from Elba back to Paris in 1815, and today it is clearly marked as the Route Napoléon. From Grasse it zig-zags for many kilometres over empty highlands where the views are stupendous (especially at the Pas de la Faye); then it dips down into the Verdon Valley at the busy little market town of Castellane, a centre for touring the Verdon Gorges (see p. 175). There's a fifteenth-century bridge, parts of old ramparts, and a church, St Victor, that was built in the twelfth century by monks from St Victor in Marseille (see p. 161). Looming over the town is a high rock, topped by the pilgrimage chapel of Notre-Dame-du-Roc: you can climb up to it by a steep footpath from behind the parish church, whose presbytery will lend you the key.

On 31 January, the Fête des Pétardiers celebrates a victory in 1586 over Huguenots who were besieging the town.

Wednesday and Saturday are market days.

Ma Petite Auberge; tel. 92 83 62 06. A typical little auberge (18 rooms) in the main square, popular with locals as well as tourists. Provençal cooking, served in a rustic *salle* or out under the lime trees. Open April to November.

Nouvel Hôtel du Commerce, Place de l'Église; tel. 92 83 61 00. Excellent Provençal cooking at this friendly 44-room hotel in the town. Open April to October.

Just off the N85 north-west of Castellane, this ancient tiny village (population 200) was, incredibly, the seat of a bishopric from the fifth century until the Revolution. Its former cathedral still survives, partly Provençal Romanesque, with later additions (the pulpit, choirstalls and tapestries are sixteenth to eighteenth century). Long disused, it is now a bit decrepit, but worth a visit (the curé at nearby **Barrème** will lend you its key).

Vence, St-Paul-de-Vence and the Loup valley

This section deals with the hinterland west of Nice and north of Antibes, an area full of interest – notably, the wonderful Maeght museum of modern art outside St-Paul, the craft shops of Tourrette, the macabre 'dance of death' painting in the church at Bar-sur-Loup, and the majestic scenery along the 'circuit of the clues' behind Vence.

Vence
06140

This pleasant little town north-west of Nice (population 13,428) stands on a hillside facing south, amid orchards, olive groves and flowers of all kinds, and is backed to the north by the high rocky escarpment of a sub-Alpine plateau. Its sheltered position has made Vence attractive to invalids (D. H. Lawrence died of tuberculosis here in 1930), and it is still very popular with retired people and other well-to-do immigrants. But it pays a price: the lush hilly countryside to the south, once so lovely, has today been spoiled by the random building of villas, hotels and flats. However, in Vence itself the oval-shaped *vieille ville* remains beguiling – a network of old alleys, full of boutiques and antique shops. In the Place du Peyra is an urn-shaped fountain, while the Romanesque cathedral has carved fifteenth-century choirstalls that are quaintly satirical, as well as a baptistry with a recent mosaic by Marc Chagall (he lived in Vence for many years, and died here in 1985).

What to see
Chapelle du Rosaire (Matisse)

Matisse was aged eighty when in 1950 he planned and decorated this enchanting, serene little chapel, in the suburbs beside the D2210 to St Jeannet. An agnostic himself, he gave it as a gift to the nuns of the adjacent Dominican convent who had nursed him through an illness. It is best seen on a sunny day, when the light falls luminously through stained-glass windows of yellow, green and blue, on to white ceramic walls covered with simple line drawings.

Festival

A Provençal folklore festival is held in the town on Easter Sunday and Monday.

Where to stay
Top price

Relais Cantemerle, 258 Chemin Cantemerle; tel. 93 58 08 18. In the quiet southern outskirts, a smart and attractive modern hotel in Provençal style, with split-level apartments (20) round a swimming pool and lovely garden. Good food and service. Open March to October.

Medium price

Diana, Avenue des Poilus; tel. 93 58 28 56. Fairly central, an efficient modern hotel; no restaurant, but the 25 rooms have kitchenettes.

La Roseraie, Avenue Henri Giraud; tel. 93 58 02 20. The Ganiers, from the Dordogne, run this friendly and sympathetic little hotel on the outskirts – it's a converted villa in a garden with a small swimming pool. Twelve cosy, pretty rooms. Open mid-March to mid-October.

Where to eat
Upper-
medium price
Medium price

Le Vieux Couvent, 37 Avenue Alphonse-Toreille; tel. 93 58 78 58. Good local cooking at this converted seventeenth-century monastery near the town centre. Closed early January to mid-February.

La Farigoule, 15 Rue Henri-Isnard; tel. 93 58 01 27. A lively bistro with a shady patio and decent local cooking. Closed Friday.

Places of interest
St-Paul-de-Vence
06570

Going clockwise and starting to its south, the following are the main places of interest around Vence.

Today one of the most heavily-visited tourist spots in Provence, this famous hill village was once a French frontier-post facing rival Savoy across the Var Valley; its sixteenth-century ramparts are intact and you can walk round them, semi-enjoying the views of that superb landscape which has been marred by over-building. Semi-enjoyment may also be your response to the village itself, so prettified that some alleys are now paved with mosaics – and trendy boutiques are legion. But the old fountains are genuine, as is the thirteenth-century hilltop church whose works of art include a painting of St Catherine thought to be by Tintoretto. There's a small museum of Provençal folklore in a sixteenth-century house, and another of mechanical musical instruments. Many notable artists frequented St-Paul between the wars: today they are somewhat put off by the tourist throng. Yet the legacy of modern art in St-Paul remains exceptional.

What to see
Foundation
Maeght

Its setting, its contents and its architecture conspire to make this one of Europe's finest and most evocative museums of modern art. Just off the Vence road, it was built in 1964 by Aimé Maeght, a Paris dealer, with the aim of spreading appreciation of contemporary art. His architect was the Catalan J. L. Sert, whose highly original building blends with the landscape; its roof of two inverted domes lends a touch of fantasy. Inside are a number of paintings by Kandinsky and Chagall including the latter's joyous life-loving 'La Vie'. The other pictures on show are often changed, but are likely to feature Pierre Bonnard, Georges Braque, Pierre Soulages and others.

In the lovely terraced garden, murals and sculptures have been set harmoniously amid the patios, lawns and pines, to wonderful effect. Mobiles by Alexander Calder and sculptures by Jean Arp and Barbara Hepworth stand in the front garden; behind, Joan Miró contributes a display of fanciful fountains, mosaics and sculptures, while the chapel has windows by Braque and Raoul Ubac. Giacomettis are strikingly aligned in the courtyard like giant skeleton chessmen. The Foundation puts on special exhibitions and has a library, art shop, and a cinema that shows films on art daily in summer. In July and August there are concerts of modern music.

Where to stay
Top price

La Colombe d'Or, Place des Ormeaux; tel. 93 32 80 02. This classy auberge at the entrance to the village is world famous for its collection of modern paintings and sculptures that any museum would envy. This was amassed by the hotel's founder, the late Paul Roux, art lover and friend of local painters, many of whom paid him in kind for his hospitality. It was thus that he acquired the Picasso, Georges Rouault and Maurice Utrillo now in the graceful dining-room, the César and Miró in the snug lounge, the Braque and Alexander Calder by the lovely swimming pool set amid cypress trees. To inspect these delights, you cannot just stroll in, but must at least take a meal: the food is only average, but the setting is what matters, especially the idyllic terrace with its Fernand Léger mural. Beautiful bedrooms (15), many with old beams and balconies. Closed mid-November to mid-December, one week January.

Medium price

Le Hameau, 528 Route de la Colle; tel. 93 32 80 24. Inexpensive and untrendy bliss: an old white-walled farmhouse, delightfully converted and truly rural, set amid trellised arbours, vines and fruit trees; comfortable lounge, 14 rustic-style rooms. No restaurant. Open mid-February to mid-November.

Where to eat
Medium price

La Brouette, 830 Route de Cagnes; tel. 93 58 67 16. Two Danes, Ole and Birgitte, run this intimate and convivial bistro, up on the hills above St-Paul, serving Nordic dishes such as Lapland reindeer and home-smoked trout, pork and eel. Modish clientele; swimming pool. Closed mid-October to end November, Tuesday.

Tourrette-sur-Loup
06140

West of Vence the landscape becomes wilder and more open, and the new building is less obtrusive. Tourrette, on a hill above the Loup Valley, is a splendid fortified village whose name comes from its three old towers. Its fifteenth-century church has gilded wood sculptures: most curiously, behind the altar is a first-century Gallo-Roman pagan shrine with an inscription to the god 'Mercurio'.

Shopping

More artists and craftsmen have settled in Tourrette than in any other village of the region. Through the medieval gateways, the sloping horseshoe-shaped Grande Rue (in fact an alley) is lined with their studio-boutiques. Among the best: A. M. and J. François, at no. 106, for puppets; Patrice Karquet, no. 35, for ornamental tinwork; Hélène Chenard, no. 10, for woven clothes; Yvette Lamoureux, no. 73, for sculptures and bronzes.

Where to eat
Medium price

Le Petit Manoir, 21 Grande Rue; tel. 93 24 19 19. A chic little place in the old village with good, interesting dishes that may include horse steak (yes, the French still eat horse). Closed Monday, Sunday dinner, mid-November to mid-December, February.

Le Bar-sur-Loup

This village amid the unspoilt wooded scenery of the Loup valley is noted for the extraordinary fifteenth-century painting known as the 'Danse Macabre' (dance of death), displayed in its old Gothic church. One lady falls, smitten by an arrow from Death, the archer; a man beside her lies slain, while from his mouth a demon is extracting his soul, a tiny naked figure; lords and ladies dance joyfully, but on the head of each is a little black devil, warning of the doom to come; St Michel weighs the souls and casts them into the jaws of hell. A text warns sinners to repent. It is thought that this haunting work was painted at the time of the plague.

Gourdon

Perched high above the deep Loup Valley, this ancient village of whitish houses looks from a distance indistinguishable from the rock on which it sits. It is much visited, both for its dramatic site and for its restored thirteenth-century castle, which holds two museums. One has historical items such as armour and old furniture; the other is devoted to the appealing, if minor, genre of 'naïve painting' (see p. 78), including a work by le Douanier Rousseau.

Below the village are the spectacular **Gorges du Loup**: you can peer down into them from the D3 north of Gourdon, or take the D6 that winds along their verdant bed from Pont-du-Loup.

Circuit of the 'clues'

These *clues* have nothing to do with crosswords or detectives, but are rocky clefts with rushing torrents. You will find them along parts of this 160 km round-trip, through the wild mountains north-west of Vence, that passes through superb and constantly changing scenery, as fine as any in Provence. Most of the way, you will see hardly a house save the odd hill hamlet, and hardly a soul (out of season) save for a few tourist cars – it is hard to believe that Nice and the madding coast are just a few kilometres away. The route described below starts at Vence, but you could equally start from another point, such as Grasse or Entrevaux.

Coursegoules

Climbing up from Vence by the D2 to Coursegoules, you are at once in another world – a desolate rock-strewn plateau with stunning views.

Where to stay and eat Inexpensive

Auberge de l'Escaou; tel. 93 59 11 28. A simple, modernised auberge in a mediaeval village setting. Young, cheerful owners, good simple food.

After the Col de Vence the scene again changes, for you enter a region of lush meadows, then wind down into the wooded vale of the upper Loup, to **Gréolières** where the church has a tenth-century Virgin in sculpted wood. Then the road loops up the side of a sheer gorge, on to a wide majestic plateau with pinewoods and sub-Alpine meadows: one turning leads to the modest ski resort of **Gréolières-les-Neiges**, another to the ski resort of **Thorenc**.

At the '4 chemins' crossroads, turn right along D5, over the Col de Bleine with its views of high rock-peaks; then if you wish make a detour west to the deep **Clue de St Auban**. Our circuit follows the narrow, winding D10 along the side of the deep Estéron Valley, in face of the stark Cheiron heights. The silent, empty uplands roll to far horizons, yet the valley vegetation is lush, with some farming on the steep hillsides – and the sun can beat hot. At the **Clue d'Aiglun**, you can bathe in the clear pools left by the torrent. Next, you can make another detour, to the **Clue du Riolan**, or follow the circuit past the ancient village of **Roquesteron**, down into a deep wooded valley and then again on to the plateau, with yet more majestic views. Finally, at Le Broc, the modern world abruptly re-emerges as sheer below you lies the ugly built-up plain of the Var. The road then winds via attractive **Carros**, with its castle, to Gattières and so back to Vence.

St Jeannet

This village east of Vence lies below the Baou, grandest of the high limestone rocks of the area: a mule-track leads to its top.

Where to stay
and eat
Medium price

Auberge St Jeannet; tel. 93 24 90 06. The Falstaffian Antoine Plutino lends ambience to his jolly Bohemian bistro where the food is so-so, but there's live music in summer. Nine pleasant rooms. Closed mid-January to mid-February.

La Gaude

South of St Jeannet, a small town amid flowers and orchards (and too many new villas), best known for the big IBM Research Centre, a star-shaped building of bold design.

Antibes and the coast from Nice to Cannes

Whereas east of Nice the coast is mountainous and lovely, to the west it is flatter and duller, for the hills are set back from the sea. To make matters worse, almost the whole of this 35-km sector between Nice and Cannes is now one messy conurbation, crammed with ill-assorted buildings and prone to heavy traffic jams. However, it does secrete a number of places of real interest and beauty – for example, the delightful old quarter of Antibes, the gorgeous peninsula of Cap d'Antibes, and just inland the little towns of Haut-de-Cagnes, Biot and Vallauris, all of them associated with great modern painters. My personal favourite is Renoir's house at Cagnes.

Cagnes-sur-Mer
06800

Easily confused with Cannes, but very different, this sizeable town (population 35,426) straggles inland from the sea in three parts, becoming more attractive as it does so. Cros-de-Cagnes, once a fishing village, is now a swollen and hideous coastal resort, full of hyper-markets, shabby hotels and high-rise flats. Just inland is the dullish commercial district of Cagnes-Ville, notable only for its Renoir Museum (see below). And above this, in total contrast, is the old hill village of Haut-de-Cagnes, squeezed within its ramparts and topped by its medieval château. This charming place has long attracted artists, writers and Bohemians: Cyril Connolly, among others, stayed here in the 1930s, and under the name of Trou-sur-Mer he made it the setting of *The Rock Pool*, his lurid novel about louche expatriates on the Riviera.

What to see
'Les Collettes':
Musée Renoir
'Les Collettes', up a quiet road on the edge of Cagnes-Ville, is the simple villa in a garden full of olive trees where Auguste Renoir spent the last years of his life, 1907 to 1919. It is now an atmospheric little museum – and there can be few other former homes of the great, anywhere in Europe, that evoke so vividly and movingly the spirit of the man of genius who lived there.

The artist's studio has been reconstructed as it was, with his coat and cravat, his invalid sticks, his easel and wheelchair: the only addition is a portrait of him at work in that same room with the same belongings, thus giving today's visitor an uncanny sense of time-warp. Renoir had severe arthritis, and his brushes were tied to his paralysed fingers so that he could paint by moving his arm. The writer Georges Besson has evoked the scene: 'This was the wretched and splendid period of suffering and glory, of magnificent inventiveness. The paintbrush was slipped between his gnarled, deformed fingers. He painted non-stop, pell-mell – flowers, fruit, landscape, nymphs, naiads, goddesses, garlanded necks, bounding bodies, expressed with a harmony ever more bold and vibrant.' The museum holds only one of Renoir's paintings, but has a number of his drawings and sculptures including a bronze bust of his wife, and in the garden his bronze 'Venus'. There are letters and photos of his family and friends, including his film-director son Jean and his faithful servant and favourite model, Gabrielle. His adored olive grove is intact: but the coastal view that he loved is now heavily blemished by new building.

*Château-
Musée*
The high castle at Haut-de-Cagnes was built in 1309 as a hill-fortress by the Grimaldi family of Monaco, who ruled here until 1789. Henri Grimaldi converted it into an elegant château in 1620; and in 1939 it was bought by the town of Cagnes, which has turned it into a varied and fascinating museum. Soft music plays as you enter via a triangular seventeenth-century courtyard, with an old pepper tree on one side. On the ground floor is a museum of the olive tree, including old olive presses and full details of the olive industry. Upstairs, the high ceiling of the seventeenth-century Salle des Fêtes bears a remarkable *trompe l'œil* fresco of the *Fall of Phaeton* by Carlone of Genoa. The second floor, where the Grimaldis lived, brings another sharp change of subject: a museum of modern artists who were born or worked by the Mediterranean, including Chagall, Raoul Dufy and Vasarély. In the Marquise de Grimaldi's boudoir is a striking curiosity – forty portraits of the cabaret singer Suzy Solidor, by various artists who knew her, including Cocteau, Dufy, Foujita and Kees van Dongen. Solidor, the flamboyant Bohemian, never shy of publicity, spent her final years at Cagnes. Lastly, you can climb on to the castle tower for a wide view of the coast and hills.

Below the castle, outside the walls, is the old chapel of Notre-Dame-de-Protection whose sixteenth-century frescoes are appealing.

What to do
An international art festival is held in the castle from June to Sep-

109

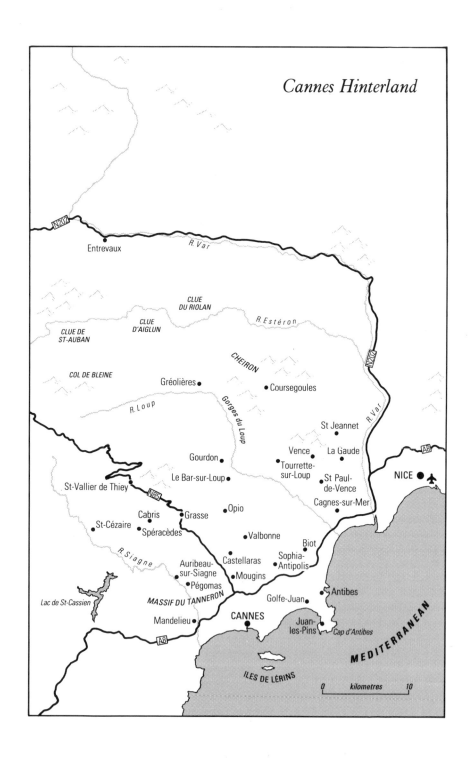

Cannes Hinterland

tember. In a different vein, the hippodrome down on the coast is the foremost on the Côte d'Azur and has frequent horse races.

Where to stay
Upper-
medium price

Le Cagnard, Haut-de-Cagnes; tel. 93 20 73 21. St-Exupéry and Sartre were among past guests at this sophisticated and well-known little hotel with superb views. It was artfully converted out of some thirteenth-century houses by the ramparts: the 20 rooms combine modern comforts with period decor, but they vary greatly in size.

Medium price

Les Collettes, 38 Chemin des Collettes; tel. 93 20 80 66. Near Renoir's house, a functional but cheerful modern hotel; the 13 rooms have balconies and many have kitchenettes – useful, as there's no restaurant. Closed mid-November to mid-January.

Where to eat
Top price

Le Cagnard (see above). Very chic and fashionable. On the lovely terrace, or in a graceful candlelit hall, you can enjoy excellent adaptations of regional dishes. Closed November to mid-December.

Upper-
medium price

Josy-Jo, Haut-de-Cagnes; tel. 93 20 68 76. A charming place with good honest cooking; you can dine under a vine arbour. Closed Sunday, mid-December to mid-January.

**Villeneuve-
Loubet**
06270

The largest new building complex in the Côte d'Azur was erected here by the beach in the 1970s, amid much controversy. It is the **Marina Baie des Anges** – four long, tall and curiously curving ziggurat blocks of flats, which are visible looming up along the shore from far away. Many local people protested loudly that they were hideously out of scale with the landscape: but for others, myself included, these twisting concrete pyramids do possess a sculptural elegance and even exert a strange fascination. The amenities include shops, a marina and a salt-water cure centre.

In the old part of town, at 3 Rue Escoffier, is the **Fondation Auguste Escoffier**, in the house where 'the king of sauces' was born in 1846. After a heavy Provençal lunch, you might think a visit to a gastronomic museum a bit much: but it would be wrong to miss this appetising array of memorabilia, including an icing-sugar model of Azay-le-Rideau château in the Loire, menus dating back to 1820, and many of the kitchen utensils that Escoffier invented, such as a device for stoning fruit and olives. You can even buy a set of forty lantern slides about bouillabaisse.

Biot
06410

Just inland from the cluttered coast north of Antibes, Biot (population 3,680) is a most attractive little town set serenely above a valley that grows roses, carnations and table grapes. It has an arcaded square, sixteenth-century gates and ramparts, and a church with fifteenth-century retables. For centuries Biot has been a major centre of Provençal ceramics and glass-making, thanks to its rich clay deposits: Novaro and the Verrerie de Biot are two glassworks whose products you can inspect and, if you wish, buy.

What to see
Musée Fernand
Léger

Besides glass-making, Biot's main claim to fame is this large and handsome museum, built by Léger's widow soon after his death in 1955. It stands amid trees on a hillside by the D4 from the town to the coast. Across its façade is a striking, brightly-coloured mosaic representing sport, while the spacious interior has big windows designed to attract maximum sunlight. Here over 300 of Léger's idiosyncratic paintings are finely displayed – a plethora of machines, cubes, cogs, girders and big robot-like figures. These works make it possible to trace his evolution, from the early flirtation with Impressionism ('Portrait de l'Oncle', 1905), through his creation of Cubism together with Braque and Picasso ('La Femme en Bleu', 1912), to his growing preoccupation with machinery. His later work was more human, much of it concerned with factory workers and their lives (for example, 'Les Loisirs sur Fond Rouge, 1949). The big mosaics and sculptures in the garden were created to Léger's design by some of his disciples.

Where to eat
Upper-medium price

Auberge du Jarrier, 30 Passage de la Bourgade; tel. 93 65 11 68. Christian Metral's *nouvelle cuisine* is superb (he spent five years with the great Senderens in Paris), and his wife's welcome is charming, at this very popular and classy auberge, which has a garden. Closed early December, most of March, Monday in winter.

Medium price

Café des Arcades, 16 Place des Arcades; tel. 93 65 01 04. The art-collecting *patron* helps to create a Bohemian atmosphere at this amusing café-bistro in an arcaded square. Slapdash service, but goodish Provençal cooking. Closed November, Sunday dinner, Monday.

Antibes
06600

The Côte d'Azur's third largest town (population 63,248) began life as a Greek trading-post. They called it Antipolis, 'the city opposite', for it faced their colony at Nice across the bay, and this setting has dictated much of the town's history: until the eighteenth century it was the frontier fortress-town of the French kings when their rivals, the Dukes of Savoy, controlled Nice. Of those defences, little remains today save the sea ramparts (you can walk along them, for fine views) and the big sixteenth-century Fort Carré north of the harbour. The modern town is hectic and commercial, but the medieval quarter by the castle has charm; and though Antibes' few sandy beaches are too crowded for a good seaside holiday, culturally the place is full of interest.

What to see
Château/
Musée Picasso

The Grimaldis ruled for centuries in this venerable thirteenth- to sixteenth-century castle on the sea-front, now a civic museum with one of the world's finest Picasso collections. When Picasso returned to his beloved Mediterranean in 1945, after spending the war years in Paris, he had difficulty in finding a studio – until the Mayor of Antibes lent him the castle museum for this purpose. Here Picasso worked with exuberant fecundity for six months, and in gratitude he later gave his entire output of that period on permanent loan to the museum, together with some of his tapestries and sculptures, and 200 of the lively ceramics that he later created at Vallauris (see p. 116). On the first floor are works inspired by the sea and by Greek mythology, full of fish and fishermen, fauns and centaurs, as well as some of

Picasso's best-known larger paintings such as 'La Joie de Vivre' and 'Ulysse et les Sirènes'.

This well laid-out museum also contains works by other modern artists, including tapestries by Jean Lurçat and Fernand Léger, four statues by Germaine Richier out on the terrace by the sea, and some abstract works by Nicholas de Staël who killed himself at Antibes in 1955.

Musée archaeologique

Along the coast south of the castle, this former Vauban bastion contains pottery, jewels, and so on, that mark Antibes' long history.

What to do
Marineland

At La Brague, 4 km north of Antibes, Marineland features performing dolphins, sea lions and Icelandic whales, while its zoo has penguins, an aquarium, and a children's play area. Often crowded.

Shopping

In the old town, you'll find plenty of boutiques around the Rue James-Close, and locally-made pottery and other handicrafts at La Colombelle, opposite the castle. The big outdoor food market in the Place Masséna is open daily except Monday.

Beaches and watersports

The small sandy beach in the southern suburbs gets very crowded, as do those at Cap d'Antibes. Just north of town, at La Brague, **La Siesta** is a huge and well-known beach-club (imported sand), with wind-surfing, water-skiing and even water-parachuting.

Nightlife

At night, when the bathers have gone, **La Siesta** becomes a night-club, one of the biggest and most exotic on the Côte: you dine and dance outdoors amid waterfalls and flaming torches. Odd wave-shaped casino. Open mid-May to mid-September.

Where to stay
Medium price

Mas Djoliba, 29 Avenue de Provence; tel. 93 34 02 48. In a quiet suburban street near the beach, a villa in a nice garden with friendly staff, pretty rooms (14) and an air of privacy. You can dine in a vine-arbour when it's fine (no meals served in winter).

Where to stay and eat
Medium price
Where to eat
Lower-medium price
Medium price

Mas de la Pagane, 15 Avenue Mas-Ensoleillé; tel. 93 33 33 78. Old farmhouse with a garden, quiet but near town centre, run by friendly local people. Excellent food. 5 rooms.

Le Marquis, 4 Rue Sade; tel. 93 34 23 00. Old Provençal house with rustic decor, friendly service, good local cooking. Closed two weeks November.

La Paille en Queue, 42 Blvd. Wilson; tel. 93 67 63 82. The decor is French eighteenth-century, but some dishes are exotic and spicy, for the owners are from La Réunion. Closed Sunday dinner, Wednesday.

L'Oursin, 16 Rue de la République; tel. 93 34 13 46. A lively bistro in the old town. Closed August, Monday, Sunday dinner.

Cap d'Antibes
06600

South of Antibes lies this beautiful pine-forested peninsula, long a favourite haunt of the rich and even now mainly given over to stately private villas with sub-tropical gardens. It was here in the 1920s that a few smart Americans first set the fashion for passing summers on the Riviera, which till then had been solely a winter resort. Cole Porter was one such visitor; others were Gerald and Sara Murphy, socialite art-lovers from Boston who bought a house just below the lighthouse and called it the Villa America (it is still there, under another name). Here they entertained Dorothy Parker, Gertrude Stein, Picasso and suchlike; their friends Scott and Zelda Fitzgerald came to stay with them (the Murphys were to an extent the originals for the Divers in *Tender is the Night*) and they would all go bathing at the Plage de la Garoupe on the east side of the Cap. This was then almost empty, for summer bathing was still a novelty. Today it is largely unrecognisable, a fenced-in private beach where you pay to enter: but Fitzgerald fans can enjoy the thrill of bathing on his 'bright tan prayer rug of a beach'.

What to see
La Garoupe
sanctuary

This unusual sailors' chapel near the lighthouse has a fine medieval Russian side-altar, but above all is famous for the array of votive offerings on its walls – paintings done by amateurs to give thanks for deliverance from some disaster. Their naïvety is most appealing. Of the sailors' ex-votos (votive offerings) down one aisle, note the self-portrait by a convict giving thanks to Our Lady for helping him escape from Toulon gaol to Martinique. The next aisle is filled with miraculous escapes on dry land – a man falling from a tree in 1865, another saved from an angry dog. The most bizarre picture is of a road accident: the car is on its back in the ditch, while the family kneel in the middle of the road (will they *never* learn?), offering thanks to Our Lady who has appeared in the sky.

Jardin Thuret

This garden was founded in 1856 as one of the first in Europe for the acclimatising of eucalyptus trees and other tropical vegetation now common on the Côte. It has many unusual plants and trees.

Musée Naval
et Napoléonien

Down near the south cape, this museum has souvenirs of Bonaparte's landing at Golfe-Juan in 1815 (see p. 116). He had also been based at Antibes in 1794, in charge of the coastal defences.

What to do
Beaches

The few beaches are sandy but private. Apart from La Garoupe (see above), the best place is the Maison des Pêcheurs at Port Gallice on the west coast – a complex that includes a lido and nightclub.

Where to stay,
or maybe not
Very top
price

Le Cap Eden Roc, Blvd. Kennedy; tel. 93 61 39 01. The most expensive, exclusive and glamorous of all Côte d'Azur hotels is as much a monument of social history as a mere place to stay, and contains famous ghosts even more numerous than bedrooms (130) for them to haunt. Since its opening in 1870 until recent days it was *the* smart rendezvous for royalty and celebrities, from G. B. Shaw to J. F. Kennedy, from Haile Selassie to Betty Grable. The Murphys, before they bought their villa, stayed here in 1923, persuading the owner to keep it open in summer for the first time. The Fitzgeralds stayed often: it's the Hôtel des Etrangers of Scott's novel, though in the manner of novelists he jumbles the topography (the hotel itself has no sandy beach).

Today owned by Dr Oetker, the fabled German puddings tycoon, this stately white palace is no longer socially quite what it was, though it's still popular with top German industrialists, Arab oil billionaires and American showbiz types. Even if you're not in that money bracket, why not pop in for a drink if you dare, to gawp at the marble floors, tapestries, great bowls of roses, and the clients who seem to be waiting for some *Vogue* fashion photographer to turn up? – and, of course, you should walk down through the majestic palm-clad park to the **Eden Roc** restaurant with its swimming pool by the sea, where Scott, champagne glass in hand, would watch poor mad Zelda diving from the rocks.

Medium price **La Gardiole**, Chemin de la Garoupe; tel. 93 61 35 03. This is more suitable for us ordinary folks – a friendly little family hotel with a garden, near La Garoupe beach. Many of its 21 rooms have balconies. Service can be slow, but the Provençal food is good, served on a flowery terrace in summer. Open March to October.

Where to eat (The ultra-renowned **Eden Roc**, see above, still luxurious, does not have cooking equal to its vertiginous prices.)

Top price **Le Bacon**, Blvd. Bacon; tel. 93 61 50 02. The high prices here *are* justified by the superb fish dishes, especially bouillabaisse, and by the lovely elegant terrace with its wide sea views. Closed mid-November to January, Sunday dinner, Monday.

Juan-les-Pins
06160

Its sheltered position on the Gulf of Juan has brought vast success as a resort to this suburb of Antibes, first made fashionable in the 1920s by the American millionaire Frank Jay Gould, who enticed here Harpo Marx, Mary Pickford, the as-yet-unknown Wallis Simpson and others. Fitzgerald found it 'a constant carnival . . . where the night was musical and strident in many languages' (not exactly *tender*). Today, apart from two luxury hotels, most of the sophistication has vanished and the town is now a haunt of the young and noisy: the little streets near the casino are crammed with fast-food bars, boutiques, discos, and cafés with frenzied orchestras (see below: maybe Scott was being prophetic). Frantic in summer, Juan in winter is much deader than other resorts on the Côte.

What to do There's an international jazz festival in July.

Beaches As at Cannes, you pay for the better ones, but you can find free ones away from the central area. All are sandy.

Nightlife **Le Festival** and **Le Pam-Pam**, two big terrace-cafés on the Blvd. Wilson, near the casino, vie with each other in ear-splitting rivalry, generating most of Juan's decibels. Each has garish lighting, flamboyant 'Brazilian' decor and a Brazilian orchestra; each serves expensive alcoholic ice-cream cups and fruit cocktails; each nightly attracts a crowd of onlookers all down the street. This street-theatre goes on till 3 or 4 a.m. in summer (bring ear-plugs if you're booked into a hotel nearby). In comparison, Juan's many discos and its casino are tame indeed.

Where to stay **Pré Catelan**, 22 Avenue des Lauriers; tel. 93 61 05 11. Pleasant

Medium price

villa-style hotel (18 rooms) with a garden, 200 m from sea. Good cooking.

Inexpensive

Eden, 16 Avenue Louis-Gallet; tel. 93 61 05 20. Near the seafront. Welcoming, clean and cosy. 17 rooms. No restaurant. Closed November to January.

Where to eat
Top price

La Terrasse. The elegantly romantic garden terrace of the luxury Hôtel Juana makes a perfect setting for some of the finest and subtlest cooking on the Côte. Chic clientele to match.

Upper-
medium price

Auberge de l'Esterel, 21 Rue des Iles; tel. 93 61 08 67. Fabrice Knoettler provides delicious food, charmingly served, in a lovely garden or dullish *salle* (the ground floor of a small hotel under separate management). Closed November, early February.

Golfe-Juan

This next-door bathing resort on the Gulf of Juan, sheltered by hills with orange and mimosa trees, has long sandy beaches (mostly free) and a marina. Napoleon landed at Golfe-Juan with 800 men on 1 March, 1815, on his return from exile in Elba, and began his march to Paris. A monument by the harbour marks the event.

Vallauris

Vallauris (population 21,217), just inland from Golfe-Juan, is linked, above all, with Picasso. It had been a pottery centre for centuries, but its industry was moribund by the time he came on a visit in 1947. He found one good potter still at work, Suzanne Ramié, and his admiration for her work led to his own involvement in ceramics. During the six years he lived at Vallauris, he shaped and decorated a vast amount (some of that output is now in the Antibes Museum, see p. 112). His biographer, Sir Roland Penrose, has written, 'To see his hands as he moulded the clay, small and feminine yet strong, gave a pleasure akin to watching a ballet.'

Picasso's presence gave new life to the local industry, as talented potters arrived to work in his aura, and local craftsmen made copies of his originals. Today, however, his influence is waning: Vallauris still has many potters, but few are gifted – as you can see from the shop windows full of inferior work in the main street. By far the best gallery is that run by Suzanne Ramié's family, the **Madoura**: its elegant museum-shop sells the work of its own pottery as well as copies of Picasso's ceramics.

What to see
Musée
National 'La
Guerre et la
Paix'

One of the most powerful of all Picasso's paintings, 'La Guerre et la Paix' is not unlike 'Guernica' in its evocation of the evils of war, and it covers the entire walls and vaulted ceiling of this small twelfth-century chapel, long deconsecrated. Asked by the town council to decorate the chapel, Picasso painted the work on plywood panels in his studio at Vallauris in 1952, when he was seventy, then screwed them on to the chapel walls. The adjacent municipal museum has some modern paintings by Alberto Magnelli and others.

In the square outside is another striking work by Picasso: a bronze statue of a naked man holding a sheep. He made this in Paris during the war, then donated it to the town.

Where to eat
Medium price

La Gousse d'Ail, 11 Avenue de Grasse; tel 93 64 10 71. Rustic decor, charming service and good Provençal cooking. Closed mid-November to mid-December, Monday evening out of season, Tuesday.

Cannes

06400

Cannes' all-year population is only 72,000, one-fifth that of Nice: but the size and splendour of its tourist industry make it seem much bigger, lending it a metropolitan air. Set along a lovely bay, backed by wooded hills, it claims to be the most glamorous and sophisticated of Europe's larger resorts – and certainly its famous palm-lined sea-promenade, La Croisette, wears all the trappings of glamour. Here luxury cars draw up outside the giant hotels, and elegant ladies slip into boutiques with famous names. But away from this super-elegant façade, Cannes is a commercial town like any other, not especially expensive, with an old quarter full of character. And in high summer, or at film-festival time, even La Croisette becomes too hot and bustling to be truly glamorous. In some ways, I enjoy Cannes most in wintertime.

Getting there

Nice international airport (see p. 72) is 25 km away, and is served by a minibus shuttle. The main station is linked to Paris by the same two daily TGV express trains as Nice (journey time six and three-quarter hours); there are also fast trains along the coast to Marseille, Nice, and further. The A8 autoroute, just north of the town, connects Cannes with these and other cities. A good bus network goes into the suburbs and to nearby towns. The main tourist office is at the new Palais des Festivals; tel. 93 39 24 53.

History

Cannes has little history, unlike Nice, and was just a fishing village on that momentous day in 1834 when Lord Brougham, a British ex-Minister, was obliged to halt there on his way to Italy, as the frontier west of Nice had been closed due to a cholera epidemic. He was so delighted by the warm climate and attractive setting that he built a villa, and there spent the next thirty-four winters. He was thus the creator of modern Cannes: he persuaded the French king to finance the building of a proper port, and soon hundreds of other aristocrats and royals were following his example as regular visitors, including the Prince of Wales and the tsar. Later, the great hotels grew up along the Croisette, and by the 1920s Cannes had outshone its local rivals and was chanting the arrogant rhyme: 'Menton's dowdy, Monte's brass, Nice is rowdy – Cannes is class!'

Cannes today

Under its assertive lady mayor, Anne-Marie Dupuy of the neo-Gaullist RPR party, Cannes today has set its cap at the lucrative new trade in conventions, industrial fairs and business tourism, and is more dynamically successful with this than Nice. The Palais des Festivals on the sea-front, opened in 1982, is the largest French convention centre outside Paris, with several huge auditoria and 14,000 sq metres of exhibition space. Its main annual event is, of course, the Film Festival in May, inaugurated in 1939 and the foremost event of its kind in the world: the big stars still come, and the publicity-hungry starlets still behave outrageously, although the festival is now little more than a glorified trade fair. Apart from this, Cannes all year round hums with congresses, tournaments, galas and festivals of all kinds. Its big hotels keep afloat mainly on this organised tourism, much of it in the form of business incentive trips. But the town also retains some faithful clientele of aristocrats and *rentiers*, most of them elderly, bringing echoes of former days. And many very rich people, Arabs especially, have villas on its suburban hillsides.

Main areas

The town is in two main parts, with the Palais des Festivals as its hub. To the west is the former fishing port and old quarter, crowned by the hill of Le Suquet with its eleventh-century tower, finely floodlit at night; in the narrow alleys, around here and Forville market, many old people still live in poverty. East of the Palais is modern Cannes. Here, behind La Croisette and its luxury palaces, are other, smaller hotels, around the Rue d'Antibes, the main shopping artery. La Croisette curves eastwards along the bay to the Palm Beach Casino on its headland – an area of smart flats and villas. This elite eastern sector extends up the wooded slopes behind, to the well-named La Californie and to Super-Cannes, where the tower of the Observatory (a lift will take you up) offers one of the grandest views in France – as far as Corsica on a fine day. All Cannes lies at your feet: but its sheltering hills are today marred by countless new blocks of high-rise, high-price flats, many occupied for just a few weeks a year. The rich live or stay in La Californie, the petit-bourgeois in Le Cannet to the north, and the workers, such as they are, in semi-industrial La Bocca to the west.

Traffic in central Cannes is horrifically dense in summer. There are some big multi-storey car parks – if you can ever reach them.

What to see

Cannes is not rich in museums or churches, and the best local 'sights' are outside the town itself.

Musée de la Castre

A citadel on the hill of Le Suquet, built in the twelfth century by monks from St Honorat (see below), is now a museum of antiquities donated to the town in 1873 by an eccentric Dutch traveller, Baron Lycklama. Besides portraits of him in oriental dress, you can see Egyptian mummies, and items from Polynesia, Peru and elsewhere.

Iles de Lérins: Ste Marguerite and St Honorat

These two lovely wooded islands just offshore, easily reached by regular boat services, are full of interest. In the fourth century the monk St Honorat founded a monastery on the smaller island, which bears his name. By the seventh century it was one of the key centres of Christendom, with 4,000 monks and a fine library that made it a vital centre of learning in the Dark Ages. Among the 120 saints and 600 bishops from St Honorat was Ireland's St Patrick, who trained there. It owned 100 castles and priories in France, but later declined, until in 1869 it was bought by Cistercian monks from Sénanque who restored it and still run it today.

St Honorat is a quiet, remote island with lush flowers and foliage, ideal for a picnic. The big nineteenth-century monastery, still active, has a small museum with relics of the founder saint. Alone by the sea on the south side, like a romantic fairy-tale castle, stands the eleventh-century keep of the old fortified monastery, where the monks took refuge from Saracen invaders. It has a fine chapel and arcaded cloisters, and, curiously, a Roman marble cistern.

The **Ile Ste Marguerite** is named after St Honorat's sister who ran a nunnery there. The fort that Richelieu built, for centuries a state prison, still survives: its most notable inmate was the Man in the Iron Mask (in fact velvet), from 1687 to 1698, a mystery figure who was possibly the bastard brother of Louis XIV, then on the throne. Visitors are shown his cell, also that of Marshal Bazaine who in 1870 surrendered Metz to the Prussians (he then escaped from prison disguised as a woman). You can also see the memorial to six Huguenot pastors who were locked here in solitary confinement after the Revocation of the Edict of Nantes (all but one went mad). Today the fort is a youth, sports and cultural centre, laying on courses for teenagers in sea-sports, dance and drama. In the Roman foundations, a newly-opened marine museum contains finds from excavations on the island and on the sea-bed around it. There are three restaurants on Ste Marguerite, and one on St Honorat.

What to do
Festivals

All through the year, various events are laid on for tourists, summer residents and the conference trade. Among the more important: in January, a major international fair of record and music publishing (MIDEM); in April, an international market of television programmes; in May, the film festival, also a gymkhana; in June, a café-théâtre festival; July/August, concerts and opera at Le Suquet and on Ile Ste Marguerite; 1 August, fête of the fishermen; June to September, *son et lumière* in the fort of the Ile Ste Marguerite.

Sport

There are some renowned golf clubs in the area, notably the smart and exclusive Country-Club de Cannes-Mougins, at Mougins, tel. 93 75 79 13, and Cannes-Mandelieu, tel. 93 49 55 39. Forest Hill Montfleury, 19 Avenue Beauséjour; tel. 93 38 75 78, is a large sports club with tennis, squash and swimming. The big new marinas offer plenty of scope for sailing, surfing and so on; ask at any hotel.

Beaches

Cannes has kilometres of sandy beaches. Most of La Croisette's is split into some twenty paying beaches with neat rows of parasols and mattresses: best and smartest are those run by the Carlton and other big hotels, but open to all. There are public beaches west of Le Suquet, or east of the Palm Beach Casino which has a fine large swimming pool. Some beaches will arrange wind-surfing or water-skiing.

Shopping | Modern boutiques as smart as any in Paris are to be found on or near La Croisette or in the Hôtel Gray d'Albion; in and around the Rue d'Antibes, just behind, is a good range of somewhat cheaper shops. The Rue Meynardier, further west, has many traditional shops for local products: here Ceneri is one of France's greatest cheese shops (300 different kinds, and the cellars are open to visitors); Aux Bons Raviolis makes marvellous pastas; Ernest is a remarkable charcutier. The nearby Forville market, colourful and inexpensive, is open mornings only, closed Monday.

Nightlife | Of the many discos, currently the most fashionable is **Studio Circus**, 48 Blvd. de la République, large, loud and ambitious. **Whisky à Gogo**, 115 Avenue des Lérins, also gets packed out with trendy teenagers, while the **Galaxy** in the Palais des Festivals is a little more sedate, and so is the select and comfortable **Jane's** in the Hôtel Gray d'Albion, which has dinner-dances.

The bars of the hotels Carlton, Majestic and Martinez are all chic and stylish. The Carlton's bar has long been a smart social rendezvous, while that of the Martinez has a super-star American pianist, Jimmy McKissic, who makes friends with all the guests.

Cannes' summer casino is the **Palm Beach**, a white 1920s' pomposity described by Archibald Lyall in *The Companion Guide to the South of France* as 'rather as though a Foreign Legion Fort had had a flirtation with the Doge's palace'. Besides the usual gambling, it has a smart dinner-dance cabaret in a glamorous hall opening wide on to the swimming pool. The less glamorous winter casino (November to May) is in the Palais des Festivals.

Where to stay | What cathedrals and palaces are to other cities, great hotels are to Cannes: they are grandiose monuments, not just places to stay. The three deluxe titans along La Croisette are in constant much-publicised rivalry, as they vie to gain the edge on each other through refurbishments, new amenities, changes of chef or manager: currently, the Martinez is coming up, pushing ahead of the mighty Carlton, while the Majestic has fallen back, its place threatened by the flashily revamped Gray d'Albion in the street behind. And now a new challenger has just been built on La Croisette, on the site of the former festival hall – the Swiss-owned deluxe Noga-Hilton, which has the advantage of a rooftop swimming pool. For those who want to lay their head more cheaply, the choice is massive: the streets behind La Croisette are chock-a-block with middle-price hotels, while others are out in the suburbs. Here is a brief selection:

Top price | **Carlton**, 58 La Croisette; tel. 93 68 91 68. Built in 1912 in ornate *belle époque* style, and sold in 1988 by Britain's Grand Metropolitan to the Japanese Seibu-Saison group, the Carlton is the most famous and imposing of the great white wedding-cake palaces along the front. Bedrooms (325) are light and pretty, many with sea-facing balconies. Despite the gilded luxury, the ambience is relaxed, for the clientele though sophisticated is informal (many top film stars stay at festival-time). Three restaurants: La Côte is very smart, the grill a bit cheaper; and a smart beach.

Martinez, 73 La Croisette; tel. 93 68 91 91. Built in 1929, the Martinez was bought in 1982 by the excellent Concorde group which has renovated stylishly, restoring many of the public rooms and 420 bedrooms to their original Art Deco style, and adding a sporty touch: the hotel has tennis courts, a smart new beach with many amenities such as a restaurant, and a spa centre. Superb service. Closed mid-November to Christmas Eve, February.

Upper-medium price

Novotel Montfleury, 25 Avenue Beauséjour; tel. 93 68 91 50. Up on a hillside in its own big garden, a breezy and relaxed modern hotel: 180 spacious rooms, many with balconies; outdoor heated pool; spa centre; two restaurants. The Forest Hill sports club is close by.

Medium price

La Madone, 5 Avenue Justinia; tel. 93 43 57 87. What a contrast with La Croisette, yet only 400 m away! Up a quiet suburban road, this comfortable little family hotel has a swimming pool in a pretty garden. No restaurant; 22 rooms, some with kitchenettes.

Campanile, Aérodrome de Cannes-Mandelieu, 06150 Cannes-la-Bocca; tel. 93 48 69 41. Just west of Cannes along the N7, a well-run comfortable motel, part of the new Campanile chain. Buffet breakfasts and fairly-priced meals. 98 rooms.

Inexpensive

Châlet de l'Isère, 42 Avenue de Grasse; tel. 93 38 50 80. A small personal *pension* on a hillside in the suburbs, quite near the sea. Delicious meals served in a small garden. 8 rooms.

Chanteclair, 12 Rue Forville; tel. 93 39 68 88. Quite central, near Forville market. Friendly owners, pleasant rooms facing a quiet patio. 14 rooms. No restaurant.

Roches Fleuries, 92 Rue Georges-Clémenceau; tel. 93 39 28 78. One and a half km from the centre; very attractive rooms (24) and terrace; good value. No restaurant. Closed mid-November to Christmas.

Where to eat

As you might expect, Cannes has several 'gastronomic' high-priced restaurants, mostly in the big hotels. More surprising is the large number of excellent much cheaper places, offering good value: you will find them notably around the port and Le Suquet, where the Rue St-Antoine is lined with trendy bistros (on my last visit the fullest here by far, but not the best, was American – the Pacific Express, serving 'Tex-Mex' food to the local *beau monde*).

Top price

Palme d'Or (see Hôtel Martinez, above). Distinguished inventive cooking by chef Christian Willer, a glamorous first-floor setting on a wide terrace facing the sea, open to the stars – and a starry clientele to match. The downstairs **Orangeraie** is also good – and cheaper.

Royal Gray, 2 Rue des Etats-Unis; tel. 93 68 54 54. The Hôtel Gray d'Albion's restaurant, under the brilliant young chef Jacques Chibois, narrowly out-classes the Palme d'Or in Cannes' gastronomic stakes, according to most pundits. Both the food and decor are elegant and modern; the palm-shaded terrace is pretty but lacks a sea view. Closed February, Sunday, Monday.

Upper-medium price

Gaston Gastounette, 7 Quai St-Pierre; tel. 93 39 47 92. An open terrace by the port, comfortable seating, live music at dinner – and excellent fresh fish. Closed three weeks in January.

La Mère Besson, 13 Rue des Frères-Pradignac; tel. 93 39 59 24. This serious, rather formal place, down a quiet street, is a stronghold of classic local cuisine (soupe au pistou, aïoli). Closed Sunday, and lunchtime in July/August.

Inexpensive

Au Bec Fin, 12 Rue du 24-Août; tel. 93 38 35 86. A delightful old-style family-run bistro: good local dishes served in generous portions with a smile. Closed Saturday dinner, Sunday.

Le Bouchon, 10 Rue de Constantine; tel. 93 99 21 76. A bit cramped, but the simple cooking is fine and the service friendly. Closed Monday, late November to mid-December.

Le Refuge, 13 Quai St-Pierre; tel. 93 39 34 54. One of the best of several touristy but reliable fish restaurants by the port. Big open terrace, often crowded. Closed mid-November to mid-December.

Grasse and the Cannes hinterland

Grasse
06130

Known as 'the balcony of the Côte d'Azur', Grasse (population 38,360) lies terraced along the southern slopes of a rocky plateau that shields it from the colder winds. In the twelfth century it was a small, Italian-style republic, linked with Genoa and Pisa. Then in the last century it became a smart winter resort, thanks to its mild climate: Queen Victoria spent several winters here, in the Rothschild Villa or at the Grand Hôtel, now closed. Grasse is not my favourite town in the region – I find it rather too sedate. But there is plenty worth seeing. And there are interesting villages nearby – Valbonne, Auribeau, and fashionable Mougins – in the lush, hilly hinterland of Cannes between Grasse and the coast.

The flower and perfume industry

Tanning and glove-making were the main local industries until the sixteenth century, when Catherine de Medici introduced scent-making from Italy because of the fashion at that time for perfumed gloves. So the growing of flowers began in the wide, warm vales to the south, to supply the new factories; and until recently some 85 per cent of the world's flower essence for scents was treated at Grasse. Today, the factories prefer to import the flowers more cheaply from North Africa, or to use synthetic essences, which are also less costly, while many growers find that they can earn more money by selling or renting their land for new holiday building. So the growing of jasmine, roses and carnations for perfume has declined: but use is still made of wild mimosa from the Tanneron hills, orange blossom from the Vence area, and lavender from the plateaus to the west. And this is even now the foremost area of France for the cut flower market. Each flower has its own season, lending splashes of bright colour to the hillsides.

In the 1970s the thirty local factories together were using annually some 490 tonnes of roses, 250 of jasmine, 250 of violet, 200 each of orange blossom and mimosa, 130 of lavender: this may seem an awful lot, but it takes 1,000 kilos of rose petals, or 150 of lavender, to produce 1 kilo of perfume essence. The factories primarily are bulk wholesalers to Dior, Chanel and the other major fashion houses of Paris, New York and so on, which then blend them into their own varieties. However, much research is done in Grasse, where the experts of the big Fragonard firm claim to be able to identify 1,500 different scents – a skill requiring a nostril more subtly tuned than any wine connoisseur's palate. It is a traditional skill handed down from father to son, today in danger of dying out.

What to see
Vieille ville

Grasse is a sprawling hillside town with long, looping boulevards, confusing at first for the motorist. At its heart are appealing ancient narrow streets and steep-stepped alleys, notably the Rue Fontette and the arcaded Place des Aires. It's an area now full of Algerian immigrants, with their lively shops and cheap restaurants. You get fine views of the valley from near the cathedral, or from the broad promenade of the Cours Honoré-Cresp.

Notre Dame,
former
cathedral

Set imposingly on a hilltop of the old town, this fine church dates from the twelfth century and was restored in the seventeenth, while its curving double stairway in front is eighteenth-century. Inside, despite the massive stone pillars, the ambience is cosy and intimate, and the decoration is rich. Note the three paintings by Rubens and, in a side chapel, Fragonard's 'Washing of the Feet' – one of his few religious works and quite lacking in any feeling of piety.

Musée d'Art
et d'Histoire
de Provence
Musée de la
Marine

The handsome eighteenth-century Hôtel de Cabris now houses a collection of Provençal art and handicrafts, including ceramics, tapestries, furniture and domestic objects, of limited interest.

Maps, scenes of naval battles, model warships, and other souvenirs of the career of Admiral de Grasse (1722-88), born in the area, the French naval hero who helped America win the War of Independence by blockading the British at Yorktown, Virginia.

Villa-Musée
Frangonard

Jean Honoré Fragonard, son of a local glove-maker, was born in Grasse in 1732, but lived most of his life in Paris. His one return visit was during the Terror, when he spent a year in this graceful home of relatives: it is now a museum, containing none of his major paintings but a few minor ones, such as a self-portrait in Renaissance costume. He brought to Grasse with him the famous series of large canvases, 'The Pursuit of Love', which he had made for Madame du Barry and she had rejected as being too frivolous: the originals are now in the Frick Museum in New York, but there are good copies in this villa.

Maison
Fragonard

What to do
Festivals
Markets

Nightlife

Where to stay
Medium price

Inexpensive

Where to eat
Medium price

Opio

Where to stay
and eat
Upper-
medium price

Where to eat

The *trompe l'œil* decoration on the stairway may be the work of Fragonard or of his son Evariste.

The town's largest perfume factory, named after the painter, operates fascinating conducted tours that attract thousands of tourists daily. You can see the staff at work, and are shown and explained the main processes of making scent from flowers, as well as being told about the use of animal fluids as 'fixatives' – for example, civet from Ethiopian cats, and whale vomit which provides the crucial ingredient of ambergris. This may sound ghoulish: but the tours are charmingly done by expert polyglot guides, and when finally you are brought into a shop full of tempting Fragonard products, you are put under no pressure to buy. There's a small museum of the history of the perfume industry, with bottles, machines and cosmetic aids dating back to the ancient Greeks. The Molinard perfume factory also puts on guided tours.

There's a rose festival on the second weekend in May and a jasmine festival on the first Sunday in August.

The daily market in the Place des Aires is colourful, and on Sunday there's a lively one in the Place Jean-Jaurès.

Don't expect too much in this rather sedate town. However, a new casino has just been built.

Panorama, 2 Place du Cours; tel. 93 36 80 80. Grasse has very few good hotels: this one is modern, efficient and quite central, with a garden; 36 rooms. No restaurant.

Campanile, Le Pré du Lac; tel. 93 42 55 55. Five km north-east of Grasse, just off the D2085 to Nice, a member of the Campanile motel chain, modern, efficient and comfortable, with good, simple meals and buffet breakfasts; 41 rooms.

Maître Boscq, 13 Rue de la Fontette; tel. 93 36 45 76. True Provençal cooking, including Grassois specialities such as stuffed cabbage, at this bistro in the old town. Closed Sunday.

Near this village east of Grasse is the Roger Michel olive oil mill, which is worth a visit. The mill is still actively in operation: visitors are shown how the olives are crushed to make oil, and can buy the olive oil and other olive-based products. Down a track to the south, off the D3, the semi-ruined eleventh-century chapel of Notre-Dame stands alone in the fields, and next to it are the remains of a sixth-century baptistry.

Club Méditerranée, Domaine de Latour; tel. 93 09 71 00. This luxurious new Club Med 'village', opened in 1989 just south of Opio, marks a further step in its relentless expansion upmarket. Beads for money are replaced by electronic cards, but some classic Club features survive, such as the all-inclusive fees and shared tables for eight. You can book just for one night, or for the day, to enjoy the gargantuan buffet meals with wine ad lib, the huge pool, tennis, golf, fitness centre, and so on. The views are glorious and the Provençal rural style of the buildings is attractive; 500 rooms.

Mas des Geraniums; tel. 93 77 23 23. Good honest food in a rural

Medium price

Valbonne
06560

Where to stay
Upper-
medium price
Where to eat
Medium price

Sophia-
Antipolis
06560

Where to stay
Upper-
medium price
Mougins
06250

What to see
Notre-Dame-
de-Vie

Musée de
l'Automobile

setting, with a garden where children can play. There are seven simple but pleasant bedrooms, too. Open February to September.

This pretty little town 9 km south-east of Grasse has a fine thirteenth-century church and a seventeenth-century arcaded square; its narrow but straight streets are laid out on a grid pattern, unusual for the period. Here we are out of the orbit of Grasse and into the wealthy Cannes hinterland, where smart private villas and hotels lie amid a rolling landscape of pines and olives, vines and flower fields – all rather too built-up to be still really beautiful.

Around 3 February there's a festival of grapes and olives.

Hôtel des Armoiries, Place des Arcades; tel. 93 12 90 90. A seventeenth-century building, stylishly restored, in the arcaded main square. Warm ambience. No restaurant.

Caves St Bernardin; tel. 93 42 03 88. A dark-panelled restaurant, always crowded and popular; good local cooking. Closed Sunday, Monday, mid-November to mid-December.

This, the largest and fastest-growing 'technology park' in France, has been developed since the mid-1970s on a wooded plateau between Valbonne and Antibes, and it marks a state bid to promote the Côte d'Azur as a centre of modern science and research. This 'silicon valley' got off to a difficult start, but has now attracted such investors as Digital Equipment, Dow Corning, Toyota and Wellcome, as well as Air France's central reservation centre. Today it's quite a town, with numerous banks, hotels and business centres, a big private boarding school, and ochre villas arranged in tiers like a pastiche of a local hill village. For the bold modern planning and architecture alone, it's worth a visit.

Novotel; tel. 93 65 40 00. Primarily for business people: but with its garden, swimming pool, tennis courts and breezy decor, this modern chain hotel has quite a holiday ambience, too; 97 rooms. Restaurant.

This most fashionable and sophisticated of all French hill villages is today the garden-suburb of Cannes, 7 km away. The rich and famous have villas here, or they come to eat at one of the many superior restaurants, or to play golf at the nearby Cannes Country Club. The whole place is incredibly neat and well-manicured, but the narrow streets of the old village have not lost their charm: there are bits of ramparts, a fifteenth-century fortified church, and a museum of photography. Go up the tower of the old Romanesque church for a sweeping view over this stretch of the Côte d'Azur, too urbanised but still spectacular.

This beautiful old chapel, once a hermitage, stands alone on a hill just east of the village, up a narrow track off the D3. It is usually closed, but through the window you can glimpse the fine Baroque altar, while outside is a fifteenth-century stone cross. Close by is the *mas* where Picasso spent part of his old age.

This modern museum, well signposted, lies just north of the A8 autoroute, south-east of Mougins, and can be reached also from Le

Cannet or Vallauris. A huge collection of modern rally-winners and vintage cars, the oldest being an 1894 Benz, are exhibited in rotation, seventy at a time, and there's a film show on automobile history.

Shopping   L'Herbier de Provence sells local herbs and food products, but is expensive.

Where to stay   **Mas Candille**, Blvd. Clément-Rebuffel; tel. 93 90 00 85. On a
Top price   hillside just outside the village, a lovely seventeenth-century farmhouse lined with cypresses, now a graceful auberge, English owned and run by Alan Kimber. Small but rustically pretty rooms (22), some with balconies; English-style bar; nice garden. The food can be erratic, however, and the small tree-enclosed swimming pool is a bit unkempt. Closed two weeks in January.

Where to eat   **Le Moulin de Mougins**; tel. 93 75 78 24. A sixteenth-century olive
Top price   oil mill south-east of the village, owned since 1969 by Roger Vergé, one of the most renowned of modern French chefs: he has built it into the most fashionable eating place on the Côte, popular with American film stars during the Cannes Film Festival. You eat from real Limoges in the luxurious dining-room, or under parasols in the garden. And the Master, lordly and handsome in his white robes, will pass among his guests at the end of the meal, to acknowledge their applause like an opera star. Does the cooking justify this high drama? Some might feel not – but it's still tirelessly inventive, with sauces light and subtle, salads gaily coloured and originally flavoured. Five bedrooms. Closed February, March.

Upper-   **La Ferme de Mougins**, 10 Avenue St-Basile; tel. 93 90 03 74. An
medium price   idyllic converted farmhouse: attentive service, pampered comfort, a wide terrace above the swimming pool, classy customers, and excellent original cooking. Closed mid-February to mid-March, Thursday.

Medium price   **Le Bistro de Mougins**, Place du Village; tel. 93 75 78 34. A seventeenth-century vaulted cellar, always crowded; good authentic Provençal and Niçois dishes. Closed December, January, Tuesday, Wednesday.

    Le Feu Follet, Place du Village; tel. 93 90 15 78. Quite smart and trendy, but very good value. Closed November, March, Monday.

Castellaras   Down a sideroad between Mougins and Valbonne, this looks from afar like yet another old hill village: but it's a recent pastiche, by the same architect as Port-la-Galère (see p. 130). The hilltop 'château' was built in the 1920s for a rich American, then the unusual 'sculpted houses' around it were added in the 1960s, neatly blending with the landscape. Today Castellaras is a luxury holiday village and country club: to rent a villa, ring 93 75 24 13.

Pégomas   A village north-west of Cannes, on the River Siagne.
06580   **Le Bosquet**, quartier du Château; tel. 93 42 22 87. Simone
Where to stay   Bernardi runs her friendly, idiosyncratic little hotel (18 rooms) with
Inexpensive   panache, creating a jolly, communal ambience: but don't expect smartness. Lots of British guests. Swimming pool and garden, but no restaurant. Closed November.

Auribeau-sur-Siagne

A pretty hill village south of Grasse. From the terrace beside its eighteenth-century church there are fine views over the lovely hills all round, with their woods, vineyards and flower fields. This is mimosa country, and in late winter the slopes of the Tanneron massif to the south are a blaze of yellow. You can go on scenic drives through the massif, from Mandelieu to the Lac de St Cassien.

Where to eat
Upper-medium price

Auberge Nossi-Bé, Place du Portail; tel. 93 42 20 20. Waitresses in fancy dress serve excellent food at this stylish auberge. There are six inexpensive bedrooms, too. Closed January, February.

Cabris
06530

The 'balcony' of Grasse continues west to the village of Cabris on a hilly spur above the verdant Siagne Valley. From the terrace beside the ruined castle the views towards the coast are stunning. Cabris has long attracted writers and artists (Gide and Herbert Marcuse had villas here), and today it's a sophisticated, much-restored show place, its ancient alleys burgeoning with boutiques and bistros.

Where to stay
Inexpensive

L'Horizon; tel. 93 60 51 69. A modest family pension with a noble pedigree: Sartre, Camus and St-Exupéry used to stay here, as did Leonard Bernstein who would sit and compose in the delightful walled, flower-filled garden. All remains as simple as they knew it: Bedrooms (22) are dullish, but some have balconies facing over the valley. No restaurant. The cultured owner, Jean Roustan, talks eagerly to guests about literature and history. Open March to October.

Where to eat
Medium price

Vieux Château; tel. 93 60 50 12. Good regional cooking at this pretty auberge built out of the castle ruins; the vine-covered terrace has fine views. Closed February, first half of December.

Spéracèdes
Where to eat
Medium price

A quiet, untouristy village just west of Cabris.

La Soleillade; tel. 93 60 58 46. Run by a former circus artist, a charming auberge offering excellent value on its cheaper menus; 8 inexpensive bedrooms. Closed October, Wednesday in winter.

St Cézaire

A fairly unspoilt village set dramatically on a cliff above the deep Siagne Gorge (good views). The twelfth-century chapel on the outskirts contains a Roman sarcophagus.

What to see
St Cézaire
caves

Discovered by chance in 1890 by a local peasant, these caves 3 km north-east of St Cézaire were formed by a glacier four million years ago, and they go 60 m deep into the limestone plateau. Their reddish hue comes from the presence of iron oxide. They are now very touristy and comic names ('the fairy's bed', 'the gulf of hell', and so on) have been given to the bizarre shapes formed by the stalagtites and stalagmites, all artfully lit. They have musical gifts, and your ever-helpful guide will tap out tunes on them, as on a xylophone.

St Vallier de Thiey
Where to stay
and eat

A summer resort on a wide plateau behind Grasse, backed by woods and mountains: clear, bracing air and lots of amenities.

Le Préjoly; tel. 93 42 60 86. The Pallanca family's lively auberge is noted for its good and copious home cooking. There are twenty bedrooms, some with private balcony: those facing open fields at the back are the quietest. Closed mid-December to mid-January.

*The Coast from Cannes
to Marseille*

CANNES
Mandelieu
La Napoule
MASSIF DEL'ESTEREL
Agay
Fréjus
St Raphaël
St Aygulf
Corniche de L'Esterel
Ste Maxime
La Garde-Freinet
Grimaud
St Tropez
Port Grimaud
Collobrières *DES*
M A U R E S
MASSIF
MARSEILLE
LE GROS CERVEAU
Cavalière
Cassis
La Ciotat
Toulon
Le Lavandou
Bandol
Hyères
Ile des Embiez
Giens
ILES D'HYÈRES

M E D I T E R R A N E A N

0   kilometres   30

The Coast West from Cannes to Marseille

Introduction

West of Cannes the coast becomes rather less heavily urbanised, for this is no longer the true original Côte d'Azur with its big towns. The main resorts, St Raphaël, Ste Maxime, St Tropez, Le Lavandou, Bandol and Cassis, are newer and smaller than such places as Cannes, and there are no big towns save the naval base of Toulon and, to the west, Marseille. The coast is hilly, heavily indented and mostly beautiful – but of course crowded in summer.

The Esterel coast, St Raphaël and Fréjus

Just west of Cannes is the booming resort of La Napoule, very popular with yachtsmen. And just beyond it you'll come to the rugged red rocks of the Esterel coast, one of the strangest sights in Provence. It also contains a fascinating new architectural development, Port la Galère. Further on, sprawling, car-clogged St Raphaël I find rather a humdrum resort; but Fréjus with its Roman and medieval remains is not to be missed.

Mandelieu/ La Napoule *06210*

What to see Fondation Henry Clews

Mandelieu (population 14,333) is an ugly little town just inland, west of Cannes; La Napoule, more attractive, is its seaside extension, a lively resort with three sandy beaches, a casino, and a large marina with excellent boating facilities.

This curious place, a great hulk of a fourteenth-century harbourside castle, floodlit a lurid orange at night, was bought by eccentric American sculptor Henry Clews in 1917 and then restored to suit his own fanciful taste. He lived and worked here, and was buried here on his death in 1937. Today the château contains a museum of his work, notably of his carved grotesques of birds, animals, people and gnomes – inspired, it is said, by medieval, Negro and pre-Columbian carvings.

And if you don't like them, you can still enjoy the gardens. Concerts and exhibitions are held at the American-run Clews Foundation in summer.

Where to stay
Medium price

Parisiana, Rue Argentière; tel. 93 49 93 02. In a quiet sidestreet near the beach, clean, comfortable and friendly; breakfast in a leafy patio. Just 12 rooms. Open April to September.

The Esterel massif and coast

One of the most distinctive sights in Provence is this single mass of volcanic rock which fills the whole coast from La Napoule to St Raphaël. Mainly red porphyry, the mountain range has been eroded into craggy shapes over the millenia. Along its northern fringe the Romans built their Aurelian Way (from Rome to Arles) which until early this century was the only through route in the area. It was a dangerous road, for highwaymen and escaped convicts would use the lonely ravines as hideouts. The most notorious of these bandits was Gaspard de Besse in the eighteenth century, a Robin Hood figure who dressed in a smart red costume with silver buckles, and would rob the carriages of the rich to feed the poor. His favourite haunt was the Auberge des Adrets, still there beside the N7. Finally, in 1781 he was captured and broken on the wheel, aged twenty-five; his head was then nailed to a tree by the road. Today the main danger is not from brigandry but from forest fires, which for several summers since the war have ravaged the forests of oak and pine and the wild shrubs. Arson is often suspected – or mere carelessness by picnickers.

The coast road was not built till 1903, and you should take this lovely scenic route, past coves and cliffs, to enjoy the contrasts in colour of red rocks, blue sea and green foliage. Better still, if you don't mind rough driving, take one of the narrow hill roads into the wild heart of the Esterel, and from them you can trek on foot to the tops of the main peaks, the **Pics de l'Ours** and **du Cap Roux** (near the coast) and the **Pic Vinaigre** (inland, near the N7). The views are splendid. Also worth exploring is the grandiose rocky gorge of **Le Mal Infernet**, north of Agay.

Along the coast, the following are the main resorts of the Esterel.

Théoule and Port-la-Galère
06590

Théoule itself is a humdrum bathing resort with reddish sandy beaches and woods rising steeply behind, 3 km south of La Napoule. Its main interest, just further south, is the astonishing new holiday village of Port-la-Galère, designed in the 1970s by architect Jacques Couelle, who also built Castellaras (see p. 126) and the Aga Khan's holiday complex in Sardinia. Couelle, known with reason as 'France's Gaudí', has created 420 flats and villas in a honeycomb of irregular façades, yellow, pink and white, some looking like cave-dwellings or as if moulded out of plasticine. The influence of Le Corbusier is evident too. Some of Couelle's white villas recall Greece or Morocco, for he has imaginatively blended different Mediterranean styles, to create a sensuous extravaganza which harmonises with the landscape. This exclusive estate is not open to the public: but you might be able to

Miramar
06590
Théoule

Where to stay
Upper-
medium price

Agay
83700
St Raphaël

Where to stay
Upper-
medium price

Medium price

St Raphaël
83700

walk round if you said you were thinking of buying a property. Alternatively, you can get a good view from a boat offshore.

As at Théoule to the north and Le Trayas to the south, the steep coast round here is heavily built-up with villas and hotels.

La Tour de l'Esquillon, Avenue de Miramar; tel. 93 75 41 51. A pleasant, classic holiday hotel on the cliffside, with a funicular that swoops you down over its lovely gardens to its private rock lido (good for bathing, but no sand). Cheerful decor, nice bedrooms (25) with sea-facing balconies; food unremarkable. Open February to October.

St Christophe, 47 Avenue de Miramar; 93 75 44 83. With a similar setting and prices and 40 rooms, this is also good.

Beyond Le Trayas, towards Agay, the coast becomes wilder and less populated, though there's plenty of traffic along the road and adjacent main railway. At Agay suburbia re-emerges: it's a sizeable bathing resort in a deep bay with a fine sandy beach, below the red crags of the Rastel d'Agay. Roman pottery dug up from the seabed suggests that this calm bay has sheltered boats since ancient times. To the south, the headland of Le Dramont with its semaphore offers fine views; by the main coast road just to its west is a tablet marking the spot where the 36th US Infantry Division landed on 15 August, 1944.

Sol e Mar, Le Dramont; tel. 94 95 25 60. A modern rectangular hotel by the sea: it is no beauty, but has a private beach, panoramic roof-restaurant, 47 bedrooms with sea-facing balconies, and a breezy modern ambience. Open mid-April to mid-October.

Beau Site, 98 Cap Long; tel. 94 82 00 45. A neat German-run pension, across the road from a sandy beach. No lunches. In the forecourt is a replica of the city of Brussels' 'Manneken Pis'. Closed November to mid-December.

This big, long-established bathing resort (population 24,310) is today a rather characterless place, always crowded, and is hardly worth a visit except for its good museum and its golf courses. It was first settled by the Romans, who built villas on the site of the present-day casino. Later, Bonaparte landed here in 1799 on his return from Egypt, and set sail for his Elba exile in 1814. St Raphaël's birth as a resort, in the 1860s, was due largely to the Parisian journalist Alphonse Karr (1808–90), ex-editor of *Le Figaro*, who settled here and urged his friends to follow him. Among those who responded were Dumas, Maupassant, and Charles Gounod, who composed *Romeo and Juliet* here. In our own day, Françoise Sagan set *Bonjour Tristesse* in a 'large white villa' on the Esterel coast.

Today the best hotels are just outside the town – in the seaside suburb of Boulouris to the east, or up on the Esterel slopes at Valescure where large villas lie scattered amid the pines. Valescure used to be popular with rich English as a winter health resort, and its famous golf course dates from 1891. Now the massive Edwardian hotels have been pulled down or turned into flats: but there is plenty of modish new development and this spacious hilltop resort remains fashionable – unlike St Raphaël itself.

The **Musée Archaeologique**, Rue des Templiers, includes a large collection of Roman anchors and Greek and Roman amphorae, most of them found locally, while in the garden are two cannons from eighteenth-century warships. One room is devoted to nostalgic souvenirs of Alphonse Karr's stay. Next door, the austere twelfth-century **Romanesque church** of St Raphaël has a watchtower probably built by the Knights Templar.

Golf is a major local sport: the grand old Golf de Valescure remains excellent (for membership, apply to the Golf Hôtel, see below), while other less exclusive courses are being completed. St Raphaël has a new yacht marina and several good sandy beaches, one opposite the main promenade. There are various clubs for tennis, gymnastics, and so on: for example, at the Hôtel La Potinière (see below).

There's a folklore festival in May, a well-known jazz festival in early July, a jolly *corso nautique* (water festival) in August.

The lively Casino, besides gambling, offers nightly dancing to an orchestra in season, and has a disco. The smartest local disco is **La Réserve**, Promenade René Coty; **Coco-Club** is a trendy piano-bar at the new marina.

San Pedro, Avenue du Colonel-Brooke, Valescure; tel. 94 83 65 69. A big villa in a pinewood, with sumptuous mock-baronial decor, nice garden with swimming pool, pleasant bedrooms (28), outdoor dining-terrace, good but pricey *nouvelle*-ish cuisine. Closed January. The **Golf-Hôtel** and **La Chêneraie**, both a little cheaper, are other useful places up at Valescure; the former adjoins the golf course.

La Potinière, Boulouris; tel. 94 95 21 43. In its own wooded park ten minutes' walk from the sea, 5 km east of town: a modern ranch-like hotel, geared towards sport, with a breezy club-like ambience. Lovely outdoor restaurant under the pines; or you can eat by the swimming pool. The bedrooms (25) may lack charm, but do have balconies with deckchairs. Closed November and December.

Provençal, 197 Rue de Garonne; tel. 94 95 01 52. 28 rooms, closed January, and **La Liberté**, 56 Rue de la Liberté; tel. 94 95 53 21, 25 rooms, closed mid-October to mid-March, are two serviceable little hotels, each about ten minutes' walk from the beach. Neither has a restaurant.

Pastorel, 54 Rue de la Liberté; tel. 94 95 02 36. Charles Floccia provides excellent traditional Provençal cooking (for example, aïoli on Fridays), in a friendly atmosphere, with a shady patio for summer. Closed August, mid-December to mid-January, Sunday night, Monday.

Fréjus (population 32,698) forms one conurbation with St Raphaël, but is utterly different – a historic city noted for its Roman relics and distinguished medieval religious buildings. Today it is just inland, on a plain, but in Roman times it was a major port, Forum Julii. Julius Caesar founded it in 49 BC as a military post on the Aurelian Way, then it became a key naval base under Augustus who built there the warships with which he defeated Antony and Cleopatra at Actium in 31 BC. Fréjus in those times was a busy town of 25,000 people, little fewer than today: but when Roman influence waned its port declined and later silted up. Sacked by the Saracens in the tenth century, Fréjus never properly recovered from this. However, today it is again go-ahead in its way, under its ambitious mayor, Francis Léotard, a leader of the French Centre-Right.

What to see
The Roman
remains

There are fewer grand buildings here than at Nîmes, Arles or Orange, but some interesting relics. Augustus' port was near the modern town centre, and is believed to have had 2 km of quays, plus a lighthouse. It was ringed by ramparts, of which one tower remains on the west side, the Porte des Gaules. The old theatre also still partly survives, as does the Porte d'Orée, an arcade that was probably part of the old baths. Outside the walls is the arena, the oldest in Gaul, built to seat 10,000 and still well preserved (see p. 134). To the east, the Lanterne d'Auguste is a medieval tower on a Roman base that probably stood at the harbour entrance.

Cité
Episcopale

This superb fortified early-medieval ensemble in the town centre consists of a cathedral, cloister, baptistry and bishop's palace. At its entrance, your guide will open the shutters of the Renaissance doors on which are sixteen carved walnut panels with scenes of Saracen massacres and the Virgin's life. To the left is the marvellously well-preserved fifth-century octagonal baptistry, with a sunken font and two doors: catechumens, all adults in those days, would enter by one door, be washed and anointed by the bishop, then go out through the other door to their first Communion in the cathedral. This building shows early Gothic influence and is harmonious but a bit austere: it has a fifteenth-century retable and sixteenth-century painted wooden crucifix. The elegant steeple of the bell-tower, covered with coloured patterned tiles, rises above the graceful twelfth-century cloister, whose colonnade of slender twin marble pillars is typical of Provence; alas, most of the tiny painted panels of animals on its beamed ceiling were destroyed in the Revolution. The museum by the cloister contains some delightful small Greek vases, also Roman sculptures and a mosaic.

Mosque and
pagoda

On Fréjus' northern outskirts you will find two exotic oddities. By the D4 road to Bagnols is a mosque built in the First World War by soldiers from the former French Sudan, as a replica of a famous mosque at Djenne. Today empty and a bit decrepit, it is painted a garish purple-red and resembles a raspberry cake. The Buddhist pagoda by the N7 is better cared for: it was built as a shrine in the cemetery of 5,000 troops from Annam in Indo-China killed from 1914 to 1918. Nearby, down a turning, is a modern chapel decorated by Cocteau.

Further away from Fréjus, 11 km to the west, is the hill village of **Roquebrune-sur-Argens**, surmounted by the solitary rocky crest of the Roquebrune mountain, visible from afar. And 11 km north of Fréjus are the grim ruins of the infamous Malpasset dam which burst in December 1959, killing hundreds of people as it flooded the town. Huge pieces of concrete still lie strewn in the area.

What to do The **Parc Zoologique**, off the D4 to the north of the African mosque, is home to 250 species of bird and animal, including elephants and zebras, in a big safari park.

Bullfights and popular concerts are held in summer in the Roman arena. On the third Sunday after Easter there's a *bravade* (local costume procession) in town.

Where to stay and eat There aren't many good hotels or restaurants, but for a night stop you could do worse than the moderate-priced **Palmiers**, Blvd. de la Libération; tel. 94 51 18 72, down by the sea. The **Toque Blanche** at Fréjus-Plage; tel. 94 52 06 14, and the **Auberge du Vieux Four** in town; tel. 94 51 56 38 both offer decent cooking at upper-medium prices.

The coast from Fréjus to St Tropez

Between Fréjus and Ste Maxime, the wooded hills of the Massif des Maures (see p. 141) slope down to the sea. This once-lovely stretch of coast, with its sandy coves and umbrella-pines, has been ruined by ill-planned new holiday building; **St Aygulf** is an especially tawdry resort. However, by the sea at **Les Issambres** are two good medium-price restaurants, **Chante-Mer** and **La Réserve**.

Ste Maxime 83120 At this point the coast improves, for Ste Maxime (population 7,364) on the Gulf of St Tropez is an attractive traditional resort, large, friendly, unpretentious and not expensive, popular with families and young people who are drawn by its long sandy beaches and sheltered climate. It has a tree-lined promenade with busy cafés, and a new town centre modelled by Ricardo Bofil.

What to see Ten km inland on the D25 to Le Muy, at the park of St Donat, is a fascinating large museum of phonographs and old mechanical musical instruments, installed in an old farmhouse. The items include an accordion from 1780, a 'singing bird' from 1860, and an early audio-visual machine for teaching foreign languages.

What to do Sports include wind-surfing, water-skiing, yachting (good marina) and golf (nine-hole course at Beauvallon, 5 km to the west). There's also a casino, five nightclubs, and various festivals including a Fête Votive on 15 May.

Where to stay **Hostellerie de Beauvallon**, at Beauvallon (5 km to west); tel. 94

Upper-
medium price

43 81 11. A series of small modern Provençal-style buildings, grouped attractively around a big swimming pool, 200 m from the sea. Bright, spacious rooms (27). Good food. Open Easter to October.

Calidianus, Blvd. Jean-Moulin; tel. 94 96 23 21. Pleasant modern bed-and-breakfast hotel (27 rooms) on western outskirts, c. 200 m from sea; smart swimming pool, garden, tennis. Closed January.

Inexpensive

Préconil, Blvd. Aristide-Briand; tel. 94 96 01 73. This is one of the best of several small, modest, family-run hotels close to the promenade. 19 rooms; no restaurant. Open mid-March to end Ocober.

Where to eat
Upper-
medium price

La Gruppi, Avenue Charles-de-Gaulle; tel. 94 96 03 61. A somewhat formal place on the promenade; very good fresh fish including bouillabaisse and bourride. Closed Mondays out of season.

Medium price

Sans Souci, Rue Paul-Bert; tel. 94 96 18 26. Up a sidestreet near the harbour, a charming family-run bistro with friendly service, good food and an outdoor terrace. Open April to September.

Grimaud
83310
Cogolin

Six km inland from Port Grimaud, and crowned by the impressive craggy ruins of its eleventh-century Grimaldi fortress (you can explore these any time), the old hill village of Grimaud has been fashionably restored and many of its aged houses are now sleek summer homes. There's a fine eleventh-century Romanesque church.

Where to stay
Medium price

Le Coteau Fleuri, Place des Pénitents; tel. 94 43 20 17. A twelfth-century chapel, now a pleasant auberge with terrace and rambling garden (good views), piano, and a log-fire for chilly days; 14 bedrooms. Good Provençal cooking. Closed February and November.

Where to eat
Top price

Les Santons, Route nationale; tel. 94 43 21 02. Claude Girard's subtle mix of classic and modern cuisine is superb, the service is stylish and the Provençal decor most elegant, at this very distinguished place, much frequented in summer by the St Tropez smart set. Closed November to March, and Wednesday.

Cogolin
83310

This small town 3 km south of Grimaud remains a lively centre of traditional cottage industries: briar pipes and clarinet pipes, carpets, corks and fishing rods are all made here. You can buy bamboo furniture at Girodengo, or carpets and fabrics at Les Tapis et Tissus, which also puts on guided tours of its factory.

La Garde-
Freinet
83310
Cogolin

An unspoilt village up in the Maures massif, reached by a wide road that runs up through the cork forests from Grimaud. Above the narrow streets, the ruined castle on the hill (worth the walk) was once a Saracen stronghold: they vandalised this coast in the tenth century, but also taught the Provençaux medical skills and how to utilise the cork bark. Cork is still the village's main industry. Many writers and actors have villas here, including Jeanne Moreau.

Port-
Grimaud
83310
Cogolin

On the coast west of St Tropez is this remarkable example of the 1970s' return to the vernacular in architecture – a luxury holiday village, geared towards sailing, with no roads, only broad canals and alleys linked by arched bridges. The houses are in local fishing port style, painted in a variety of pastel shades and no two alike; and the overall design of this small-scale latterday Venice is most harmonious. It was built during the 1970s and 1980s, designed by the Alsatian architect François Spoerry who conceived it as a real village: around its main square are cafés, shops, banks, a post office, and an ecumenical church whose tower you should climb for a good view of the port and coast. Port Grimaud today has a lived-in ambience: people play boules, go shopping, laze in cafés. Tourists can visit it (on foot), and can tour the canals on a sightseeing cruise, or hire a self-drive boat. The houses, individually owned and not cheap, appeal especially to yachting people, for each has its own mooring by its door: the British are much in evidence, and there's an English yacht agent, Robin Brandon.

Where to stay and eat **La Giraglia** is a glamorous, rather artificial, very expensive hotel, with a private beach and a good restaurant, **L'Amphitrite**, also expensive. **La Résidence du Port**, a hotel on the main square by a canal, is cheaper and pleasant. You can eat well at medium price at **La Gitoune**, or at the British-owned **Salad Table**, which offers Cheddar, Stilton and Aberdeen Angus beef as well as French fish dishes. Both have tables right by the water. **L'Atelier du Crabe**, also by the water, is a charming créperie/tea-room/ice-cream parlour.

St Tropez

83990 Despite everything, St Tropez, that legend of our times, is still like nowhere else in France – hypnotising and infuriating, romantic and over-commercialised, glamorous and tawdry, beautiful and impossible. It remains a charming old fishing port, long beloved of artists, cradled by green hills and facing out across its blue bay towards the Maures hills. In season, it attracts a sophisticated high society of screen stars and other glitterati; and it's a stage for show-off Bohemian eccentrics, from Paris and elsewhere. But it's also become a brash fairground besieged in summer by tourist mobs from the world over who come, some of them, in search of its elusive legend.

St Tropez is best on the fringes of the season, in April/May or September/October, when it's lively enough to be fun, but not too much so. In winter it almost shuts down, and the chill Mistral blows (this is the only resort on the Côte to face north). Avoid August. Being relatively new as a resort, and a fairly small place (population 6,248), St Tropez is very different from the older, bigger towns on the Côte such as Cannes or Menton. It's more picturesque, garish and provocative; and it has not yet been engulfed by the business convention trade. However, maybe inevitably, this New Jerusalem of the modern religion of arty-smarty hedonism is no longer quite what it was in its heyday of the Swinging Sixties, when the young Bardot and Vadim first created its legend.

Getting there

St Tropez is less easy of access than Provence's other major resorts. It is 100 km from Nice Airport and 50 km from Toulon Airport (see pp. 72 and 146), along coast roads crowded in summer. The Nice-Marseille autoroute is 40 km away. There is no railway (the nearest main station is at Fréjus, 34 km away), but regular buses go to Fréjus and other coastal towns. The tourist office is on the harbour front, Quai Jean-Jaurès; tel. 94 97 45 21.

History

Long before its modern notoriety began in the late 1950s, St Tropez already had an ancient and lively history. Initially a Greek trading-post, it acquired its name from one Torpes, a Roman officer beheaded under Nero for his Christian faith, whose corpse, according to legend, found its way here across the sea (he is honoured today in the *bravade* festival, see p. 138). Devastated by the Saracens in 739, St Tropez was rebuilt by the Genoese in the fifteenth century and then for 200 years was a self-governing republic. Its citizens were gifted for naval warfare, routing a Spanish fleet in 1637: so it is apt that France's leading admiral, the Bailli de Suffren (1729-88), should have been born here (his statue stands incongruously in a terrace-café on the Quai de Suffren).

St Tropez was just a quiet fishing village in the late nineteenth century when its career as a focus of culture first began. Guy de Maupassant discovered it by chance, then the painter Paul Signac settled here, quickly followed by Matisse, Bonnard and others who came in summer and painted prolifically. After 1919 the town then filled up in summer with artists and writers from Paris, notably Colette who bought a house and set her novel *La Treille Muscate* (1932) in St Tropez. In August 1944 the retreating Germans blew up the port: today the pretty pastel-shaded houses lining the quay are careful copies of the old ones.

Finally, in the 1950s, an industrialist called Louis Bardot bought a house here, and his aspiring actress daughter Brigitte married a young film director, Roger Vadim. That was why Vadim chose St Tropez in 1957 as location for his film *Et Dieu Créa la Femme*, starring his wife – and so, almost by chance, it all began. The film was a worldwide *succès fou*: not only did it mirror a new permissive, hedonistic epoch, it also helped to create that epoch, and it started a cult for Bardot and St Tropez. Everyone flocked to the town – the Vadims' showbiz and literary friends, such as Françoise Sagan, as well as hordes of hangers-on, including the *paparazzi*. The habitués used to meet at the Café des Arts (see p. 139), Tahiti beach, or L'Escale bar by the harbour. In 1965 I met a Dominican priest in Lourdes who told me: St Tropez 'is a kind of Lourdes. Young people feeling a lack in their lives want to be cured of their desolate yearnings, so they come here to be touched by magic and reborn. But they leave disappointed. All they find is each other.'

St Tropez today

St Tropez in summer remains an extraordinary melting-pot, a sartorial jumble of the elegant, the outré and the dowdy, harmless day trippers, drop-outs and petty criminals. A surprising number of the truly famous and/or distinguished still remain loyal to the place, though today they live much more privately than in the Sixties. Bardot still spends part of each year behind the walls of her villa, La Madrague, near the Cap St-Pierre: but she seldom appears in public. Others with villas in or near St Tropez include Joan Collins, Gunter Sachs and the French pop stars Johnny Halliday and Eddie Barclay; some other celebrities, such as Harold Robbins and Sam Spiegel, bring their yachts into the harbour. Such people will dine in the smart restaurants, but you'll not see them strolling along the quayside. Many of the swagger yachts by this quay are London-registered, but few are British-owned.

Main areas

This quayside of the Vieux Port, no longer used for fishing, remains the focus of tourism: but though it still has one or two smart bars and restaurants, mostly it's become a tatty place, lined with trashy stores. Far pleasanter is the network of little streets just inland, going up towards the hilltop Citadelle: here you'll find many small romantic bistros, quaint boutiques and amusing galleries. To the south are the residential quarters, where the most entertaining spot is the Place des Lices, popular for *boules* and lined with lively Bohemian cafés. Further south are the beaches of Pampelonne. There are large guarded car-parks at the main entrance to the town, near the new port: it is unwise to leave your car in the street overnight, for petty theft is rife.

What to see
Musée de l'Annonciade

A converted sixteenth-century chapel by the port now houses one of the finest of all collections of French late nineteenth- and early twentieth-century painting, featuring many of the artists who lived and worked in St Tropez at that time – Paul Signac, Matisse, Bonnard and others. The 100 or so canvases include bathing scenes by Henri Manguin, delightful van Dongen portraits of girls, lively Dufys, and bright Provençal landscapes by Braque and Maurice de Vlaminck. St Tropez itself appears often – in gouaches and drawings by Dunoyer de Segonzac, a colourful Charles Camoin, a pointillist Signac. Spacious and well lit, the museum also has bronze and marble sculptures by Charles Despiau and Manguin.

Citadelle

On a hill in the eastern outskirts stands this seventeenth-century fortress, complete with moat and ramparts. Its keep contains a naval museum (reconstructed Greek galley, seventeenth-century maps, old engravings of St Tropez, and details of the 1944 Liberation).

What to do

Festivals

The *bravade* is a folk-festival peculiar to Provence, and St Tropez has two that are famous. The Bravade of St Torpes, on 16–18 May, dates from the sixteenth century (see p. 137): the saint's bust is taken from the church and carried around the town, amid much mirth and music, with a guard of men in seventeenth-century uniform who fire salvoes of blank cartridges. A more modest *bravade* is the Fête des Espagnols on 15 June, marking the victory over the Spanish in 1637. Late June sees the Fête des Pêcheurs, while in July and August classical concerts are held occasionally in the citadel. In early October there's an ambitious regatta, the Nioulargue.

Beaches The superb sandy beach that stretches for 6 km along the bay of **Pampelonne**, south of the town, is one of the main reasons for St Tropez' great popularity. Almost all of it, as at Cannes, is divided into some thirty privately-run sectors, where you must pay a fee (there are good free beaches further south, beyond Cap Camarat); and as no road goes along the shore, the beaches are reachable only down winding lanes, not all clearly signposted.

As you might expect, the beaches are exotically hedonistic, some a paradise of sweet sensuality, others vulgarly outré. **Tahiti**, since the 1960s one of the world's most famous beaches, is still fashionable and stylish, though its chic is now tinged with decadence. It is today less *à la mode* than **Moorea**, or **Club 55**, which is also very select. **La Voile Rouge** is what the French call *chaud*, that is, not for families. And **Blouch** is decently nudist.

Bars, cafés and nightlife These are all constantly changing. Of the cafés and bars along the harbour, Sénéquier used to be trendy but is now tawdry, and l'Escale, which used also to be trendy, is today dull. Much the best bars are inland – that of the **Hôtel Byblos**, very chic, that of the **Hôtel Yaca**, and that of **Chez Nano**, a favoured haunt of the St Tropez smart set. The most amusing arty-Bohemian bars are on the Place des Lices – that of the famous **Café des Arts**, and that of the **Bistro des Lices** where the maître d'Charles Roux is a captivating after-dinner comedian and conjurer.

Of discos and nightclubs, the famed **Papagayo** is now 'out', but **L'Esquinade** remains 'in' (especially in the wee hours), as does **Le Bal** where gays and heteros cheerfully mix and blonde Sophie is the hostess with the mostest. **Le Pigeonnier** has a gay show and is often crowded. **Les Caves du Roy**, in the Hôtel Byblos, remains one of the two or three most fashionable discos on the Côte – but you'd better dress trendily if you want a chance of being let in.

Where to stay Good hotels are numerous, most of them in the medium and upper price brackets. Some lie inside the town, but more are spread around the countryside just outside.

Top prices **Byblos**, Avenue Paul-Signac; tel. 94 97 00 04. Only St Tropez could have spawned a luxury hotel as bizarre and exotic as this one, created in 1967 by a rich Lebanese with the utterly improbable name of Prosper Gay-Para. It's a pastiche of a local hill village, with little white houses grouped intimately around a lovely swimming pool. The interior, a labyrinth of alcoves, archways and patios, contains a wealth of genuine Levantine *objets d'art* such as an Arab salon transferred from a Beirut palace. The studied glamour is mind-blowing – and some of the guests live up to it. There are 107 rooms; very good restaurants. Open March to October.

Résidence de la Pinède, Plage de la Bouillabaisse; tel. 94 97 04 21. Small (35 rooms) but charming luxury hotel right by the sandy beach, just out of town. Superb food. Open April to mid-October.

Upper-medium price

Treizain, Domaine du Treizan, Gassin; tel. 94 97 70 08. Just outside town, a new building in local rustic style, informal but sophisticated, run by a friendly Dutch family: lovely swimming pool, bedrooms (17) with balconies. No restaurant, but lunches are available. Open April to mid-October.

Medium price

Lou Troupelen, Chemin des Vendanges; tel. 94 97 44 88. Amid vineyards on the edge of town: another new hotel in the style of an old mas, with a cosy ambience, nice views and a pretty garden; 44 rooms. No restaurant. Open Easter to mid-October.

Les Palmiers, 26 Blvd. Vasserot; tel. 94 97 01 61. Very central, family-run, comfortable, with a patio; 22 rooms. No restaurant.

Inexpensive

Lou Cagnard, Avenue Paul-Roussel; tel. 94 97 04 24. Good cheap hotels in town are few, but this is maybe the best – in a side-street seven minutes' walk from the port. 19 rooms; no restaurant. Closed mid-November to Christmas.

Where to eat

St Tropez has many attractive, good value restaurants of all kinds. If you want amusing, romantic, inexpensive ones, get away from the crowded harbour-front into the small streets behind – such as the Rue de la Citadelle, where I can recommend the **Rascassou** or the **Citadelle**.

Top price

Chabichou, Avenue Foch; tel. 94 54 80 00. Crammed with the smart and trendy, this beautiful modern restaurant beside the Hôtel Byblos is owned by patron/chef Michel Rochedy whose inventive cooking is among Provence's best. Open mid-May to early October.

Upper-medium price

La Marine, 22 Quai Jean-Jaurès; tel. 94 97 04 07. Today the most fashionable of the eating places on the harbour front, much used by visitors from the posh yachts. Closed mid-November to mid-December.

Chez Nano, Place de l'Hôtel-de-Ville; tel. 94 97 01 66. Very 'Tropézien': a prime haunt of the chic set whose chattering deafens, even on the terrace. Energetic service, pretty lighting, and average food. An experience. Closed mid-January to end March.

Café des Arts, Place des Lices; tel. 94 97 02 25. The most idiosyncratic of the town's 'in' places: just a simple café until it was taken up by the *beau monde* in the 1960s, it remains Bohemian-sophisticated, full of crazy characters who booze in the weirdly-decorated bar or eat simple, decent dishes in the flowery *salle* at the back. Open March to mid-October.

Medium price

Le Blé en Douce, 9 Rue Citadelle; tel. 94 97 57 57. Good fish and local dishes at this simple place with an outdoor patio, in the old town.

Closed January, February.

Le Girelier, Quai Jean-Jaurès; tel. 94 97 03 87. Much more conventional: an attractive place with an open terrace facing the harbour. Good for fish. Closed mid-January to end February.

La Ponche, Place du Révelin; tel. 94 97 02 53. A popular little place whose tables are spread across a charming tiny square by a beach behind the harbour. Open April to mid-October.

Inexpensive   **Trattoria da Roma**, Avenue du Général-Leclerc; tel. 94 97 51 97. Good pasta served to hungry tourist crowds; near the bus station.

Around St Tropez   St Tropez stands on the north side of the lovely Ramatuelle peninsula, its hillsides cloaked in vineyards and thick woodlands of pine and oak: despite the influx of tourism, much of it remains remarkably unspoilt. **Ramatuelle** is a pleasant old hill village: the noble elm in its square was planted in 1598. The actor Gérard Philipe (1922–59) used to live here, and he lies buried in the cemetery. On a hilltop to the north-west are the three ruined mills of Paillas: it's worth driving up here for the marvellous view of the coast and mountains. To the south, at **L'Escalet**, **La Bastide-Blanche** and **Gigaro**, are a whole series of splendid sandy beaches in rocky inlets – all free, and quite unlike the St Tropez beaches.

Where to stay and eat Top price   **Le Baou**, Avenue Georges-Clémenceau, Ramatuelle; tel. 94 79 20 48. A smart, sophisticated hotel on a hillside, with superb views, lovely swimming pool, 36 rooms, ambitious new-style Provençal cooking. Open mid-March to early November, and Christmas/New Year.

Where to stay Upper-medium price   **Hôtel de Marres**, Route des Plages; tel. 94 97 26 68. Provençal *bastide* with large garden, swimming pool and tennis courts, near sandy beaches. No restaurant. 21 rooms. Open mid-March to end October.

Gassin   North-west of Ramatuelle, Gassin is another well-known old hill village, set high on a ridge above the plain. Its church, floodlit at night, is a landmark for kilometres around. **Bello Visto** and **Les Microcouliers** are two outdoor restaurants where you can enjoy the view and eat quite well at medium price. Just north of Gassin, the Château Minuty, tel. 94 56 12 09, produces one of the best-known Côtes de Provence wines, and is open to visits.

The coast from St Tropez to Toulon: Massif des Maures, Hyères and its islands

The Massif des Maures is a beautiful wooded mountain range that follows the coast from Fréjus to Hyères, some 55 km. Many people imagine that its name comes from *les Maures* (Moors or Saracens),

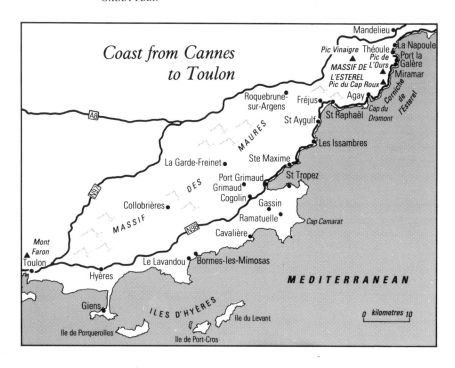

Coast from Cannes to Toulon

who ravaged and occupied this area in the tenth and eleventh centuries: but in fact it's derived from *maouro*, a Provençal word meaning 'dark', referring to its woods of chestnut, cork oak and Aleppo pine. The making of wine-bottle corks and of *marrons glacés* (glazed chestnuts) remain today two local industries. It is well worth leaving the busy coast to explore the wild and unspoilt interior; the glorious winding coast, a succession of small bays backed by steep woods, is inevitably crammed with resorts, but its new developments are at least less ugly than in the St Aygulf area further east, and everywhere there are good sandy beaches. Further west, south of Hyères, are two of the loveliest and strangest of all Mediterranean islands: Porquerolles and Port-Cros.

Cavalière
83980 Le Lavandou
Where to stay
Top price

A small, lively resort backed by pinewoods, in a sheltered bay.

Le Club; tel. 94 05 80 14. There is indeed an exclusive club-like ambience at this, the most smart and sophisticated hotel between St Tropez and Marseille. Private beach, swimming pool and tennis; dancing by the sea. Some of the 32 luxurious bedrooms are bungalows with their own patios. Open May to September.

Where to eat
Top price

Le Club (see above). A supremely elegant place with a lovely sea-facing terrace. The great Roger Vergé (see p. 126) was once the chef, and Alain Gigant is a worthy successor, creator of distinguished fish

Le Lavandou
83980
Where to stay and eat
Top price

Where to stay
Upper-medium price
Medium price

Inexpensive

Where to eat
Upper-medium price

Bormes-les-Mimosas
83230

Where to stay
Upper-medium price

Where to eat
Upper-medium price

Collobrières
83610

dishes such as loup with caviar butter.

An old fishing port (the name comes from *lavandières*, washer women), today expanded into a biggish holiday resort, with much new high-rise building: but the animated harbour area still has charm.

Hôtel Les Roches, at Aiguebelle, just east of le Lavandou; tel. 94 71 05 07. Stylishly glamorous luxury hotel by water's edge. Lovely views, food and bedrooms (42), with good paintings. Sun-terrace, disco. Open April to October.

La Calanque, 62 Avenue du Général-de-Gaulle; tel. 94 71 01 95. A white Provençal villa (38 rooms) above the harbour, comfortable, cheerful and newly redecorated. Nice garden. Open May to October.

Belle Vue, at St Clair (3 km to east); tel. 94 71 01 06. Round the cape from Le Lavandou, on a hillside just above the beach: a delightful homely villa run by three sisters, with flowers everywhere, parasols in the pretty garden, small but pleasant rustic-style bedrooms (19), some with sea-facing balconies. Goodish food. Open April to mid-October.

Neptune, Avenue Général-de-Gaulle; tel. 94 71 01 01. Very central, in a main street near the front, but facing inland; clean and good value. 33 rooms; no restaurant.

La Calanque (see above). Friendly waitresses, and some good and unusual fish dishes, at the hotel's modern and very attractive restaurant 'Algue Bleue'.

Other good restaurants in town are **Au Vieux Port** (expensive) and **La Bouée** (medium price).

Mimosa trees bright yellow in February, as well as eucalyptus groves and cypresses, surround this graceful old village which stands up on a hill 5 km behind Le Lavandou, with fine views of the coast. The pastel shades of its house façades, pale blue, pink and yellow, make a change from the usual severe grey stone of Provençal hill villages. Artists and intellectuals have summer homes here, and there's a small museum of local history. By the coast to the south, the offshore fortress of Brégançon is an official summer residence of the French President.

Les Palmiers, Cabasson; tel. 94 64 81 94. Down a sideroad 8 km south of Bormes, but inside its commune, this sympathetic holiday hotel stands amid oaks and pines in an isolated position near the beach. Pleasant well-modernised rooms (21), many with balconies; cheerful ambience, charming Madame, good classic cooking.

La Tonnelle des Délices, Place Gambetta; tel. 94 71 34 84. This well-named 'arbour of delights', in the village square, is a bistro with a shady vine-terrace; the Gedda brothers' 'delights' include skilful variations on Provençal dishes. Open April to September.

Try also **L'Escoundudo** (medium price).

From Bormes, several scenic roads wind up into the heart of the lonely Maures massif. You can drive 8 km north-east to the craggy Pierre d'Avenon peak, for a marvellous view of the coast; or 23 km north over the Col de Babaou to the picturesque old village of

Collobrières, where shops sell the local *marrons glacés*. From here a narrow road leads 13 km to the Chartreuse de Verne, an ancient monastery in a wild and grandiose setting, well worth visiting. It was built of local brown stone in Romanesque style in the twelfth century, then much revamped in the eighteenth. It lost its monks after the Revolution, but is today again the home of a monastic community.

Hyères
83400

A few kilometres west of Bormes the N98 highway leaves the Maures hills and enters a built-up coastal plain of some ugliness. Here, just inland, is Hyères (population 41,739), a sizeable place with a varied history. The coast was colonised both by Greeks and Romans, whose relics can be studied in the **Musée Municipal**. Later the town was a port for the Holy Land (St Louis – Louis IX – stayed here in 1254 on his way back from the Seventh Crusade): the sea was then much closer to the town, and the port has since silted up.

Hyères is also the oldest of all *Côte d'Azur* resorts, dating from the eighteenth century: its devotees have included Napoleon, Queen Victoria, R. L. Stevenson and Tolstoy. Today its broad boulevards lined with date-palms survive as memorials of its past splendour, but the resort is now quite out of fashion and has no good hotels. Excuse the pun, but Hyères indeed belongs to *hier*. The old medieval part of town, on a hillside below the ruined castle, has interesting reminders of its past, mainly in and near the Place Massillon where there is a lively weekday market. Here it is worth visiting the twelfth-century Tour St Blaise, part of an old fortified Templars' church, and the twelfth-century church of St Paul, beside a fine turreted Renaissance mansion. In June, Hyères stages a Provençal festival, and in July and August there are street concerts. In the south-east suburbs, the large **Jardin Olbius-Riguier** has a profusion of exotic plants.

At La Londe-des-Maures, 7 km east of Hyères, the Clos Mireille is one of the principal vineyards of Ott, a prolific but reliable producer of Côtes de Provence wines. To visit, first ring the firm's head office in Antibes, tel. 93 34 38 91.

Where to stay
Medium price

Relai Bleu, 45 Avenue Victoria; tel. 94 35 42 22. Part of a modern motel chain, clean, functional, convenient; just south of the town centre, on the bypass. 44 rooms; restaurant.

Where to eat
medium price

Try **Le Delphin's**, 7 Rue Roux-Seignoret; tel. 94 65 04 27, or the **Auberge du Vieux Puits** at La Bayorre; tel. 94 65 01 05.

Giens
83400 Hyères

This old village, topped by a ruined castle (fine views from its terrace), stands on a hilly peninsula that would really be one of the Iles d'Hyères (see below) were it not now joined by a narrow isthmus to the mainland south of Hyères. The Nobel prize-winning poet St-John Perse spent his later years here. On the isthmus, La Capte is a busy camping resort, its pinewoods full of blue and orange tents in summer. Just to the north, high piles of white salt mark the big Pesquiers saltworks; along the flat, built-up coast round here there is prosperous market gardening, thanks to the warm winter climate.

Where to stay
Medium price

Le Relais du Bon Accueil; tel. 94 58 20 48. A small informal hotel on a rocky headland, with a neat garden and fine sea views. Rooms (10) of varying size; interesting food. Closed November.

Iles d'Hyères

Porquerolles, Port-Cros and the Ile du Levant are three strange, fascinating and very lovely islands, where rugged coasts contrast with lush sub-tropical vegetation; they are known also as the Iles d'Or, because of the way their southern cliffs glint gold in the sunlight. Geologically, they are an outcrop of the Maures massif. They have been colonised by everyone from Ligurians to Turks and were for long a haunt of corsairs. François I granted the right of asylum there to convicts and criminals, but they repaid his kindness by becoming pirates, and the islands were not pacified until the time of Louis XIV. Today they are sparsely inhabited, and though tourist-besieged in summer they are well worth a visit (regular boat services from the mainland: see below).

Porquerolles
83400 Hyères

This, the largest of the three islands, is thickly covered with heather, pines, eucalyptus and exotic shrubs and is excellent for walking (or bicycles can be hired). From the one village, where the boats land, you should walk across to the lighthouse on the south coast, for a superb view of the cliffs. The village was built in the nineteenth century as an army garrison, and with its wide main square it still has the look of a former French army compound in North Africa; in the little church, the wooden Stations of the Cross were sculpted by a soldier whose amateur artistry was remarkable. (Frequent boat services from La Tour Fondue, near Giens, fifteen-minute voyage; services also from Hyères-Plage, Le Lavandou, Cavalaire.)

Where to stay
and eat
Top price

Mas du Langoustier; tel. 94 58 30 09. Handsome converted manor house, secluded in its wooded park. Superb food and service, great comfort; tennis courts, sandy beaches. 53 rooms. Open May to mid-October.

Where to stay
Medium price

Relais de la Poste; tel. 94 58 30 26. In the village, clean and modern, with a library and 28 rooms; no restaurant, but salad lunches served.

Port-Cros
83145

Hilly, beautiful and mysterious, this very special island has few beaches but a lush bright-green vegetation watered by springs, and it enjoys the status of National Park (nature reserve). You arrive at the tiny port, with just a few bistros and fishermen's cottages, and from here you can go on a variety of strenuous walks over the rough terrain – through the Vallée de la Solitude (alas, unsuitably named in high season), or to the cove of Port-Man, or the Plage de la Palud from where a *sentier botanique* leads through exotic sub-tropical foliage.

Guided tours in summer include botanical rambles and underwater explorations, with scuba-masks, of the fish life and marine fauna. (For information, ring 94 65 32 98 or 94 05 90 17). Port-Cros has an unlikely literary souvenir too: D. H. Lawrence once stayed here with a well-born young Englishwoman, who told him of her fleshy romance with a local labourer. Lawrence stole this theme for his best-known book, simply changing the locale. (Regular boat services from Le Lavandou, some also from Hyères-Plage, Cavalaire. No cars allowed on the island.)

Where to stay
Upper-
medium price

Le Manoir; tel. 94 05 90 52. Quietly secluded in its own park, by a creek near the port, this graceful white eighteenth-century manor is totally in keeping with Port-Cros. Pierre Buffet's family used to own the whole island; now he and his charming wife just run this manor as a private hotel, to make ends meet. But the ambience is that of a cultured house-party, for most of their guests are personal friends and habitués, many of them writers, musicians or theatre people, French or foreign. Simple but spacious 'period' bedrooms (26), delightful service, good cooking without frills. You may need to book months ahead, but it's worth it for the experience, in a wistful romantic atmosphere, perhaps less Latin than Celtic, despite the palm trees.

**Ile du
Levant**

A long, thin island with dense foliage and high inaccessible cliffs. Most of it is a French naval base, closed to visitors. The rest is **Héliopolis**, a large and famous nudist village dating from the pioneering 1930s, which you can visit (boat services from Le Lavandou).

Toulon

83000

France's leading naval base after Brest is a big commercial city (population 181,405), third largest in Provence; and it occupies a superbly theatrical setting, around a deep natural harbour sheltered by a ring of high bare hills crowned by old forts. I like it a lot: though not obviously a tourist venue, it in fact offers a lot to see and is fun for a short visit, with the added bonus of the lowest prices on the coast. There is much ugly new building, and many sidestreets are crumbling and dirty: but like most big ports Toulon is a spicily characterful place, and can provide louche excitement for those looking for it. The bars and bistros in the district by the port, not all of them so innocent, are thronged with the sailors of many nations.

**Getting
there**

There are daily scheduled flights to Paris, and some to other French cities, from the airport of Toulon-Hyères (tel. 94 57 41 93), 21 km to the east, south of Hyères. The main station, quite central, offers fast rail connections to Marseille, Nice, Paris (three TGVs a day, six-hour journey) and elsewhere. An autoroute goes west to Marseille, Paris, and so on and a highway (part autoroute) goes east to Nice. The tourist office is fairly near the station at 8 Avenue Colbert; tel. 94 22 08 22.

History

Despite its fine harbour, Toulon had little importance in Roman and medieval times. Its era as a naval base began soon after Provence's attachment to France in 1487: Louis XII then built the *vieille darse*, the oldest part of the port. But it was Louis XIV who turned Toulon into a major base, by creating the Arsenal (*darse neuve*) and transferring the royal galleys from Marseille; at the same time the military engineer Vauban began work on the ring of massive hilltop forts. A plague in 1720 cut the town's population from 26,000 to 17,000, but it soon recovered. The seventeenth and eighteenth centuries were the terrible era of the galley-slaves until galleys were abolished in 1748. Convicts, African captives and political prisoners such as Huguenots were forced to row the royal galleys, with feet bare and heads shaven, chained in groups to their seats where they also ate (miserably) and slept. As if this were not enough, the slaves became a tourist attraction in that cruel age, and people would gawp and giggle at them as shackled together they shuffled through the streets.

It was at Toulon in 1793 that the young Bonaparte, then an unknown artillery captain, first gained distinction. The town, having declared for the Royalists, was being protected by the English fleet which had set up a strongpoint at Tamaris, near the mouth of the harbour. But Napoleon blasted the invaders with such a storm of cannonfire that they withdrew – and he was promoted to brigadier-general. More recently, Toulon has again been in the wars. In November 1942, when the Germans moved to occupy the *zone libre* of southern France, the Vichy fleet of sixty ships scuttled itself to avoid capture – even though its commander, Admiral Laborde, was a firm Anglophobe. In 1943 to 1944 the port was heavily bombed by the Allies; then, after the landings in Provence in August 1944, the Germans before surrendering blew up the citadel and most of what remained of the harbour. Since 1945, with the inevitable decline of its naval role, the city and its port have diversified and acquired new industries, so the Arsenal today has a civil role too.

Main areas

The central part of town is dissected by a broad east-to-west street (Blvd. de Strasbourg, Avenue du Général-Leclerc): to its north, the commercial area round the station, to its south the port, the *vieille ville*, and other areas of tourist interest. Downtown Toulon has numerous car parks, as well as meter parking. The port extends a long way round the bay, with the old Arsenal to the west, the residential suburb of Le Mourillon to the east. Across the harbour stands the industrial town of La Seyne (population 58,146) whose big shipbuilding yards have closed since 1986, like those of La Ciotat (see p. 153). Further south is the suburb of Tamaris, where Georges Sand often stayed. The northern suburbs with their villas climb

What to see

The port

up the steep hillsides towards Mont Faron.

The harbour front, the Quai de Stalingrad, was completely destroyed in the war; the tall concrete blocks built hurriedly in the late 1940s are singularly hideous. Fortunately, the two magnificent stone telamons (*atlantes*) sculpted by Pierre Puget, that once adorned the door of the old town hall, had been put away for safe keeping, and these powerfully impressive figures are now back in place on a new building. From the Quai there are frequent guided tours by boat round the vast harbour, and the modern dry docks, the arsenal and other installations are all explained. The port remains the headquarters of France's Mediterranean fleet, though much of its traffic is now commercial: the arsenal employs 10,000 civilians.

Musée Naval

This museum, at the west end of the Quai de Stalingrad, contains some huge models of seventeenth-century warships, giant ships' *atlantes* sculpted in wood, paintings of naval battles and other souvenirs to fascinate lovers of naval history, plus some modern weaponry such as a real torpedo built at Toulon.

Vieille Ville

So accurate were the Allied bombers that while flattening the waterfront they left largely intact the network of narrow old streets just behind it. Part of this area is now a trim pedestrian precinct, with boutiques, bars, bistros, and little paved squares adorned with flowers and plants: the Rue d'Alger is the favourite evening strolling place of young Toulonnais, while just north in the place Puget is the curious **Fontaine des Trois Dauphins** (1782), 3 m wide and covered with dense foliage. To the east stands the gloomy cathedral, part Romanesque and Gothic inside, and next to it is the **Musée Historique du Vieux Toulon**, somewhat decrepit, but with interesting souvenirs of local history. The covered **fish-market** (*poissonnerie*), to the south, is rich in fishy sights, sounds and smells, notably at dawn. Eastwards you come to the broad leafy Cours Lafayette, and further on to a run-down area where washing hangs out high across the alleys.

Tour Royale

On a headland at the east side of the harbour mouth, this broad stone tower was built by Louis XII as part of its defences, and was long used as a prison. It is now an annexe of the Musée Naval, housing two curious black *atlantes* taken from men o' war, and the cannon used by Lafayette against the British at Rhode Island. There are fine views from the tower's terrace.

Musée d'Art

On the Avenue du Général-Leclerc south of the station, this excellent museum of painting and sculpture has recently been attractively renovated. It has works by Provençal artists such as Fragonard, Claude Joseph Vernet and Pierre Puget, others by Rodin and Félix Ziem. The collection of contemporary art is especially good, but as space is limited the works are exhibited in rotation.

Mont Faron

Toulon's major landmark and well worth a visit, this 500 m-high rocky ridge rises directly behind the city and can be reached by funicular from beside the Hôtel Frantel, or by car up a steep winding road. The view from the top is stupendous – the sweeping coastline, the entire city and harbour where brown tankers and grey warships lie like small toys. In an old fort below the summit is the **Musée-Mémorial du Débarquement en Provence**, which vividly sets out and explains the Allied landings on this coast in August 1944 – somewhat exaggerating the French role in what was foremost an Anglo-American operation. Nearby is a small zoo with lions, tigers and monkeys.

What to do

Festivals and music

The main events are the music festival in June/July, and the international dance festival also in July at the new cultural centre of Châteauvallon, north-west of the city, which has all-year activities too. There is good opera in winter in the stately Opera House, whose interior is richly ornate. Of wider popular appeal are the flower parade in April, the circus performers' festival in the old town in high summer, and the *santons* fair in November.

Market

There's a big open-air market daily on the Cours Lafayette.

Beaches

Le Mourillon in the south-east suburbs, Tamaris and Les Sablettes in the south-west suburbs, all have sandy beaches.

Nightlife

Two fashionable places, opened recently, both on the Littoral Frédéric-Mistral, are **Côte Jardin** and **La Lampe à Pétrôle**.

Where to stay

Upper-medium price

Altéa La Tour Blanche, Blvd. Amiral Vence; tel. 94 24 41 57. Splendidly situated on the slopes of Mont Faron, this biggish modern hotel (92 rooms) is one of the best of the Altéa chain, very good value, and catering alike for business and pleasure. There are lovely views from the outdoor bar-terrace and bedroom balconies.

Medium price

La Corniche, 1 Littoral Frédéric-Mistral; tel. 94 41 35 12. This newish hotel facing the tiny port at Le Mourillon has original rustic-style decor, including a flagged patio with mimosa, and plenty of comfort at very fair prices; 22 rooms.

Inexpensive

Campanile, Zone des Espalins, 83160 La Valette; tel. 94 21 13 01. Useful modern chain motel just off A57, 7 km east of Toulon. Good breakfasts, inexpensive meals; 40 rooms.

Strasbourg, 10 Rue Leblond St-Hilaire; tel. 94 92 84 78. Family-run, helpful and comfortable; between station and port. 19 rooms.

Where to eat

Upper-medium price

La Corniche (see above). The hotel's restaurant has been built around three big umbrella-pines whose broad trunks push up through its middle. Almost as innovative is Patrick Suere's excellent cuisine. Closed February and Monday.

La Tour Blanche (see Altéa, above). You get fine panoramic views from the hotel's elegant restaurant, which is best for fish, poor on desserts. A buffet lunch is served by the swimming pool in summer.

Inexpensive

Madeleine, 7 Rue des Tombades; tel. 94 92 67 85. The friendly Bellomeau family offer outstanding value on the excellent set menu at this cosy little bistro in a very old house of the *vieille ville*. Closed Tuesday evening and Wednesday.

The coast from Toulon to Marseille

This coast is just as rugged and indented as that of the Maures, and more thickly populated. There are two major resorts, Bandol and Cassis, and a shipbuilding town, La Ciotat, that has seen better days. Just inland is some wild and unusual mountain scenery – notably around the bizarre half-ruined clifftop village of Evenos. A good zoo, some unusual offshore islands, and the lovely fjord-like 'calanques' west of Cassis all add to the diversity and interest.

Sanary
83110

Twelve km west of Toulon, this unremarkable sailing and fishing port (population 11,689; market Wednesday) has a sandy beach and a few hotels. Aldous Huxley lived here in the early 1930s, at the Villa Huley (sic). After 1933 Sanary became a place of exile for some prominent anti-Nazi German intellectuals, notably Thomas and Heinrich Mann, whom Huxley insensitively described as 'rather a dismal crew'. Did he expect them to be jumping with joy?

Embiez

Just south of Sanary, the 97-hectare island of Embiez has been

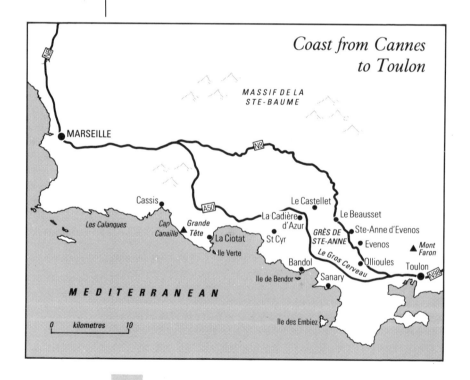

Coast from Cannes to Toulon

developed by Paul Ricard, the pastis tycoon (see p. 152) as a major sea-sports centre: it has a large new marina for sailing and powerboats, a luxury hotel and sports amenities. It also houses the **Fondation Océanographique Ricard**, a research centre run by Alain Bombard, the leading marine biologist. Here the remarkable aquarium displays some 100 kinds of Mediterranean fish and shellfish, many brilliantly coloured, all in their natural habitat. It's a good place to get to know the inhabitants of your bouillabaisse.

Further round this rocky shore at Cap Sicié, south-west of Toulon, the old clifftop chapel of **Notre-Dame-du-Mai** contains sailors' ex-votos and offers epic views over this majestic coast. A pilgrimage is held every 14 September.

Ollioules and Le Gros Cerveau

Just inland from Sanary is some of the wildest and most dramatic mountain scenery in Provence. From Ollioules, a steep narrow road winds up along the high ridge of the Gros Cerveau, offering awesome views over the coast and the hills inland towards the Ste Baume massif. All around are the stark barren limestone heights, contrasting with the lush valleys below and the shining sea. North of Ollioules, the N8 highway from Toulon winds through the lunar landscape of the arid Ollioules gorges, to emerge within sight of giant stone-quarries and the jagged rocks of the Grès de Ste Anne. Many of the rocky cliffs of this region are popular with climbers, and in season great crowds of onlookers assemble to watch the teams of daredevil *alpinistes* with their ropes and picks.

Evenos

At Ste Anne-d'Evenos a narrow road climbs up east to the half-ruined crag-top village of Evenos, an amazing place. It is rather like Les Baux (see p. 210), but smaller and less touristy. A few years ago it had become totally deserted, but now a few of its ancient stone houses have been restored as summer homes: there is a café and an old church, but no shops. As at Les Baux, the village is surmounted by the gaunt ruins of a castle (very feudal-looking though in fact it's only sixteenth-century); its keep with massive walls stands on an extinct volcano whose lava deposits are clearly visible. The view from the terrace is dramatic.

Le Castellet
83330 Le Beausset

North-west of Evenos, beyond the little town of Le Beausset, a side-road leads to the charming ancient village of Le Castellet, perched on a hilltop above a rolling pastoral landscape full of vineyards. It has well-preserved medieval ramparts, a twelfth-century church and an old castle, all carefully restored to create a showpiece ensemble. There are numerous craft boutiques of local artisans. So 'authentically picturesque' is Le Castellet that several feature films of traditional Provençal life have been shot here, including some scenes of the 1986 remake of *Manon des Sources* (see p. 168).

Where to eat Upper-medium price

Castel Lumière; tel. 94 32 62 20. Beside the medieval gateway, a small elegant restaurant whose good food can be accompanied by splendid views alike from the indoor *salle* and the pleasant leafy patio.

**La Cadière
d'Azur**
83740

Five bedrooms. Closed November, and Tuesday out of season.

West of Le Beausset, this big, fairly unspoilt hill village has an animated local life and is less of a museum-piece than Le Castellet, while sharing the same lovely setting. Among the many local artisans who sell their wares, try Surlier for ceramics, Bonhomme for dried flowers, L'Atelier de l'Acacia for wool fabrics. Better still, out on the St Cyr road the Moulin de St Côme is an old watermill still making olive oil (in winter, you can watch this process); it also will sell you its oil, and other local products.

*Where to stay
Upper-
medium price*

Hostellerie Bérard, Avenue Gabriel-Péri; tel. 94 90 11 43. One of my own favourite hotel/restaurants in all France, this old inn in the main street has been converted into a stylish modern *auberge*, run with skill and charm by René and Danièle Bérard: he, shy, does the cooking; she, exuberant and flirtatious, is front-of-house, ruling her efficient young female staff like a busy headmistress. New beamed ceilings, a spacious bar, small swimming pool, comfortable bedrooms (36) mostly in nearby annexes (one is a former monastery); lots of British guests. Closed January.

*Where to eat
Upper-
medium price*

Hostellerie Bérard (see above). René's cheaper menus include classic Provençal dishes, the dearer ones are more *nouvelle* and innovative, but all are excellent. The waitresses are charming, and the spacious dining-room has lovely views over the valley.

Bandol
83150

The largest resort on this part of the coast, Bandol (population 6,713) was a sleepy, little-known place when D. H. Lawrence and Katherine Mansfield stayed here in the 1920s. Today it is big and bustling, but still quite stylish. It has a sizeable yacht marina, three sandy beaches (best is the one in sheltered Renecros bay), and a profusion of handsome villas on its hillsides where the only blemish is the long concrete scar of new holiday flats. These hillsides also produce the reputed Bandol wines (see p. 52). The sea-promenade, lined with cafés, shops and palm-trees, is a mix of old-style sophistication and brash modern commercialism. At weekends it gets crammed with day-trippers from Toulon and Marseille.

What to see

The tiny rocky island of **Bendor**, 2 km from Bandol (frequent boat services), belongs to Paul Ricard, the pastis tycoon, eccentric philanthropist and innovator. He has planted it attractively with pines and flowers, and today he runs it as a centre for sport, culture and tourism. Here you will find an imitation Provençal fishing port, a group of artisans' craft shops (lacquer painters, jewellers, and so on), a nautical club with a diving and a sailing school, an excellent modern art gallery, and most notably a museum of wines and spirits that includes 7,000 bottles from forty-five countries (closed Wednesdays). All quite fun, and worth a visit.

What to do

The **Zoo-Jardin Exotique**, just beyond the autoroute 2 km northeast of Bandol (clearly signposted), is a small but very well-kept zoo where the animals look properly cared for – and alas that's not always the case in French zoos. There are no large animals, but plenty of bright-plumed birds such as cranes and flamingoes, also monkeys, puppy-like fennecs, and two hideous Vietnamese pigs called Romeo and Juliet who probably think each other beautiful. The well-landscaped park contains exotic plants and pretty trees.

Bandol has a lively outdoor market by the promenade on Tuesdays. At St Cyr, 8 km west of Bandol, Aqualand is a big swimming pool with artificial waves and water games enjoyed by children of all ages.

Bars and cafés

The fifteen or so terrace-cafés edge-to-edge along the promenade all have the same kind of wicker chairs with cushions – monotonous, but quite elegant. Nicest are the **Bistro du Port**, **Café Latin** and **O'Don Quichotte** (sic), outclassed only – but by far! – by **Tchin-Tchin**, a very chic, stylish bar, romantically lit, that serves nothing but champagne, whisky and cocktails. Caviar and foie gras, too.

Nightlife

The Casino, recently remodelled with chintzy 1930s' decor and lots of mirrors, is trying hard to rival the one at Cassis (see p. 154). It's open daily, from 4 p.m., and has a nightclub, **Stars Circus**. **Black Jack** is a lively summer disco on the beach. **Le Club** and **Le Privé** are good discos at nearby St Cyr, while **Mai Tai** out on the Sanary road has a reputation for orgiastic naughtiness.

Where to stay
Medium price

La Ker Mocotte, Rue Raimu; tel. 94 29 46 53. A big pink villa on a cliff above Renecros beach which was once the home of Raimu, the great Provençal actor. Now it is a pleasant and unusual holiday hotel run by a cultivated Alsatian couple, the Goetzes, who hold special *soirées* for their guests, and provide watersports on their private beach. However, they are planning to sell, so all this may change. Closed mid-October to February; 19 bedrooms.

Les Galets, Montée Voisin; tel. 94 29 43 46. A good small hotel, quite cheap, by the beach 2 km to the east.

Where to eat
Upper-medium price

Auberge du Port, 9 Allées Jean-Moulin; tel. 94 29 42 63. A large, elegant place with modern decor and an open terrace facing the promenade. Best food in town, especially the innovative fish dishes.

Medium price

La Grotte Provençale, 21 Rue du Dr-Marçon; tel. 94 29 41 52. Good local dishes at this cramped but friendly little auberge in a side-street near the front.

La Ciotat
13600

Originally a Greek colony, this sizeable town (population, 31,727) has long been a major shipbuilding centre: but in 1986 the decision was taken to close the shipyards, which for years had been doing badly, like so many in Europe. There are good beaches at La Ciotat-Plage. The offshore Ile Verte, with its small fort, can be visited.

Cassis
13260

One of the most typical and attractive of Provençal coast resorts, Cassis (population 6,318) is an old fishing port secluded in a deep bay and surrounded by the high limestone cliffs that are characteristic of this area. It gets very crowded in summer, notably with weekenders from nearby Marseille: but it still keeps its charm, and mercifully the port area is now a pedestrian zone. As at Bandol, the beautiful pine-clad hillsides behind have been disfigured by new blocks of holiday flats.

Cassis first attracted attention in the 1860s when Mistral published his epic poem *Calendau* (1867), about a local fisherman. Early this century, the port and its setting have inspired work by the Fauve painters, André Derain, Dufy, Matisse and Vlaminck, and by Salvador Dali. The municipal museum is of interest, the local dry white wine (see p. 52) goes well with the local shellfish, and there is an arts festival in July and August.

What to see
Les Calanques

The local word *calanque* means a deep creek or small fjord, and there are several on the rugged coast just west of Cassis. In their setting of white cliffs covered with heather and gorse, they are very beautiful indeed, and their clear deep water is ideal for bathing – but not in rough weather. You can go by car from Cassis to the creek of **Port-Miou**, where there are rock quarries (the hard white stone was used to build part of the Suez Canal). Further west, about 6 km from Cassis, the **Port-Pin** and **En-Vau** creeks can be reached only on foot: the paths are well marked, but it's a steep scramble down to the water. Alternatively, there are regular boat excursions to the *calanques* from Cassis.

Cap Canaille

This limestone cliff, rising 360 m sheer above the sea, dramatically dominates the bay of Cassis on its east side. From the town you can drive to the summit, then along the clifftop to La Ciotat, via the Grande Tête (396 m), France's highest cliff. The views are stunning, but don't go too near the edge.

Nightlife

The **Casino**, a sumptuous new building with modern sculptures, marble floors and a floodlit Japanese garden, contrasts strikingly with the Côte's usual rather *démodé* Edwardian gambling palaces. Its main clients are Marseillais, who are great gamblers: that's why it's so very active and prosperous. **Big Ben**, near the port, is a lively disco.

Where to stay
Medium price

Hôtel de la Plage du Bestouan, Plage du Bestouan; tel. 42 01 05 70. Breezy, modern and family owned, by the beach. Good cooking, breakfasts poor. 30 rooms. Open April to October.

Le Liautaud, 2 Rue Victor Hugo; tel. 42 01 75 37. The author of this book spent the honeymoon of his first marriage here, back in 1952. It has since been much modernised (it needed it), but remains a friendly family-run place (32 rooms) by the quayside, with good food and a bar popular with locals. Closed November to mid-December.

Les Roches Blanches, Route de Calanques; tel. 42 01 09 30. Superbly situated on a rocky headland 1.5 km west of the port, this creeper-covered villa has a spacious garden sloping to its stone bathing terrace (no sand). A most civilised hotel, apart from the dull bedroom decor (35 rooms). Good food. Closed December, January.

Inexpensive

Commerce, 2 Rue St-Clair; tel. 42 01 09 10. Quite central, a friendly, family-run *Logis de France*; very good value; 16 rooms.

Where to eat
Upper-medium price

La Presque'île, Route de Port-Miou; tel. 42 01 03 77. The luxury and beauty of the setting, with wide windows and a big terrace all facing the sea, compensate for some ups and downs in the cooking (many local dishes). Closed January, February, Sunday dinner, Monday.

Inexpensive

Commerce (see above). Sound home cooking is served in this pleasant restaurant.

Marseille

13000

A fine town, Marseille. This human ant-heap, this smutty vulgarity, this squalor. They don't kill each other as much as it's said, in the alleys of the Vieux Port – but it's a fine town all the same.

Thus spoke the enigmatic Monsieur Henri in Jean Anouilh's play *Eurydice [Point of Departure]*. Poetic exaggeration, maybe, but with a gleam of truth. Marseille *is* a fine town, a great town, if only for its setting – spread around a wide, blue bay, circled by high, barren, limestone hills. It has a mighty history, too, dating back to 600 BC; in the nineteenth century it was the most important port of Europe, 'the gateway to the East', and though its port has now declined, this strident capital of the Provence/Côte-d'Azur region is still the second city of France (population 878,689), equal to Lyon, which has larger suburbs but is a smaller commune.

Like other great Mediterranean seaports (for instance, Naples and Alexandria), it's a place of vivid contrasts. The climate varies from torrid summer heat to the icy gales of the winter Mistral. Some districts by the coast to the south are spacious and elegant, but much of the downtown area is noisy, congested and dirty, with fearful traffic jams and run-down buildings. It's a social melting pot, a steamy cosmopolitan mix, with large Levantine and North African elements; and though drug-trafficking may have declined, there's still enough sporadic gangsterism and racial tension to sustain the city's reputation. Of course, the ordinary Marseillais are industrious and (fairly) law-abiding, but they are also hot-blooded, rough-mannered and earthily humorous – much as Pagnol described them in his 1930s' *Marius* trilogy. In short, Marseille is a town with a strong personality that I always find exciting, if infuriating; and though it may not seem an obvious tourist venue, in fact it has quite as much of cultural interest as the smaller, more gracious nearby cities such as Aix and Arles. You could spend whole weeks here and never get bored. And the restaurants are among France's best.

Getting there and transport

The big international airport (tel. 42 89 90 10) is at Marignane, 28 km to the north-west; it has scheduled direct flights to some seventy French and foreign cities, with about twenty daily flights to Paris. Allow twenty-five to forty minutes for the bus journey from town: buses go every fifteen minutes from the central railway station, the Gare St-Charles, which itself is linked to Paris and Lyon by TGV express train (twelve TGVs a day to Paris, a four and a half-hour journey). Buses to nearby towns leave from the equally central Gare Routière, Blvd. d'Athènes.

Within the city, there's an efficient and frequent new Métro, usually the fastest way of getting about: but it has only two lines, one north-south, one from the north-east suburbs to the centre. It links in with the dense and effective bus service (buses are few after 9 p.m., while the Métro goes on till 12.30 a.m.). There are some forty taxi ranks: or call 91 02 20 20 or 91 49 91 00. Local cab-drivers are not famous for their helpfulness or courtesy. The main tourist office is 4 La Canebière; tel. 91 54 91 11.

History

France's oldest town was founded in 600 BC by Greeks from Phocea in Asia Minor who named it Massilia. It became the main Greek colony in the west and then played some role in Roman history, siding with the hapless Pompey against Caesar and thus suffering reprisals. Commerce has always been Marseille's lifeblood: it prospered greatly in the time of the Crusades, becoming a trade rival of Venice and Genoa. Then in 1721 a plague originating from Syria wiped out half of its 100,000 population, but it recovered quite quickly. After 1789 it welcomed the Revolution and sent troops to Paris, where so ardently did they sing the new battle anthem composed in Strasbourg that this was dubbed *La Marseillaise* – and the nickname has endured.

Industry and politics today

Marseille's greatest epoch of commercial prowess came in the later nineteenth century, after the opening of the Suez Canal in 1869 and the French conquest of North Africa. Most of the city's grandiose buildings date from that era, when new heavy industries sprang up and the port was greatly extended. Since about 1918, however, the port has declined, hastened since the 1950s by France's loss of her overseas empire (notably in Africa) and more recently by the world shipping slump: many docks lie idle, repair yards have closed and unemployment is above the French average. What is more, much of the city's own industry is in traditional sectors such as textiles, soaps and heavy engineering, and many of these firms have been doing badly.

However, food processing continues to thrive (Marseille is the world capital of pastis-making as well as of pastis-drinking, home of a number of Paul Ricard's factories: see p. 152). In the past thirty years, new modern industries have developed out to the north-west, around the Étang de Berre (see p. 223). And the city is now setting its cap at a high-tech future, by building a big new science park ('technopole') to house an institute of robotics and other advanced research bodies. The success of Comex, the famous diving firm, ensures that Marseille remains a world leader in oceanography.

And so, despite economic problems that have been only partly its own fault, this city since the Second World War has remained intensely active and dynamic. Much of its success has been due to the leadership of the powerful Gaston Defferre, who was mayor for thirty-three years until his death in 1986. This Socialist autocrat and wealthy bourgeois, owner of the two main local daily papers, may have been a wheeler-dealer not entirely above the taint of corruption: but he also did a great deal to modernise and develop the city, as witness the new Métro and road tunnels, the vast universities and hospitals in the suburbs, the much-needed blocks of council flats that tower up on the hillsides. Defferre was succeeded as mayor by Robert Vigouroux, a local surgeon, and in the municipal elections of March 1989 this popular independent Socialist managed to retain the post by defeating an official Socialist Party candidate – thus proving once again that in Marseille a charismatic personality carries more weight than a political party. Very Provençal.

With so many Muslim immigrant workers from North Africa, and so many French *pieds-noirs* repatriates from the same area, racial animosity in the city is above average; and Marseille in recent years has been a stronghold of Jean-Marie Le Pen's National Front party. Occasionally there has been violence, with beatings-up of Arabs by young French thugs. However, this problem should not be exaggerated: most of the gangsterism in the city is not racist, but due simply to local feuds, often connected with the Mafia and drug-trafficking. True, the 'French Connection' drug-trade is now on the wane, thanks to police efforts. But petty crime, such as mugging, remains worse than in most big cities.

Main areas

Hemmed in by the bare limestone heights, the city sprawls for 20 km around its bay, and stretches some 10 km inland down the valley towards Aubagne. But its focus remains the narrow inlet of the Vieux Port, where the ancient Greeks built their colony. High on a hill to the south of this stands the ugly church of Notre-Dame-de-la-Garde, Marseille's major landmark and as much its emblem as the Eiffel Tower is of Paris. On the north side is a medieval quarter, much rebuilt, and beyond it lies the vast modern port. Inland from the Vieux Port runs La Canebière, once one of Europe's grandest streets, now much run down but still the main artery: to its south are the best shopping streets and entertainment areas; to its north is the Gare St-Charles, plus a red-light and immigrant quarter around the Rue Thubaneau, sinister at night, where women visitors especially should not walk alone after dark.

Further out, to the west and south of Notre-Dame, a corniche road runs along the rocky, much-indented shore. This is the smarter part of

Marseille, where villas and neat modern flats fill the Roucas-Blanc and Périer districts. South again, more housing stretches through Le Cabot and Ste Marguerite to the huge new university campus at Luminy. The main working-class and factory districts are north of the centre, towards La Rose and St Antoine.

Downtown there is some meter parking, much in demand, and plenty of guarded car-parks. Car theft is rife, and it's most unwise to leave anything visible in the car.

What to see

The many sights to see range from the ancient Greek and Roman to Le Corbusier and beyond. Some of them are scattered wide, but the majority are within easy walking distance of the centre, especially on the north side of the Vieux Port. The list below follows a geographical order, starting north of the Vieux Port, going east, then west and south round the coast.

The centre and north side

Vieux Port

Until the nineteenth century this quay-lined inlet was the main port; today it's used just by pleasure craft and a few fishing boats, but in a sense it's still the city's hub. At its mouth are two old forts – St Jean to the north and St Nicolas on the south side, the latter built under Louis XIV to control the turbulent Marseillais. Pagnol set his *Marius* trilogy on the Quai de Rive Neuve, but the area has since been so much rebuilt that there's little sign of where César's fictitious 'Bar de la Marine' might have been.

North of the Vieux Port

This ancient quarter of narrow alleys, once patrician, had by the 1930s degenerated into a low-life slum (as described by Anouilh). In 1943 the Wehrmacht, finding its inhabitants impossible to control, expelled 40,000 of them overnight and blew up the sector between the Vieux Port and the Rue Cassière. Then after 1945, to meet the housing shortage, it was hastily rebuilt with rows of hideous rectangular blocks. However, the area north of the Rue Cassière remains much unchanged and truly Mediterranean – steep steps and old alleyways, where washing hangs like faded bunting between the tall houses, teeming with Arabs and gipsies. Even down near the quai, a few lovely old buildings have survived the 1943 holocaust, including the Baroque seventeenth-century town hall. Here also are two splendid museums – one of Old Marseille, and one of the Roman Docks.

Musée du Vieux Marseille

The sixteenth-century Maison Diamante ('diamond-studded'), named after its faceted façade, has a main stairway with a richly-carved ceiling. More to the point, it houses a superb folk-art museum, including paintings, maps and models of the city's life through the centuries. One floor contains Provençal porcelain and furniture; another has a fine collection of Camoin playing cards. Best of all, in my view, is the room full of Provençal and Neapolitan *santons* and nativity cribs. Most are eighteenth and nineteenth century: but a modern craftsman, Georges Prost, has contributed a colourful tableau of local traditional life, with hundreds of tiny *santons*.

Musée des Docks Romains

Massilia's old Roman docks first came to light as a result of the 1943 destruction. A block of flats was then built on top: but on its ground floor this museum cunningly contains the docks in their real setting, so it's less a museum than a true Roman remain. The quai and the grain storage jars (*dolia*) can be seen just as they were; Roman amphorae and anchors have been added, mostly found in wrecks off-shore. All is clearly explained, with maps and panels that trace Massilia's trading role in classical times and the recovery of wrecks carried out locally by Jacques Cousteau's team.

Vieille Charité (Museum of Archaeology)

Up behind the slummy alleyways stands this magnificent seventeenth-century almshouse, designed by the great Pierre Puget. For years it had been left to decay: but recently the city council has restored it, as a multi-purpose cultural centre – a fine example of inner-city renovation. All in creamy gold stone, it has a graceful courtyard with three tiers of arcades, surrounding a domed church. Special art exhibitions are held here, and the city's main **archaeological museum** has just been transferred from the Château Borély (see below). This important collection includes mummies and other relics from Egypt, also Etruscan bronzes, Greek and Roman ceramics, and a Minoan wine-pitcher of the fifteenth century BC. In the lapidary section, the star exhibit is a reconstructed Celto-Ligurian sanctuary from Roquepertuse, near Aix: note its portico decorated with skulls, and the two-headed Hermes.

Twin cathedrals (Major and Ancienne Major)

Just to the west, near the port, are Marseille's two adjacent cathedrals, each utterly different. The newer one, a huge nineteenth-century neo-Byzantine monstrosity with cupolas and striped stone, looks like a marzipan gâteau. Tucked beside it is the tiny Ancienne Major, as it's called, a delightful example of pure twelfth-century Romanesque. The interior is ill-lit, but you can just about discern the porcelain bas-relief by Della Robbia and the superbly-sculpted fifteenth-century altar of St Lazarus in the left transept.

The port

With its 19 km of quays, the great port stretches north for 6 km from the Vieux Port. Work on it began in 1844. Despite its recent decline, it still handles some 100 million tonnes of traffic a year (together with Fos, see p. 224), plus 800,000 passengers, mostly Algerian workers. It is open to visits only on Sundays and public holidays, but you can get a good bird's-eye view by car from the elevated Autoroute du Littoral (N568B).

The centre and east side

La Canebière

In the days before air travel, this was one of Europe's great streets – 'If Paris only had a Canebière, it would be quite a little Marseille', was the local boast – and it had some grain of sense, for the terrace-cafés with their live orchestras were chic meeting places for the maharajahs, princes and emirs who used the port on their way to or from Paris or London. But today they go by air, the orchestras have vanished, and Marseillais can hardly feel proud of this tawdry boulevard, its grand cafés replaced by cheap bars and cafeterias, cut-price stores and sleazy fun-arcades.

And yet, the boulevard is still the focus of business and cultural life. To its south is the Opéra; and on its north side is the former Bourse, now housing a dull maritime museum, with behind it the new World Trade Centre. It was just in front of the Bourse that in 1934 a Macedonian shot dead King Alexander of Yugoslavia.

Jardin des Vestiges The recent redevelopment of the area behind the Bourse laid bare the remains of the original Greek port and town, which have now been cleverly transformed into a little public garden: here you can walk amid the ruins of quays, towers and ramparts, all Greek from the third to second centuries BC, with Roman additions. They are clearly explained and most attractively set out, floodlit at night.

Musée d'Histoire de Marseille Adjoining the garden, this modern museum traces the city's history from earliest times. Its showpiece is the hull of a large Roman merchant vessel, discovered in 1974 entirely freeze-dried.

Palais Longchamp At the end of the tree-lined Blvd. Longchamp, 2 km east of the Vieux Port, stands this typically grandiose 1860s palace whose two wings, linked by a curved colonnade, each house a museum. In the middle there cascades a majestic moss-covered fountain.

Musée des Beaux-Arts This, the more important of these two museums, is the city's main art gallery, full of treasures. The most arresting, on the first floor, are Michel Serre's two huge paintings of Marseille during the plague of 1721, its streets filled with the dead and dying. These closely-observed scenes have a graphic documentary impact. On the stairway above are two vivid cartoon-like frescoes by Parvis de Chavannes, another local artist, showing Marseille first as a Greek colony, then as 'gateway to the East'.

Foreign artists displayed on the first floor include Jan Brueghel (a fantasy with cupids), Rubens (an 'Adoration of the Shepherds' and other works), and Caracci's charming 'Village Wedding'. Marseille's great sculptor Pierre Puget is fully honoured, with designs of his never-achieved town-planning projects for the city, and casts of six of his major sculptures, imaginatively lit (the originals are in the Louvre and in Genoa). On the second floor are some sharp caricatures by another Marseille-born artist, Honoré Daumier, as well as works by Corot, Courbet, Millet, David, and so on.

Musée d'Histoire Naturelle The second Longchamp museum contains stuffed animals of all kinds, skeletons of elephants and whales, and gaudy tropical fish in a small aquarium. For those who prefer live animals, the city's large but rather unkempt zoo is just behind the palace.

Musée Grobet-Labadie This delightful small 1870s' house at 140 Blvd. Longchamp was the home of local violinist and art-lover Louis Grobet, and on his death in 1919 he bequeathed it to the city, together with his remarkable collection of *objets d'art* – oriental carpets, porcelain, antique tapestries, old musical instruments and microscopes, German fifteenth-century paintings, works by Jean Baptiste Greuze and Corot, and much else. For all the eclecticism, the cosy rooms convey a feeling of harmony.

South side

Musée Cantini

In the Rue Grignan, south of the Canebière, is this seventeenth-century mansion that holds a large display of Provençal porcelain, also modern works of art by the Marseille-born sculptor César and others.

Notre-Dame-de-la-Garde

Built in the mid-nineteenth century in the neo-Byzantine style then in vogue, this monstrous church with its huge statue of the Virgin stands high on its hilltop south of the Vieux Port, and is floodlit at night. You can climb up, or go by car or trolleybus: the trip is worth it, for the intriguing array of sailors' votive offerings inside, also for the majestic view of the city, coast and hills.

St Victor basilica

Just as Marseille's two cathedrals are chalk and cheese, so this fascinating ancient church, near the south entrance to the Vieux Port, is a total contrast to Notre-Dame. It brings early Christian history vividly alive: built first by St Cassien in the fifth century (in honour of the early martyr St Victor), it was wrecked by the Saracens, and the present fortifed Gothic church, with its crenellated fort-like tower, was superimposed on it in the eleventh century. The remains of St Cassien's old abbey are now the large crypt, restored and still used for worship: it contains catacombs and sarcophagi both Christian and pagan, as well as the tomb of two obscure early martyrs whose skeletons and other relics were discovered in 1965 and dated to AD 250. According to an early legend, St Mary Magdalene and St Lazarus (see p. 227) sheltered in the grotto which is now this crypt.

The coastal corniche

Just outside the Vieux Port, by the sea, is the public Parc du Pharo whose imposing château belonged to the Empress Eugénie. Beyond here, the Corniche Président Kennedy winds far along the coast, past little coves and modern bathing lidos. Eventually, at the far edge of the urban sprawl, this road reaches the semi-derelict fishing hamlets of Les Goudes and Callelongue, amid stark limestone hills: the buildings are gloomy, but the coastal scenery is eerily majestic. Tough walkers can climb from here to the summit of the Marseilleveyre massif, where the views are outstanding.

Château Borély

This severe white eighteenth-century mansion in a dusty park, near the corniche road, houses a collection of drawings by Fragonard, Jean Baptiste Greuze, Ingres and other eighteenth- to nineteenth-century artists of the French School. Its archaeological treasures have just been transferred to the Vieille Charité (see p. 159). Inland along the broad Avenue du Prado, a neat residential district, is the big Palais des Congrès where trade fairs are held.

Le Corbusier's 'Unité d'Habitation'

South from here, on the Blvd. Michelet, is a seventeen-storey block of flats designed by Le Corbusier and built in 1952. Intended to be part of a six-block 'Cité Radieuse', it was a pioneering work in its day, but now looks old hat and unkempt – far from 'radiant'.

Château d'If

Many visitors will want to make the boat trip from the Vieux Port to this infamous fortress, 3 km offshore on a rocky isle. Built by François I in 1524 as a defence bastion, it was long used as a state prison: among its inmates were 'The Man in the Iron Mask' (see p. 119) and, in fiction, Dumas' *The Count of Monte Cristo*. You can see the memorial to the 3,500 Huguenot prisoners brought here, and the carvings they have left; also the terrible windowless cell where those with life sentences were left to die. There's a fine view of Marseille from the upper terrace.

What to do

Culture

The cultural scene is lively: events are listed in the weekly *Marseille Poche*. The Opéra's regular company performs all year except summer, and has a good standard; the famous Roland Petit ballet is also based here. The leading theatre company is the state-backed rep, Théâtre de la Cité. There are some ten other theatres, and a satirical café-théâtre, La Maison Hautée. The newly-created Orchestre Philharmonique de Marseille is rather good. Concerts are often given in St Victor and other churches; in summer, there are outdoor concerts and ballet at the Parc du Pharo. The Paris cinema shows 'art' films and subtitled foreign ones.

Fairs and festivals

A famous *santons* fair, lively and picturesque, is held at the top of the Canebière from the last Sunday in November until 6 January. In July there's an international folklore festival at Château-Gombert, and in August a *boules* tournament in the Parc Borély. Big trade fairs are held at the Palais des Congrès (Parc Chanot) in early April and early September, when the city gets very crowded.

Sport

The nearest eighteen-hole golf course is 22 km north, at Les Milles. The better tennis clubs in town are exclusive, not allowing temporary membership: but try Raquette Club. There is regular horse-racing at the Parc Borély course. For sailing, go to the Centre Municipal de Voile on the Promenade de la Plage, near Borély, where there's also a large public bathing beach, often crowded. The best swimming pool is at Luminy in the southern suburbs.

Zoo

Marseille's big but not-so-attractive zoo is just behind the Palais Longchamp (see above).

Shopping

Small shops selling local produce include Marrou, 15 Place Castellane, Bataille, 18 Rue Fontange (wines, cheeses, etc.), La Taste, 73 Cours Julien (local herbs and spices), Marcel Carbonel, 84 Rue Grignan (he makes his own *santons*), Les Olivades (fabrics and *santons*). The best daily open-air markets are in the Avenue Prado (food and clothes) and at the Vieux Port (fish, seafood).

The smartest modern boutiques are in the Rue Paradis, Rue St-Ferréol, Rue de Rome, all running south from La Canebière. Nearby, the Centre Bourse is a huge modern shopping centre.

Nightlife

Of the various discos, **Le Duke**, 6 Rue Lulli, is the most sophisticated and **Satellite**, Corniche Kennedy, the most sedate; other goodish ones are **Domingo**, 60 Corniche Kennedy, and **Golf**, 3 Rue

Sénac. **L'Abbaye de la Commanderie**, 20 Rue Corneille, is a cosy cabaret/bar with Marseille songs and ribald jokes – but you need to know the patois. South of the Canebière, there are amusing bars on and near the Cours Julien, known as 'the Montmartre of Marseille'. The nearest casino is 23 km to the east, at Cassis (see p. 154).

Where to stay

Of the few really good hotels, some are modern and functional, others small and classically elegant. Some are downtown, but others are out along the Corniche, and for these you really need a car. The cheap hotels near the station are best avoided.

Top price

Le Petit Nice, Anse de Maldormé, Corniche J. F. Kennedy, 13007; tel. 91 52 14 39. By the sea, 3 km from the centre, this nineteenth-century villa in Hellenic style is now a very select little hotel (18 rooms), owned and run with lordly pride by the Passédat family. Elegant, classical-style bedrooms and suites; pretty palm-shaded garden above the rocks. Closed January.

Upper-medium price

Pullman Beauvau, 4 Rue Beauvau, 13001; tel. 91 54 91 00. Right by the busy Vieux Port (but there's double-glazing), this famous eighteenth-century *relais de poste* counts Chopin, Georges Sand, Cocteau and Hemingway among its past guests. It has just been finely restored by the Pullman group, with period-style bedrooms (71), and has real warmth and character; opera stars and other such celebrities stay often. The snug English-style bar has a pianist. No restaurant, but light meals are served, in the bar or bedrooms.

Concorde Palm Beach, 2 Promenade de la Plage, 13008; tel. 91 26 20 00. By the sea, 5 km south of the centre, an unusual modern hotel with a breezy, club-like ambience, popular both with tourists and business people. Built on the site of a mineral spring, it was formerly a chic spa centre (note, in the basement, the amazing late-Victorian photos of people taking their cures); and a spring still bubbles out of the rocky cliff inside the foyer! All bedrooms (161) have sea-facing balconies. The large pleasant bar opens on to the sun-terrace and swimming pool, whose warm water comes straight from the spring. Lunchtime buffet by the pool in summer. Watersports.

Medium price

La Résidence Bompard, 2 Rue des Flots-Bleus, 13007; tel. 91 52 10 93. What a delightful surprise! – a quiet villa in its own big garden, high on the hill above the sea yet only ten minutes' drive from the city centre, and quite inexpensive. Cheerful modern bedrooms (47), some in bungalows with patios and kitchenettes. You can breakfast idyllically under the trees. No restaurant.

Lower-medium price

Ibis, Avenue E Triolet; tel. 91 72 34 34. Near Parc Borély, off corniche road, a useful and efficient member of the modern Ibis chain; 88 rooms. Simple grill-type restaurant.

New Astoria, 10 Blvd. Garibaldi, 13001; tel. 91 33 33 50. This nicely renovated city-centre hotel, with biggish rooms (58) and an unusual foyer, is under the same ownership as the Bompard. No restaurant.

Inexpensive

Edmond Rostand, 31 Rue du Dagon; tel. 91 37 74 95. Simple but friendly, and very central – just off the Rue du Paradis. 18 rooms, no restaurant.

Dijon, 33 Allées Léon Gambetta; tel. 91 62 22 22. Central, off the Canebière and near a car-park. 12 rooms. No restaurant.

Where to eat

Good restaurants in Marseille are legion, and they come in all price ranges – save that it's harder to eat really cheaply and well than in many big French towns. Maybe this is because fresh fish and seafood are the mainstays of local cuisine, and these are never inexpensive, certainly not bouillabaisse (see p. 49). Try the simple-looking places down by the coast for really good fish. The best central area for eating is south of the Canebière: but beware of the tourist traps near the fish market south of the Vieux Port.

Top luxury price

Le Petit Nice (see Hôtel Le Petit Nice, p. 163). A sumptuous clientèle attends the hotel's sumptuous restaurant, where the Passédat family's inspired cooking is rated the city's best and among Provence's best. Pampered comfort, and a lovely setting, with sea views alike from the intimate *salle* and the pretty garden. Closed Monday out of season.

Maurice Brun, 18 Quai Rive-Neuve; tel. 91 33 35 38. This highly idiosyncratic place is a real experience. Up a gloomy stairway by the Vieux Port, you reach a graceful dining-room where pure Provençal cuisine at its finest is served by the Brun family in a solemn hieratic style: one unchanging menu, and no smoking allowed. Glorious hors d'/oe/uvres, spit-roasts. Closed Sunday, Monday.

Upper-medium price

Calypso, 3 Rue des Catalans; tel. 91 52 64 00. By the sea beyond the Vieux Port, family-run, down-to-earth and very traditional, this restaurant serves some of the best fish in town, notably bouillabaisse. Closed Sunday, Monday, two weeks in February.

L'Oursinade, Rue Neuve St-Martin; tel. 91 91 91 29. The dull Hôtel Mercure secretes this exciting gastronomic haunt, where chef René Alloin concocts *nouvelle* variations on classic local dishes. Spacious comfort; a shady patio for summer. Closed Sunday, August.

Miramar, 12 Quai du Port; tel. 91 91 10 40. On the Vieux Port; small, chic and comfortable; superb fish including bouillabaisse. Closed Sunday, three weeks in August, Christmas and New Year.

Les Arcenaulx, 25 Cours d'Estienne-d'Orves; tel. 91 54 77 06. An old arsenal just south of the Vieux Port has been transformed into a stylish culture centre, with an art gallery, bookshop, tearoom and restaurant. Owned and run by the Laffitte sisters, local trend setters, it has become a venue for the intelligentsia. The food is good, too; and the decor is charmingly unusual, with book-lined walls. Closed Monday, Sunday dinner.

Medium price

Chez Madie, 138 Quai du Port; tel. 91 90 40 87. Popular bistro on the Vieux Port; excellent *bouillabaisse* and other fish dishes. Closed August.

Paprikas, 24 Rue Sainte; tel. 91 33 64 37. If you're bored with

French food, try Paprikas' genuine Hungarian cuisine, with soft music and candlelight at dinner. Closed Sunday, Monday, August.

Brave Margot, 22 Rue de la Guirlande; tel. 91 90 83 41. And if you're bored with Provençal food, try the Lyonnais dishes at this unassuming place near the town hall. Closed Monday, September.

Inexpensive

La Charpenterie, 22 Rue de la Paix; tel. 91 54 22 89. Good traditional local cooking. Closed Saturday, Sunday, high summer.

Avant-Scène, 59 Cours Julien; tel. 91 42 19 29. At this pleasant Bohemian place, open late, the tiny stage provides theatre shows during the meals. Closed Monday night, Sunday.

Dent Creuze, 14 Rue Sénac; tel. 91 42 05 67. Copious help-yourself salads and swift service at this popular eatery off La Canebière. Closed Monday, Saturday.

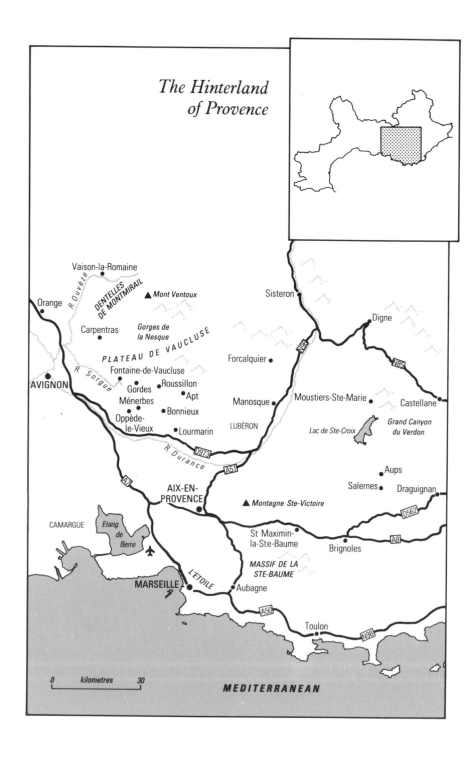

The Hinterland of Provence

The Hinterland of Provence

This chapter takes in the entire hinterland of Provence comprised roughly of the Var, Vaucluse and Alpes-de-Haute-Provence departments. It is a vast region of limestone heights and rolling hills, pastoral and often vine-clad in the south, towards the coast, much wilder to the north beyond the River Verdon and on the Vaucluse plateau. There are no big towns here: a place like Digne, with less than 17,000 people, has the semblance of a capital.

Inland from Marseille and Toulon

Aubagne and Pagnol country

The urban sprawl in the valley east of Marseille leads to the ugly industrial town of Aubagne (population 38,571) where the French Foreign Legion today has its headquarters: there's a museum, with photos and documents that relate the Legion's history and exploits.

In the town's Syndicat d'Initiative is a huge *tableau vivant* full of *santons* depicting the stories and films of Marcel Pagnol, including likenesses of Gérard Depardieu as Jean de Florette and Yves Montand as the wily Papet. Here, far more than in Marseille, we are in the heart of Pagnol country. He was born in Aubagne in 1895, son of a teacher; and though the family moved to Marseille, they would return for long summer holidays to a cottage up above **La Treille**, a hamlet northwest of Aubagne, on the edge of the wild limestone hills. Here, talking to local people, Pagnol found the material and the inspiration for his rural films such as *Manon des Sources* and *La Femme du Boulanger* (1939), and for his trilogy of memoirs (*Souvenirs d'Enfance*) that so vividly evoke his pastoral boyhood. When he turned to film-making, he created an open-air studio on the east side of the Barre St Esprit, a high ledge of rock between La Treille and Aubagne: you can reach it by car and on foot from Aubagne, and see the buildings he created for filming his *Regain* and *Angèle*, based on books by Giono. Across the wild valley is Manon's cave; and at La Treille you can see the village fountain that he used for his own film of *Manon*. It is just above the cemetery where he lies buried, and below the simple house at the top of the road that was his holiday home. This mingling of fact and fiction I found rather moving and quite uncanny. What is more, La Treille is actually *inside* Marseille's city borders, although out in the wilds and not much changed since Pagnol's day. Claude Berri's two-part 1986 remake of the Manon story, a world-wide box-office success, was filmed further east, near **Cuges-les-Pins**.

North-west of La Treille, framing the northern Marseille suburbs, is the high limestone range of l'Etoile. Here the Col Ste Anne offers fine views of the city, while the village of **Allauch** has old windmills, and there's a folk-art museum at **Château-Gombert**.

Gémenos

13420

Where to stay and eat Upper-medium price

A small town just east of Aubagne.

Le Relais de la Magdeleine; tel. 42 82 20 05. A marvellous hotel in the outskirts of Gémenos, set in a big walled garden. It's a seventeenth-century mansion, luxurious yet unpretentious, with civilised owners, charming staff, and good Provençal food served outside by candlelight under the trees; 20 bedrooms; swimming pool. Open mid-March to October.

OK Corral

On the N8 3 km east of Cuges-les-Pins, OK Corral is a big Dutch-owned amusement park offering fun for all ages, with such amusements as a ghost train, Wild West train and big wheel. Sometimes live actors play out the exploits of Buffalo Bill and other heroes.

Circuit Paul Ricard

Six km further along the N8, north of Le Beausset, is Provence's best motor-racing track, created and owned by the pastis tycoon Paul Ricard. Major races are held several times a year, notably the Grand Prix de France (first weekend in July) and the Bol d'Or (mid-September); tel. 94 93 55 19.

Massif de la Ste Baume

From Gémenos you can make an excursion up into the most spectacular of all Provence's rocky limestone massifs, and one that also enshrines the mystery of early Christian legend. St Mary Magdalene is said to have spent the last thirty years of her life alone in a cave on these windy heights (see p. 227), and the name 'baume' comes from the Provençal *baoumo*, meaning cave. Thickly wooded on its southern slopes, arid to the north, the range runs for some 16 km from Aubagne to St Maximin.

The best route through its wild heart is the D2 from Gémenos, which first passes the Parc de St Pons, with lovely trees and the ruins of an old Cistercian abbey. The narrow road then loops up giddily into a lunar landscape of gaunt white crags – the toothy pinnacle of the Forcade rock, and the broader Pic de Bertagne with its domed white observatory. The views all round, to Marseille, the coast at Cassis and Montagne Ste Victoire to the north, are stunning.

Near Plan d'Aups you reach a serene upland plateau, as the landscape changes abruptly to cultivated fields and neat farmsteads. Farther on is an old hostelry, L'Hôtellerie, with a Renaissance fireplace and statues of Louis XI and his wife; it's now run by Dominicans as a religious and cultural centre. All around is the forest of Ste

Baume, whose giant beeches are trees seldom found in southern France. And to the south rise the massif's high crests, where a stone monument crowns the topmost peak, St Pilon (1,150 m).

Just below this peak is the large, dimly lit cave of Mary Magdalene: from the hostelry below, you can walk up to it through the forest, along well-marked paths, and then climb the final steep flight of 150 steps. In the Middle Ages, this was one of the most venerated sites in Christendom, and kings and popes would make the pilgrimage up to this lonely spot, where a candlelit midnight mass attracting large crowds is still held every 22 July. It's an impressive, mysterious place, well worth the trek.

St Maximin-la-Ste Baume

This busy market town (population 5,552) on the N7 Aix-Nice main road is known mainly for its great basilica of Ste-Marie-Madeleine, which is regarded as the finest Gothic building in Provence. The tombs in its crypt have been venerated as those of Mary Magdalene and St Maximin, who is said by legend to have come from Palestine with the three Marys (Mary Magdalene, St Martha and the Virgin Mary, see p. 227) and then to have been martyred in Aix. The abbey was built at a slow pace in the fourteenth and fifteenth centuries, and even today the west façade is unfinished. During the Revolution, the abbey was saved from destruction by the lucky chance that Bonaparte's younger brother Lucien was stationed in the town, took the church over as a warehouse, and enjoyed playing its fine eighteenth-century organ.

Unlike many great churches in Provence, this one has a feeling of space and light, with its high vaulted nave and polygonal apse. Apart from the organ, its fine works of art include the sculpted seventeenth-century choir screen; the huge eighteenth-century pulpit carved from a single piece of wood; and above all, to the left of the high altar, an unusual sixteenth-century Venetian retable, whose sixteen painted panels depict the life and Passion of Christ against such backdrops as the Colosseum and Avignon's papal palace. Down in the crypt, originally the burial vault of a Roman villa, are four very early Christian sarcophagi, and a bronze reliquary holding a skull that was long worshipped as Mary Magdalene's.

The organ plays a big part in the classical music festival held each August in the church and adjoining buildings.

Where to eat
Medium price

Chez Nous, Blvd. J.-Jaurès; tel. 94 78 02 57. A friendly, rustic-style bistro; good local dishes, fine value. Closed Wednesday.

Brignoles

Another market town on the N7 highway, Brignoles (population 10,894) lies amid vineyards and is one of Provence's main wine-producing centres. It is also France's capital of bauxite mining (2 million tonnes a year), while white marble too has been quarried in the area since Roman times. In the old town, the much-rebuilt feudal château of the Counts of Provence now houses the Musée du Pays Brignolais, whose oddly eclectic collection includes a third-century sarcophagus, a concrete rowing boat, dinosaurs' eggs and a mechanical crib. The church of St Sauveur has a fine Romanesque doorway and a painting by Parrocel.

What to do — The Parc Minifrance, on the Nice road, has some seventy scale models of well-known French buildings and sites: you can hire a portable cassette-player with an English tape that will guide you round. Very educational – and there's fun for kids, too, with a mini-train and playing area.

The upper Var

The northern part of the Var department is a wide, beautiful, fairly thinly populated area, typical of the hilly Provençal hinterland. It stretches from the Maures hills just behind Toulon and St Tropez, right up to the Gorges du Verdon. My own favourite spots in this area are the hill villages of Seillans, Mons and Tourtour, the lovely Cistercian abbey of Le Thoronet and the bizarre museum at Entrecasteaux castle. I also enjoy the equally bizarre festival at Barjols.

Draguignan
83300 — Until 1975 the capital of the Var department, this dignified market town (population 28,194) has broad avenues and a lively medieval quarter crowned by a seventeenth-century clock tower.

What to see — The municipal museum contains some Flemish and Italian paintings, and watercolours by Rodin. If you are interested in local social history and life styles, visit the newly-created Musée des Arts Populaires – it has well set-out displays of old farm tools, costumes, furniture, and photos of peasant life.

Clockwise from Draguignan, starting to its east, the following are the main places of interest in the upper Var region.

Bargemom — The rolling open countryside between Draguignan and Grasse is extremely beautiful – a succession of lush wooded valleys, wide vistas, and ancient villages clinging to the hillsides. There is plenty of space, and not too much new building. One of the finest of the villages is Bargemon: it has shady avenues and squares where fountains play, as well as twelfth-century fortified gateways, and built into its ramparts a fourteenth-century church with a flamboyant Gothic doorway. Many of the summer residents are British. There's a folk festival on the first Sunday in August, while **Chez Pierrot** and **Maître Blanc** are two good medium-priced Provençal restaurants.

Seillans
83440 Fayence — Max Ernst used to live and paint in this delightful hill village east of Bargemon, still popular with artists and writers. It has steep paved alleys, fountains, and a twelfth-century ruined château whose ramparts were a defence against the Saracens; 1 km along the Fayence road

is the Romanesque chapel of Notre-Dame-de-l'Ormeau, with a remarkable sixteenth-century polychromatic wooden altarpiece. There's a local fête on the last Sunday in July.

Whereto stay **Hôtel des Deux Rocs**; tel. 94 76 87 32. An eighteenth-century
and eat mansion, converted by its Parisienne owner into a chic and intimate
Medium price little hotel (15 rooms). Cheerful lounge and bedrooms. The service can be slow and the food unremarkable; but it's a delight to eat outdoors under plane trees in the cobbled courtyard. Open April to October.

Hôtel de France–Clariond, Place Thouron; tel. 94 76 96 10. Pleasant family-run hotel with lovely pool, good food served outdoors around an old fountain. 20 rooms. Closed January.

Fayence A small town on a hillside, with a pleasant medieval quarter. To its
83440 east, **Callian** and **Montauroux** are also attractive hill villages, the latter much frequented by artists and craftspeople.

Where to stay **Moulin de la Camandoule**, Chemin de Notre-Dame-des-Cyprès;
and eat tel. 94 76 00 84. An old olive mill out on the Draguignan road, set
Medium price idyllically by a stream and charmingly converted. Bedrooms (11) in Provençal style; big swimming pool where barbecues are held. The new chef was trained at London's Le Gavroche, no less, but his skills have yet to be tested by us. Closed January, February and early November.

You can eat cheaply but well at the modest **Centenaire** in Callian.

Mons A tiny unspoilt hill village in a wild and spectacular setting, 14 km north of Fayence; old arcaded streets, and a stunning view from its terrace. You can see Corsica on a clear day.

Lac de For swimming or watersports without the hassle of driving to the
St Cassien coast, try this big artificial lake south-east of Fayence, built after the Malpasset dam disaster (see p. 134). There are bathing, windsurfing and sailing (no motor boats), but the rocky shore is not ideal for sunbathing.

Les Arcs This small town south of Draguignan lies amid vineyards and is a leading centre of Côtes de Provence wine production: the Château Ste-Roseline, tel. 94 73 32 57, and the Château St-Pierre, tel. 94 47 41 47, are two leading local growers and both are open to visits. Les Arcs has a Roman bridge, and in its church are a curious mechanical crib and a lovely sixteenth-century altarpiece in sixteen panels. The newly-restored Romanesque chapel of Ste Roseline, 4 km to the east, was once part of an abbey on this site: it contains the well-preserved remains of Ste Roseline (born at Les Arcs in 1267), as well as sixteenth-century choirstalls, and some modern works including a Chagall mosaic and a bronze bas-relief of the life of the saint by Diego Giacometti.

Abbey of Le Of the three great abbeys built in Provence by Cistercian monks in
Thoronet the twelfth century (see also Sénanque and Silvacane, pp. 188 and 222), this is the loveliest and the one that reflects most perfectly,

through the purity of its Romanesque style, the austere and humble spirit of the Order. Like the others, it is in an isolated spot – amid woodlands, some 30 km south-west of Draguignan. In the Cistercian style, the church with its high vaulted ceiling is devoid of decoration or furnishing, apart from some frescoes added in the seventeenth century and now faded. On its north side is the graceful little cloister, with cypresses and a hexagonal washing-house in the centre. This leads to the early Gothic chapter-house, the library, refectory and dormitories, all finely proportioned. The strange niche on the outer south wall is where local people could place their dead before burial.

After the monks were driven out during the Revolution, the abbey fell into disrepair. It was bought by the State in 1854 and has since been finely restored, using the original golden-brown stone from a nearby quarry. In the late afternoon, the sunlight shining through the bare windows makes the stone glow softly, and this is the best time to visit the abbey: you are welcome also to attend vespers in the simple chapel beyond the cloister. Services are held by nuns who live nearby. It is all inspiringly peaceful.

Entre-casteaux
The tall, severe-looking seventeenth-century castle in this village west of Draguignan is a real curiosity. It used to belong to local lords, the Brunys, one of whom in the eighteenth century spent many years in a Portuguese jail after murdering his young wife. Finally, the château fell into ruins, but in 1974 it was bought by the astonishing Ian McGarvie-Munn, Scottish nationalist born in India, avant-garde painter, soldier and adventurer, former commander-in-chief of the Guatemalan Navy and married to the granddaughter of a former Guatemalan president. He restored the place at his own expense, and since his death in 1981 the work has been continued by his son Lachlan who runs it as a delightfully informal and eclectic museum (including Scottish bagpipes, pre-Columbian ceramics, Murano goblets and Provençal kitchenware) which you enter via the family's private kitchen. There are many special exhibitions, and classical concerts in summer on the lovely terrace. But it's a pity that Lachlan has hidden away his father's bold surrealist paintings, which he judges too provocative for local taste.

Where to stay
Medium price
Lachlan offers three rooms bed-and-breakfast (tel. 94 04 43 95): one has an amazing colonnaded Roman bathroom, built by his father.

Cotignac
83570 Carcès
An attractive small town amid vineyards, at the foot of a brown tufa cliff holed like an Emmenthal cheese with curious caves, some once inhabited. Outdoor theatre festival in July, August.

Where to stay
and eat
Medium price
Lou Calen, 1 Cours Gambetta; tel. 94 04 60 40. A friendly family-run place, with bedrooms (12) in rustic style, a large swimming pool, wild garden and lovely dining-terrace: lavish hors d'/oe/uvres buffet and goodish local dishes. Open April to October.

Barjols
This charming little town amid a circle of hills, 15 km west of

83670 Cotignac, is a key centre of Provençal folk tradition. It is almost the only place where the old instruments, the *tambourin* and *galoubet* (see p. 29), are still made, though the principal craftsman, Marius Fabre, is now around eighty and has no real successor.

Barjols is known also for its curious stumpy moss-covered fountains, aptly called *champignons*: there is one in the big main square, another outside the *mairie* in the enchanting Place du Capitaine-Vincens, shaded with unusually broad plane trees.

What to see One of the most curious of Provençal folk festivals, the Fête de St Marcel, is held on the third weekend in January, to mark the burial in 1350 of a local saint. A procession of costumed dancers and musicians, with traditional instruments, winds through the streets and enters the church, where the people continue to dance and play, singing the old refrain, '*St Marcel, les tripettes!*' [tripe]. On certain years a cow joins the fun – to its cost. Decked with ribbons, it is led through the town, blessed by a priest then slaughtered; the next day, after a high Mass, it is roasted on a spit in the main square, amid much Provençal festivity, and its meat is consumed by all. The origin of this odd episode is that in 1350 the saint's funeral cortège met some peasants who were ritually washing the entrails of a cow they had killed – hence the song about tripe.

Salernes This modest town 29 km west of Draguignan uses its clay deposits
83690 for the production of coloured enamel tiles, for bathrooms and other home uses. You can watch these tiles being made, and buy them if you wish, at some workshops: Emphoux and Polidori are among the best. Pierre Boutal, the largest firm, has a big salesroom and showroom, but its factory is not open to the public.

La Fontaine is a good, modestly-priced restaurant in the shady main square.

Villecroze A pleasant medieval village on a wooded hillside north-east of Salernes. In its outskirts, off the D51 to Tourtour, you can inspect the curious caves from which Villecroze (that is, *ville creusée*, 'hollow') takes its name: in the sixteenth century they were used as hide-outs by local seigneurs, and the windows they built in the rock are still visible. **La Marmite**, a pleasant medium-price rustic-style restaurant with a terrace, offers some local dishes.

Tourtour Just east of Villecroze, this ancient village stands on a hilltop amid
83690 woods of pine and cypress, oak and olive, with wide views all around.
Salernes Today it has been neatly restored and is something of a self-conscious showpiece, its façades of local golden stone all scraped clean; there are several fancy hotels nearby, and a new upmarket holiday estate of bijou villas, St Pierre. The two giant elms in the main village square, planted in 1638 to mark the birth of Louis XIV, are just as they always were. There are fêtes on the first Sunday in August and 4 September.

Where to stay **La Bastide de Tourtour**, Route de Draguignan; tel. 94 70 57 30.
Top price Set in its own wooded park, this recently-built château-like hotel is

stylish but a shade pretentious, with baronial fittings such as old tapestries. Large cheerful bedrooms (25), many with good views; large swimming pool too. Unusual collection of 200 peasant bonnets and hats. Open March to October.

Medium price

Auberge de St Pierre; tel. 94 70 57 17. This eighteenth-century stone-floored manor is now an unusual hotel (15 rooms), set amid the meadows of its huge home farm where horses, cows and gazelles graze. The owners, the Marcellins, believe in local tradition: there are *santons* everywhere, and a mossy fountain in the dining-room. The former chapel is now a television salon. Open April to September.

Where to eat
Top price

La Bastide de Tourtour (see above). Refined versions of local dishes, served stylishly in the heavily vaulted dining-room or out on the lovely terrace.

Upper-
medium price

Auberge de St Pierre (see above). The cuisine is 'biological' (organic), and the Provençal dishes, often unusual, taste delicious. Dinner is served to residents only.

Aups

A big village in the wilder part of the upper Var, with quaint old streets and remains of ramparts. It's an odd place to find a Museum of Modern Art, installed in a former Ursuline convent: 250 paintings, many from the Ecole de Paris. Alas, few are much good.

To the north and north-west of Aups the scenery of the Var changes sharply. The pastoral vine-clad valleys and gentle hills of the Draguignan/Salernes sector give way to a much wilder landscape of broad plateaus covered with scrub and gnarled trees, stretching towards the deep gorges of the Verdon.

Moissac-
Bellevue
Where to stay
Medium price

Small hilltop village in rolling *garrigue* country.

Hôtel Le Calalou; tel. 94 70 17 91. Characterful old *mas*, well converted; good food, nice pool. 38 rooms. Open March to November.

Comps-sur-
Artuby and
Trigance

These two villages to the east of the Verdon gorges are separated from Draguignan by the big military camp of Canjuers. The views of the encircling bare mountains are austerely majestic. A grey limestone thirteenth-century church, in early Gothic style, stands on a hill outside Comps.

Where to stay
and eat
Upper-
medium price

Château de Trigance; tel. 94 76 91 18. A battlemented medieval pile on a spiky hill, not easy of access, but stylishly converted into a small (10 rooms) château-hotel by its jovial ex-Parisian owner, Jean-Claude Thomas. Canopied beds; fairly good varied food in the atmospheric vaulted restaurant. Open April to October.

Inexpensive

Grand Hôtel Bain, Comps; tel. 94 76 90 06. Not a large spa hotel as its name might imply, but a modest country inn, run by the friendly Bain family since 1737. Bedrooms simple but serviceable; good food and smiling service. Closed mid-November to end December.

Upper Provence: Gorges du Verdon, Digne, Sisteron and Manosque

This is the northernmost stretch of the central Provençal hinterland, a wild, spreading region of grandiose vistas. Just west of the vast Verdon gorge is the porcelain-making town of Moustiers, and further north is Sisteron with its spectacular citadel. Across the Durance we come to the *pays* of that wonderful writer Jean Giono, whose novels are suffused with the spirit of rural Provence: his vision is utterly different from Pagnol's.

Grand Canyon du Verdon

Few landscapes in Europe are as dramatically impressive as this mighty canyon, 700 m deep and 21 km long, formed by an ancient fault in the wide limestone plateau of upper Provence. The River Verdon surges through it, on its way from the high Alps to join the Durance. The riverbed is impassable: but along the clifftops, tourist roads wind on both sides, and there are spots where you can park safely and then gaze giddily into the depths below. You must drive cautiously, for the roads are not wide and in some parts there are no railings. To avoid driving on the cliff side of the road, those wary of heights had best take the north road from east to west or the south road from west to east.

You can approach the canyon from Castellane or Comps to the east, or from Moustiers or Aups to the west. Along the north side, coming from the east, the first good view is at the Point Sublime. Further on, you can turn left along the Route des Crêtes with its fifteen belvederes above the gorge. Or else – if you fancy a dizzily exciting hike – you can park at the Point Sublime and take a footpath that winds down the cliff and along a series of ledges above the river, rejoining the Route des Crêtes at the Châlet de la Malène. This eight-hour trek can be made in either direction. It is only for hardy, experienced hikers unafraid of heights; they should take climbing boots, warm clothes and torches, for there are many tunnels. The bed of the canyon can be tackled only by trained mountaineers with an official guide.

On the south side, the road from Moustiers winds up first to **Aiguines**, a village whose attractive seventeenth-century château has four pepperpot towers and a polychromatic tiled roof; there are good views over the long artificial Lac de Ste Croix, a widening of the Verdon that has a hydro-electric dam at its far end. The road climbs up past the Cirque de Vaumale, then follows the Corniche Sublime, with splendid views at the Falaise des Cavaliers. The finest viewpoint is at the Balcons de la Mescla, just beyond the Pont de l'Artuby, where

Gorges du Verdon, Var

you look down vertically to the point where the Verdon and Artuby gorges meet.

Moustiers-Ste-Marie
04360

Popular with visitors, this old village north-west of the canyon is set dramatically at the foot of a deep ravine, between whose cliffs there hangs a 210-m iron chain with a glittering star in its middle: it was placed there by a local knight, on his return from the Crusades after a long captivity.

Moustiers, however, is famous less for this oddity than for its faience, based on rich local clay deposits. An Italian monk is said to have brought the secret of its white glaze from eponymous Faenza. The pottery industry flourished at Moustiers in the seventeenth and eighteenth centuries, then declined, but has been revived since the 1920s. Its porcelain, mostly white and pale blue, rather expensive and not always of good quality, is on sale at shops in the village; the museum of pottery has a display going back to the seventeenth century. You should also climb up inside the ravine to the chapel of Notre-Dame which has a Romanesque porch and tower and a sculptured Renaissance door. **Les Santons**, tel. 92 74 66 48, is a good traditional restaurant, fairly expensive.

Riez

Fifteen km west of Moustiers, Riez was once a busy Roman settlement, then a major centre of early Christianity. Now it is just a pleasant little town, but a few relics of its great days remain. Alone in a meadow on its west side there stand, somewhat incongruously, the four Corinthian columns of a Roman temple, probably Apollo's. And just across the river, beside the D952 to Allemagne, is one of the oldest surviving Christian buildings in France – a small fifth-century Merovingian baptistry not unlike those as Fréjus and Aix (see pp. 133 and 218). Its hexagonal interior has eight columns, with marble capitals. It is lit up at night, and you can easily inspect it from across the barred gate without needing to go inside. A board gives historical details.

Riez, and the village of **Valensole** to its west, lie in the middle of a broad flat plateau, a contrast to the generally hilly Provençal hinterland. This is France's main lavender-growing area, best seen in July when the fields are a blaze of purple.

Digne
04000

As fans of the smash-hit rock musical may know, it was at Digne that Valjean stole the bishop's candlesticks in the opening scenes of Victor Hugo's *Les Misérables*. Today this capital of the Alpes-de-Haute-Provence department (population 16,391) is as dignified a town as its name implies, popular with elderly *curistes* for its thermal baths are good for rheumatism. The Blvd. Gassendi, shaded with tall plane trees, is close to a picturesque pedestrian zone of narrow streets. The municipal museum has items of local natural history, such as butterflies, and some mediocre paintings. Of much more interest is the former cathedral of Notre-Dame-du-Bourg, a yellowish twelfth-to thirteenth-century building in the north-eastern outskirts, now used only for funerals. It has a façade in Lombard style and a graceful Romanesque nave.

Digne holds a lavender fair in early September.

Where to stay
Medium price

Grand Paris, 19 Blvd. Thiers; tel. 92 31 11 15. A seventeenth-century monastery, now a clean and quiet little hotel of character, though the decor is a bit sombre; 27 rooms.

Inexpensive

Coin Fleuri, 9 Blvd. Victor-Hugo; tel. 92 31 04 51. Friendly little Logis de France, quite central, good food; 15 rooms. Open March to October.

Where to eat
Upper-
medium price

Grand Paris (see above). Excellent traditional cooking. The dining-room is formal, but when the weather is fine you can eat out on a lovely shady terrace. Closed January, February, Sunday night, Monday.

Château-
Arnoux

This small town (population 5,662), with a ruined medieval château, lies on the Durance 25 km west of Digne, at the junction of the main roads from Marseille and Nice to Grenoble. The wide valley here is ugly, for the river flows torpidly between mud-flats in the dry season, and the industrial plant – notably the huge electro-chemical works at St Auban – hardly improves matters. But to the north-east is the picturesque hill village of **Volonne**, also with a high-towered feudal castle; and across the river to the south are the bizarre limestone pinnacles of Les Mées.

Where to stay
and eat
Upper-
medium price

La Bonne Etape, Chemin du Lac; tel. 92 64 00 09. A seventeenth-century coaching inn, luxuriously and stylishly converted, owned and run by the friendly anglophile Gleize family. The main-road setting is a bit cramped (front rooms can be noisy), but at the back are open fields. Sumptuous bedrooms (11) in period style; lovely patio and heated pool. In the elegant dining-room, the cooking is among the very finest in Provence – light and subtle variations on regional dishes. Closed one week November, January and early February, Sunday night and Monday out of season.

Sisteron
04200

Located at a point where the Durance drives its way through a defile between rocky peaks, ancient Sisteron (population 6,572) forms a natural gateway to Provence from the north. So it's little surprise that it possesses a mighty citadel, perched on a peak just opposite the jagged precipice of La Baume.

Sisteron was heavily bombed by the Allies on the day of the landings in Provence, 15 August 1944, because German troops were occupying the citadel: some 400 people died, many of them civilians, and many old houses were destroyed. So parts of the town are now modern, though a few medieval streets remain between the Place du Dr-Robert and the river. Here, at 20 Rue Saunerie, is the house where Bonaparte breakfasted on his return from Elba along the Route Napoléon. Three isolated towers stand as relics of the fourteenth-century ramparts, next to the former cathedral of Notre-Dame, which is twelfth-century Romanesque with Lombard influences.

The Citadel | Henri IV called this massive structure 'the most powerful fortress in my kingdom': its upper ramparts are twelfth century, while the lower ones were reinforced by Vauban in the seventeenth. It's worth making the steep climb to the top, if only for the view from the upper terrace that takes in the Dauphiné Alps to the north and shows strikingly that Sisteron has always been a natural frontier-point. You should also inspect the **Tour de l'Horloge**, once a prison, and the remarkable **Guérite du Diable** (devil's watchtower), perched giddily above the river. On top of the rock, the fifteenth-century Gothic chapel was destroyed in the 1944 bombing but has since been rebuilt, with attractive stained glass. The guardroom at the citadel's entrance, where French patriots were held captive by the Germans, is now a museum of the local Resistance. On summer nights the citadel is impressively floodlit.

What to do | An open-air theatre on the north slope of the citadel's hill is the venue for a drama and dance festival, mid-July to mid-August.

Where to stay
Medium price | **Grand Hôtel du Cours**, Place de l'Eglise; tel. 92 61 04 51. There are 50 rooms and no restaurant.

Tivoli, Place du Tivoli; tel. 92 61 15 16. Somewhat cheaper than the Grand Hôtel, it has 19 rooms and a restaurant.

Giono country | Jean Giono (1895-1970), the novelist, spent most of his life in Manosque (see p. 180): but it was in the wild country to the north-west of the town that he set many of his best-known books, which evoke so poetically his feeling for nature, for the landscapes of upper Provence and the life of its peasantry. As a young man he had a job with a bank that involved touring the hilly area around the village of Banon. Later, during the summers of 1935 to 1939, Giono and a group of friends held a series of much-publicised seminars or non-religious retreats, on the themes of ecology and pacifism, in the remote hamlet of **Contadour** up on a glorious plateau between Banon and the Montagne de Lure. The old stone farmhouse that they bought is still there, just south of the hamlet; nearby is a *ferme auberge* that will feed and lodge you at modest cost. Wild, lovely and almost totally unpopulated, it's a great area for upland hiking and for imbuing oneself with Giono's back-to-nature ideals. (But, considering that Giono was such an ardent pacifist, it's a savage irony that today France's leading nuclear missile base is a mere 10 km away, on the Plateau d'Albion to the south-west).

Regain (1930), his remarkable novel about a young peasant and his girl who triumphantly build a new life in an abandoned hill village, was based in part on the deserted hillside hamlet of Redortiers, just south of Contadour, and also on Carniols, south of Banon. A scene in the book takes place at Banon market, still held weekly.

Forcalquier
04300 | Splendidly set on a steep hillside, overlooking luxuriant countryside, this venerable town (population 3,790) was an independent state in the twelfth century, and later the capital of upper Provence and a major cultural and economic centre. Today it's an unassuming place,

but full of very diverse interest. The thirteenth-century Couvent des Cordeliers, one of the first Franciscan monasteries in France, contains a museum of early religious art. There's another small museum in the town hall, opposite the Romanesque twelfth-century church of Notre-Dame. In the narrow Rue d'Orléans, in striking contrast to these antiquities, is a modern art centre that puts on enterprising exhibitions. The cemetery up the hill to the north has lines of tall box-hedges of clipped yew, forming archways – an unusual sight in France.

Where to stay and eat Medium price

Hostellerie des Deux Lions, 11 Place du Bourget; tel. 92 75 25 30. A delightful coaching inn with rustic-style rooms, very friendly owners and excellent local dishes, plus an unusually wide range of cheeses. Open March to mid-November; closed Monday out of season.

Lure and Lurs

There are interesting places all around Forcalquier. To the north, beyond St Etienne, a road zig-zags up through dense forest to the crest of the long ridge of the Montagne de Lure: here a stiff fifteen-minute walk from the road will bring you to the Signal de Lure (1,826 m), where the panoramic views as far as the coast and the Cévennes are fantastic. South-west of Forcalquier is the Observatoire de Haute-Provence, a State-run astronomical centre whose site was chosen for the purity of the air (it is open to visits only occasionally: enquire locally). And down in the Durance Valley east of the town is the spot on the main road by the village of Lurs where the Drummond family, from Nottingham, were murdered while camping in 1954. Suspicion fell on an elderly local farmer, Gaston Dominici, who was tried, but never found guilty.

Manosque
04100

A lively market town (population 19,546) on a slope above the Durance. A circular boulevard now replaces the old ramparts, of which two fortified fourteenth-century gateways survive: the tall Porte de Saunerie is impressive, especially when floodlit at night. The *vieille ville* is a maze of narrow streets, some closed to traffic, and has two twelfth-century churches. Jean Giono was born and died in Manosque, and lived there for thirty-nine years – on a hill in the outskirts, down a road now suitably called le Chemin des Vraies Richesses (the title of one of his books). His aged widow lives there still, and the house is due to become a museum after her death.

Where to stay and eat Upper-medium price

Hostellerie de la Fuste; tel. 92 72 05 95. Across the Durance, 6 km east of Manosque on the D4, this seventeenth-century coaching inn, set in its own park, is now a famous and stylish luxury restaurant, with clientèle to match. Patron/chef Daniel Jourdan gives his own interpretation to classic local dishes. There are nine spacious bedrooms. Closed January, early February, and Monday out of season.

Where to stay Medium price

Campanile, Route de Volx; tel. 92 87 59 00. Well-run, comfortable modern motel in the eastern outskirts; meals and buffet breakfasts; 30 rooms.

Inexpensive

François Premier, 18 Rue Guilhempierre; tel. 92 72 07 99. A clean little commercial hotel, with obliging service. No restaurant; 25 rooms.

South-east of Manosque is the little spa-town of **Gréoux-les-Bains**, which has soothed rheumatism and arthritis since Roman times. Downstream on the Durance is the Cadarache hydro-electric dam, next to a big nuclear research centre; and upstream, the village of **Volx** is overlooked by a looming white rock.

The Lubéron

The Lubéron, full of unlikely curiosities, is one of the most appealing corners of Provence, and in many ways my own favourite. It consists of a beautiful range of hills that runs for some 55 km between the Coulon Valley to the north and the Durance to the south. The higher and wilder stretch to the east, the Grand Lubéron, is a national park: from the village of Auribeau you can hike up on foot to the peak of Mourre Nègre (1,100 m) for a splendid view stretching from the Alps to the Rhône. The Petit Lubéron, west of the Apt-Lourmarin road, is a gentler region – a fertile plateau with vineyards, lavender fields and

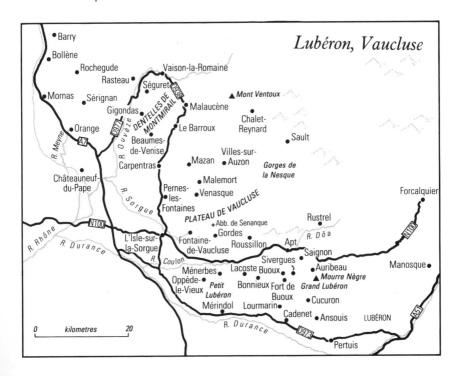

beehives for honey. The northern slopes of the Lubéron are covered with a marvellous variety of trees, mostly deciduous, such as oaks, poplars and cherries. The landscape is lovely from spring through to autumn, but brown and more sombre in winter. The southern slopes are warmer in winter and more meridional, with conifers and olive trees. A scenic road follows the crest of the hills, from Bonnieux down to Cavaillon, past a forest of giant cedars.

An early Protestant sect, the Vaudois, who had somewhat similar beliefs to the Cathars (see p. 14), used the Lubéron as their stronghold from the twelfth to sixteenth centuries. Their main settlements were at Sivergues, south of Apt, and at Mérindol, west of Lourmarin. Though devout, these 'heretics' were sometimes violent and would pillage churches in the area. Finally, in 1540 François I launched a Crusade against them, which was enthusiastically taken up locally by the cruel Baron Meynier of Oppède, and by 1545 over 3,000 Vaudois had been tortured, massacred or sent to the galleys.

Today the Lubéron attracts a different kind of settler: it has become just about the most popular part of Provence for actors, intellectuals, politicans and others, from Paris and elsewhere, who have bought summer homes here, in and around Bonnieux, Ménerbes and other hill villages. One of them is the English writer Peter Mayle, who lives near Ménerbes and has given his own quizzical view of the local scene in his best-selling books, *A Year in Provence* and *Toujours Provence*. Naturally, this invasion has greatly altered the Lubéron's social character. However, although old houses can be converted, no new building is permitted: so the villages have preserved their outward aspect. This restriction has pushed up house prices, adding to the area's trendiness.

Almost all of the many villages in the Lubéron are attractive and worth a visit. The main ones on the north side, east to west, are given below.

Saignon
84400 Apt

An old hill village on a promontory beside a high rock. The Romanesque church, restored in the sixteenth century, has bricked-up 'blind' arches. La Mandragoule, in the tiny main square, sells good local pottery. Broux, nearby, makes and sells leatherwork – you can watch the craftsmen at work in the shop.

Where to stay
Rock-bottom
price

Regain, 3 km to the south-east of Saignon, off the Auribeau road (signposted); tel. 90 74 39 34. This is one of the oddest recommendations in this book. In fact it's a youth hostel, but an unusual one, for the young-in-heart of all ages, and it's famous across Europe. Its owner is the veteran François Morenas, a droll and engaging character, former friend and disciple of Giono, and he runs it on Gionesque lines (hence the name, *Regain*). The hotel attracts Paris intellectuals, German Greens and the like, who will happily debate with you into the night, about nature, ecology and the joys and woes of our age. It's an old farmhouse, built into the rock down a steep hillside in the middle of nowhere, simply but attractively converted, its walls lined with Madame Claude Morenas' remarkable paintings. Solidly rural food is served. François, a great film buff, has an indoor and an outdoor cinema and a fantastic collection of old feature films, which he shows regularly. In summer, you can watch a Pagnol rural comedy projected against the backdrop of a real Pagnolesque landscape, so that the two merge – a magical experience.

Fort de Buoux

The D113 turning off the Apt-Lourmarin road leads east into the wild heart of the Grand Lubéron, past a tall Romanesque bell-tower that survives from the priory of St Symphorien. A little further on, in the wooded gorge of the Aigebrun, there are Palaeolithic cave dwellings, as well as all-too-modern workers' holiday dwellings owned by the Ville de Marseille. Up on the rocks above, reached by a stiff thirty-minute climb, stands the ruined fortress of Buoux, a haunting place. This natural defence point was used in turn by Ligurians, Romans and Vaudois, then destroyed on the orders of Louis XIV. Its relics include a Ligurian sacrifice stone, a keep, and silos hewn out of the rock.

Where to eat
Medium price

Auberge de la Loube; tel. 90 74 19 58. In the nearby village of Buoux, a delightful place run by Parisians, serving good local dishes. Closed January and Thursday. The owners also have some old horse-drawn carriages in which they will take you on excursions.

Bonnieux
84840

A large and animated village on a spur, with good views to the north. Its twelfth-century church is now seldom used; down the hill is a large nineteenth-century one, rather ugly, but worth a visit for the four fifteenth-century German paintings, formerly in the old church, which stand behind the altar and depict the martyrdom of Christ. Looking fresh and new, they are painted on wood panels in vivid greens and reds. At 12 Rue de la République, an old bakery has just been turned into the remarkable Musée de la Boulangerie, full of documents on the history of bread-making, such as old letters relating to a lawsuit that began in 1429 and went on for centuries. There are antique ovens, and examples of unusual loaves.

Where to stay
Upper-medium price

L'Aigebrun; tel. 90 74 04 14. In an isolated spot just off the Apt-Lourmarin road, 6 km south-east of Bonnieux, a small nineteenth-century manor beside a stream has been turned into a most beguiling hotel, now under friendly new owners. It's run more like a private home: a lounge with country antiques, a log fire blazing, classical music playing. Nice bedrooms (8), and utter peace. Open mid-March to mid-November.

Inexpensive

César, Place de la Liberté; tel. 90 75 80 18. A friendly little hostelry (11 rooms) on the main street.

Where to eat
Upper-medium price

L'Aigebrun (see above). Very good food, served outside by the river when fine. Reasonable set menu, but the *carte* is over-priced.

Lower-medium price

César (see above). A lively and attractive local meeting place, offering good food at fair prices.

Lacoste

This pleasant hill village is dominated by the ruins of a castle, part eleventh-century, that for long belonged to the de Sade family. The infamous Marquis (1740–1814) lived here for thirty years and has described it in *Cent-vingt jours de Sodom* and other writings; he would take refuge here, after his spells in prison for sexual crimes. After the Revolution the castle was sacked, but the ruins are now open to visitors, and the present owner or his guides will gladly show you where the Sadist orgies took place. More wholesome fun is provided by the summer concerts in the village, and in a nearby quarry. Lacoste is home to an American art school, and the life of the village has been candidly described by a former teacher there, Michael Jacobs, in his book *A Guide to Provence* (1988).

Ménerbes

Strung out along the spur of a hill, Ménerbes is a beautiful and very fashionable village, packed full of artists and art lovers, such as Dora Maar, the Yugoslav photographer who was Picasso's mistress. There is an old castle, and at the far end of the spur a small fourteenth-century church in a lovely, quiet setting.

Where to eat
Medium price

Pascal; tel. 90 72 22 13. A down-to-earth auberge near the village centre with a shady garden and plain dining-rooms, serving good, copious lunches (no dinners) to hungry locals. Open Easter to October.

Oppède-le-Vieux

One of the most curious of all the curious places in the Lubéron, this old village stands on a limestone crag below its ruined twelfth-century castle. By 1910 it was totally abandoned, when its last inhabitants moved to Oppède-les-Poulivets down in the valley. Then in the 1940s a group of artists and architects, including Antoine de St-Exupéry's widow, began to take over some of the semi-ruined houses and restore them for their own use – some decades before this practice became as fashionable as it is today in Provence. So the ghost-village has come back to life: in its rough cobbled alleys, tastefully restored homes alternate with dilapidated ruins too far gone to be repaired. But happily there are still very few boutiques or souvenir shops. The much-restored twelfth-century church is worth a visit, and so is the over-grown château.

The main villages along the Lubéron's south side, west to east, are given below.

Lourmarin
84160
Cadenet

An attractive village in the valley, just below the point where the main road to Apt winds up through a gorge on to the plateau. Albert Camus lived here for three years before dying in a car crash near Paris in 1960; he lies buried in the cemetery. The Provençal novelist Henri Bosco also had a house nearby, and has described the area in *Le Mas Théotime* (1944) and other books.

The stately château on the edge of the village, part Renaissance, part earlier, is notable for its splendid stairway and decorated fireplaces. It was bought and restored in the 1920s by an art-loving industrialist, Laurent Vibert, who imposed his own eclectic taste – Chinese musical instruments, Spanish furniture, and other items still on display for visitors. The château holds concerts in summer, and runs residential courses for young artists.

Where to eat   In the village, **Ollier** is smart and fairly expensive, **Le Bistro** is cheaper and has Lyonnais specialities, while **Le Récré** is cheap and fun, with an outdoor terrace.

Cucuron   The church with its Romanesque nave and Gothic apse has a sixteenth-century painted wooden pietà and an eighteenth-century marble altarpiece. Nearby is a small museum of local folklore and archaeology. Cucuron features in one of Daudet's funny stories in *Lettres de mon Moulin* when the curé of Cucuron who goes to look for his parishioners in Heaven finds that they are all in Hell.

Ansouis   This old village amid wooded hills is surmounted by the interesting Château de Sabran: it has belonged to the same ducal Sabran family since the thirteenth century, and today it is long-serving family servants who show you round. The northern part is medieval and fortress-like, the south façade is elegant Renaissance, while all around are formal eighteenth-century hanging gardens. Inside, some rooms still have a medieval aspect, others are eighteenth-century in decor: note the Flemish tapestries in the dining-hall and the fine Provençal kitchen, still in use.

The old Romanesque village church, fixed to the castle walls, was originally its court of justice. Nearby is the **Musée Extraordinaire**, which fully lives up to its name: it belongs to a Marseillais, Georges Mazoyer, who loves sea-diving; and beside some curious pieces of old furniture it includes his own bizarre marine paintings, some rare seashells and shellfish, and the weirdest of sub-marine grottoes. It's all somewhat surprising for a hill village. But then, as we've seen, anything can be expected in the Lubéron.

Below the Vaucluse plateau: Apt, Roussillon and Gordes

The limestone Plateau de Vaucluse, wild and hilly, part barren, part thickly forested, stands opposite the Lubéron on the north side of the broad and fertile valley of the Coulon. Along its southern flank are a number of interesting places – the hill villages of Gordes and Roussillon, the superb Cistercian abbey of Sénanque, the Fontaine de Vaucluse where Petrarch nursed his hopeless love for Laura, and – especially fascinating – the double museum of stained glass and of olive oil, just south of Gordes.

Apt   This busy little town (population 11,560) in the broad Coulon
84400   Valley has a lively market on Saturdays and makes candied fruits and

lavender essence; the new high-rise apartment blocks on its hillsides are used by Army personnel who work at the Plateau d'Albion missile base.

In Roman days, too, Apt was a military centre, named 'Colonia Julia Apta' after Julius Caesar, and Roman traces remain today: beneath the *sub-préfecture* are Roman baths, while vestiges of the arena can be reached underground from the museum of archaeology (this has Roman coins, oil lamps, sarcophagi and other objects found locally, as well as Provençal faïence).

Another Roman relic lies 8 km west of Apt, just off the N100 – the **Pont Julien**, a fine triple-arched bridge across the Coulon, on the old Domitian Way from Italy to Spain.

Above all, Apt is associated with Ste Anne, mother of the Virgin, whose body, according to legend, was brought here. The former cathedral of Ste Anne, in the old part of town, has a fourteenth-century stained-glass window representing the saint, and a reliquary bust of her in a side-chapel. In the sacristy is the so-called 'shroud of Ste Anne', in reality an eleventh-century Arab standard brought from the First Crusade. The sacristy also houses many other treasures, including early medieval manuscripts and enamelled reliquaries. The church's lower crypt is pre-Romanesque, one of the oldest Christian buildings in France.

A pilgrimage of Ste Anne is held on the last Sunday in July.

Where to stay
Inexpensive
Colorado
de Rustel

Aptois Hôtel, 6 Cours Lauze de Perret; tel. 90 74 02 02. Central, suitable for a night stop. 26 rooms. No restaurant. Closed February.

Twelve km north-east of Apt, near the village of Rustrel, are these huge ochre quarries, mostly abandoned; some are in strange shapes, such as the *'cheminées de fées'* (fairies' chimney stacks). To visit, leave your car by the River Dôa, off the D22, and follow the yellow arrows for thirty minutes.

Roussillon
84220 Gordes

This very pretty hilltop village is the main centre of the ochre country, which extends also to Apt. All around are russet rocks, ochre quarries still in use, and expanses of pine and heather with their roots in the red earth. Roussillon ('russet') has houses built of local stone in many shades of red, pink and orange. The quarrying has produced cliffs in bizarre shapes, given coy names such as 'Needles of the Fairy Vale' and 'Giants' Causeway': you can visit them by taking a path from the main car-park.

The American sociologist William Wylie, who lived in Roussillon, made it the subject of his famous book *Village in the Vaucluse*. He charted the impact of the modern world on a warm but somnolent peasant community. Roussillon today, somnolent no more, has become a trendy residential centre for writers and artists, and teems with summer visitors.

What to do

There's a 'festival of ochre and colour' on Ascension weekend, a local fête on the last Sunday in July, and a market every Wednesday.

Exhibitions by artists are frequent, while the Galér'e des Ochres at the top of the village sells some good local pottery, notably by Gisèle Buthod-Garçon.

Where to stay
Upper-
medium price

Mas de Garrigon; tel. 90 05 63 22. Three km out on the St-Saturnin road, a delightfully converted old farmhouse, with rooms (7) in Provençal style, a fine swimming pool, good cooking and lovely views.

Medium price

Résidence des Ochres, Route de Gordes; tel. 90 05 60 50. A comfortable, modern, family-run hotel (15 rooms). No restaurant. Closed February, mid-November to mid-December.

Where to eat
Medium price

Tarasque, Rue R.-Casteau; tel. 90 05 63 86. A woman ex-journalist from Lorraine serves good Provençal food at this charming rustic restaurant; pretty terrace. Closed Wednesday, mid-February to mid-March.

Gordes
84220

Gordes (population 1,607), one of the biggest and best known of Provençal hill villages, stands visible from afar on a rocky spur above the Coulon Valley, its stone terraced houses rising up to a Renaissance castle. It was badly damaged in August 1944, when the Germans blew up many old houses in retaliation for an attack by the Resistance, but it has since been restored. Gordes has been popular with artists since the 1930s, when the Cubist André Lhote began to come here, and today more than ever it attracts the Paris intelligentsia in summer. Various craftsmen work here too.

What to see
Château and
Musée
Vasarély

Though austere-looking from without, the fortified château has a true Renaissance elegance within, with a fine gateway, ornate mouldings and chimneypiece. The Hungarian-born artist Victor de Vasarély, who spends the summers at Gordes, restored the building recently in return for permission to install in it his Musée Didactique – and indeed it *is* even more didactic than his Fondation at Aix (see p. 219). Automatic sliding panels expound his theories, notably in two rooms full of his brightly-coloured geometric designs in the form of mosaics and tapestries – a feast for those who admire this idiosyncratic artist. An upper room is devoted to his more figurative Picasso-like work of the 1930s.

Village des
Bories

Borie is the local name for a beehive-shaped hut made of rough stones without mortar, and in Provence you find them, standing singly or in clusters, on the north slopes of the Lubéron and the south slopes of the Vaucluse plateau. None of the extant ones is older than the eighteenth century, but there is evidence that similar *bories* existed in Megalithic times and were in fact an early kind of Provençal man-made habitation. Newer ones continued to be inhabited until the early nineteenth century: and it is thought that they were sometimes used by town-dwellers fleeing the plague. But their full history remains a bit of a mystery. The Village des Bories, down a rough track 3 km south-west of Gordes, is a group of a dozen huts now converted into a museum of traditional rural life.

Moulin des Bouillons and Musée du Vitrail

A remarkable place. Here, 5 km south of Gordes on the Beaumettes road, are two museums in one, both unusual and fascinating but entirely different, and owned by the stained-glass artist Frédérique Duran. The Moulin des Bouillons is an ancient olive-oil mill that has existed on this spot since Roman times and was even described by Pliny the Elder (it was the Romans in the first century AD who brought the cultivation of the olive into Provence). The stone floor of the mill and the base of the olive press are Gallo-Roman, though the giant oak of the press itself dates from the fifteenth-century when the wood needed to be changed; close to it is a circular fifteenth-century olive crusher, which was horse-drawn. In this sixteenth-century building the history of olive cultivation is beautifully set out.

In the lovely garden, Madame Durand has created a small museum of stained-glass that charts its history and manufacture across the centuries and also displays some of her own colourful works (she has pioneered new techniques). Everything is clearly explained, and sometimes the artist herself is present to contribute her own forceful enthusiasm.

What to do

Gordes has a market on Tuesdays, and a theatre and music festival in the first half of August. The Aumonerie St-Jacques, an old alms-house behind the church, holds interesting temporary exhibitions. L'Atelier, in the Rue Baptista-Picca, sells curious locally-made jewellery and other trinkets.

Where to stay
Medium price

La Mayanelle, Route de la Combe; tel. 90 72 00 28. In an old house built on the cliff with views over the valley, a friendly, unpretentious little hotel (10 rooms) with a wide sunny terrace and a salon/bar in antique style. Sound regional cooking. Closed January, February.

Where to eat
Top price

Les Bories, Route de Sénanque; tel. 90 72 00 51. Believe it or not, a group of *bories* just north of Gordes has been transformed into a chic and comfortable restaurant serving some of the best food in the area. There are four sleek bedrooms, too. Closed December, Wednesday, lunchtime on Thursday, Friday, Saturday, evenings on Sunday, Monday, Tuesday.

Medium price

La Renaissance, next to the castle, with tables out on the square, provides good local dishes such as daube and aïoli.

Abbey of Sénanque

Sénanque, set alone in a wild and narrow valley, 4 km north of Gordes, is one of Provence's three superb Cistercian abbeys (see also Silvacane and Le Thoronet, pp. 222 and 171) and illustrates the Order's love of isolated sites. Built in 1148, it is also the best preserved of the three, maybe because its history has been the calmest: its one grave drama was in 1544, when it was attacked and damaged by Protestants from the Lubéron, but it was later restored. It was sold at the Revolution, but the Cistercians bought it back in 1854, and they still own and run it today.

The arcaded cloister, the chapterhouse and monks' dormitory, with their Romanesque arcaded ceilings, are all delightful. The large harmonious church is typically bare of decoration: but its carpets and rows of new chairs indicate that today it is very much in use. In fact, despite its remote location, Sénanque is full of activity, for it houses a busy cultural centre, both lay and religious. There are medieval concerts, mainly of Gregorian music; lectures and study groups; and exhibitions of modern art. In the old refectory is a display of Cistercian history and a remarkable sequence of 'symbolic photographs' that counterpoints unusual landscapes with philosophical and biblical quotations.

Most important, the Centre for Saharan Studies has an excellent museum here, with details of life and art of the Touareg tribe, and of the Tassili N'Ajjer cave paintings. All in all, Sénanque's ambience contrasts strikingly with that of its two sisters, enclosed in their ancient spiritual stillness.

Fontaine de Valcluse
84800 L'Isle-sur-la-Sorgue

Over a million visitors come each year to this famous spot west of Gordes, where the River Sorgue surges up from a cavern below a limestone cliff. In the dry season there's really not much to see: but in winter or spring, notably after heavy rain or when the snows are melting, the 'fountain' is a mighty spectacle. It is a short walk from the ultra-touristy village of the same name, where little now remains of the romantic serenity that enticed the Italian poet Petrarch to spent sixteen years here, from 1337 to 1353, brooding over his beloved Laura (see p. 200). On the site of his house is a small museum with manuscripts of his poems and many pictures of Laura. There's also a speleological museum (with fine stalactites), a ruined hilltop castle, and a Romanesque church that holds the tomb of St Véran, a sixth-century bishop who rid the village of a monster.

What to do

Son et lumière is held every evening at the fountain, mid-June to mid-September.

Where to stay and eat Lower-medium price

Hostellerie du Château; tel. 90 20 31 54. Pleasant old hostelry beside the river, with a shady terrace and good food. 5 rooms.

L'Isle-sur-la-Sorgue
84800

The River Sorgue here divides into five branches, making this delightful market town (population 13,205) into a place of running streams and grassy, tree-lined banks. The seventeenth-century church has a lavish Baroque interior, rare in Provence; the old hospital has eighteenth-century wood-carvings in its chapel; and the house at 20 Rue du Docteur-Tallet holds ambitious art shows. The poet René Char (1907-88) was born and spent most of his life in the town, and wrote about it.

What to do

In July a *festival de la Sorgue* (music, theatre, dance) is held in this town and four nearby villages. There's a lively flea market on Sundays, good for antiques.

Where to stay

Hostellerie de la Grangette; tel. 90 20 00 77. Six km to the north

Upper-medium price

on the Carpentras road, alone in open country, this finely-converted manor has oak beams, antiques, sophisticated food and courteous service, as well as a swimming-pool and tennis.

Inexpensive

Pescador, Partage des Eaux; tel. 90 38 09 69. One-star Logis de France in the outskirts; modest but comfortable; goodish food; 10 rooms. Closed December to mid-March.

Carpentras, Mont Ventoux and Vaison-la-Romaine

Roman colonial officers and patricians, like Parisian bourgeois today, liked to make country homes for themselves in the Vaucluse: hence, in the north of the department, the important Roman residential centre of Vaison, just below the windy heights of Mont Ventoux. The western foothills of this mountain are very beautiful, around the jagged Dentelles de Montmirail, and the edge of the plain has some of the very best Côte du Rhône vineyards, notably Gigondas. Don't miss the fountains of pretty Pernes, the seventh-century baptistry at Venasque and the quaint hill village of Séguret. And why not consider eating a dinner of wild boar *chez* a Parisian engineer up in the hills?

Carpentras
84200

This prosperous old market town (population 25,886) is full of interest. It is ringed by boulevards on the site of its medieval ramparts, of which nothing now survives save the Porte d'Orange. From 1320 until 1791 it was the capital of the Comtat Venaissin, an area east of the Rhône with much the same boundaries as modern Vaucluse, that was ceded to the Papacy in 1274 and not returned to France until the Revolution: it still preserves its individuality.

What to see
St Siffrein

This former cathedral has a richly decorated interior, with some notable works of art – to the left of the altar, a triptych of St Siffrein (the town's patron) from the fifteenth-century Avignon School; in the chapels of the north aisle, paintings by Mignard and Parrocel; gilded sculptures by Bernus behind the altar. The Trésor also holds precious objects. The west door is Renaissance, but the south door is flamboyant Gothic and is known as the Porte Juive, for Jewish converts passed through here to be baptised.

The synagogue

The town's former important Jewish colony began to be influential when Jews were financiers to the Avignon Popes: it then went into decline, but revived in the eighteenth century. The synagogue, opposite the town hall, reflects these fortunes. The oldest in France, it dates from 1327 and was rebuilt in the eighteenth century: it is still used today even though few Jews remain in Carpentras. It has a rich Rococo interior: note the purification baths and the oven for unleavened bread. In 1990 the Jewish cemetery was horribly desecrated by right-wing

Hôtel-Dieu

vandals, and all France was shocked.

This vast eighteenth-century building outside the ring boulevard is still used as a hospital: its main artistic interest is the Baroque chapel, also the Rococo pharmacy whose cupboards contain Moustiers porcelain and are covered with quaint paintings of monkeys.

Other sights

The Roman era at Carpentras is marked by a small triumphal arch beside the cathedral, decorated on one side with strange bas-reliefs of captives. Of the town's museums, the Musée Comtadin deals with local history and folk art, the Musée Duplessis has works by Provençal artists, while the Bibliothèque Inguimbert (not open to the public) houses the massive library of a famous local eighteenth-century scholar and cleric, Bishop Inguimbert.

What to do

There is an international theatre, music and opera festival (mostly Offenbach), mid-July to mid-August.

Shopping

The Friday morning open-air market is famous.

Where to stay
Medium price

Safari, Route d'Avignon; tel. 90 63 35 35, is a well-run modern hotel in the outskirts; its food is nothing special.

Where to eat
Inexpensive

L'Orangerie, 26 Rue Duplessis; tel. 90 67 27 23, and **La Rapière du Comtat**, 47 Blvd. du Nord; tel. 90 67 20 03, are superb value.

Pernes-les-Fontaines
84210

So named because it has no less than thirty-six fountains, most of them eighteenth-century, this delightful and historic old town (population 6,961) was the first capital of the papal Comtat, earlier than Carpentras. Some medieval walls and Renaissance gates survive: one of these, the Porte Notre-Dame, is charmingly set by a river bridge with a tiny sixteenth-century chapel on it. The Tour Ferrande, part of a former palace, contains on its upper floor some well-preserved thirteenth-century frescoes, which are not to be missed.

Venasque

Perched on a cliff on the edge of the Vaucluse plateau, south-west of Carpentras, the ancient village of Venasque preceded Carpentras as bishopric of the Venaissin, to which it gave its name. The thirteenth-century church has a fine fifteenth-century painting of the Crucifixion by the Avignon school. Next door is an old four-sided baptistry with slim marble columns: it possibly dates from the Merovingian period (seventh century), but was certainly rebuilt in the eleventh. It is beautifully set out for the visitor, with an intelligent guide, soft religious music playing, and clear explanations, including details about the mysterious St Siffrein.

Gorges de la Nesque

East of Carpentras, around Mazan and Malemort, there is large-scale quarrying of clay and gypsum. Beyond Villes-sur-Auzon, a scenic road climbs up through the wild gorge of La Nesque, past the jagged rock of Cire, and finally reaches **Sault**, a village on a rocky spur, known for its honey and lavender (it has a market on Wednesday).

Where to eat
Medium price

La Lauze; tel. 90 61 83 23. If you fancy eating wild boar, try this unusual restaurant 6 km east of Villes-sur-Auzon, along the D942 to Sault and then up a bumpy track on the left (watch out for the Asterix signboard). Raymond Cafournelle was a Paris engineer who tired of the rat-race, so he bought a tumbledown farm up in the wilds, where he now breeds little black *sangliers* (wild boar). His rustic auberge offers just roast *sanglier* on the set menu, but it's very good and the ambience is jolly. You can also go to inspect the herds of boar – *after* the meal, I suggest. There's *gîte* accommodation too.

Mont Ventoux

The lofty pyramid of Mont Ventoux has a symbolic power in western Provence and has fired the imagination of many of the region's writers, including Petrarch and Mistral, both of whom climbed to its summit. Rising to 1,900 m and visible from far away, it is Provence's highest peak apart from the Alps, and is the major south-westerly spur of the Alpine massif. Even in summer its white crest seems from afar to be snow-capped, but in fact this is limestone. Up near this crest you find alpine and even polar flora, such as the hairy Greenland poppy and the Spitzbergen saxifrage.

Today easy roads lead to the top, both from the west and the east. The drive is worth it, for on a clear day the panorama is stupendous, among the finest in France – from the Alps to the Cévennes, even to the Pyrenees on some days, while at night lighthouses can be seen flashing along the coast. In summer it is best to go in early morning or late afternoon, for at midday there is often haze. In winter the skies tend to be clearer, but this 'windy mount' is best avoided if the Mistral is blowing.

Near the summit are some humdrum modern tourist facilities such as snack bars; also a military radar post and a weather station. In winter you can ski at Mont-Serein or Chalet-Reynard. In some years during July the Tour de France cyclists must struggle to the very top (a roadside memorial marks the spot where England's Tom Simpson collapsed and died during the 1967 race).

Le Barroux
84330 Caromb

The little town of **Malaucène** (where there is an interesting Romanesque church) is the best starting point for excursions into Mont Ventoux. Six km to the south, just off the road to Carpentras, is the tiny unspoilt hill village of Le Barroux, topped by a massive Renaissance castle now much restored. The views are superb. Le Barroux is known for its pink apricots (there's an apricot market daily in July). On a hill to the north, the Benedictines are building a large unisex monastery/convent for monks and nuns. Remarkable.

Where to stay and eat
Inexpensive

Les Géraniums, Place de la Croix; tel. 90 62 41 08. A charming, unspoilt village auberge, run by friendly local people. The bedrooms (22) are small but comfortable, especially in the annexe. Good food is served in a beamed *salle* or on the terrace. Closed January, Wednesday.

Crillon-Le-Brave
Where to stay and eat
Upper-medium price

A small hill-village on the slopes of Mont Ventoux.

Hostellerie de Crillon-Le-Brave, Place de l'Église; tel. 90 65 61 61. A lovely old mansion stylishly converted, owned and run by a young Canadian ex-lawyer, Peter Chittick. Old beams and antiques, colourful Provençal fabrics, fine views, sophisticated ambience. Good food. 22 rooms. Closed January, February.

Dentelles de Montmirail

North of Carpentras, this spur of the Ventoux range consists of high toothy limestone crests – hence the name, 'lace-point'. They are a bold sight from the Rhône plain to the west. To their east you will find exceptionally lovely hilly landscapes, best seen from the road that winds from Malaucène to prettily-named **Beaumes-de-Venise**. It is good hiking country.

Gigondas
84190
Beaumes-de-Venise

This pretty village nestling in the foothills of the Dentelles produces some of the best, and best-known, Côtes-du-Rhône wine. One place you can visit for tasting and buying is the Château de Montmirail, Cours Stassart-Vacqueyras, tel. 90 65 86 72. The wines of Gigondas, both the red and the excellent but lesser-known white, are fairly dry. However, nearby Beaumes-de-Venise produces a sweetish muscat wine, which you can taste and buy at the Château Redortier, tel. 90 62 96 43.

Where to stay
Medium price

Hôtel Montmirail; tel. 90 65 84 01. Set amid vines near Vacqueyras, a friendly family-run holiday hotel with swimming pool in a garden amid ancient trees. Good local cooking. 44 rooms. Open April to November.

Les Florets, Route des Dentelles; tel. 90 65 85 01. A pleasant little country auberge, with a delightful terrace facing vineyards and hills; 15 rooms. Closed January, February, Wednesday.

Séguret
84110 Vaison-la-Romaine

On a hillside above the Rhône plain south of Vaison, this tiny, very pretty village of cobbled traffic-free alleys is today something of a showpiece, crowded in summer. There's a twelfth-century church and a fine fifteenth-century fountain. The Provençal Midnight Mass and torch parade *pegoulado* on Christmas Eve are a great attraction; so is the Provençal festival in the third week of August. Among the many craftsmen at work in Séguret, some make *santons*, notably the Oustan dei Santoun and P. Fournier. The Atelier de Séguret is a well-known residential international art school, run by a painter from Berlin: it has seen better days.

Where to stay
Upper-medium price

La Table du Comtat; tel. 90 46 91 49. A fifteenth-century house on a hill above the village, now a spruce and comfortable restaurant with rooms (8) and a delightful small swimming pool beneath a sheer rock. Closed February, late November/early December, Wednesday.

Where to eat
Upper-medium price

La Table du Comtat (see above). A sophisticated clientèle, largely foreign, comes here to enjoy some of the finest and most subtle cooking in the region, superbly served in a spacious and elegant setting, above the wide valley.

Rasteau
84110
V-la-R
Where to stay
and eat
Medium price

A wine-growing village situated across the River Ouvèze from Séguret.

Bellerive; tel. 90 46 10 20. Amid vineyards by the river, a bright and cheerful modern hotel (22 rooms) with a big swimming pool. Good, interesting food is served on an outdoor terrace with fine views of the hills. Closed January to mid-March.

**Vaison-la-
Romaine**
84110

Whereas Orange, Nîmes and Arles were Roman cities with great public buildings, Vaison was mainly residential, a town of rich patrician villas; and recent excavations in this 'French Pompeii' now provide a vivid insight into what daily life was like in Roman Gaul. Even before that time, Vaison was a Ligurian centre of some importance. Then the Romans built it into a wealthy place where merchants and retired officers bought handsome villas.

In the early Christian era, Vaison soon became a major religious centre, and was a bishopric from the fourth century. But the mighty Counts of Toulouse became jealous, and in the twelfth century they took the Church's land and built their own castle across the river. The townsfolk began to take refuge here from marauders, so that a medieval town grew up below the castle. Later they moved back, creating the present eighteenth- and nineteenth-century town (population 5,864) next to the Roman quarter. So Vaison today is in three distinct parts, from different epochs. Parts of the town and some of the Roman remains were badly damaged by floods in 1992.

*What to see
Roman
Vaison: La
Villasse area*

Two districts of the Roman town have been excavated – the Puymin quarter, near the tourist office, and the smaller quarter of La Villasse, by the post office. The latter has a main street with pavements, parallel to a colonnaded path once lined with shops. Next to it, the big Maison de la Buste en Argent is a graceful villa with peristyle (colonnaded courtyard), baths, paved hall and traces of hanging gardens. The nearby Maison du Dauphin is somewhat similar.

Puymin area

You come first to the Maison des Messii, the mosaic-floored home of a wealthy Roman family, with its salon, baths, lavatories and kitchen all discernible. The adjacent Portique de Pompée, a stately colonnade with three statues, once had a garden with pavings and murals. Beyond you can see traces of servants' and poor people's homes, while above is the Nymphée, a trough above a spring that supplied Vaison's water. Close by, a Roman tunnel leads to the theatre, up on the hillside facing away from the town. Its amphitheatre still has its rear colonnade, but little survives of the stage, which was cut out of the rock.

The Puymin quarter contains the excellent modern museum, where the main finds from the excavations are clearly laid out and explained in French, English and German. Note the statues of Hadrian and his wife Sabina; the silver bust of the owner of La Villasse villa; the marble statue of an armour-plated emperor (probably Domitian); and a charming double-faced statuette, one side a bearded noble, the other a laughing satyr.

*Former
cathedral of
Notre-Dame*

Set alone near the La Villasse quarter, this austere but graceful twelfth-century Romanesque building stands on the visible foundations of a sixth-century Merovingian church. Behind the present apse are traces of an arcaded Merovingian one, while the table-shaped marble high altar is also pre-Romanesque. The pretty cloister contains a lapidary museum, with early Christian sarcophagi and inscriptions.

The castle and medieval town

Across the river, terraces of narrow cobbled streets line the hillside below the castle. By 1950 this district was derelict and deserted, but it has since been restored to life by the fashion for turning old Provençal houses into chic summer homes. With their creepers, flower pots and neat façades, the upper streets such as the Rue des Fours are now most attractive. From here you can climb up a steep path to the twelfth-century castle: it is closed and empty, but the view over Mont Ventoux and the Ouvèze Valley is stupendous.

What to do

An important drama and music festival is held mid-July to mid-August in the Roman theatre. Every third year (1992, 1995, and so on) there's an international choral festival, too, in August.

Where to stay
Medium price

Le Beffroi, Rue de l'Evêché; tel. 90 36 04 71. Up in the old town, next to a belfry (hence the name), a rambling sixteenth-century mansion, with beamed ceilings and uneven floors, has been converted into a cosy and friendly hotel (21 rooms, some in an annexe). When fine, you eat on a leafy terrace, with lovely views. Open mid-March to mid-November, Christmas and New Year.

Where to eat
Medium price

Le Bateleur, 1 Place Th.-Aubanel; tel. 90 36 28 04. This is quite good and worth a visit.

Orange and the Rhône Valley

The broad River Rhône flows into Provence from the north, and the first town of importance that it encounters is Orange, site of two of the most majestic Roman monuments in France. To its north and south on the wide Rhône plain lie some other interesting places, such as wine-growing Châteauneuf-du-Pape. But let us begin further north, at Grignan, which lies some way east of the river.

Grignan
26230

The village so closely associated with the Marquise de Sévigné is today not in Provence but in the Drôme department (Rhône-Alpes); however, its character and history are Provençal, so it merits a mention here. On a rock above the village stands the massive Renaissance château that for centuries belonged to the Adhémar family, Counts of Grignan. In 1669 one of them married the Marquise de Sévigné's beloved daughter Françoise, and took her to live with him at Grignan. The Marquise was so pained by the resulting separation that she began to write to her daughter almost daily – and her renown as a letter-writer stems quite largely from this. She herself stayed at Grignan three times: her letters from there speak of her love for Provence (save for the Mistral), of her enjoyment of the melons and figs, the fat quails and partridges, and of the views from her window. Visitors today can visit her bedroom, and her tomb in Saint-Sauveur church (she died here in 1696).

Bollène
84500

This old town beside the Rhône lies close to the important industrial complex of Donzère-Mondragon, with its huge hydro-electric dam and nuclear power station. Up on a hill to the north is the strange deserted castle and village of **Barry**, built into the rock: it offers fine views over the Rhône Valley and the Ardèche mountains. South of Bollène, towering above the motorway to Avignon, is another medieval curiosity – the ruined village and fortress of **Mornas**, built atop a sheer cliff.

Where to stay
and eat
Top price

Château de Rochegude, 26790 Rochegude; tel. 75 04 81 88. By the village of Rochegude, 7 km east of Bollène, this old stone château in its own park is now a smart and attractive hotel, full of antiques. Excellent food and service in a lovely dining-room. Heated swimming pool, tennis. Closed January, February.

Sérignan

In this village 5 km north-east of Orange is the villa where the great entomologist Jean-Henri Fabre (1823–1915) spent the last thirty-six years of his life. He was famous for his studies of the anatomy and behaviour of insects, and did much of his field research in the garden of this villa. It is now a museum housing his collections: but alas it's all so badly run and decrepit that it's hardly worth a visit.

Orange
84100

The name comes not from orange trees but from Arausio, the town that the Romans founded here in 46 BC – on the site of a Celtic settlement – for veterans of the VIIth Legion. Here they built two of their greatest monuments: a theatre, and a triumphal arch. By Augustus' time Arausio was a busy city with temples, baths, stadium and arena. Later it suffered from Barbarian invasions, then in the twelfth century it became a small principality within the Comtat Venaissin. In the sixteenth century it passed by inheritance to William, Prince of Nassau, ancestor of today's Dutch royal family. He liked the place so much that he named his dynasty the House of Orange, as it's still called today. And so, through former Dutch influences abroad, the name Orange is now borne by the Protestant movement in Ulster, towns in America, and a state and a river in South Africa. Orange was annexed to France by the Treaty of Utrecht in 1713.

If little now remains of the temples, baths and arena, it is largely because in the seventeenth century Prince Maurice of Nassau used their stones for fortifying the town; but because they formed part of his defences, the theatre and arch were spared. Set amid the vineyards of the Rhône Valley, Orange today (population 27,502) is a pleasant town of shady avenues, with a kernel of narrow streets. For a panoramic view, especially of the theatre, drive up to the colline St-Eutrope along the Montée des Princes d'Orange.

What to see
Roman
theatre

This massive edifice near the town centre – a great wall of brown-red sandstone, 90 m long by 35 wide – is the finest and best-preserved of all extant Roman theatres and the only one whose stage façade remains. Built to hold over 7,000 people, it's a majestic sight, especially on its inner side: here the three rows of columns and statues have alas disappeared, but the big statue of Augustus with his general's baton is still there. Above are the stone blocks that held the poles carrying awnings to protect spectators from the sun. The acoustics are superb

– as anyone attending today's music and drama events can discover. Recent excavations on the west side have revealed the foundations of a temple, the largest yet found in Gaul, and traces of a huge sports field. On the hillside above stood the stately Capitol, with three temples of which traces can be seen. This whole complex was probably the most grandiose in Roman Gaul, dwarfing Arles and Nîmes.

Triumphal arch

Traffic swirls on either side of this mighty arch, which stands in the main road going north from the town. It was built to commemorate Julius Caesar's victories over local Gauls and over the Greek fleet at Massilia which had joined Pompey. It's the third biggest surviving Roman arch of its kind and one of the best preserved; on its north side, detailed bas-reliefs above the main arch depict battles with Gauls.

Musée de la ville

This excellent museum opposite the theatre contains local Roman remains (notably, marble fragments of a Roman cadastral survey, relating to the boundaries and subdivision of land), souvenirs of the Nassau period, and – curiously – works by the British Edwardian painter Sir Frank Brangwyn.

What to do

One of Provence's major annual festivals – of opera and classical music – is held in the Roman theatre in the last two weeks of July.

Where to stay
Medium price

Arène, Place de Langes; tel. 90 34 10 95. A hotel of charm in the heart of town, with good service; 30 rooms; no restaurant. Closed November to mid-December.

Inexpensive

Français, 21 Avenue F.-Mistral; tel. 90 34 00 23. Welcoming and well-run, near the station; 16 rooms, no restaurant. Closed November.

Château-neuf-du-Pape
84230

The Popes at Avignon in the fourteenth century began to grow vines round here and build summer residences: hence the name of this big Rhône Valley village (population 2,060) and of its famous red wine. There's an interesting small wine museum, the Caves du Père Anselme, in whose cellars you can buy wine. Producers in the village whose *caves* are open to visits include Armand Establet, tel. 90 83 70 54, and the Domaine Trintignant, tel. 90 83 70 95. Of Pope John XXII's residence only one tower remains: from its top you get a splendid view of Avignon and its Palais des Papes.

Where to stay
Upper-medium price

Château des Fines Roches; tel. 90 83 70 23. This nineteenth-century mock-medieval 'castle', on a low hill south of the village just off the D17, was the home of the Marquis de Baroncelli, and a meeting-place of Mistral, Daudet and other writers of the time. Today it's a fancy hotel (7 rooms), heavily mock-baronial, but cosy and comfortable, although service is a bit impersonal. Open mid-February to c. 23 December.

Inexpensive

Mère Germaine, Place de la Fontaine; tel. 90 83 70 72. Tiny (6 rooms), a bit basic, but clean and central. No restaurant.

Where to eat

Château des Fines Roches (see above). Quite good, sophisticated cooking, served in an elegant setting; panoramic terrace.

Le Mule du Pape; tel. 90 83 70 30. This village restaurant offers interesting local dishes at a range of prices.

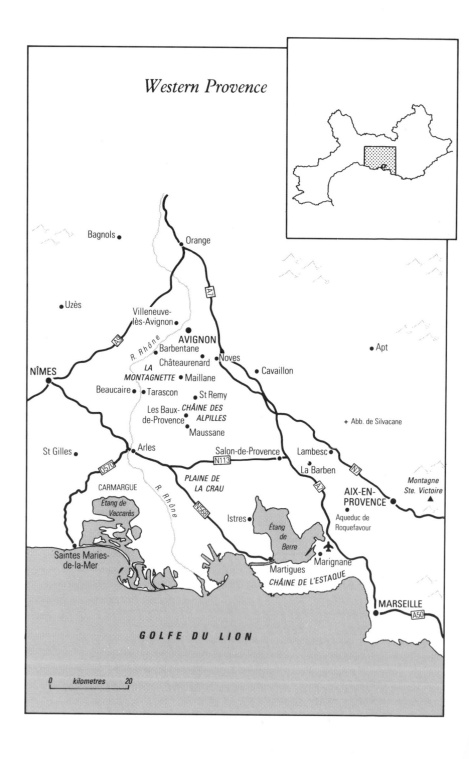

Western Provence

Bagnols

Orange

Uzès

Villeneuve-lès-Avignon

R. Rhône

AVIGNON
Barbentane
Châteaurenard • Noves
LA
MONTAGNETTE • Maillane
Cavaillon

Apt

NÎMES

Beaucaire • Tarascon • St Remy

Les Baux- CHÂINE DES
de-Provence • ALPILLES
Maussane

+ Abb. de Silvacane

St Gilles •

Arles

Salon-de-Provence
N113

Lambesc •
La Barben

Montagne
Ste. Victoire

CARMARGUE

R. Rhône

PLAINE DE
LA CRAU

AIX-EN-
PROVENCE

Étang de
Vaccarès

Istres •

Étang
de
Berre

Aqueduc de
Roquefavour

Saintes Maries-
de-la-Mer

Martigues
CHÂINE DE L'ESTAQUE

Marignane

MARSEILLE
A50

GOLFE DU LION

0   kilometres   20

Western Provence: the Lower Rhône

This chapter covers the broad plain between Avignon and the sea, between the Camargue and the Durance Valley. This, more than the hilly coast and uplands to the east, is the true heartland of old Provence, the *pays* of Frédéric Mistral. And here are the three 'A's – Aix, Arles and Avignon – that are perhaps its most typical cities. Aix was for centuries Provence's capital; Arles has long been the focal centre of Provençal folk tradition; Avignon still remembers with pride its Papal past.

Avignon

84000

In the days when the Popes ruled here in the fourteenth century and built their mighty palace, Avignon was briefly one of the great capitals of Europe, a place given over to gaiety and luxury as much as to religion. Today the Popes are long gone, and it's just a provincial town (population 91,474) – but one of the most sophisticated and fashionable outside Paris, and its citizens retain their old reputation for ebullience and hedonism. The shops are smart, and life goes on well past midnight in the cafés and bistros around the Place de l'Horloge – especially in July, during the theatre festival, one of Europe's great cultural events.

Avignon has always attracted writers. It was in St Clare's church that Petrarch first met Laura in 1327; he adored the city at first, but later became shocked by its corruption (see below). In the nineteenth century, it was the main centre of the Félibrige movement, founded by Frédéric Mistral and other writers. Dickens and the Brownings came here, also John Stuart Mill who spent some years here and died and was buried in the city. In our own time, Lawrence Durrell in his novel *Monsieur or the Prince of Darkness* has been inspired to typical flights of fancy: 'Avignon! Its shabby lights and sneaking cats . . . It has always waited for us, floating among its tenebrous monuments, the corpulence of its ragged bells, the putrescence of its squares . . . It haunted one although it was rotten, fly-blown with expired dignities, almost delinquescent among its autumn river damps. There was not a corner of it that we did not love.'

Getting there

The airport, 7 km to the south-east along the N7, has daily flights to Paris, and some other regular connections (tel. 90 88 43 49). There are good rail links to nearby cities, and eleven daily TGV express trains to Paris (four-hour journey). Motorways, quite close, lead east, west and north. The tourist office is at 41 Cour Jean-Jaurès; tel. 90 82 65 11.

History

Set strategically where the Durance meets the Rhône, Avignon has been a trading post since pre-Roman times. Its great Papal era in the fourteenth century happened almost by chance. In 1274 the Papacy had acquired the nearby Comtat Venaissin district (see p. 190). Then, when the Papacy felt that its life in Rome was being made impossible by the feuding between rival noble families, it decided to look for another home. The Comtat itself had no town suited to being a capital: but the French king, Philippe-le-Bel, persuaded the newly-elected Pope Clément V, a Frenchman, to move to Avignon, and this he did in 1309. Philippe hoped thereby to increase French influence over the Papacy.

The old episcopal palace was at first the seat of Papal rule. Then Benedict XII, elected in 1334, decided to build a bigger palace so as to make the move from Rome more permanent: this was completed by 1352. So Avignon for a while was the capital of Christendom, in an era when the Papacy enjoyed high pomp and lavish living, and was tolerant of carnal weaknesses. Diplomats, prelates and artists flocked in from all over Europe to join the Cardinals and Curia – and prostitutes and spongers came too. Avignon became a town of joyous luxury, also of vice and crime – to the horror of some in the Papal entourage, including Petrarch. The Italian poet had moved to the Papal court as a child with his lawyer father, and later joined the service of a cardinal. At first he enjoyed the life of sophisticated dissipation, but then grew shocked at the corruption. He wrote of Avignon: '. . . an abode of sorrows, the shame of mankind, a sink of vice . . . a sewer where all the filth of the universe has gathered. There God is held in contempt, money is worshipped, and the laws of God and man are trampled underfoot. Everything there breathes a lie: the air, the earth, the houses and above all the bedrooms.' Into Laura's bedroom Petrarch never went, it seems, for he was religious and she married and virtuous.

By 1377, when seven Popes, all of whom were French, had reigned in Avignon, Gregory XI was persuaded to return to Rome. But some cardinals refused to go, so they stayed in Avignon where they elected their own Pope. This led to the Great Schism of the West, as Popes and anti-Popes hurled insults and excommunications at each other, and bickered over Papal lands and incomes. Avignon's last anti-Pope was removed by force in 1403, but he fought on in his native Spain, and the Schism persisted until 1449. Avignon was next governed by a

Main areas

Papal legate, until the Revolution when it was united with France. Since then it has had the modest role of capital of the Vaucluse.

The ramparts, built in the 1350s by Pope Innocent VI, were much restored by Viollet-le-Duc in the nineteenth century and are thus intact. They measure little more than a kilometre in diameter, and today four-fifths of the city spreads outside them: but nearly everything of tourist interest is inside, except for the town of Villeneuve-lès-Avignon (see p. 241), just across the Rhône.

The focal point of the inner city is the broad Place de l'Horloge, which with its buskers and roundabouts often has something of a fairground ambience. From here it is easy to see the main sights on foot, after parking in one of the big car-parks (there's one below this square, another just outside the ramparts to the north-west, a third near the station). The main avenue, the Rue de la République, runs south from the Place de l'Horloge; on either side of it are networks of ancient streets, full of interesting museums, churches and other old buildings. To the north-west of the square is a newly-rebuilt area; to the north-east stands the Palais des Papes.

What to see

Palais des Papes

Going anti-clockwise, the town's main sights are as follows.

This is one of the most imposing medieval buildings in Europe, though it is not exactly beautiful: from the outside, with its turreted towers and great bare walls, it looks more like a fortress than a holy place. It is really two palaces, created by two very different Popes. The Palais Vieux (1334–42), simple and sober, reflects the austere approach of Benedict XII; the Palais Nouveau, to the south, built a few years later (1342–52) by Clément VI, lover of pomp and art, is more ornate. The building was damaged in the Revolution and its furniture abducted; then until 1906 it was used as a barracks, and many of its frescoes were spoilt. It has now been restored as far as possible, but still lacks most of the sumptuous furnishings and decor that must have made it look splendid in its Papal days.

The guided tour takes over an hour, through a labyrinth of halls and chapels. You visit first the Consistoire, where the Pope received important visitors and conferred with his cardinals; some faded frescoes are all that remain of its original decor, and it's now hung with eighteenth-century portraits of the nine Avignon Popes. In the adjacent chapel of St Jean, the frescoes are much brighter: they show scenes from the lives of the two St Johns. You then go upstairs to the Grand Tinel, a banqueting hall where up to 150 people would sit down to a meal lasting as long as eight hours, with minstrels and jugglers. Today it contains six Gobelin tapestries, some of them based on works by Raphael. Off this hall, the little chapel of St Martial is lined in part with lovely dark-blue frescoes by Giovanetti, showing St Martial's miracles.

The Papal antechamber holds a scale model of the palace as it was in the fourteenth century. Its vaulted roofing suffered badly from a fire in 1413, but traces of it remain. The adjacent Pope's bedroom, small and ornately decorated, has blue and gold frescoes of squirrels, birds and foliage. Its tiled mosaic floor is a recent copy of the original, now in the palace museum. Pope Clément's study, the 'Room of the Deer', gives some evidence of the secular tastes of that Pope and his court – for example, it has amusing frescoes of fishing and hunting scenes, games and bathing parties. The Grand Chapel has seventeenth-century paintings by Parrocel and Mignard, while in its sacristy are casts of the tombs of Clément VI and other Popes. Here the guided tour ends, and you are left to explore other rooms on your own. The Indulgence Window, where the Pope would bless pilgrims in the courtyard below, is at the top of the stairway leading from the Grand Chapel; below is the Grand Audience, a state room for tribunals, while on the way out a graceful gallery leads to the Conclave room where, just as in the Vatican today, the cardinals were locked up to elect a new Pope.

Cathedral and Rocher des Doms

The Palais des Papes faces on to the broad traffic-free Place du Palais, lined with other fine buildings, too. Just opposite the palace is the Hôtel des Monnaies (the former Mint), a seventeenth-century mansion with an ornamented Baroque façade; and on the palace's north side is the cathedral of Notre-Dame-des-Doms, partly twelfth-century, containing an archbishop's throne in white marble and the flamboyant Gothic tomb of Pope John XXII. North again is the Rocher des Doms, a rocky plateau above the river, which is now a pleasant flowery garden and a great place to stroll and admire the wide views.

Musée du Petit Palais

At the north end of the Place du Palais, this former archbishops' palace, built in 1317, is now an excellent museum of thirteenth- to sixteenth-century art of the North Italian and Avignon schools. The Italian primitives are charming; Venice is represented notably by Carpaccio's 'Holy Conversation'; and the fine Florentine paintings include Botticelli's 'Virgin and Child', a superb triptych by Lorenzo Monaco, and vivid miniatures by Ambrogio di Baldese. Best of the many works of the Avignon School is Enguerrand Charenton's retable.

Pont St-Bénézet

This is the famous 'Pont d'Avignon' of the old song. Built for horses and pedestrians, it was in reality too narrow for dancing 'in a circle': most probably this dancing took place *'sous le pont'*, on the Île de la Barthelasse, a traditional local recreation spot. Dating from the twelfth century, the bridge used to stretch right across the river to the tower of Philippe-le-Bel in Villeneuve, and was one of the very few solid bridges across the lower Rhône in early days. However, floods carried away most of it in the seventeenth century, and now just four arches remain. Beside one of them is the tiny chapel of St Nicolas, Romanesque below, Gothic above.

Vieille ville,

West and south-west of the Place de l'Horloge is an interesting area *west side* of old narrow streets. Here the Palais du Roure has a delightful fifteenth-century courtyard, while the church of St Agricol's sculptured façade is also fifteenth-century. Near the ramparts to the west, at 17 Rue Victor-Hugo, the **Musée Louis-Vouland** contains some fine eighteenth-century ceramics and furniture.

Musée Calvet This eighteenth-century mansion in the Rue Joseph-Vernet has a courtyard full of peacocks where Stendhal once found serenity. Recently renovated, it is full of oddly diversified treasures. These include Roman, Greek and Egyptian vases and sculptures, dating from the fourth century BC; and a large display of iron locks and wrought-ironwork, also including dental equipment and instruments of torture. The bulk of the museum is devoted to French sixteenth- to twentieth-century painting, notable more for its range than its high quality. Indifferent landscapes by the eighteenth-century Joseph Vernet of Avignon co-exist with works by Manet, Renoir, Géricault, a good Corot, and David's famous 'Barra', the portrait of a drummer boy, who was killed in the Revolution for shouting *'Vive le Roi'*. Of the modern artists, Dufy and Utrillo are outshone by Chaïm Soutine, and by the little-known Albert Gleizes whose three vivid paintings have a Picasso-like quality.

In a building next door is the **Musée Requien**, devoted to local natural history and famous for its herbarium, a large collection of pressed plants. John Stuart Mill once gave it a donation.

Musée Lapidaire This former seventeenth-century Jesuit chapel, 27 Rue de la République, contains a number of local Roman and pre-Roman finds, most notably the famous 'Tarasque of Noves', a statuette of a man-eating monster that dates from the second Iron Age.

Vieille ville, east side The elegant heart of old Avignon, east and south-east of the Place de l'Horloge, is a honeycomb of winding streets and tiny squares, many of them now closed to traffic: it's a rewarding area for a stroll, for exploring the cafés and smart boutiques, and for looking at the many old churches and mansions. Some of these date from the Papal period, and some from the sixteenth century when Avignon prospered under the benevolent rule of the Papal legates. Many of the chapels and churches have altarpieces or other paintings by the local artists Pierre Mignard and the Parrocel family.

Just north of the Musée Lapidaire, the fourteenth-century church of St Didier has fine frescoes dating from the same time and a famous bas-relief of the 'Bearing of the Cross' by the Italian sculptor Laurana (note the realistic looks of anguish on the faces of the Virgin and other onlookers). East from here, the Rue Roi Réné and Rue de la Masse lead past imposing old mansions into the attractive Rue des Teinturiers, a cobbled street beside the River Sorgue that might almost be in Bruges; its one surviving paddle-wheel was used until the late nineteenth-century to power the local textile workshops (hence the name, 'street of the dyers'). Beyond the ramparts here, in the St Véran cemetery, is John Stuart Mill's grave.

East of the Papal Palace, the church of St Symphorien (Place des Carmes) is worth a look for its sixteenth-century gilded wood sculptures, while the Chapelle des Pénitents Noirs (Rue Banasterie) has rich carvings both inside and on its façade. The church of St Pierre is notable for the fine sculptured woodwork in the choir and the elaborate Renaissance carvings on its inner folding doors.

Musée
Aubanel

Down an alley behind the church of St Pierre is this evocative little family-run museum, in the former home and office of the Félibrige poet and publisher, Théodore Aubanel. It is still the family's home, and they run their printing and publishing firm from here; Madame Aubanel herself will show you the museum, which is devoted to the history of printing and to souvenirs of the poet and his literary friends. A very personal collection.

Fondation
Jean Vilar

Close by, in the Rue de Mons, is this institute founded in 1981 in honour of the great theatre director who founded the Avignon Festival and led France's drama revival of the 1950s. It mounts temporary theatre exhibitions, and has a video library and documentation centre of interest to theatre specialists.

What to do

International
Theatre
Festival

The major European event of its kind, founded in 1956 by Jean Vilar and Gérard Philippe, this spans the last three weeks of July and features some 400 productions, large and small. Some of the main 'official' ones are staged in the Great Courtyard of the Papal Palace or other such prestigious venues; they compete with hundreds of 'fringe' shows, held all over the place, often in the streets. Great crowds turn up, and the town wears a carnival air. As at the Cannes Film Festival or Frankfurt Book Fair, there's also a trade fair aspect, for many European and American theatre owners come to spot talent and book shows for their programmes. For seats, apply: Bureau du Festival, 8 Rue de Mons; tel. 90 82 67 08.

Other annual
festivals

There's a three-day horse festival at the end of January, a dance festival in February, a Baroque Music Festival in March, and in August a jousting festival on the Rhône.

Year-round
culture

Because of the influence of the Festival, Avignon has better year-round theatre than most French provincial towns. Of the dozen permanent companies, mostly small and experimental, the best are Le Chien qui Fume, Le Chêne Noir, Les Carmes, Les Halles and Le Moulin à Paroles. The permanent opera and ballet companies are quite good, and the Utopia cinema club has enterprising programmes.

Nightlife

Le 5-5, Porte St-Roch, is a pleasant piano-bar. **Le Baracuda**, in the south-west suburbs, is a disco and nightclub on a barge in the Rhône. The best and trendiest disco, a big 'exotic' place with oriental restaurant and swimming pool, is **Le Sholmès**, 10 km to the west at Rochefort-du-Gard.

Shopping

Roumanille, 19 Rue St-Agricol, is an outstanding antiquarian bookshop, strong also on books about Provence. Souleiado, Rue Joseph-Vernet, is good for Provençal fabrics (but expensive), and Les Olivades for local food products. Les Halles, the big covered market in the Place Pie, has good shops of all sorts. In the Place des Carmes there's a flower market on Saturday mornings and a flea-market on Sunday mornings.

Where to stay

Of Avignon's many hotels, in all price ranges, there are several quite good modern or refurbished ones near the Palais des Papes, and others out along the Marseille road. Here's my own short list.

Upper-medium price

Europe, 12 Place Crillon; tel. 90 82 66 92. This sixteenth-century nobleman's house, now the city's best and most characterful hotel, was already an inn when Napoleon stayed here in 1799. It's in a small square just west of the Palais des Papes (some back rooms may be noisy). There are grandiose public rooms with marble floors and tapestries; period furniture in the bedrooms (53). Friendly, helpful staff.

Medium price

Cité des Papes, 1 Rue Jean-Vilar; tel. 90 86 22 45. New and functional, but efficient and very central, near the Palace; 63 rooms. Closed mid-December to late January. No restaurant.

Danieli, 17 Rue de la République; tel. 90 86 46 82. Also central; cheerful modern decor, nice rooms (34), amiable staff.

Inexpensive

Angleterre, 29 Blvd. Raspail; tel. 90 86 34 31. Unexciting but efficient, in a quiet but central street; 40 rooms. Closed mid-December to late January. No restaurant.

Mignon, 12 Rue Joseph-Vernet; tel. 90 82 17 30. Charming, quaint and tiny, with small but comfortable rooms (15). Delightful owner.

Where to eat

Upper-medium price

The best areas for good restaurants of all kinds are the networks of little streets west and south-east of the Place de l'Horloge.

Hiély-Lucullus, 5 Rue de la République; tel. 90 86 17 07. The Hiély family's famous, long-established place has simple decor but superb classic cooking, certainly Avignon's best. Impeccable service. Closed late June, early January, Tuesday.

Le Vernet, 58 Rue Joseph-Vernet; tel. 90 86 54 83. An eighteenth-century mansion with an intimate, elegant *salle* and a shady garden for summer. Claude Clareton's cuisine is excellent, if almost *too* innovative – for example, lobster with mango, goat with aubergine, pancake of curried frogs' legs. Closed January, February, Sunday in winter.

Vieille Fontaine. The Hôtel Europe's restaurant (see above) serves rich classical food most elegantly, and is best for summer, when you can dine out on the lovely patio beside a fountain. Closed Saturday lunch, Sunday.

Medium price

La Fourchette II, 17 Rue Racine; tel. 90 85 20 93, and **Salon de la Fourchette**, 7 Rue Racine; tel. 90 82 56 01. The Hiély family's move into a lower price-range has yielded these two delightful restaurants, prettily decorated, where Avignon's *beau monde* queues up eagerly for food that is superb value and gracefully served. Fourchette closed late June, Saturday, Sunday; Salon closed November to March, Sunday, Monday.

Lower-medium price

Le Petit Bedon, 70 Rue J-Vernet; tel. 90 82 33 98. Excellent cooking and exuberant service at this ever-popular bistro. Closed latter half August.

Arrête tes Salades, 4 Rue Pavot; 90 85 24 34. Near the Place St-Didier, a friendly little Franco-American place; very good value. Closed November to March.

There are some brunch and light-lunch places, charming and quite cheap, west of the Place de l'Horloge: try the very pretty **Barbotine**, 15 Rue Racine, and **Simple Simon**, 28 Rue de la Petite-Fusterie, like a pastiche of a cosy Devon teashop, serving some English dishes.

South of Avignon: Tarascon, Les Baux and St Rémy

The area south of Avignon, where the parched and craggy Alpilles hills rise dramatically out of a broad plain, contains a number of famous little towns and villages that are the very quintessence of Provence. Among the highlights are Mistral's home at Maillane, the Renaissance castle at Tarascon, Daudet's windmill at Fontvieille, the haunting clifftop ruins of Les Baux and the Roman monuments outside St Rémy.

This suggested route is roughly circular, beginning and ending at Avignon. The main points of interest are given below.

Barbentane

On the wooded northern slopes of the Montagnette hills, south-west of Avignon, Barbentane is a fortified village with several fine old buildings, including a Romanesque church. Its jewel is its château, owned by the Marquises de Barbentane ever since it was built in 1674: its Baroque interior is sumptuous.

St Michel-de-Frigolet

This large and unusual monastic centre with a curious history lies secluded in a hollow of the Montagnette hills, amid rocks, pines and fragrant flowers. It was founded in the tenth century by Benedictine monks from nearby Montmajour (see p. 209), and became a popular halt on the pilgrims' way to Santiago de Compostela. Later it declined, and was dissolved at the Revolution, to re-emerge as a small school where Frédéric Mistral spent two years as a boy. Then in 1858 the monastery was bought by the Order of Premonstratensians who, despite some vicissitudes, are still its owners. They run it as a kind of hostel and educational centre, untidy but lively, often thronged with teenagers. Concerts are held here, too.

The monks of the Order also rebuilt it radically, in a typical nineteenth-century neo-Gothic style complete with crenellated gates, so it hardly retains the serene medieval ambience that one might expect of an ancient Provençal monastery. Nonetheless, the new church with its gaudily-coloured interior woodwork and *tableaux vivants* is attractive in its own way, and next to it are some survivors from the earlier times – a much-restored twelfth-century church, and at the back a Romanesque chapel that contains some fine Baroque panelling donated by Anne of Austria in 1638. Until 1880 the monks used to make a herb-based liqueur that features in Daudet's story, *The Elixir of Père Gaucher*, and you can see the distillery they used. The monks will still sell you a liqueur of that same name, but it is no longer made on the premises.

On Christmas Eve there's a Provençal Midnight Mass and Nativity pageant, as at Les Baux.

Maillane   This sleepy village on the plain north-west of St Rémy owes its fame to the poet Frédéric Mistral, who was born on a Maillane farm in 1830, and spent nearly all his life here until his death in 1914: in the cemetery is his tomb, which is a replica of the Pavillon de la Reine Jeanne at Les Baux (see p. 211). In the village centre, the little house where he lived with his mother for twenty years stands opposite the larger one that he built as his home after his marriage, and where he died. This is now an evocative museum, with photos of the poet amid his family, dogs and admirers. Upstairs, outside his bedroom, is a plaque from the Vichy period, with an inscription by General Pétain praising Mistral as 'a precursor of today's great French renewal'! Mistral admittedly did have Right-wing sympathies, and it is not surprising that the Vichyists sought to enlist him posthumously in their cause. Even so, it is disturbing that today's owners of the museum have refused to remove the plaque.

Despite Mistral's charismatic appeal, the village remains oddly untouristy, though it bursts into life each 9 September with a folk festival and Mass in Provençal to mark the poet's birthday.

Tarascon   Famous alike for its storybook castle, its Tarasque monster, and the anti-hero Tartarin devised by Daudet, Tarascon (population 11,024), an otherwise ordinary little town, stands beside the wide Rhône that until Good King René's death in 1480 was the frontier between 'free' Provence and France across the river. That is why René fortified the castle, where he spent much of his later life.

The story of the Tarasque, theme of a festival in June, links in with the legend of the three St Marys and their landing in Provence (see p. 227). St Martha, one of the party, went to Tarascon and found it terrorised by this amphibious dragon-like monster which would leap out of the river to eat children and kidnap their mothers. The knights of Provence had failed to overcome it: but the saint simply made the sign of the Cross, ordered it back into the river, and it disappeared for ever.

What to see
The castle

Beside the Rhône stands this splendid example of a Renaissance castle, with moat and turreted towers. The foundations are twelfth-century, but the main part was King René's work in the fifteenth. Though for centuries used as a prison, until 1926, it has survived in near-perfect condition. The square-towered lower courtyard is surmounted by the *logis seigneurial*, a high, neat fortress with two square and two round towers. Here the small and charming inner court has a loggia (restored) from which the king and queen would look down on miracle plays, troubadours and jugglers. The minstrels' gallery, giving on to both court and chapel, was used for religious services as well as secular singing.

A spiral staircase leads up to the lovely rooms on the three higher floors: mostly they are bare of furniture, but in two of them an apothecary and a museum of seventeenth-century tapestries have recently been installed. The big banqueting hall with its fireplace for roasting has a ceiling covered with tiny paintings. Higher up is a priest's bedroom, with a wall-oven for bread, and above it a chapel with separate oratories for king and queen. The strange graffiti on the walls of several rooms were done by prisoners, some of them English sailors captured in the eighteenth century – 'Here be three Davids in one mess / prisoners we are in distress', runs one sad inscription. The guide will gleefully show you the 'ecological toilets' where excreta would drop into the river through holes in the floor, then take you to the flat roof, from where prisoners were hurled during the Revolution – also straight into the water.

Church of
Ste Marthe

A graceful but much-restored twelfth-century church, opposite the castle. The fifth-century sarcophagus in its crypt is venerated as being that of St Martha, who is said to have remained in Tarascon after her scuffle with the monster. Above the tomb, the fine marble sculpture of the saint is seventeenth-century Genoese.

Musée Tartarin

Daudet made Tarascon the home town of the absurd Tartarin, in his trilogy of novels that genially satirise the Provençal character. The Tarasconnais at first felt insulted: but today Tartarin has passed quietly into local folklore and even plays a role in the annual Tarasque parade. The small, newly-opened museum has souvenirs of Daudet and some clever *tableaux-vivants* of scenes from the book.

Festival

It was King René, a lover of popular festivity, who created the Fête de la Tarasque, still held on the last Sunday in June. The green, scaly, papier-mâché monster, its head and tail waved by the men standing inside, parades through the streets amid much jollity.

Where to stay
Inexpensive

Confort, Quai A.-Sylvestre; tel. 61 05 61 90. Too simple to live fully up to its name, but fine for a night's stop. By the river; 14 rooms; no restaurant.

Fontvieille
13990

On a hilltop outside this little town south of Tarascon is the venerable old windmill that inspired Alphonse Daudet. He never owned it, and his *Lettres de mon Moulin* were in fact written in Paris,

Daudet's mill

where he lived. But he would often go to visit friends in Fontvieille, where he would collect anecdotes and bits of folklore from local people as material for his stories. Daudet would love to sit and muse in this mill, and in two others across the road. Today it's a much-visited tourist sight, where up in the rafters there sits a stuffed replica of his 'silent tenant', the owl. The little museum below displays numerous photos of the writer with his droopy moustache and sad, spaniel eyes. And the mill has an exhilarating site, on a bare rocky hill with wide views of the Alpilles and the Rhône plain – marred only by the huge papermill outside Tarascon, which smells when the wind blows from the north.

Where to stay and eat

Top price

La Régalido, Rue Frédéric-Mistral; tel. 90 97 60 22. An old oil-mill, converted into a delightful family-run auberge, warm and friendly, with log fires in winter and a lovely garden. Superb classical cuisine, served in a flowery patio or a vaulted *salle*; 14 rooms. Luxury without pretentiousness. Closed December, January.

Medium price

Le Val Majour, Route d'Arles; tel. 90 97 62 33. A spacious, unassuming rustic-style hotel with a big swimming pool, run by pleasant local people; 28 rooms. Closed January, early February.

Abbey of Montmajour

Dating from the tenth century, this former Benedictine abbey stands north-east of Arles on a low hill that was then an island amid the marshes. It was wealthy and powerful in the Middle Ages, owning

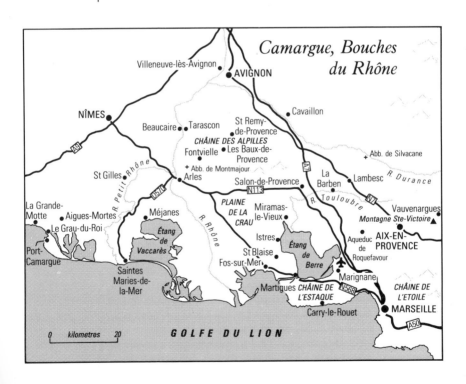

priories all over Provence. Then it declined, and was partly pulled down after the Revolution, but has now been semi-restored. The high fourteenth-century *donjon* was made for defence against marauders. Below it is the cross-shaped twelfth-century church of Notre Dame, whose crypt is built out of the rock. The charming cloister has carvings of animals on the capitals of its marble pillars. Just down the Fontvieille road is the curious burial chapel of **Ste Croix**, topped by a bell-tower.

Maussane
13520

A pleasant village on the southern edge of the Alpilles. To its south stretches the wide plain of La Crau, where Mireille caught sunstroke in Mistral's poem.

Where to stay
Medium price

Hôtel Le Pré des Baux, Rue du Vieux Moulin; tel. 90 54 40 40. The 10 bedrooms encircle a swimming pool at this neat, cheerful B&B down a quiet road near the main square. Closed mid-January to end February.

Les Baux
13520
Maussane

'. . . That dusty pile of ruins, sharp rocks and old emblazoned palaces, crumbling, quivering in the wind like high eagles' nests,' wrote Daudet. Today, well over a million tourists a year visit this, the most renowned of all Provence's hill villages: they cram its crumbling alleys, and jostle in its souvenir stalls. So you should come early, or out of season – or, better still, visit this ghost-realm by moonlight. At all events, Les Baux is not to be missed – it is one of the most unforgettable sights in France.

Haunting and mysterious, the half-ruined village stands on a southerly spur of the craggy Alpilles, below the remains of its grisly castle. The best views of it are from the D27 to the north-west or the D5 in the valley to the east, where the whitish-grey castle walls seem to be part of the huge white rock on which it sits. The village's name comes from *baou*, meaning rock in Provençal, and has spawned the word 'bauxite', first found here in 1822 and still quarried in Provence, but not at Les Baux itself.

History

From the eleventh century the lords of Les Baux were a feudal family of exceptional power and arrogance, extending their sway over much of Provence and as far afield as Albania and Sicily. By the thirteenth century the castle had become a leading 'court of love', where troubadours sang for lovely ladies. But in 1372 the cruel Raymond de Turenne became its ruler – a classy brigand whose sport was to kidnap people from nearby towns, then force them to jump to their deaths from his clifftop, while he wept with mirth. In 1400 the king sent an army against him, and he was drowned in the Rhône.

Les Baux was then incorporated into Provence, and later became a Protestant enclave under its new seigneurs, the de Manvilles. This displeased Louis XIII and Richelieu, who in 1632 razed the castle and ramparts, thus putting an end to Les Baux' great days. In its prime it had 6,000 inhabitants; today, just 433.

What to see
The village

You should park just below the village, and enter it on foot by the Port Mage. Amid all the touristy boutiques, there are some fine

Renaissance buildings in the old alleys, notably the Hôtel des Porcelets, now a museum of archaeology, and the Hôtel de Manville, now a museum of none-too-desirable modern art. In the tiny Place Vincent is the lovely twelfth-century church of St Vincent where the famous shepherds' fête is held (see below). From its terrace, you can look down on to the valley, where between the luxury hotels there stands incongruously the tiny Pavillon de la Reine Jeanne, built in 1581 by the Baroness Jeanne des Baux who was not actually a queen.

The castle ruins

At the top of the narrow rock-lined Rue Turcat stands the fourteenth-century Tour de Brau, now a lapidary museum with a good display of local finds. Here you enter the castle ruins, past the barren south end of the spur with its memorial to the poet Charloun Rieu. In a good light, the view eastwards here is lyrical: the stark peaks of the Alpilles, and below them the golden pastoral valley full of olive groves, poplars and a myriad other trees. The path then winds back to the north end of the spur, where the gaunt wreckage of the castle is a macabre sight: the thirteenth-century keep is where de Turenne watched his victims leap to their doom below.

Cathédrale d'images

Just north of the village, some gigantic caves formerly used as stone quarries have been ingeniously converted for use as a kind of non-stop *son et lumière* show, where lantern-slides are projected on to the high, smoothed-out concrete walls. The show's theme, usually cultural or ethnographic, changes annually.

Festival

Every Christmas Eve since the sixteenth century, a Midnight Mass in the form of a Provençal pageant of the Nativity is held in St Vincent's church. It's the best known of several of its kind in Provence, and is immensely popular: you should get there early.

Shopping

In the Hôtel de Manville, there are attractive wood engravings by local artist Louis Jou, whose workshop is here.

Where to stay and eat
Top luxury price

L'Oustaù de Baumanière; tel. 90 54 33 07. Probably the most famous of France's small rural hotel/restaurants: Queen Elizabeth and Prince Philip stayed here on their State visit to France in 1972. Its legendary owner-chef, the great Raymond Rhuilier, died in 1993 aged 96, and it is now run by his grandson. It offers pampered luxury in a spectacular setting: a large garden with peach, fig and olive trees, fine swimming pool, elegant terrace, regal bedrooms (15) – and the rocks behind are floodlit at night. Served in high style, the much-praised cuisine is defiantly classical – *no* concessions to the *nouvelle* mode. Closed mid-January to early March, Wednesday in winter.

Medium price

La Benvengudo, Vallon de l'Arcoule; tel. 90 54 32 54. A creeper-covered farmhouse, also in the valley below the village, far cheaper than the Baumanière, but with its own touch of glamour. Excellent meals (dinners only) are served in a cosy room with antiques, or on a floodlit patio; 18 rooms. Large swimming pool. Closed mid-November to mid-February.

The Alpilles

Running for some 30 km between Rhône and Durance, this distinctive range of arid hills does not rise above 450 m, but its jagged white peaks wear the aura of ancient mountains. The highest point, **La Caume**, is reachable by car and offers fine views. Alternatively you can take a bracing three-hour scenic walk, along a clearly-marked path, from St Rémy up to the summit and down to Les Baux. Some of the wildest scenery is the rocky gorge of **Val d'Enfer**, near Les Baux.

St Rémy-de-Provence

13210

This agreeable little market town (population 8,439), set in a fertile plain, has shady avenues and several interesting old buildings. One, a Renaissance mansion, houses the **Musée des Alpilles Pierre de Brun**, devoted to local folk art and souvenirs of Mistral and of Nostradamus (the great astrologer was born in the town, in 1503). There's a lively market on Wednesday mornings.

What to see

St-Paul-de-Mausole

This former monastery out on the Les Baux road has been a mental home since 1605 and remains so today. Van Gogh spent a year here as a voluntary patient, from 1889 to 1890, after cutting off his ear in Arles. His room is not open to visits: but you can see his bust in the drive, also the peaceful garden where he continued to paint ('The Sower', among other works). The twelfth-century cloister and Romanesque chapel, both lovely, are well worth a look.

Another notable inmate was Dr Albert Schweitzer (1875–1965), the theologian and missionary doctor. In 1913 he founded his famous hospital at Lambaréné in Gabon, French West Africa. Being Alsatian, he was a German citizen at the time, and so in 1914 he was arrested as an enemy alien and then transferred to St Rémy where he spent most of the war in internment. Later he returned to Lambaréné where he passed much of his later life, being awarded the Nobel Peace Prize in 1952.

Glanum and Les Antiques

These, St Rémy's major sights, lie just beyond the hospital, at the foot of the Alpilles. Glanum is a Gallo-Roman settlement, excavated only since 1921, and fascinating because it reveals the varied impact of first the Greeks, then the Romans in Provence. It was never a Greek colony, but its second-century BC houses were built to Greek design, thus showing the influence of the Massiliot Greeks. The Romans later settled at Glanum and probably used it as a spa and hill-station. The town was wrecked by Barbarians in the third century AD, and today nothing of much height is left standing: but the ground lay-out is clearly visible. **Greek-style houses**, most notably those of Atys and Antes, each with columns, peristyle (colonnaded courtyard) and fine mosaics, lie to the west of a central Roman-built street. On its other side are the Roman buildings, including a sizeable **forum**, **baths** with a covered gallery, and temples. To the south is a **nymphaeum** still full of fresh spring water, next to six altars dedicated to Hercules.

212

Les Antiques, two of the most appealing Roman monuments in France, stand just opposite the entrance to Glanum: not enclosed, they can be inspected freely. Dating from c. 20 BC, they were clearly part of Roman Glanum, but somehow survived the Barbarians' onslaught. The triumphal arch, celebrating Caesar's victories over Gauls and Greeks, bears sculptures of prisoners chained to a tree. Its top part is missing. The adjacent cenotaph, however, is well preserved. It was long believed to have been a mausoleum, but scholars are now certain that it was a memorial to Augustus's grandsons, Gaius and Lucius, who died young. Beside the cupola are their toga-clad statues, while the square base has ornate bas-reliefs of a boar hunt and cavalry and infantry battles. The lapidary museum in St Rémy contains a fine bust of the boys' mother, Julia, as well as many other finds from Glanum.

Where to stay
Upper-
medium price

Château des Alpilles, Route Départementale; tel. 90 92 03 33. Somewhat similar: also just west of town, also a graceful manor house with lovely gardens and fine decor, also with no restaurant (but lunchtime grills are served by the pool). When it belonged to a leading local family, Lamartine and Chateaubriand were among its guests. Now it's a well modernised hotel (16 rooms). Open April to mid-November, Christmas.

Medium price

Les Antiques, 15 Avenue Pasteur; tel. 90 92 03 02. By a main road inside the town, a nicely-converted nineteenth-century mansion (marble floors, tapestries) with a park and swimming pool. Very friendly owners; 27 rooms. Again, no meals. Open April to mid-October.

Lower-
medium price

Hôtel du Soleil, 35 Avenue Pasteur; tel. 90 92 00 63. Beamed ceilings, well-kept pool and outdoor terraces amid flowes, at this central but quiet B&B. 18 rooms. Closed mid-November to February.

Inexpensive

Les Arts, 30 Blvd. Victor-Hugo; tel. 90 92 08 50. A cheerful café-pension, popular with the young, artists and writers. Beamed ceilings and a pretty patio; bedrooms (17) in rustic style. Closed early November, all February and March.

Where to eat
Inexpensive

Yes, there *is* food to be had in St Rémy-de-Provence, despite all the above B&B recommendations. Best places are the lively, crowded **Les Arts** (see above), or the quieter **France,** 2 Avenue Fauconnet; tel. 90 92 11 56.

Cavaillon
84300

A major trading point since Roman times, wealthy Cavaillon in the fertile Durance Valley (population 20,830) is a leading market centre for fruit and vegetables: its pink melons are famous. It has some interesting buildings, too. The well-known eighteenth-century synagogue contains a museum of the Jewish community, once powerful in Vaucluse; the nearby former cathedral of St Véran has a Romanesque nave and cloister, and in its side-chapels some seventeenth-century gilded wood carvings. In the Place du Clos is a reconstructed Roman arch, while the archaeological museum has important Gallo-Roman finds.

Noves
13550

A quiet and ancient market town between Cavaillon and Avignon. Noves was the birthplace of Laura de Noves, a local noblewoman thought probably to have been the Laura who inspired Petrarch (see p. 199).

Where to stay and eat
Top price

Auberge de Noves; tel. 90 94 19 21. Set amid pastoral country west of the town, this nineteenth-century manor is now a luxurious and stylish hotel, owned and run by the friendly André Lallemand, and noted for its superb *nouvelle*-ish cuisine. Delightful staff, magnificent bedrooms, lovely shady patio for drinks and meals: but the swimming pool and gardens are unkempt. Closed January, February.

Château renard

Like Cavaillon, a major centre for fruit and vegetables. Above it stands a ruined feudal castle, containing a small museum. Bucolic folk festivals are held on the first Sundays of July and August.

Aix-en-Provence

13100

Aix (population 124,550), capital of Provence from the twelfth to the eighteenth centuries, is a town with a brilliant past. Today, politically, it is merely a *sub-préfecture* of the Bouches-du-Rhône department; but it remains an important centre of learning, with a big university, and it's a delightful place to visit (apart from the dense traffic). In fact, many foreigners regard Aix as their favourite town in the South of France (I slightly prefer Montpellier). You have only to walk along its famous main avenue, the Cours Mirabeau, lined with cafés, or through the lively old streets nearby, to notice how Aix's modern student ambience somehow blends harmoniously with its many beautiful buildings of the Classic period: it is a town both proud and intimate, full of dark-eyed southern grace, not unlike the nobler cities of Italy such as Florence or Bologna. So intense is the life of the womb-like ancient city centre that you hardly notice its wider setting, on the edge of the Rhône plain, with Cézanne's hills rising up to the east.

Getting there

Marseille's international airport at Marignane (see p. 156) is halfway to Aix (27 km), and there are regular bus connections. Aix itself is not served by the TGV, but there are good rail links with Marseille, Nice and other places. It is right beside a major *autoroute* junction, leading to the main Provençal cities and to Grenoble. There are good suburban and local bus services. The tourist office is at Place Général-de-Gaulle; tel. 42 26 02 93.

History

Aix was the earliest Roman settlement in Gaul. Its name comes from the Latin *aquae*, for it has thermal springs (for curing aches?): here the consul Sextius founded a spa in 123 BC, after subduing local Ligurian tribes. Aix became a major Roman centre, but then went into long decline as later Roman emperors favoured Arles. It revived in the twelfth century when the Counts of Provence made it their capital, and it knew its greatest epoch under 'Good King René' from 1442 to 1480. Though in fact a count, as exiled King of Naples and Duke of Anjou he kept his royal title. He was a true man of the Renaissance – patron of the arts, linguist, mathematician – and he also promoted Provence's economy, introducing the muscat grape and the silkworm. A kindly man with the common touch, he loved organising festivals for his people – and to this day he remains something of a popular cult-figure in Aix. You will see shops, cafés, even dry-cleaners named after him.

In the seventeenth and eighteenth centuries, Aix was the seat of the *parlement* of semi-autonomous Provence, and thus it acquired its many elegant mansions of that period, built by wealthy magistrates and nobles. This was a new golden era. Then in 1790 Marseille was made capital of Provence, as a result of which Aix again went into some decline. But since 1945 its population has tripled, as new suburbs and factories have spread across the plain, together with new campuses for its important university (founded in the fifteenth century, and today very popular with foreigners: many Americans especially regard Aix as their favourite French town). Thanks in part to the proximity of the new high-tech industries of the Marignane area (see p. 223), Aix today is a wealthy place. However, its society has some tensions. Its older patrician families, the true Aixois, mostly lawyers and doctors, form an enclosed and snobbish milieu that will not mix easily with the new business and scientific elites that have settled in the town. Aix till recently had a reactionary Right-wing mayor, but in 1989 the *mairie* fell to the Socialists.

Main areas   Aix shares the familiar shape of many old cities of southern France: an ancient and compact nucleus of narrow streets, girt by a ring boulevard, and outside this the sprawling new suburbs. The focus of the old town, and its one broad street, is the Cours Mirabeau, flanked on its south side by the once aristocratic Mazarin quarter, largely seventeenth-century, and on the north by Le Vieil Aix, a maze of graceful streets, many of them medieval, leading towards the cathedral. All the major sights of Aix, with about three exceptions, are within this charmed circle of the old town and are best visited on foot, after leaving the car in one of the many guarded parks (in summer these tend to get very full).

Outside the ring boulevard, the main university campus is to the south, near the station, and the main industrial estate further out to the south-west, at Les Milles. East of the town towers the white rock of Mont Ste Victoire, beloved of Cézanne (see p. 223). The itinerary below, of places to see, follows first a tour on foot in the old town and then takes in those sights further out for which a car or taxi could be

What to see

*Cours
Mirabeau*

needed: the Vasarély Museum, the Vendôme pavilion, Cézanne's studio, and Celto-Ligurian Entremont.

Aix's central avenue, short but elegant, was built in the seventeenth century on the site of the old ramparts, as a promenade for the town's patrician families. Later it was named after the Marquis de Mirabeau, the Revolutionary leader who spent some years in Aix and was elected to the States General as its deputy. Shaded by four rows of tall plane trees which meet to form an arbour, it is still the busy focus of the town's life, full of people in every kind of dress, mostly students and tourists. The north side is lined with bookshops and cafés (see below). The south side, despite some infiltration by banks, offices and cinemas, is mostly a preserve of seventeenth- and eighteenth-century mansions: note the bearded half-naked atlantes holding up the balcony of no. 38.

The Cours has four fountains. At its west end, the huge three-tiered Fontaine Grande, surrounded by swirling traffic in the big Place du Général-de-Gaulle; then the Fontaine des Neuf-Canons (1691); then the Fontaine d'Eau Chaude, squat and mossy, with running warm spring-water; at the far end, the Fontaine du Roi René with its nineteenth-century statue of the king holding muscat grapes.

South of the Cours is the quiet **Mazarin** quarter, built in the seventeenth century on an austere but harmonious grid pattern, by Michel Mazarin, Archbishop of Aix. Here is the **Musée Paul Arbaud**, devoted to local history; the charming seventeenth-century fountain of the four dolphins; and, next to the Musée Granet, the former priory church of St John of Malta, with a lovely thirteenth-century interior.

Musée Granet

Named after a local nineteenth-century painter, François Granet, this interesting and varied art collection is housed in a seventeenth-century priory of the Knights of Malta. The Dutch and Flemish works include a Rembrandt self-portrait, David Vinckeboons' curious 'Wedding in Cana' and David Teniers' delightful 'Night Fête in a Village'. Of the French paintings of the Renaissance and Provençal schools, many are by François-Marius Granet himself, or Jean Baptiste van Loo. The nineteenth-century works, rather badly lit and hung, include a remarkable Ingres, 'Jupiter and Thetis', and Guillemot's large, colourful 'King René Signing a Reprieve'. The only Cézannes are some minor drawings and water-colours.

The archaeology collection on the ground floor has remarkable Celto-Ligurian sculptures from Egremont (see below), including death-masks and warriors' torsos. There are also Greek and Roman sculptures, and an Egyptian mummy of the Twelfth Dynasty.

Le vieil Aix

The comparison with Florence is here most apt: this oldest part of Aix, north of the Cours Mirabeau, its narrow streets lined with graceful old buildings, remains an animated centre of the city's daily life, full of chic shops and shoppers. It's a delightful place to stroll, especially as much of it is now traffic-free. Several of the fine sixteenth- to seventeenth-century houses are now museums. In the **Hôtel Boyer d'Eguilles**, 6 Rue Espariat, is the museum of natural history.

Next door is a tiny eighteenth-century cobbled square with a fountain, the Place d'Albertas, that has been carefully preserved in its old state, without any modern shops or cafés. To the north is the Place de l'Hôtel de Ville, with its flower market: here the old cornmarket, now a sub-post office, has fine eighteenth-century carvings by Chastel. The seventeenth-century town hall houses the renowned Méjanes library, whose 300,000 volumes, many of them rare works of the fifteenth and sixteenth centuries, were donated by the Marquis de Méjanes in the eighteenth century: they are kept locked up, but can be inspected by scholars, who should write to the curator. In one wing of the town hall is a tiny museum of the poet and Nobel prize-winner St-John Perse, containing letters, photographs and other souvenirs that he donated to Aix before his death in 1975. The sixteenth-century clocktower beside the town hall has an unusual belfry with four statues representing the seasons: they rotate, each in turn showing its face for three months. At 19 Rue Gaston de Saporta, the **Hôtel de Châteaurenard** where Louis XIV once stayed is now a citizens' advice bureau: during office hours it is worth going inside to see the seventeenth-century *trompe l'/oe/il* murals around its staircase.

Church of Ste-Marie-Madeleine

The modern façade is dull, but the interior of this big seventeenth-century church is ornate: besides the paintings by Rubens and Van Loo, do not miss the fifteenth-century 'Annunciation', a fine work of the Avignon School, the centrepiece of a triptych whose side-panels are in Belgium and Holland (but there are copies in the sacristy).

Musée du Vieil Aix

Housed in a seventeenth-century mansion with a fine staircase, this absorbing folklore museum contains nativity cribs, *santons*, mechanical dolls and puppets, all richly costumed and once used in local fêtes. Note also the unusual paintings on velvet by a local artist, Grégoire. The charming frescoed boudoir at the back houses a chest which Louis XIV left here on a visit to the house.

St Sauveur cathedral

This extraordinary treasure trove of a cathedral is in a great jumble of styles, from the fifth to sixteenth centuries, and it also houses a bewildering variety of works of art. The main Gothic building is fourteenth-century, but its right aisle was previously the nave of an older Romanesque church: so the west front, too, has a Romanesque bit to the right while the rest is flamboyant Gothic (all of its original sculptures were destroyed in the Revolution, save for the Virgin in the middle, spared because a cap of Liberty was stuck on her head; the others are later replacements). Off the right aisle is a fine fifth-century

Gallo-Roman baptistry, very like that at Fréjus; and further along the nave are the clearly visible traces of the old Roman forum, recently excavated. Outside is a charming Romanesque cloister, roofed over.

As for the works of art, two of the finest are kept under lock and key for safety, but the sacristan will show you and explain them: the intricate sixteenth-century wood carvings on the west doors, showing four prophets and twelve pagan sibyls; and Nicolas Froment's famous 'Burning Bush' triptych, a masterpiece of minutely-observed realism, painted for King René in 1475. Hardly less splendid are the set of fifteen Brussels tapestries, woven for Canterbury Cathedral in 1511, then sold by Cromwell and later bought cheap by a canon of Aix: after some had been stolen recently, the remainder were shut away from the public, but thanks to a new security system they are now back on view, behind the altar. Lastly, you should go into the chapel of St Mitre, also behind the altar, to see the astonishing fifteenth-century strip-cartoon series of the legendary life of this patron saint of Aix, including one painting of him carrying his own head.

Musée des Tapisseries   A famous set of eighteen Beauvais tapestries, seventeenth- to eighteenth-century, is housed in the former Archbishop's Palace: they were found in its roof in 1849, probably having been hidden there in the Revolution. The most appealing are nine scenes from the life of Don Quixote, gangling and wild-eyed, from designs by the Rococo artist Natoire.

Joseph Sec memorial   At 4 bis Avenue Pasteur, just north of the cathedral, is this bizarre piece of exhibitionism by a local Catholic freemason, Joseph Sec – a memorial that he erected to himself in 1792, *before* his death. Its allegorical sculptures and allusions, part serious, part tongue-in-cheek, trace the ascent of his soul.

Atelier Cézanne   Paul Cézanne was born in Aix and spent much of his life here. He lived in the town, at 23 Rue Boulegon, but he would come daily to paint on the first floor of this modest house in the northern outskirts, with its wide windows. Here his untidy studio has been restored to what it was at his death in 1906 – and it gives a fair impression of his dour, obsessive personality. There are few of his own works, although you can see his easel, palette and other personal belongings, as well as some of the objects that he painted (skulls, bottles and glasses). The effect is a bit sinister, very different from the warmth and lyricism of Renoir's house at Cagnes.

Pavillon Vendôme   Just to the west of the old town, this handsome mansion in a formal garden was built in 1667 by the Cardinal of Vendôme, Governor of Provence, as his summer home, and belonged later to the local painter van Loo. The seventeenth-century façade has atlantes holding up its balcony. The interior has paintings and furniture of the period, and is used for temporary exhibitions. Just to the east, beside the old Roman baths, is a spa centre built in the eighteenth century and still used for treating arthritis and bad circulation.

Vasarély Foundation

Not everyone admires this idiosyncratic Hungarian-born artist: but those who do will relish a visit to the modern museum that he built on a hill in the western suburbs in 1975, to house his own works. Not one for false modesty, he has decked it out with tributes to his 'genius' by Le Corbusier and others. A set of sliding panels expounds his /oe/uvre to the uninitiated (as at Gordes, see p. 187), while seven hexagonal cells offer a range of his geometric murals, tiled mosaics, rotating glass sculptures, and so on. Mathematical patterns combine with dazzling colours to reveal his experiments with the illusions of movement and light. And if you still thirst for more, you can always attend one of the Foundation's seminars.

Entremont

Celto-Ligurian tribes settled on this plateau 3 km north of Aix, in pre-Roman days. Their oppidum, sacked by Sextius in 123 BC, has recently been excavated (see Musée Granet, p. 216), and parts of its ramparts and house walls are visible.

What to do

One of Europe's leading festivals of classical music, with concerts in such venues as the cathedral cloister, is held from mid-July to mid-August: details from Bureau du Festival, Palais de l'Ancien Archevêché; tel. 43 23 11 20. There's a street festival of free outdoor concerts in the last fortnight of June, and week-long folklore festivals in March, June and July.

Festivals

Shopping

The range of specialised shops selling local produce is the best in Provence: many streets in the old town, especially the Rue Gaston de Saporta, are full of them. La Reine Jeanne, 32 Cours Mirabeau, and Brémond, 36 Cours Mirabeau, are among the best of many pâtisseries making *calissons*, the marzipan biscuits for which Aix is well known. Puyricard, 7 Rue Rifle-Rafle, produces superb chocolates as well as *calissons*. La Crémerie Canavese, 9 Rue Gaston de Saporta, sells local foods, wines and olive-oil products. Arnaud Camurat, 16 Rue des Cordeliers, makes lutes, guitars and other instruments; Paul Fouque, 65 Cours Gambetta, is the best place in town for costumed *santons*; L'Oseraie, 26 Rue Vauvenargues, sells olive-wood sculptures as well as *santons*; and for baskets and other wickerwork try Isoard, 35 Cours Sextius. Soleiado, Place des Tanneurs, is good for Provençal fabrics, but not cheap.

On Tuesday, Thursday and Saturday mornings there is a lively food market in the Place des Prêcheurs, and a flower market in the Place de l'Hôtel de Ville.

Nightlife, bars and cafés

The **Deux Garçons**, 53 Cours Mirabeau, is an Aix institution – a classic café with an old literary tradition and Empire decor. It still has its intellectual habitués, but the younger set have deserted it for the flashier **Grillon** and **Belle Époque**, in the same street. The liveliest and most amusing nightspot in town is the **Bistro Aixois**, a big terrace-café that has live jazz from 10 p.m. As for discos, the **Mistral**,

3 Rue Frédéric-Mistral, is smart and not just for teenagers; **Rétro 25**, at Luynes in the southern suburbs, is comfortable and lively. **Hot Brass**, at Célony on the north-west outskirts, is one of Provence's best jazz clubs. The municipal casino in downtown Aix also offers rather sedate dinner-dances.

Where to stay

Upper-medium price

From the large number of good hotels, most of them centrally placed and medium-priced, the following is my selection.

Augustins, 3 Rue de la Masse; tel. 42 27 28 59. Just off the Cours Mirabeau, a fourteenth-century monastery, artfully converted: rooms (29) vary in size and character, but all are quiet. No restaurant.

Le Pigonnet, 5 Avenue du Pigonnet; tel. 42 59 02 90. Aix's most seductive hotel, with an air of intimate chic, is a stately creeper-covered mansion with a large, ornate and romantic garden, and swimming pool, out in a quiet residential area. The pretty bedrooms (48) have antiques; some have balconies with views of the hills.

Medium price

Le Manoir, 8 Rue d'Entrecasteaux; tel. 42 26 27 20. In the heart of old Aix, a finely-converted fourteenth-century cloister; large rooms (43) with period furniture and pretty wallpaper. No restaurant. Closed mid-January to mid-February.

Caravelle, 29 Blvd. du Roi-René; tel. 42 21 53 05. An efficient and welcoming modern hotel on the ring boulevard; half of its 30 bedrooms face over inner gardens. No restaurant.

Inexpensive

Pax, 29 Rue Espariat; tel. 42 26 24 79. On a busy street in the heart of the old town; good value, despite some noise; 18 rooms; no restaurant.

Where to eat

The smarter restaurants are in the suburbs, while in the old town there is a wide range of good, lively, inexpensive eating places.

Top price

Clos de la Violette, 10 Avenue Violette; tel. 43 23 30 71. A quiet villa on the northern outskirts, elegantly converted, with a lovely garden for summer dining. Owner-chef Jean-Marc Banzo's cooking is the best in town. Closed three weeks in November, two weeks in March, Sunday.

Upper-medium price

Le Patio (see Hôtel le Pigonnet). Dining out under the chestnut trees may be nicer than the formal dining-room. Service is polished but a bit impersonal, and the regionally-inspired cuisine reliable.

Medium price

Le Bistro Latin, 18 Rue Couronne; tel. 42 38 22 88. Very central, very lively, very popular with Aixois in search of good food. Closed Sunday.

Auberge d'Aillane, Les Milles; tel. 42 24 24 49. After the Curto family turned their country home into this beguiling restaurant, an industrial estate grew up round it, spoiling the setting maybe, but bringing many lunchtime clients. And there's still the lovely romantic garden and rustic dining-room, where the Curto daughters serve excellent Provençal food in an informal ambience, as classical music plays. Lunches only; closed weekends and August. Hard to find, but a wonderful experience!

Le Vieu Tonneau, 6 Rue des Bernardines; tel. 42 27 86 46. A sympathetic Bohemian bistro in the old town. Good local food.

Al Dente, 14 Rue Constantine; tel. 42 96 41 03. Thronged with students, cramped and animated, good for pasta. Very central.

Charlotte, Place Ramus; tel. no unavailable. Crammed with its own habitués but friendly to outsiders, too; honest local cooking. In the old town.

The Aix area and the Étang de Berre

Aix is ringed on three sides by bare limestone hills, but to the west there stretches a wide plain, partly occupied by the huge lake of Berre, its shores today lined with modern industry. This chapter looks first at the places round Aix, starting at Salon and going clockwise; then it explores the Étang de Berre.

Salon-de-Provence
13300

A centre of the olive oil industry since the Middle Ages, this is now a sizeable market town with shady streets (population 35,845). The astrologer and physician Michel Nostradamus (1503–66), who was born at St Rémy, spent the last nineteen years of his life at a little house in the old part of town, Place de Loge, which is now a museum devoted to him; it was here that he wrote many of his famous enigmatic predictions of the future, in rhyming quatrains. He is buried in the interesting fourteenth-century church of St Laurent. The vast, looming **Château de l'Empéri**, tenth-century, former residence of the archbishops of Arles, lords of Salon, is today an important military museum, with items ranging from Louis XIV's epoch to 1918. Some 4 km to the north, by the N7, is another war souvenir: a memorial to the great Resistance hero Jean Moulin.

It was west of Salon, by the N115, that in 1973 English tourist John Cartland was murdered in his caravan. The police arrested his son Jeremy as a suspect. The way that the entire French Press at once assumed him guilty, proclaiming it under banner headlines such as '*Jeremy, assassin de son père*', caused fury in Britain and damaged Franco-British relations just after Britain had joined the EEC. Cartland was soon transferred to Britain, acquitted, then released. The crime was never solved.

In July and August there is a drama festival in Salon's château, while a big jazz festival is held in July. Wednesday is market-day.

Where to stay
Top price

Abbaye de Ste Croix, Route de Val-de-Cuech; tel. 90 56 24 55. Secluded in its own park on a low hill 5 km north-east of Salon, this noble twelfth-century abbey has been sumptuously converted and furnished with antiques. Many of its 24 bedrooms are smallish, being former monks' cells: but they have views over the pretty cloister or the far hills. Unheated swimming pool. Open March to October.

Inexpensive

Select, 35 Rue Suffren; tel. 90 56 07 17. Clean, convenient and central, good for a night stop; 18 rooms. No restaurant.

Where to eat
Top price

Abbaye de Ste Croix (see above). Dinner is by candlelight, either in a graceful stone-walled room or out under the trees, and the service and cooking are equally stylish. Closed Monday lunch.

Francis Robin, 1 Blvd. Clémenceau; tel. 90 56 06 53. Smart and comfortable, with excellent light modern cuisine. Closed Sunday night, Monday, two weeks in February.

Medium price

Craponne, Allées de Craponne; tel. 90 53 23 92, is good value.

La Barben

The crenellated medieval château near this village east of Salon has an interesting history, having belonged to a daughter of Good King René in the fifteenth century. There are paintings by Van Loo, and an Empire-style boudoir named after Napoleon's sister, Pauline Borghese, who stayed here. The grounds contain a small zoo, aviary and aquarium.

Where to stay
and eat
Medium price

La Touloubre, Pélissanne; tel. 90 55 16 85. An unassuming family-run auberge and lively local meeting place, where you can dine out by lamplight under the trees. Closed Monday, two weeks in November and January.

Lambesc

A pleasant old town of quiet streets, just off the main N7; its old buildings include a sixteenth-century gate and a fourteenth-century clocktower. To the north, a road climbs steeply into the Chaîne des Côtes, a former *maquis* hideout, where a memorial stands to Resistance fighters killed by the Nazis.

Abbey of
Silvacane

Of Provence's famous trio of lovely twelfth-century Cistercian abbeys (see also Sénanque and Thoronet, pp. 188, 171), this one has the least secluded and attractive setting – in the broad, ugly valley of the Durance – but its Romanesque architecture is just as pure and harmonious. Its name comes from *silva* (wood) and *cane* (reed), for it was built by reedy marshes. In the late twelfth century it was the most powerful of the 'three sisters', and housed 110 monks. Then its fortunes declined: forcibly taken over for a while by its Benedictine rivals in the thirteenth century, pillaged by vandals in 1590, seized by bandits in 1590, it became for centuries a mere parish church. Today, in State hands, it is still being restored.

The high-vaulted church is typically Cistercian in its bareness. The chapterhouse shows early Gothic influence, while the big, handsome refectory was rebuilt in the fifteenth century. The small cloister with its vaulted arcades is especially appealing.

The nearby village of **La Roque-d'Anthéron** has a stately seventeenth-century castle. In August there's the Fête de St Louis and, more unexpectedly, an international piano festival.

Fifteen km south-east of Silvacane, on the D13 from Le Puy-Ste-Réparade to Aix, is the Château de Fonscolombe (tel. 42 61 95 87) where the Marquis de Saporta produces some of the best Coteaux d'Aix wines, red, white or rosé, sold in bottles with smart ribbons and seals. It's worth a visit.

Montagne Ste Victoire Cézanne (see p. 218) loved to paint this high limestone ridge, just east of Aix. From the city, as he saw it, it looks like a narrow pyramid, but in fact it's a 16 km-long wall of whitish rock, as you can observe from the A8 autoroute on its south side. From the D10 west of **Vauvenargues** you can hike up a mule track to the monument of **Croix de Provence** by the summit (945 m) where the view stretches as far as the Alps and the coast. The imposing seventeenth-century château at Vauvenargues was owned by Picasso in his last years, and is still in his family's hands. Visitors are not admitted, but through the gates you can glimpse his tombstone in the park.

At Palette, 3 km south-east of Aix off the N7, you will find Château Simone, where some of the finest Coteaux d'Aix fruity red wines are produced. It makes an interesting visit, if you want to inspect and buy.

Roquefavour aqueduct South of Aix, towards the rocky range of L'Etoile, there's little of interest. But 10 km south-west of the city is this three-tier aqueduct built in 1842 to 1847 to carry water from the Durance to Marseille. It is much longer than the Pont du Gard (see p. 243), and nearly twice as high.

Étang de Berre Separated from the sea by the barren Estaque hills, this enormous salt-water lagoon is only 10 m deep and yet covers 155 sq km. Its shores have been colonised since Greek times; today they are much industrialised, notably to the south where at night the blazing flares and lit-up factories make an impressive sight. The main places of interest round the lake are the four oil refineries, big petro-chemical factories, and the terminal of the south Europe pipeline that bears crude oil to Alsace and south-west Germany.

Marignane
13700 Just outside this industrial town lies Marseille's huge airport, with several good modern hotels (in the cheaper range, try the motel-like **Campanile**; tel. 42 89 25 11, 4 km to the east, at Le Griffon, by the A7). Close to it is Europe's biggest helicopter factory, part of the State-owned Aérospatiale. In the 1970s the factory successfully pioneered a new model of labour relations, with small autonomous work units, rather like the Fiat and Volvo schemes.

Chaîne de l'Estaque Between the Berre lake and the sea, this is one of the three rugged limestone ranges that ring Marseille, under which the 6 km Canal du Rove was tunnelled in 1920, so that big barges could reach the lake. However, owing to landslip it has been unused since 1963. The village of **l'Estaque**, now part of the Marseille suburbs, was frequented by Cézanne, then by Dufy and Braque: all three were excited by the hills' wild scenery of whitish rocks and dark pines.

Carry-le-Rouet

Where to eat
Top price

Of the line of little resorts along the south side of l'Estaque, this is the smartest: it has bathing beaches, a picturesque fishing port, and many villas owned by well-to-do Marseillais.

L'Escale, Promenade du Port; tel. 42 45 00 47. Those wealthy Marseillais use this beautiful place as a kind of intimate club, notably at weekends. It has charming owners, a lovely flowery terrace above the sea, and some of the finest fish cooking in Provence. Open March to October.

Martigues
13500

The new oil-based industries on the coast at Lavéra, and at nearby Fos, have turned this fishing village into a sizeable dormitory town (population 42,039). Yet its old quarter retains some of the picturesque appeal that once drew Félix Ziem, Corot, Augustus John and others to paint it. Boats and coloured houses line the canals, the prettiest spot being the Pont St Sebastien on the central Île de Brescon. Next to it, the seventeenth-century church of Ste Madeleine has an ornamental façade and a fine Baroque organ. The newly-reopened Ziem museum, in the Ferrières district, contains paintings by Ziem and others, local Greek and Roman finds, and an amusing collection of *ex-votos*.

An impressive new suspension bridge, 292 m long, carries the autoroute over the canal in the western suburbs. Just to the north, you get a good view of the Berre lake, its industry and the hills beyond, from the hilltop chapel of Notre-Dame-des-Marins.

On the first Saturday in July there's a 'Venetian fête', with decorated boats lit up at night. During the second half of July, a popular festival includes open-air plays and concerts, and free distribution of seafood and sardines.

Where to stay
Medium price

Hotel St-Roch, le Moulin de Paradis; tel. 42 80 19 73. On the north-west edge of town, a modern, well-run hotel with good service, its main charm being its garden which contains an olive-oil mill. Restaurant.

St Blaise

Eleven km north-west of Martigues is a major archaeological site that sheds light on the early history of Provence. Near the twelfth-century Romanesque chapel of St Blaise, recent excavations have revealed a Greek fortified camp of the 7th century BC, even older than Massilia, and traces of a Christian necropolis and basilica of about the fourth century AD. It is thought that the site was an Etruscan trade centre, before the Greeks arrived, and that later the early Christians used it as a refuge against Barbarians.

Fos-sur-Mer

The ancient and modern truly co-exist in this area. On the coast a bare 8 km west of St Blaise is this gigantic new port and industrial zone, developed since 1965 by the Port of Marseille Authority as an extension of the city's own port, cramped for space and today in decline (see p. 156). The site covers 103 sq km, and the port can handle tankers of up to 400,000 tonnes: it claims to be Europe's leading port after Rotterdam. Because of the post-1973 oil crises and the slump in the European steel industry, Fos has not developed as fast or far as planned: even so, it has some important refineries, steelworks, petro-chemical and other factories, and annually handles 3 billion cubic metres of imported liquid gas.

At **La Fossette**, 8 km inland beside the N568 to Arles, the Centre de la Vie information centre has full details about Fos including scale models. You can go on a guided tour of Fos if you give prior notice (tel. 42 05 03 10 or 91 91 90 66).

Istres   On the west shore of the étang de Berre, this town (population 30,360) has an interesting museum of local history, including archae-ology and folklore. The huge military airport west of the town dates from before 1914, and was used for very early flights.

Miramas-le-Vieux   An old town on a rocky spur at the north end of the lake, with a thirteenth-century ruined castle and fifteenth-century church. Five km to the south-east, beyond the village of St-Chamas, is the **Pont-Flavien**, a handsome first-century single-arch Roman bridge that bestrides the River Touloubre. Of its four sculpted lions, only one is original.

The Camargue

This wide expanse of lagoon and marshy plain, within the delta of the Rhône, is a mysterious area like none other in France, and it contrasts sharply with the rocks and hills of the rest of the coast of Provence. Here orange-purple sunsets glow and linger; herds of black bulls and half-wild white horses roam the salty marshes, where there are few buildings save the lonely thatched cottages of the local gipsy-like herdsmen, the *gardians*; and at dusk a flock of flamingoes may suddenly fly up from the reeds of a lagoon.

The Camargue consists of 770 sq km of the Rhône delta between Arles and the sea. Outside the tourist season, it can be very lonely, for apart from its 'capital', the seaside village of Les Saintes-Maries, there is nowhere bigger than a hamlet. The northern part, towards Arles and St Gilles (see pp. 228, 244), has been desalinated since the Second World War and is now devoted to rice-growing. To the south, the big étang de Vaccarès and the mass of islands that separ-ate it from the sea are now a nature reserve, full of birds of many species and a huge variety of rare flowers and plants. Most of the Camargue's bird life is inside this reserve, which is open only to accredited students and naturalists: you should apply in advance, stating your case, to the Réserve Nationale, La Capelière, 13200 Arles; tel. 90 97 00 97.

You can, however, get near to the reserve, and thus see something of the birds and flowers, if you drive beyond the south-east corner of the lake and then turn west to where the road ends at the lighthouse of La Gacholle: from here the intrepid can take a long, bracing walk along the dyke (impassable in wet weather) to Les Saintes-Maries. The best time to see the birds is early morning, or just before dusk, and you need patience, for they do not appear readily. The migratory flamingoes come in summer to the lagoons around La Gacholle, and are a marvellous sight as they rise up from the water's edge in a flurry of pink.

The best time to visit the Camargue is spring or early summer, before the high season; in autumn mosquitoes can be a pest, and in winter the Mistral can be icy. There are good roads close to the lake, where the plain is divided into some thirty ranches: each owner has his *manade* (herd) of sturdy white horses, stocky but sure-footed, and black fighting bulls (see p. 54). You can see plenty of these animals from the car.

What to see There are several small museums of Camarguais life. The best is at the **Pont de Rousty**, 10 km south-west of Arles on the D570, where a handsome old farm building, long and low, displays interesting details of local history and folklore; from here a signposted footpath will lead you into the marshes. To the south, 5 km before you come to Les Saintes-Maries, the Camargue Information Centre at Ginès offers a free slide show; next door is a small, rather unkempt aviary – but the owls are interesting. South again, the **Musée du Boumian** has not-too-convincing waxwork tableaus of traditional local life.

What to do The Camargue is just the place for a riding holiday. Numerous ranch-hotels (see below) have their own horses, and many other little firms (details at any tourist office) will take groups out for horseback excursions through the marshes, led by *gardians*: it costs about 60 francs an hour. These *gardians* are lithe, tough men and women with weather-beaten faces, and they spend much of their time in the saddle, rounding up their herds with long staves; some still live out in the marshes in remote whitewashed thatched cottages topped with a cross.

For non-riders, there are trips by Land Rover. Or you can observe the area's wildlife by taking a seventy-five-minute boat-trip up the Petit Rhône from a landing-stage 3 km west of Les Saintes-Maries. Tourists can also attend a *ferrade*: these are ranch ceremonies where the yearling bulls are branded with their owner's mark.

Méjanes is a ranch on the north-west shore of Lake Vaccarès, now a holiday centre owned and run by Paul Ricard. It offers horse-riding, mock bullfights, horse displays, a scenic railway and some *ferrades* – all very commercialised, but fun.

Les Saintes-Maries Tawdry, down-market bathing resort, focal point of Camarguais and Provençal folk tradition, gipsy pilgrimage-centre still wrapped in
13460 mystic legend – this odd little town (population 2,045) is a mix of all these things, and more. It lies at the heart of the legends about Chris-

tianity's arrival in Provence, and has thus become a place of pilgrimage. A boat without sails or oars is said to have left the Holy Land and drifted ashore here, bearing a saintly cargo – the Virgin's sister St Mary Jacobe, St Mary Salome the mother of James and John, St Mary Magdalene, Saints Martha, Lazarus, Maximin and Sidonius, and their African servant Sara. According to the legend, the saints then went off to evangelise Provence – Martha to Tarascon, Lazarus to Marseille, Mary Magdalene to Ste Baume, Maximin and Sidonius to Aix (see p. 207 and 168). Sara and the other Marys stayed here (hence the town's name) where they built an oracle. They were buried on the spot where the great church now stands, so the story goes.

Despite this ancient legacy, this is not an old medieval town like so many in Provence, and apart from the church it has few old buildings. Its windswept little streets of white houses, looking rather like Andalusia, have their own charm despite the scores of trashy souvenir shops. There's a mock bullring, and kilometres of fine beaches backed by dunes, while behind stretch lagoons and marshes.

What to see
The church

Built in the eleventh century as a fortified defence against Saracens and other marauders, this unusual church with its crenellated parapet does indeed look like a fort. It is topped by a five-arch belfry (worth climbing, for the view) which can be seen from afar, across the plain. The sombre nave is almost empty, save for its case of naïve *ex-votos*, and the 'boat of the Stes-Maries' that is borne in procession in festivals. The reliquary said to hold the bones of the saints is in a chapel above the apse, and is kept closed. However, you can visit the fifteenth-century crypt, where Sara's reliquary stands across the altar from a much-petticoated statue of this grave-faced lady. The many burning candles indicate how much she is venerated. It is in this haunting, atmospheric church that Mireille dies of sunstroke at the end of Mistral's epic poem.

Musée
Baroncelli

This small old-fashioned museum next to the church contains a Camargue folklore and wildlife collection that was put together by the eccentric Marquis Folco de Baroncelli, a follower of Mistral. He was a poet from Avignon who went to live the life of a *gardian* on the marshes, and did much to preserve and revitalise Camarguais tradition. You will see tableaus of Arlesian costumes, old photos of the gipsy festival, and three-dimensional scenes of Camargue bird life.

What to do
Festivals

The gipsy pilgrimage on 23 to 27 May is the great event of the European gipsy year. The gipsies long ago chose St Sara as their patroness; and each May they still converge here in thousands, from France, Spain and elsewhere, bringing their caravans which today are nearly all motorised, not horse-drawn. On 23 May they hold a night vigil in St Sara's crypt. The next day, at a special service, the reliquary of the two Marys is lowered from its high chapel. Then, on 25 May, a procession of clergy, gipsies, *gardians* and others, all in fine costume, carries the pink and blue statues of the two saints, in their little boat, as far as the sea, then back to the church in the afternoon. There follow two days of Provençal merriment, with bull-races, horsemanship and folk-dancing. The brightly-clothed gipsies are a fine sight – even if today it's commerce, as much as religion or tradition, that entices them to this very touristy festival.

The same ceremonies, on a more modest scale, take place on the weekend nearest 22 October, and the first Sunday in December. Early in November there's a newly-instituted Journée de Mireille, with folk activities – all to prove that the town is very much a living centre of Provençal folk tradition.

Where to stay

In the town and near the beach are some goodish seaside hotels. Just to the north, near the lagoons, you'll find a number of modern ranch-hotels that cater for riding and other sports: as well as the two featured below, I can recommend the **Pont de Bannes** and the **Mas du Clarousset**, both upper-medium price.

Top price

Mas de la Fouque, Route du Petit Rhône; tel. 90 47 81 02. By a lagoon, 4 km out of town, the Camargue's most luxurious hotel is sophisticated but informal – a whitewashed ranch with heated swimming pool, a herd of white horses, and private verandas where you can birdwatch. Friendly owners, good but simple food; 10 rooms. Open April to November.

Upper-medium price

L'Etrier Camarguais, Chemin Bas-des-Launes; tel. 90 47 81 14. In the same area, and much cheaper, this ranch-hotel has a breezy, club-like ambience, proving that *l'après-cheval* can be as much fun as *l'après-ski*. Log-cabin decor, a big swimming pool and sun terrace, the usual white horses – and a disco just out of earshot. The bedrooms (27) are chalets in the garden. Hearty local cooking. Open April to mid-November.

Medium price

Le Galoubet, Route de Cacharel; tel. 90 97 82 17. A pleasant, more conventional seaside hotel on the edge of town; 20 rooms. No restaurant. Open March to November and New Year period.

Where to eat
Medium price

Pont de Gau, Route d'Arles; tel. 90 47 81 53. On the main road 5 km north of town. Good authentic Camarguais cooking (for example, conger eel in garlic sauce) at very fair prices, served in a spacious barn-like setting. There are 9 cheap bedrooms, too. Closed January to mid-February.

Inexpensive

Plage, Avenue de la République; tel. 90 97 84 77. Very central; clean and old-fashioned, with 19 rooms; no restaurant. Open May to September.

Arles

13200

On the northern edge of the Camargue plain, astride the broader of the two arms of the lower Rhône, stands the mellow and seductive old city of Arles (population 50,772), one of the supreme centres of Provençal history and tradition. It is a much smaller place than Aix or Avignon, and is generally engulfed by tourists who come to visit its exceptionally rich and varied ensemble of Roman and early Christian splendours. However, though full of fascinating museums, it is no mere museum-piece, and has a vigorous and engaging personality of its own. It's easy to see why Arles held such an appeal for Van Gogh and other artists – even if its women, in my humble view, are not *quite* as beautiful as their reputation.

Getting there   The best airport to use is Nîmes, 25 km away (see p. 235). There are good rail connections with Avignon, Marseille and other cities, and with Paris, the journey by TGV (change at Avignon) taking nearly five hours. The nearest *autoroute* is at Nîmes. Regular buses go to most nearby towns.

History   Its geographical situation made Arles a key Roman centre. It became a major maritime port after the consul Marius dug a canal to the sea near Fos; as it was also at the lowest point where the Rhône was bridgeable, it carried much of the land traffic between Rome and Spain, and was at the junction of the Agrippan Way leading to Lyon with the Aurelian Way going west. Arles benefited, too, from taking Caesar's side against Pompey and Marseille. So when Caesar punished Marseille in 49 BC, Arles took over its influence and for a time was the capital of Roman Provence. Later, in the fourth century, Constantine the Great built a palace at Arles and made it briefly the capital of the Roman Empire; after it lost this role, it was the capital of the 'three Gauls' (Gaul, Spain and England).

Next, the town became a crucial focus of early Christianity: St Augustine was consecrated Archbishop of Canterbury here in 597. In the Dark Ages, Arles suffered badly from the Barbarian hordes, and it never recovered its power, even though it was the capital of a kingdom of Provence in the ninth to tenth centuries (Frederick Barbarossa was crowned Holy Roman Emperor here in the twelfth century).

Arles today   Ever since this period Arles has played a minor role in Provençal affairs compared with Aix or Avignon. Since the eighteenth century its reputation has been due mainly to its prowess as *the* heartland of Provençal folk tradition: much of the old Provençal furniture that you still find in the region derives from eighteenth-century Arlesien craftsmen, and this is one of the few parts of Provence to have retained its own folk costume, notably the women's elegant lace head-dresses. Today, this attire is still worn for festivals, but seldom for daily use, for it takes a long time to put on.

Nor is Arles any longer the magnet for artists, musicians and writers that it was in the last century. Daudet, who wrote *L'Arlésienne* here in 1872, and Bizet, who set that play to music, were among those drawn by the romantic appeal of its folklore. Van Gogh lived here from 1888 to 1890 (see p. 232); and Arles was the favourite town of

Mistral, who created here his famous folk museum (see p. 231). Today, what remains of this great cultural tradition? Well, both State and city are at least now making efforts to revive it. In 1988 to 1989 the centenary of Van Gogh's visit was marked by major exhibitions, and by the conversion of the old Hôtel Dieu into the new Espace Van Gogh, an ambitious cultural centre that houses, among other things, a newly-created national institute of translation. Jack Lang, as Minister of Culture, also founded a college of photography here in 1984, and the city can now claim to be the leading French centre of that art.

Main areas

The old part of town, a compact and delightful area of narrow streets, lies on the east bank of the Rhône: nearly all the main museums and monuments are here, so close together that they are easily visited on foot, after parking your car either in the broad Place Lamartine to the north or in one of the car-parks off the Blvd. des Lices to the south (it's best to buy a combined ticket for all the main sights). The tree-lined Blvd. des Lices, with its terrace-cafés, is the main focus of modern Arles. Beyond it stretch the suburbs, while across the river is the Trinquetaille quarter.

What to see

Starting at the Roman arena, here is a suggested circular tour of the main places of interest.

Roman arena

One of the oldest arenas of the Roman world (46 BC) and one of the largest, too, this was built to hold over 20,000 spectators. There were gladiatorial combats; also fights with wild beasts, as is clear from the tunnels that led to their cages and from the height of the wall round the ring. After the Roman era the arena was made into a fortress, containing a church and some 200 houses. For this its own stones were used, and not till the nineteenth century was it rebuilt and restored. Today it is in fair condition, though unlike Nîmes' arena it has lost its third storey which supported a canopy-like roof. The three towers were added for defence in the twelfth century; there is a good view from the top of the one by the entrance. Bullfights and concerts are today held in the arena (see p. 233). To its south are remains of the city ramparts: parts date from the Dark Ages.

Théâtre antique

This theatre, built in Augustus' time and holding 7,000 people, was pillaged in the Dark Ages and used as a stone quarry for churches and the ramparts. So it is badly ruined: only two tall columns survive from its stage wall, once elaborately decked out with rows of statues. There are also twenty rows of its original seating, today used for summer cultural events (see p. 233).

St Trophîme

St Trophime, to whom this lovely former cathedral in the Place de la République is dedicated, was sent by St Peter to evangelise Provence, according to legend. Much altered in the twelfth century, the original building was Carolingian, but its stunning west portal is pure Provençal Romanesque. Here the stone carvings may have suffered from time and weather, but they include a frieze full of curiosity: on the left, the chosen, fully clad, advance towards Christ in the

230

centre; on the right, the damned are led off chained to hell.

The simplicity of the high, narrow, Romanesque nave contrasts with the choir's Gothic flamboyance. One fourth-century sarcophagus, representing the crossing of the Red Sea, is now an altar; another, in a chapel off the north aisle, is now used as a font. The two fine paintings by Ludovicus Finsonius include an 'Adoration of the Magi'.

Cloître St Trophîme

The elegant arcades round a little garden of cypresses, the elaborate Romanesque sculptures and the tranquil beauty all conspire to make this the most loved of all Provence's cloisters. The north and east arcades with their barrel vaulting are twelfth century; the others, with ogival arches, are fourteenth-century Gothic. The pillars carry ornate carvings of Christ and saints, while the capitals are decorated with biblical scenes and even some from Provençal legends (note the curious bas-relief of St Martha and the Tarasque). In a chapel off the north side are three fine seventeenth-century Aubusson tapestries of the Virgin's life, and three smaller Flemish ones.

Musée d'Art Païen

St Trophîme stands in the Place de la République, heart of the old town, next to the imposing seventeenth-century town hall and opposite this museum of Greek and Roman art (tombs, mosaics and statues, all found locally) that is housed in a deconsecrated church. The fine Greek sarcophagus of Hippolytus and Phaedra (second century AD) was found in a villa at Trinquetaille, while the statue of Augustus stood backstage in the Roman theatre. Also found in the theatre, in 1651, was the famous Venus of Arles, broken into three pieces with both arms missing; much restored, this is now in the Louvre, and the two Venuses you see here are merely casts. The earlier one, late seventeenth century, is less complete but purer than the later model.

Musée d'Art Chrétien

Just behind the pagan museum, this one is housed in a former seventeenth-century Jesuit chapel, and its array of richly-carved early Christian sarcophagi is claimed to be the world's best outside the Lateran Museum in Rome. Those round the walls are from the Alyscamps (see p. 232), but the three superb fourth-century tombs in the centre were found in 1974 in the Trinquetaille villa: they include a remarkable tomb of a married couple, the 'tomb of the Trinity', with friezes of Old Testament scenes. Inside the museum, steps lead down to the Cryptoporticus, a huge U-shaped gallery that the Romans built underneath their Forum and used as a granary for wheat.

Museon Arlaten

Installed in a sixteenth-century Gothic mansion is this large and magnificent museum of Provençal life, created by Mistral in 1896 and later enlarged with the help of money from his 1904 Nobel prize for literature. The intensely personal museum is suffused with the poet's passion for the people and culture of Provence; many of its exhibits still bear the labels that he wrote with his own hand (printed French ones are now added). The 30 rooms are filled with Provençal costumes and Arlesian coifs, or have life-size tableaux of traditional peasant scenes. Among the many portraits of Mistral himself, one shows him in the crowded Roman arena, acknowledging the acclaim of the crowd – a handsome bearded figure, clad in a black cape.

Place du Forum

Just to the north, this pleasant little square is not quite on the site of the Roman forum, but the two Corinthian columns at one corner were part of a temple adjoining it. The statue in the square is of Mistral, who often frequented its terrace-cafés.

Constantine's palace, Trouille baths

All that now visibly remains of Constantine's mighty fourth-century palace are these Roman baths, the largest in Provence, impressive by their size but partly in ruin. They are made of narrow layers of brick and stone, unlike earlier Roman buildings.

Musée Réattu

This graceful fifteenth-century building, former priory of the Knights of Malta and then the home of a local painter, Jacques Réattu (1760–1833), is now a large and eclectic museum, of uneven quality. The works by minor nineteenth- and twentieth-century artists, including Réattu himself, are mostly of little interest: but some other exhibits are splendid.

On the ground floor, beside Roman masonry, is a striking modern tapestry by Grau Garriga, from Spain. On the first floor are five astonishing seventeenth-century Brussels tapestries, imaginatively depicting five of the Seven Wonders of the World. Look out also for the set of witty cartoon-like coloured sketches by Picasso, which he donated to the city in 1971, in thanks for the many bullfights he had enjoyed here. There are works by Gauguin, Léger, Lurçat and others, and upstairs a fine display of photographs of Arles.

In the footsteps of Van Gogh

The artist's fourteen months in Arles were a period of eager fecundity, but also of descent into madness – it was here that he cut off part of his ear. Today, the Arles that he painted has also been disfigured: in the Place du Forum, his 'Café du Soir' is now a furniture shop below the Vaccarès restaurant; in the Place Lamartine, the house that he shared with Gauguin ('The Yellow House') was bombed in 1944; and his bridge south of Arles, the 'Pont de Langlois', was pulled down in 1926, though a copy has since been built near Martigues, at Port-de-Bouc. (The Arles tourist office will supply a map of the sites in the area connected with Van Gogh.)

Les Alyscamps

One of Christendom's great historic cemeteries lies in the south-east suburbs, about seven minutes' walk from the Blvd. des Lices. A long avenue lined with sarcophagi leads to a ruined Romanesque church. First established by the Romans as a necropolis on the Aurelian Way (the name probably meant 'Elysian Fields'), it became a notable burial ground in early Christian days and contained thousands of tombs. Those remaining on the site are of little artistic interest, but it's a lovely romantic spot.

What to do

Festivals

For sheer number and variety of annual festivals, Arles has few equals in France. From Easter Friday to Monday, there is a bullfight festival in the Roman arena. Around 1 May, a fête of Camargue *gardians* (see p. 225). All July, international festival of music, dance and drama in the Roman theatre. Second week in July, international photography festival, the leading one of its kind in Europe. Mid-December to mid-January, a trade fair of *santons*.

Sport

Bullfights, with *mise-à-mort* (bulls are killed), are held in the Roman arena on about two Sundays per month, from April to November. In summer there are also frequent *courses à la cocarde* (see p. 55).

Shopping

A lively and colourful market (food, costumes and antiques) is held every Saturday on the Blvd. des Lices; two stalls sell Arlesian costumes and head-dresses. Of small shops with local products, Le Cloître, Rue Jean-Jaurès, makes and sells santons and ceramics; La Taste, Blvd. des Lices, sells olive oil and dried flowers; Soleiado, Blvd. des Lices, is good for local fabrics; Milhau is a good butcher for *saucisson d'Arles*, the celebrated dried sausage.

Where to stay

Upper-medium price

The choice of good hotels isn't great; nor would I recommend the smartest, the Jules César.

D'Arlatan, 26 Rue du Sauvage; tel. 90 93 56 66. One of Provence's best-loved and best-known hotels: a fifteenth-century building of great character, former home of the Counts of Arlatan, tucked down a side-street beside Constantine's palace. Delightful walled garden and shady courtyards; bedrooms (43, some very small) with Provençal fabrics and antiques, tiled floors. No restaurant. Book well ahead.

L'Atrium, 1 Rue Emile Fassin; tel. 90 49 92 92. By contrast, a flashy modern hotel, just off the Blvd. des Lices, formed from a converted old house with new additions. Piano-bar, rooftop swimming pool, comfortable with good service. Restaurant; 90 rooms.

Inexpensive

Calendal, 22 Place Pomme; tel. 90 96 11 89. A modest but pleasant little hotel near the arena, with a lovely shady garden; 27 rooms. Open mid-February to mid-November. No restaurant.

Le Cloître, 18 Rue du Cloître; tel. 90 96 29 50. Efficient and central: some of the 33 bedrooms overlook the St Trophîme cloister. No restaurant. Open mid-March to mid-November.

Where to eat

Medium price

L'Olivier, 1 bis Rue Réattu; tel. 90 49 64 88. Very popular locally, a cool, elegant place in an old building; careful, serious cooking. Closed two weeks in April, November; Sunday, Monday.

Vaccarès, Place du Forum; tel. 90 96 06 17. Good regional cuisine, notably Camarguaise, at this handsome, classic establishment. Closed mid-December to mid-January, Sunday, Monday.

Hostellerie des Arènes, 62 Rue Refuge; tel. 90 96 13 05. A simple, usually crowded, family-run auberge opposite the arena; good value. Closed December, January, Wednesday.

Inexpensive

Lou Gardian, Rue 4-Septembre; tel. 90 96 76 15. Cramped, popular, good value.

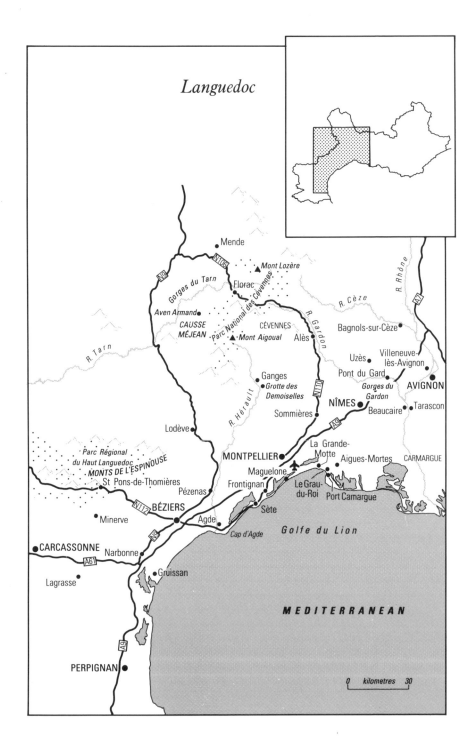

Languedoc

Languedoc

Introduction

The modern Languedoc-Roussillon region is something of a hybrid, as I mentioned earlier (see p. 8). Of its five *départements*, this chapter covers four – Gard, Hérault, Aude and Lozère. It does not include the fifth, Pyrénées-Orientales (otherwise known as Roussillon, or French Catalonia), which is outside the scope of this book. The chapter begins at Nîmes, then takes in most of the rest of the Gard, then goes west to Montpellier, capital of the region, and on to Narbonne and Carcassonne, then up into the heights of the Cévennes and Causses, such a contrast with the broad coastal plain of Lower Languedoc. This region has much in common with Provence and yet is different, marked by its own history – by the long-ago struggles of Cathars and Huguenots, of vinegrowers, too (*les Cathares de la vigne*, they have been called) in times much nearer our own. The traces of these struggles are everywhere.

Nîmes

30000 Nîmes (population 129,924) was never within the kingdom of Provence, for it lies west of the Rhône, and today it is politically part of Languedoc: but its character is in some ways more Provençal. It calls itself 'the Rome of France', for Roman colonisation has left behind some splendid buildings, notably the arena and Maison Carrée. It's a dusty, workaday town, less obviously graceful and sophisticated than its rivals, Montpellier and Avignon, yet busy with activity and innovation. Its long Huguenot tradition survives in its mistrust of Paris. In short, it's a stimulating, down-to-earth city that personally I love to visit.

Getting there The airport, 8 km to the south, has scheduled flights to several cities, including daily ones to Paris (tel. 66 70 06 88). The main station, which is quite central, is linked to Paris by eight TGVs a day (a four-and-a-half-hour journey), and is on main lines to Marseille, Toulouse and so on. The Paris–Barcelona autoroute is close to the city, and there are regular bus links with nearby towns and villages.

235

History

The tourist office is at 6 Rue d'Auguste; tel. 66 67 29 11.

The Romans found a gushing spring here, so they built a town and called it Nemausus. Augustus then settled a big colony of veterans in the town after defeating Mark Antony in Egypt: hence the crocodile chained to a palm tree that the city still bears on its crest. In the sixteenth century Nîmes opted for the Reformation and became the principal Protestant bastion in the Midi (see p. 16): for this it was then punished under Richelieu. It has been an industrial centre since early days, and in the eighteenth and nineteenth centuries its textile workshops developed greatly. A rough twill cloth for overalls was invented here, and marketed abroad as *'de Nîmes'*: American buyers shortened this to 'denim' and the name has stuck – but who today calls these trousers anything but *'le blue-jeans'*?

Nîmes today

The city remains, as it has been for centuries, an important centre of French Protestantism, and many of its leading families are Protestant. This helps to explain its long tradition of hostility to Paris, which continued in a different guise in 1965 to 1983 when the city was run by the Communists. They were conservative and unimaginative in local affairs and did little for Nîmes' development. However, since 1983 a new Right-of-centre mayor, Jean Bousquet, has brought a fresh spirit of dynamism, attracting new industries and embarking on some major civic projects – *'Enfin, ça bouge à Nîmes!'*, people say. In October 1988 a freak downpour in the hills sent a torrent of brown muddy water flooding through the town, killing eleven people and causing immense damage; but Bousquet coped with this disaster so effectively that his political reputation was enhanced. Today Nîmes is an utterly different place from even ten years ago, and is in zealous rivalry with larger Montpellier.

Main areas

The central part of the city is quite compact, containing most of the Roman remains and the pleasant streets of the Old Town. It is best negotiated on foot. North of the centre are low limestone hills, while newer commercial and residential districts stretch southwards towards the motorway and airport. Driving and parking are easier than in most larger French towns.

What to see

Roman arena

One of the best-preserved of the seventy extant Roman arenas, this majestic building is slightly smaller (21,000 spectators) than the one at Arles, but otherwise similar (they had the same architect). In the fifth century it became a fortress, and from the thirteenth it served as a tenement for 2,000 paupers, in 150 dwellings. The Romans used it for gladiatorial combats and chariot races: today's programme includes bullfights, tennis and opera (see p. 238), and in 1988 it acquired an ultra-modern movable roof so some of these activities could continue in winter.

Maison Carrée

This 'square house' (in fact, rectangular) is a temple built by Agrippa in 20 BC in Hellenic style, and is regarded as one of the most graceful and finely proportioned of all extant Roman temples, equal to those of the Greeks. It is also very well preserved – despite having been used successively since the Middle Ages as the town hall, a private home, a stable, a church and today a museum. Facing what used to be the forum, it stands on a high platform, with a peristyle of fluted columns whose carving is delicate and subtle. The interior, now walled in, holds a collection of local Roman finds, including a statue of Apollo, and the 'Venus of Nîmes' that was found in fragments and has been reassembled. The floor's mosaic centrepiece is the original one, remarkably well preserved.

The museums None of these is of great interest, except perhaps to specialists. All are in the centre of town. The Musée des Beaux-Arts, Rue de la Cité-Foulc, has indifferent works by Brueghel, Rubens, Rodin and others. The Musée du Vieux Nîmes, in the old episcopal palace, contains a large collection of traditional Nîmois furniture, porcelain and fabrics – the latter, including shawls and tapestries, are rather lovely. The Musée d'Archaeologie, in a former Jesuit college on the Blvd. Amiral-Courbet, displays Greek ceramics and a roomful of objects evoking the daily life of a Gallo-Roman family. Lastly, a new Médiathèque (cultural centre) is due to open in 1991, opposite the Maison Carrée, and will house the city's collection of (rather way-out and boring) contemporary art.

Vieux Nîmes The narrow streets of the old part of town north of the arena, graceful and picturesque, contrast with the dusty avenues of the rest of workaday Nîmes. Some of these streets, notably the Rues de l'Aspic, de Bernis and des Marchands, are now closed to traffic and have been finely restored. Here you'll find attractive surprises. Push open the door of 14 Rue de l'Aspic, and you enter a private courtyard, with a handsome seventeenth-century double stairway; at no. 8 there's a Renaissance gateway; and at 3 Rue de Bernis a fifteenth-century façade. The Passage des Marchands, off 12 Rue des Marchands, is a beautiful Renaissance gallery with low vaulted arches, now containing antique and handicraft shops. The nearby cathedral of St Castor is eleventh-century, but was much rebuilt in the nineteenth: on the frieze on its façade, the scenes from Genesis to the left are originals, but the others are copies. To the north-east is the Roman Porte d'Auguste (15 BC).

Jardin de la Fontaine Ten minutes' walk north-west from the town centre, this ornamental garden, typically French with its pools, statues and balustrades, was built in the eighteenth century to embellish some Roman remains. At its upper end, the fountain of Nemausus cascades into a clear pool; lower down, the massive ruin of a temple, possibly to Diana, is all that remains of the baths, theatre and other buildings that the Romans put on this site.

Tour Magne Above the garden, up on the wooded Mont Cavalier, stands this Roman tower, only the top of which can be seen from the garden below. It was built probably as a watchtower and has now lost its upper deck, originally some 10 m high. From its platform there's a splendid view of the mountains.

Victor Hugo visited Nîmes on one of his many tours round France. He adored puns and other word games, and one of his cleverest jokes of this kind was the following couplet, whose two lines sound identical if you speak them fast:

Galles, amant de la reine, alla – tour magnanime! –
gallament de l'Arène à la Tour Magne, à Nîmes.

(The Prince of Wales, lover of the Queen, went – generous feat! – gallantly from the Arena to the Tour Magne, at Nîmes.)

What to do

Festivals and culture

The city's various annual festivals centre on bulls, wine and music. The Feria de la Pentecôte, one of Languedoc's major annual events, lasts for five days around the Whitsun weekend: as well as bullfights and bull-races, it offers folk displays, concerts and street dancing. There's a big jazz festival in the arena in mid-July, and a folklore one in July/August. In May to October bullfights are held in the arena two or three times a month, mostly on Sunday afternoons: the toreadors are both local and Spanish, the bulls are from the Camargue and are fought to the death. The last weekend in September sees a folkloric wine festival, and October to December a series of musical events. Musical life remains lively all year, with summer concerts either in churches and châteaus or outdoors in the Jardin de la Fontaine, and opera from October to March in the main theatre or in the arena.

Sport

Forest Hill, 30 Chemin de l'Hostellerie; tel. 66 38 31 00, is a watersports and health club with tennis, saunas, and a swimming pool with wave-making machine.

Shopping

L'Huilerie, 10 Rue des Marchands, sells olive oils and local food products. You will find Provençal fabrics, but not cheap ones, at Soleiado, opposite the Maison Carrée.

Nightlife

Le Liberté, 24 Blvd Amiral Courbet, is possibly the best of the dozen or so discos and dance-halls in town.

Where to stay

Upper-medium price

Imperator, Place Aristide-Briand; tel. 66 21 90 30. Quite central, this is a dignified, classic hotel (as its name implies), with a palatial foyer, which is cheerful and newly modernised. Lovely inner garden, 62 rooms, excellent service and new-style cooking.

Medium price

Mercure, 21 Rue Nationale; tel. 66 76 28 42. A seventeenth-century building with a fine Renaissance staircase, now a charming newly converted hotel in the heart of the old town. 33 rooms.

Lower-medium price

Tuileries, 22 Rue Roussy; tel. 66 21 31 15. In city centre; nicely furnished and many rooms have balconies. 10 rooms.

Inexpensive

Majestic, 10 Rue Pradier; tel. 66 29 24 14. Near the station; clean and simple, with sizeable rooms (29). No restaurant.

Where to eat

Upper-medium price

Alexandre, Garons; tel. 66 70 08 99. The best restaurant in the Nîmes area is near the airport, 8 km from town. Elegant decor, a lovely garden, and first-rate classic cooking. Closed late August, Sunday evening, Monday. It also has 4 bedrooms.

Le P'tit Bec, 87 bis Rue de la République; tel. 66 38 05 83. Quiet and pretty place with a courtyard; interesting dishes. Closed latter half August.

Medium price **L'Alberguier**, 4 Rue Racine; tel. 66 36 13 22. An intimate, elegant little place near the Maison Carrée, with original cooking (for example, lamb with langoustines). Closed Monday lunch, Sunday.

San Francisco Wine Bar, 11 Square de la Couronne; tel. 66 76 19 59. Lively, trendy, popular with locals, but the cuisine is not so local (for example, steaks). Open late.

Inexpensive **Flunch**, 12 Blvd. Amiral Courbet; tel. 66 76 10 04. Could this be France's best self-service cafeteria? It's clean and comfortable, with *real* French dishes nicely presented, served at rock-bottom prices. A find!

Around Nîmes: Uzès and the Pont du Gard

This section covers the eastern part of the Gard department, between the Rhône and the Cévennes. From Nîmes it takes you north to the fascinating old town of Uzès, then up over the wild hills and plateaus of the *garrigue* to the lovely Cèze Valley, then down the Rhône via Bagnols (good modern art museum) and Villeneuve-lès-Avignon (superb old buildings) and so back to Nîmes. In short, an area of varied interest, much of it pleasantly off the beaten track.

Gorges du Gardon North of Nîmes the D979 to Uzès climbs up into typical *garrigue* country – the dry, stony hills, covered with scrub and wild flowers, that form much of the southern slopes of the Cévennes. The road enters the arid gorges of the River Gardon (another name for the Gard) and crosses the quaint thirteenth-century Pont St Nicolas.

Uzès In the heart of this lovely distinguished little town (population **30700** 7,826) stands a massive feudal castle, home of a great ducal family, the House of Uzées, which dates back to Charlemagne. Louis XIII proclaimed it 'the premier duchy of France', a title that it is still allowed to use. And the family live on in their castle, at the centre of a network of narrow arcaded streets lined with patrician houses. Formerly the town had ramparts, too: but it was a Huguenot stronghold, so Richelieu had them pulled down, and in their place is now a ring boulevard. However, some of the old towers survive, that were symbols of power in medieval days.

André Gide's father's family, of local Huguenot stock, had their home in Uzès, where the writer spent many boyhood holidays. In his memoirs, *Si le Grain ne Meurt*, he has written vividly of his rambles through the Gardon countryside, and of the influence on him of this

What to see
The ducal
castle

stern Protestant milieu.

There's a fairy tale quality to this massive turreted pile, where the duke's flag flies in red and gold, the Occitan colours. Once inside the courtyard, you can see that the building is a mix of different styles and epochs: on the left the eleventh-century keep, the Tour Belmonde, and beside it the fourteenth-century Tour de la Vicomté; on the right, the Renaissance façade of the part where the family now live. The chapel is Gothic, but its roof of coloured tiles bearing the ducal crest was added in the nineteenth century.

The old town

Very compact, this is best visited on foot. The many lovely buildings near the castle include the eighteenth-century town hall, with a stately courtyard; the Crypte, where one of the two bas-reliefs has glass eyes; the twelfth-century Tour de l'Horloge; and the Hôtel Dampmartin, with its Renaissance façade and round tower. Nearby is the Place aux Herbes (also called the Place de la République), a very pretty square with a fountain and broad arcades. To the east, the seventeenth-century former cathedral of St Théodorit has a fine organ. Next to it is an amazing building: the **Tour Fénestrelle**, a round twelfth-century bell-tower six storeys high, of a kind unique in France, though common in northern Italy. It is all that survives of the Romanesque cathedral sacked by the Huguenots. The Promenade Jean Racine to the south (so named because the dramatist spent two years in Uzès) offers a good view over the valley.

Festivals

There's a festival of classical and modern music in the last half of July. Several picturesque rural fairs are held in the Place aux Herbes: first Saturday in February, pig fair; second Saturday in April, spring fair; 24 June, garlic fair; first and second Saturdays in August, wine fair; 14 August, local fête; 11 October, sheep fair; 17 November, horse and poultry fair.

Where to stay
and eat
Upper-
medium price

Hôtel Marie d'Agoult, Château d'Arpaillargues; tel. 66 22 14 48. Five km west of Uzès, by the village of Arpaillargues, this stately eighteenth-century château belonged to the d'Agoult family (hence its dual name), one of whom, Marie d'Agoult, was Liszt's mistress. It's now a stylish luxury hotel, with tennis, big swimming pool, spacious park, a good library and antiques in the bedrooms (25). The cooking can be erratic, but it's elegantly served – out by the garden, or in the baronial dining-hall. Open mid-March to end October.

Medium price

Entraigues, Place de l'Evêché; tel. 66 22 32 68. Under the same ownership, but in the town centre: a sixteenth-century mansion converted with superb taste, but elegant rather than cosy; 22 pleasant rooms. Restaurant (closed January, Tuesday) is only fairly good.

Inexpensive

St-Géniès, Route de St-Ambroix; tel. 66 22 29 99. In the north-west outskirts, welcoming, neat and well modernised, with 18 rooms; no restaurant.

Méjannes-
le-Clap

The D979 goes north from Uzès over the rolling plateau of the *garrigue*, where the wide vistas are exhilarating. It passes the sleepy, unspoilt hill village of **Lussan** (here a detour can be made eastwards to a dramatic rocky gorge known as **Les Concluses**) and then comes to the spacious new holiday centre of Méjannes-le-Clap (the French are not aware of how oddly that name strikes an American or English ear). Here you'll find swimming, tennis, mini-golf, villas to rent, and scope for fishing or boating in the clear waters of the lovely River Cèze.

Méjannes-le-Clap makes a suitable base for exploring the beautiful valley of the Cèze and its many charming, unspoilt villages such as Montclus, Goudargues and La Roque (see below); also for visiting the plateau itself, where the Guidon du Bouquet, south-west of Lussan, is a notable panoramic point.

La Roque-sur-Cèze

Some way downstream from the Méjannes area, just off the D980 to Bagnols, is this ancient village, its houses clustered on a steep hillside below a Romanesque chapel. Close by is the remarkable Cascade du Sautadet, where the River Cèze swirls and foams between flat rocks, forming a series of natural jacuzzis. It's a splendid spot for picnics or unpolluted bathing – but watch out for the rapids.

Bagnols-sur-Cèze

A town in two parts (population 17,777), old and new: since the late 1950s, old Bagnols has had grafted on to it a large new suburb that acts as dormitory for the workers and scientists of the nearby Marcoule nuclear centre. The architect, Georges Candilis, won the first official Prix de l'Urbanisme for the harmony of his planning: the three medieval towers of the old town are balanced by three white tower blocks of flats in the new one. Inveterate haters of Modernism will remain unimpressed.

Modernism takes a very different form in the town's Musée d'Art Moderne, an unlikely find in such a small place. The pictures include a typical Renoir of naked girls, some good works by van Dongen and Albert Marquet, a *fauvist* who worked with Matisse; but the paintings by Matisse himself are unremarkable. Bagnols also has a small museum of archaeology, and nice old houses in the Rue Crémieux.

Some way south-east of Bagnols, just off the N580 to Villeneuve, is the village of Tavel, famous for its strong, dry rosé wine, which is rather expensive. A good place to taste and buy is the *cave* of the local producers' association, 'Les Vignerons de Tavel', tel. 66 50 03 57.

Where to stay
Lower-medium
Villeneuve-lès-Avignon
30400

Hôtel Valaurie, St Nazaire; tel. 66 89 66 22. Pleasant modern B&B on wooded hill north of town. Big garden. 22 rooms. Closed January.

Standing just across the Rhône from Avignon (*lès* means 'near'; see Avignon, p. 199), Villeneuve (population 9,535) was used by the French kings as a fortress town in the thirteenth to fifteenth centuries, when the river was the frontier between France and Provence: hence its two great military buildings, the Tower of Philippe le Bel and the Fort of St André. However, in the fourteenth century the kings did allow the cardinals of Papal Avignon, seeking an escape from that teeming city, to build themselves expensive mansions in 'foreign' Villeneuve, only two of which survive. Villeneuve today is still popular with rich Avignonnais, many of whom have villas here. It also contains some magnificent old buildings and works of art, legacies of its past. It's a delightful old place of narrow, ancient streets, well worth a visit, and very different from its larger, tourist-packed neighbour, Avignon.

What to see
The military
posts

Philippe le Bel's Tower, on a rock above the river, is thirteenth- to fourteenth-century. The massive fourteenth-century St André Fort, with its twin round towers, is a superb example of a medieval military building. From its terrace gardens there are fine views of Avignon and the Papal Palace, seen best in the late afternoon sun.

Chartreuse du
Valde
Bénédiction

Founded in 1356 by Pope Innocent VI, this charterhouse is the largest in France, covering 2.4 hectares, and housing hundreds of monks in its prime. At the Revolution it was sold and the monks evicted, but it's now being restored and has a curious diversity of uses. Part, including the biggest cloister, is municipal housing, with lots of shops and flats. And part, including the main religious buildings, is owned and run by the State as a cultural and scientific centre cum historic monument, vast and austere. All is clearly explained in three languages, with diagrams and panels that tell of the monastery in its prime. Main points of interest are the elegant tomb of Innocent VI with its white marble statue; the fourteenth-century Italian frescoes in the Papal chapel; and the bakery, washhouse and barber's shop in the monks' quarters. The cultural centre runs seminars: so don't be surprised if you find, say, engineers or biologists sipping cocktails beside the Pope's tomb.

Notre-Dame

This old church has paintings by artists of the Avignon School, and is famous for the fourteenth-century polychrome ivory statuette of the Virgin and Child, in the sacristy. This was carved from an elephant's tusk and follows its curve, which is why the Virgin is leaning awkwardly sideways.

Municipal
Museum

Housed in a seventeenth-century palace, this drab-looking little museum contains some items of furniture from the Chartreuse, and a few good paintings: there's a ghoulish Mignard of monks being hanged, and a seventeenth-century engraving of Avignon's Pont St Bénézet while it was still intact. The museum's glory is Enguerrand Charenton's 'Coronation of the Virgin', a powerful masterpiece of the Avignon School. The artist was from Laon, close to Belgium, and his landscape of mountains and cities is Flemish-influenced: as well as St Peter's, Rome, he has included local scenery, such as Mont Ventoux, and a vivid panorama of Hell and the damned.

Festivals

There's a picturesque wine festival in late April. In July/August there are concerts and plays in the Chartreuse.

Where to stay
Top price

La Prieuré, Place du Chapitre; tel. 90 25 18 20. Near the town centre, but facing quietly over fields at the back, this fourteenth-century priory is now a sleek luxury hotel, run with style by the Mille family. Of its 36 bedrooms, those in the old building have more character (including tiled floors), those in the new annexe are larger, with wide balconies. Tennis, swimming pool, lido, lovely rose garden. Open mid-March to early November.

Medium price **L'Atelier**, 5 Rue de la Foire; tel. 90 25 01 84. A graceful sixteenth-century house in the old town, with beamed ceilings and a pretty patio; 19 comfortable rooms. No restaurant. Closed January.

Where to eat **Le Prieuré** (see above). Dinner by candlelight on the lawn is the *Upper-* highlight; the classic cooking, usually good, can be erratic.

medium price Standing majestically alone amid lovely scenery, this marvellous **Pont du** three-tier Roman bridge has impressed countless travellers, among **Gard** them Rousseau, Smollett and Henry James, and is one of the great sights of France. It was built across the Gardon by Agrippa in 19 BC, as part of the aqueduct carrying water to Nîmes; and today, somewhat restored in the nineteenth century, it is still in near-perfect condition. Built of yellowish local stone, its two lower tiers have large arches, while the upper one, which carried the water, has smaller ones. Modern engineers still marvel at its construction, for its blocks weigh up to 6 tonnes, it is 275 m long and 50 m high. The best view of it is from 100 m upstream on the right bank. From here a path leads up to the top tier, which you can walk across if you do not suffer from vertigo. Notices warn that people have sometimes been blown off by strong winds.

Beaucaire Beaucaire (population 13,015) and Tarascon, the one historically in *30300* Languedoc, the other in Provence, are ancient rivals that face each other across the Rhône, each with its proud castle.

The castle Beaucaire's was built by Count Raymond VI of Toulouse in the thirteenth century. Partly demolished by Richelieu, it is now half-ruined and has not been much restored. Its lofty triangular keep still stands, however, and you can clamber to its top for a wide view: be warned, however, that two huge (and smelly) factories by the river just below are every bit as noticeable as romantic Tarascon castle. Near the castle, the old part of town has some fine buildings, notably the seventeenth-century town hall.

The fair Count Raymond also initiated the town's annual trade fair, which became the foremost in Western Europe, attracting some 800 boats and 300,000 visitors from many countries, every July. Beaucaire at that time was a major river port. The fair survived until the mid-nineteenth century, when the railway age killed it. The fairground was in the meadow between castle and river, and here at the end of July a modest little fair still commemorates it. The Musée de la Vignasse, within the castle grounds, has souvenirs of the old fair, as well as some local Gallo-Roman finds.

Where to stay **Hôtel Robinson**, Route de Remoulins; tel. 66 59 21 32. A down-
and eat to-earth family hotel with a big garden, tennis, swimming pool and
Inexpensive other amenities; 30 rooms. Good local cooking in a simple setting. Closed February.

St Gilles St Gilles the hermit, who gave his name to Edinburgh's cathedral, has long been venerated in this little town on the fringe of the Camargue, a major pilgrimage centre during the Middle Ages. St Gilles founded an abbey here in the eighth century, but the present church is twelfth-century. It was damaged during the Wars of Religion: but its ornate west front has happily survived as one of Provence's finest examples of medieval sculpture. Its three portals carry scenes from the life of Christ, plus lions, camels and even a centaur. The church's eleventh-century crypt, spacious and Romanesque, has ogival vaulting: here St Gilles tomb was discovered in 1865 and is thought to be authentic. A solitary bell-tower stands amid the ruins of the eastern part of the church: inside it is a famous spiral staircase, Le Vis, whose steps are roofed over with stone, thus giving the impression of a curved funnel.

Twelve km west of St Gilles along the N572, just north of Galician, a turning to the right along a rough road will bring you to the Château de Fonteuil (tel. 66 73 33 13). Here Jean-Pierre and Geneviève Manquillet, former Paris TV producers turned local *vignerons*, will be delighted to show you their wine-farm and sell you its produce. They even have a tiny bull-ring, occasionally in active use.

Source Perrier

All the Perrier water that is drunk around the world, some 800 million bottles a year, comes from underground springs at this site 14 km south-west of Nîmes. An Englishman, St-John Harmsworth of the newspaper family, was the first to commercialise it: he bought the spring in 1903, and modelled the tapering green Perrier bottle on Indian clubs that he used for exercise.

The spring is now owned by a French firm, which employs 2,500 people here. You can go on a guided tour of the plant, which starts with a film showing production methods, including the quarrying of sand from Mont Ventoux for making the bottles. The attractive English-style mansion that Harmsworth built for himself is today used by the company as a PR centre.

Montpellier

34000

Languedoc-Roussillon's fascinating capital is today France's fastest-growing city, and has changed dramatically in the past twenty years from sleepy old wine town to trendy modern metropolis, its population swelling to 201,067 (300,000 including suburbs). Its university is one of Europe's oldest, and the town has long been a centre of the local wine trade: now, through a number of factors, it has developed other ambitions and has acquired some bold new architecture as well as fast-growing high-tech industries and research centres. All this makes for exciting contrasts, in a lively, youthful town with a huge student population, where old-style southern grace goes hand-in-hand with zippy modernity – all under the blazing Midi sun. Best of all, the Vieille Ville, the ancient kernel of narrow streets, has been delightfully restored and partly closed to traffic: it may have far fewer grand churches, palaces and museums than Aix or Avignon, but as an elegant and animated social forum it is even more attractive. In short, Montpellier is just about my favourite town in France. But a lot of other people flock here too because they love it – and the traffic can be horrendous.

Getting there   Fréjorgues Airport (tel. 67 65 60 65), 8 km from the city centre, is linked to Paris by five daily flights, and has scheduled services to many other towns too, in France and elsewhere. There are nine TGV expresses to Paris a day (a journey of under five hours) and good rail links with many other cities. The A9 autoroute going west to Toulouse and Spain, east to Marseille and Lyon, passes right beside Montpellier. The tourist office is at 6 Rue Maguelone; tel. 67 58 26 04.

History   The town has remarkably little history. From 1204 to 1349 it was a Spanish possession, and during this time its university was founded (in 1289) and began to develop the prowess in medicine which it retains to this day. Rabelais was a student here. After the Reformation, Montpellier became a Protestant fief, but in 1622 it fell to Louis XIII's forces and Richelieu built a citadel.

Montpellier today   In the 1960s, Montpellier was a sluggish place which, like the other towns of Languedoc, looked askance at the big new State development projects for the region. However, it began to stir out of its slumber, and in 1965 IBM set up a plant which later expanded into its largest in France, with 3,000 staff. It has since suffered cutbacks, like all IBM factories. But other modern industries have been enticed here, too, and ever since the present Socialist mayor, the dynamic and super-ambitious Georges Frèche, took power in 1977, change has gathered pace furiously. The university now has 45,000 students, and there are many new firms and research centres, in electronics, pharmaceuticals, medical equipment and foodstuffs. A new optical-fibre fifteen-channel television network has been installed, which now reaches almost every home. The airport has been doubled in size, and Frèche has just completed several monumental building projects close to the Vieille Ville: one of them, Antigone, is the work of the famous Barcelona architect Ricardo Bofill. Frèche's ebullient hyperbole ('Montpellier is the Rome of tomorrow!') may have its absurd aspect, and certainly other local towns such as Nîmes and Perpignan have become vociferously critical of their capital, which they fear is 'colonising' them just as Paris used to do. But Montpellier today has almost seized from Grenoble and Toulouse the mantle of number-one French boom-city. Success breeds success – and the sunny southern location makes it easy to attract scientists and executives to come and live here.

Main areas   A ring boulevard surrounds the Vieille Ville, which is built on a low hill. On its south-east side is the broad Place de la Comédie, main focus of the city's life, and east of that the new developments, Polygone and Antigone. While the whole of this central area is striking and unusual, the rest of the city is more humdrum: a drab commercial section around the station, to the south, leads to the residential Cours Gambetta district, and further out the modern town has expanded on all sides – new hospitals and university campuses to the north, industry to the east, suburbs to the south and north-west.

The central area, quite compact and much of it pedestrianised, is best tackled on foot: there are big car-parks all round it, with colour codes to help you find your bearings. The city's lay-out can make driving confusing at first, for the inner ring-road is one-way clockwise. In the suburbs, traffic is less dense.

What to do

Vieille Ville

The narrow streets and little squares of the old town have been elegantly restored, and the stone houses are beautifully lit at night – a fine backdrop for the busy social life of this quarter with its many bars and bistros, full of students in term-time. It is as enchanting a *vieille ville* as any in France, fully the equal of Aix or Arles, even if it has fewer really important buildings or museums. Take a stroll in the streets on either side of the stately Rue Foch, or of the Rue de la Loge that descends to the Place de la Comédie, and you will see many fine seventeenth and eighteenth-century noblemen's mansions, some still homes today. Many of the city's old churches were destroyed during the Wars of Religion, but one that has survived is the massive cathedral of St Pierre, dating from 1364 and restored in the 1860s. Next to it is the Medical Faculty, and just across the ring boulevard is the Jardin des Plantes, the oldest botanical garden in France, founded in 1593. Just to the south, forming an entrance to the Old Town, is an Arc de Triomphe built in 1691 in honour of Louis XIV, leading to the Promenade du Peyrou, a stately belvedere that ends in an aqueduct.

Musée Fabre

The city's leading museum is rather fusty and not too well lit, but it does contain some fine Flemish and Dutch paintings, notably by Brueghel and Jan van Steen, as well as works by Raphael, Veronese, Courbet, Greuze and Delacroix. Note Max Leenhardt's graphic canvas of Huguenot women prisoners in the tower at Aigues-Mortes.

Polygone, Corum and Antigone

These are the modern developments. The Polygone is a shopping piazza, including the new town hall and some hotels, that in the 1970s was grafted on to the eastern end of the Place de la Comédie (known locally as 'La place de l'Oeuf' because of its oval shape). North from this square, a broad shady esplanade leads to Le Corum, where an ambitious new complex, including a congress centre and opera house, has just been completed. Stand at the point known as Le Triangle, where Esplanade and Polygone converge to join the 'oeuf', and you will discover an impressive urban vista, uniting old and new.

Behind the Polygone is Ricardo Bofill's Antigone, also just completed. This unusual housing complex, with its curvaceous colonnades, massive porticos, piazzas and gardens, slopes down grandly to the River Lez. Bofill's neo-Classical style may be too monumentalist for some tastes, including my own, and some of his critics call it 'Mussolinian'. But it is commendable that Antigone is a medium-rent social housing project, not a preserve of new homes for the rich. And it's a remarkable venture for a town of this size.

What to do

Festivals

Modern dance is a speciality, and the major annual event is an international dance festival in July, coupled with a Radio France music festival. Apart from this, there's a photography festival in May, a festival of sports films in September and – more in keeping with local tradition – an international wine fair in October.

Year-round culture

The scene is quite lively. The Théâtre Municipal (opera house) has a resident company that stages operas of average quality, October to June; this theatre is used also for modern ballet (Dominique Bagouet's local company is good) and for concerts by the philharmonic orchestra. The best drama theatre company is the State-backed Treize Vents, based just out of town at the Domaine de Grammont, where the big new Salle Zénith is used for pop and jazz concerts. Le Club and Diagonal are the best cinemas for sub-titled foreign films. The weekly *Sortir* gives all cultural listings.

Sport

For tennis, try the Club de Grammont, Route de Mauguio. The Réganéous hotel (see below) has a swimming pool. For beaches, watersports and golf, see under La Grande-Motte (p. 251).

Shopping

Small shops selling porcelain, sculpted olive-wood and other local products can be found in and around the Rue de la Loge and Rue St-Guilhem in the old town; Soleiado, Rue Voltaire, is good for local fabrics, but not cheap. For wine, if you want to taste and buy the local Coteaux du Languedoc, try the Hôtel Montpelliérain des Vins du Languedoc, 7 Rue Jacques Coeur, or the Cave Coopérative Les Vignerons, 55 Rue St Cléophas.

Nightlife, bars and cafés

This student city that lives outdoors, and lives late, is a great place for terrace-cafés and bars. The trendiest bar is **Le Café Riche** on the Place de la Comédie, while the nicest of the hotel bars is the bright and cheerful **Louisiane**, the piano-bar of the Midi, see below. **Le Puit du Temps**, 17 Rue des Soeurs-Noires, a lively pub/bar in the old town, is a popular haunt of students; **Les Chandelles**, 18 Rue de l'Aiguillerie, is a night bar with music. For a slick nightclub, try **Le Privé** in the Réganéous Hotel, and for a good casino go to La Grande-Motte (see p. 251).

Where to stay

The modern chain hotels, Altéa, Novotel and Sofitel, are efficient but characterless, while the city's premier classic hotel, the Métropole, is comfortable but a bit dull (best feature is its quiet garden). My preferred choices are as follows.

Medium price

Grand Hôtel du Midi, 22 Blvd. Victor-Hugo; tel. 67 92 69 61. Very central, a handsome old renovated building, with period furnishings but modern comfort; 49 rooms. Stylish new restaurant.

Le Guilhem, 18 Rue J.-J.-Rousseau; tel. 67 52 90 90. Recently opened, a small hotel in an old building of the Vieille Ville, well run by a charming Parisian couple: 20 small but comfortable rooms, superbly equipped; excellent breakfasts. No restaurant.

Noailles, 2 Rue des Ecoles-Centrales; tel. 67 60 49 80. In the heart of the old town, a charming seventeenth-century mansion, with friendly, helpful service; 30 rooms (back ones are quietest). No restaurant. Closed Christmas to mid-January.

Inexpensive

Majestic, 4 Rue du Cheval Blanc; tel. 67 66 26 85. Cramped rather than majestic, but clean and well-run; very central, off Grande Rue. No restaurant.

Paix, 6 Rue Loys; tel. 67 66 05 88. Quiet and central, in the old town; 26 rooms; no restaurant. Closed Christmas, New Year.

Palais, 3 Rue Palais; tel. 67 60 47 38. Small (26 rooms), friendly, off Rue Foch in the old town. No restaurant.

Where to eat

Montpellier is not an expensive town, either for dining or sleeping, and the range of pleasant good-value eating places is enormous, especially round the student haunts of the Vieille Ville.

Upper-medium price

Le Chandelier, 3 Rue Leenhardt; tel. 67 92 61 62. In a drab street near the station, an elegant, spacious restaurant with Hellenic decor, stylish service and first-class creative cooking based on local dishes. Closed Sunday, three weeks in August.

La Réserve Rimbaud, 820 Avenue de St-Maur; tel. 67 72 52 53. The cooking is heavier than at Le Chandelier, but the setting is nicer – a charming outdoor terrace by a river, in the outskirts. Delightful *patronne*. Closed Monday, first half of January.

Medium price

Le Louvre, 2 Rue de la Vieille; tel. 67 60 59 37. An intimate, classic little bistro in the old town; good regional cooking, friendly owners. Closed May, early November, Sunday, Monday.

Le Menestrel, Place de la Préfecture; tel. 67 60 62 51. A converted thirteenth-century granary; the set menu is excellent value. Closed Sunday, Monday.

Inexpensive

Among the many good cheap places in the old town, try especially **Le Bouchon**, 7 Rue de l'Université; **Marco Polo**, 8 Rue Herberie, a stylish pizzeria in a lovely building; and in the Rue Jules-Latreilhe the trendy **B/oe/uf Agile** and the tiny, charming **Piccolina**.

Aigues-Mortes, Sète and the modern coast-resorts

Of the eight big new resorts built since the 1960s along the Languedoc coast (see p. 17), three – Port Camargue, La Grande-Motte and Cap d'Agde – are in the part between the Rhône delta and Béziers. With their bold modern architecture they contrast strikingly with the older towns on this coast, notably medieval Aigues-Mortes and the port of Sète – two of the most intriguing places in Languedoc. The coast here, backed by large lagoons, is almost entirely flat and not immediately attractive. But the new road network and other amenities are excellent, and there are long sandy beaches, which naturally get crowded in summer.

Aigues-Mortes
30220

This small medieval walled town, lovely but rather melancholy, stands 5 km inland amid salty marshes and lagoons (its name comes from *Aquae Mortuae*, 'Dead Water'). As you approach it across this empty plain, the sight it presents is unexpected and unforgettable – massive ancient walls, with one high tower rising above them. Its moat is now filled in, but otherwise its aspect has changed little, and its old streets within the gates retain their original grid pattern. In medieval times some 15,000 people lived within the walls, and today there are still 4,500 inhabitants – enough to make this a lively, fascinating place to visit, but of course thronged with tourists all summer.

In those days it was on the sea, but the coast has since silted up. Louis IX (St Louis) chose this spot from which to sail for the Seventh Crusade in 1248, and then the Eighth in 1270, and it was he who built the city keep, the Tour de Constance (a statue of him stands in the Place St Louis). After his death from the plague on the Eighth Crusade, his son Philip the Bold completed the ramparts.

What to see Ramparts and Tour de Constance

The summit of the tower provides fine views over the strange coastal landscape, and from it you can walk round the ramparts. The impressive circular keep contains two vaulted rooms. In the lower one, the old Oratory of St Louis is built into the thick walls: illuminated manuscripts and other souvenirs of St Louis at Aigues-Mortes are displayed in a showcase. The upper room is even more interesting, for it contains mementoes from the fourteenth to eighteenth centuries when the tower was a political prison, first for Templars, then for Huguenots and other victims of religious intolerance: the Protestants of the Nîmes region (see p. 236) still venerate the sufferings of their martyrs in this tower. You can see the courageous words carved on the walls by eighteenth-century Huguenots – notably, *'au ciel, résistez'* (resist to the end), inscribed by Marie Durand who was imprisoned here aged eight and released thirty-eight years later, physically a wreck but spiritually triumphant.

Late July to mid-August, there's a drama festival. Late August, the fête of St Louis commemorates his creation of the town.

Hostellerie des Remparts, Place Anatole-France; tel. 66 53 82 77. A seventeenth-century house within the ramparts, tastefully converted in harmony with its setting: bedrooms (19) have stone walls but are modernised. Friendly service; restaurant. Open March to October.

Hôtel des Arcades, 23 Bld. Gambetta; tel. 66 53 81 13. Sixteenth-century building within the ramparts, full of quirky charm. Antiques, lovely garden, excellent food. 6 rooms. Closed mid-February to mid-March.

St Louis, 10 Rue Amiral-Courbet; tel. 66 53 72 68. Another pleasantly converted house in the old town, with 21 pretty bedrooms, a warm welcome, and light, excellent cooking.

L'Escale, Avenue Tour de Constance; tel. 66 53 71 14. A simple, clean and convenient place just outside the ramparts. No restaurant.

Six km south-west of Aigues-Mortes, an old fishing village somewhat over-submerged by tourism but still appealing: you'll find plenty of cheap, goodish restaurants along its quais. By the road to Aigues-Mortes are two places worth visiting: the **Salins-du-Midi**, enormous saltworks that process some 500,000 tonnes of salt a year from the marshes; and, under the same ownership, the **Listel wine-cellars** of the Domaine du Bosquet, where the well-known rosé wine is produced from marshland vineyards. You can inspect the huge wine casks as well as taste and buy the wine (tel. 66 53 60 80).

Just south of Le Grau-du-Roi, this is the most easterly of the new modern resorts on this coast, and has been created out of an empty stretch of marsh. Attractive in its way, and very spacious, it is one vast marina for some 4,000 boats, so designed that each villa has its own mooring. While geared mainly towards sailing, it also offers tennis and riding, and has two good sandy beaches.

Le Spinaker; tel. 66 51 54 93. A cheerful modern hotel on the marina's central jetty; the 21 bedrooms all have balconies facing the port. Swimming pool; and 10 moorings free to residents. Closed November, mid-January to mid-February.

Le Spinaker (see above). A light, luxurious dining-room facing the marina; charming service, and good inventive cooking with the accent on very fresh fish. Closed Sunday night, Monday.

As if competing with the old ramparts of Aigues-Mortes, the ranks of ten-storey ziggurats of this New Babylon are visible for a long way along the shore. It is the most notorious and controversial of the new resorts, also the most sophisticated and the largest, its all-year population of 4,000 swelling in high summer to some 45,000. Several of the newer blocks of holiday flats are in weird shapes and colours, notably in the Quartier du Couchant, to the west: some resemble giant fairground wheels, painted red, blue or purple. Not everyone would wish to spend a holiday in this surreal Op-art setting, however gay the colours and lavish the amenities (see below): yet La Grande-Motte is always full in season, popular with British, Germans, Dutch and Scandinavians as well as French. It has camping sites for 15,000 people and a huge marina. Woodlands have been planted just behind the resort. Details from the tourist office, Place du 1er Octobre; tel. 67 56 62 62.

La Grande-Motte has also become a residential suburb of Montpellier, only 20 km away, so to some extent it remains open all the year, and is invaded by local city-dwellers at weekends.

What to do
Sports

The range of facilities is large. There are two new eighteen-hole golf courses in a wooded setting, as well as tennis, riding, archery and gymnastics. Watersports include sailing, water-skiing and windsurfing, and for bathing you can choose between the long sandy beaches and indoor or outdoor pools. The marina has berths for 1,500 boats.

Nightlife

The casino is the best in the area, and **La Copacabana** is a trendy and animated nightclub.

Where to stay
Upper-
medium price

Altéa, Rue du Port; tel. 67 56 90 81. Large (135 rooms), comfortable chain hotel by the port, occupying one of the ziggurats. Two restaurants, swimming pool. Open March to December.

Azur, Espl. de la Capitainerie; tel. 67 56 56 00. Very attractive modern hotel, quite glamorous, in a quiet position at the end of the jetty; 20 rooms. No restaurant. Closed December, January.

Medium price

Acropolis, Quartier du Couchant; tel. 67 56 76 22. Near the sea, with bold designs and modern comforts; slick and breezy; 24 rooms; no restaurant. Open Easter to September.

Where to eat
Upper-
medium price

Alexandre-Amirauté, Espl. de la Capitainerie; tel. 67 56 63 63. Fancy period decor and a bit too much chic: but the modern cuisine is among the best in the region. Closed early November, mid-January to mid-February, Sunday night and Monday out of season.

Maguelone

L'Amiral, Avenue du Casino; tel. 67 56 65 53. One of the best of the resort's many restaurants, very good for fish. Closed mid-December to end January.

West of La Grande-Motte, and nearer to Montpellier, are the two older bathing resorts of **Carnon-Plage** and **Palavas-les-Flots**, ugly and a bit down-at-heel, so hardly worth a stop. Beyond Palavas, however, down a narrow road between the lagoon and the sea, you will come to a great surprise: the tiny former cathedral of Maguelone, serenely secluded from the tourist throng. This curious ancient site was probably a Phocaean colony in the sixth century BC, then a thriving religious community in the Middle Ages: but in the Wars of Religion it was Protestant, and so in 1622 it was sacked on Richelieu's orders and its population expelled. Today only the church survives, part Romanesque, part Gothic, restored in the nineteenth century, and still sometimes used for services. The sculptured portal bears an inscription '1178'. An austere, remote, rather moving place.

Frontignan

Here we are back to modernity indeed, for this busy town on the

Montpellier-Sète main road has a large Mobil Oil refinery. It earns its living also from a very different liquid: a reputed local muscat wine, whose distillery, the Coopératif du Muscat, can be visited.

Sète
34200

With its picturesque canals, Sète (population 40,466) brings a touch of Venice to the Languedoc, and is one of the most lively and pleasing towns in the region. Its port, the largest on France's south coast after Marseille and Fos, was first built under Louis XIV, then enlarged in the nineteenth century and is linked to the Rhône by a major canal: hence the many industries in the area, including oil refineries and chemical works. The port also handles the bulk import of Italian wines – to the indignation of local growers who have sometimes blockaded it. And it is Languedoc's leading fishing port, mostly for sardines and tunny. The most attractive area of town is the Vieux Port and the lower part of the Canal de Sète.

What to see
Paul Valéry's
tomb and
museum

The poet Paul Valéry (1871-1945) was born in Sète and remained deeply attached to it, even though he spent most of his adult life in Paris, where he died. He was laid to rest in the lovely quiet cemetery high above the sea that had inspired his best-known poem, *Le Cimetière Marin* (The Cemetery by the Sea), a meditation on the closeness of death and the difficulty of living: '*Le vent se lève!* . . . *il faut tenter de vivre!*' (The wind is rising, we must try to live) is one of its lines. And today his tomb is a fitting spot to ponder on the poem's philosophical themes (some brash modern tourist developments are happily just out of sight). The adjacent Musée Paul Valéry is disappointingly thin on souvenirs of the poet, but has a lively collection of photos relating to another famous son of Sète, Georges Brassens (1921–81). Singer, poet, and left-wing champion of the poor, he was born in Sète and lies buried here, but not in the same cemetery as Valéry. There are also some modern paintings.

Behind the museum a path leads on to the Mont St-Clair, one of the few hills that interrupts the Languedoc coastal plain. From its top there are good views, of the coast and of the huge lagoon of Thau, where oyster and mussel breeding takes place.

What to do
Festivals

Sète is famous for its nautical jousts, a tradition dating from the seventeenth century: young men dressed in white stand on platforms fixed to large rowing boats, and each team tries to knock the other into the water, amid much song and laughter. This sport takes place several times each summer, most notably during the Fête de la Saint-Louis at the end of August, which includes a procession of decorated boats – Sète's Venetian dimension, but entirely home-grown. Mid-July to mid-August there's a theatre festival, too.

Where to stay
Medium price

Grand Hôtel, 17 Quai le Lattre-De-Tassigny; tel. 67 74 71 77. Recently modernised, a sound traditional hotel facing a canal, with a patio at the back; 47 rooms. Restaurant. Closed Christmas period.

Les Terrasses du Lido, Rond-Point Europe; tel. 67 51 39 60. On the coast, near the beach, pleasant little family-run hotel with pool.

Where to eat

Medium price

Inexpensive

**Cap
d'Agde**
34300

Where to stay
Medium price
Where to eat
*Upper-
medium price*
Medium price

Agde
34300

What to do
Festivals
*Where to stay
and eat*

Good if pricey food. 8 rooms. Closed February.

Sète has a strong local tradition of cuisine, especially for fish, and even some specialities of its own, such as *rouille de seiche* (cuttlefish in garlic sauce). A number of the restaurants around the Vieux Port, although touristy, offer good value.

La Palangrotte, 1 Rampe Paul-Valéry; tel. 67 74 80 35. Some of the best fish around the Vieux Port; try the bouillabaisse for a treat. Closed mid-January to mid-February, Monday out of season.

L'Amandier, Blvd. Joliot-Curie; tel. 67 51 30 30. Copious portions, and a good choice of menus, at this lively modern bistro out on the coastal corniche road to the west.

La Rascasse, 27 Quai du Gén. Durand; tel. 67 74 38 46. A lively, popular quayside bistro, with swift service and good cooking; the fish menus are a splendid blow-out. Closed January, Monday.

Another of the big new resorts on this coast, Cap d'Agde contrasts with the modernism of La Grande-Motte, for it has been built like a pastiche of a local fishing village, with pretty, traditional houses in pastel shades – a good idea, save that with so many cafés, shops, bistros and discos along the quayfronts, the whole place has now become a bit overblown and tatty. However, there's something for everyone, including a casino, sports centre, new golf course, and moorings for 1,700 boats.

Tucked away on the outskirts is a torch-bearer of that major growth-industry of modern tourism: nudity. The nudist holiday town here, Europe's largest, has its own nightclubs, supermarkets and casino – and beds for 20,000 bodies, many of which are British and German, and quite a lot of them ageing and paunchy. Nudity is compulsory, except in bad weather. You need a special ticket to enter the town, and photography and filming are allowed only within families. There are various cult and sect activities, Oriental or Californian in style.

St-Clair, Place St-Clair; tel. 67 26 36 44. A functional but comfortable new hotel right by the port; 82 rooms. Open April to October.

Côté Jardin; tel. 67 26 33 33. Facing the port, a stylish and comfortable restaurant with a lovely terrace, cheerful service, and good, if slightly overpriced, food. Closed October to mid-March.

Le Braséro; tel. 67 26 24 75. Next door, also with a nice terrace; less elegant but better value. Closed January, February.

This old fishing port (population 13,235) on the River Hérault, 4 km inland, is notable mainly for its curious, fortified former cathedral, complete with battlements, built partly with tufa-ash from the nearby volcanic hill of Mont St-Loup, now extinct.

Agde, like Sète, has its nautical jousts, mostly in July and August. On the second Saturday in July they are held at night.

La Tamarissière, 21 Quai Théophile Cornu; tel. 67 94 20 87. A former fishermen's pub, now a chic riverside inn, near the sea south-

Upper-medium price | west of town. Inventive variations on classic local dishes, served on a flowery terrace facing the fishing boats; 33 rooms. Open mid-March to end November.

Pézenas, Béziers and Narbonne

The plain south of Montpellier, gently undulating, has more to it than its seemingly endless vineyards. Here are three historic old towns of great interest – Pézenas where Molière wittily performed, Béziers where the Cathars cruelly suffered, and Narbonne where the Romans mightily ruled. Down on the coast, and not to be missed, is the strange village of Gruissan, where bathers idly suntan.

Pézenas
34120

This distinguished old town (population 7,841) is surrounded by rolling vineyards, and by hoardings that urge you to buy *'le vin de Molière'*. Certainly he drank plenty of the local stuff when he played here with his theatre company from 1650 to 1657 – in the days when this was one of the major towns of Languedoc. After 1456 it became the seat of the governors of the province, one of whom, Armand de Bourbon, Prince of Conti, held court in such style in the Château de Grange-des-Prés (now ruined) that, with its fountains and gardens, it was dubbed 'the Versailles of Languedoc'. The Prince invited and sponsored Molière, but on his death the golden age of Pézenas ended. However, its fine ensemble of fifteenth- to seventeenth-century houses, austere but dignified, bears witness to that past.

What to see

You should park in the broad Place du 14 Juillet, and explore the old town on foot to enjoy its stylish gateways and balconies. In and near the graceful little Place Gambetta, look for the **Tribunal de Commerce** (wrought ironwork) and the fifteenth-century **Hôtel de Lacoste** (Gothic arches, beamed ceiling). Other notable buildings are the **Hôtel de Wicque** (Renaissance façade) and the **Sacristie des Pénitents Blancs** (fifteenth-century courtyard). The rather gloomy little **Vulliod St-Germain Museum** of archaeology and local arts has some seventeenth-century Aubusson tapestries. The Jewish ghetto around the Rue de la Juiverie dates from the fourteenth century.

What to do

There's an open-air Molière drama festival in July, and various cultural and folklore events from June to September. Twelve km east of Pézenas is the Abbaye de Valmagne (tel. 67 78 06 09), a lovely mellow old abbey set amid vineyards, with a fine church and cloister. You can visit the *chais*, and taste and buy the wines.

Where to stay
Inexpensive

Genieys, 9 Avenue Aristide-Briand; tel. 67 98 13 99. A pleasant, family-run Logis de France, with copious good food; 27 rooms. Closed one week November, one week February.

Where to eat

Léonce, 8 Place de la République, 34510 Florensac; tel. 67 77 03 05.

Upper-medium price

A chic modern restaurant in a village 10 km south of Pézenas, serving excellent and interesting cuisine. Seven simple inexpensive bedrooms. Closed mid-September to mid-October, Monday.

Béziers
34500

Located on a promontory above the River Orb, this large town (population 78,477) was settled in c. 35 BC by the Romans, who built a forum and temples, probably on the site of the present town hall. Its great moment in history, a tragic one, came in 1209 when Simon de Montfort's Crusaders massacred 30,000 citizens in the worst outrage of the Albigensian Wars. Since the nineteenth century Béziers has been the principal trading centre of the Languedoc wine industry. It also has one of the leading rugby teams in France. But it is not a rich town (in this area, wine is rarely a great money-spinner) and there's a good deal of poverty. For many years after the war, until 1983, its mayor was Communist.

What to see

The old quarter near the cathedral, in part closed to traffic, is attractive. From here you can stroll to the main promenade, the Allées Paul-Riquet, named after Béziers' best-known son (1604-80) who built the Canal du Midi. This leads to the Plateau des Poètes, a park with busts of poets. The former cathedral of **St Nazaire**, a large, impressive Gothic building with a high vaulted roof, was rebuilt after being sacked in 1209 and has two fortified towers and a fine rose window. There's a good view of the river from its terrace. The **Musée du Vieux Bitterois et du Vin**, at the Caserne St-Jacques, has Greek, Roman and Etruscan finds, and historical details of wine-making. The **Musée des Beaux-Arts**, close to the cathedral, is well above average for a provincial art museum. It has some quite good eighteenth- to nineteenth-century works by Corot, Delacroix and others, and on the stairway a set of curious visionary paintings on the theme of Orpheus by Marcel Feguiels. Strangely enough, there's also a sizeable collection of Greek vases found at Delos.

What to do

Spanish-style *corridas* (that is, the bull is killed) are held in the old Roman arena, from March to September. The *feria*, a folklore festival with bullfights, fills the first two weeks of August.

Shopping

There are several antique shops in the Rue Viennet area near the cathedral.

Where to stay
Medium price

Europe, 87 Avenue du Président-Wilson; tel. 67 76 08 97. Useful for a night's halt, a modern hotel on the Agde road; 30 rooms. No restaurant.

Inexpensive

Paris, 70 Avenue Gambetta; tel. 67 28 43 80. A clean, well-run little place near the station; 17 rooms; no restaurant.

Where to eat
Medium price

Le Framboisier, 33 Avenue du Président-Wilson; tel.67 62 62 57. A serious, quiet, tasteful little place; Angel Yagues' cooking is excellent. Closed Monday, parts of February and August.

Inexpensive

There are several pleasant little bistros just east of the cathedral, for example, the **Brasserie du Palais**, Place de la Révolution, and **Aux Pâtes Fraîches**, Rue Viennet.

**Oppidum
d'Ensérune**

Standing on a hilltop 6 km south-west of Béziers, this is one of the most important known pre-Roman settlements in France. It was not discovered until 1915, but excavations since then have revealed a former Celtic town dating back to at least 600 BC, with a population of up to 8,000. The foundations are clearly visible. For the non-specialist, the main point of interest on the site is the museum: as well as silos and funeral urns, this contains Greek pottery from the Aegean, suggesting that the Greeks traded here long before Roman times.

Narbonne
11100

Narbonne (population 42,657) is today a rather sleepy town devoted to tourism and the wine trade. In Roman times, however, it was a major city, one of the first to be colonised outside Italy and the capital of Gallia Narbonensis. Its port, now silted up, was then extremely busy. Charlemagne later created a duchy here, with Narbonne as its capital.

What to see

Several remarkable buildings have survived, not from Roman but from medieval times. The cathedral of **St Just**, one of the tallest Gothic buildings in France, towers over the town, visible from afar: begun in 1272, it was never finished, for when the choir had been built the local rulers would not let the nave be added, and so it remains today – something of an oddity. Its treasury contains some fine fifteenth- to seventeenth-century tapestries. Its fifteenth-century cloister leads to another mighty edifice, the thirteenth- to fourteenth-century fortified **Palace of the Archbishops**, with three square towers. The palace contains two museums, one of local antiquities and one devoted to art, with four fine Aubusson tapestries. Not far away in an old church is the **Musée Lapidaire**, with interesting Roman finds. And near to this you'll find the curious **Maison des Trois Nourrices** (three wet-nurses), a sixteenth-century building so named because the cornice of its Renaissance window is held up by buxom caryatids.

Where to stay
Medium price

La Résidence, 6 Rue du 1er-Mai; tel. 68 32 19 41. In a quiet street near the cathedral, an unusual but sympathetic little place. The decor is Victorian boudoir style, quaint and theatrical, almost kitschy (velvet curtains and so on). But comfort and service are exemplary. There are 26 rooms; no restaurant. Closed January.

Where to eat
*Upper-
medium price*

L'Alsace, 2 Avenue Paul-Semard; tel. 68 65 10 24. A big conventional place opposite the station. Not much charm, but comfort and good food. Closed Monday, Tuesday.

Inexpensive

La Brasucade, 31 Cours de la République; tel. 68 32 47 95. A lively, popular pizzeria, very central.

Gruissan

Set amid lagoons by the sea 15 km south-east of Narbonne, this very curious village-cum-bathing resort is made up of several disparate elements that somehow harmonise. First, the sleepy old fishermen's village, built in a circular pattern on a low, lagoon-girt hill and topped by the stumpy ruins of a castle (you can clamber up its tower for a good view of the marshes, the rocky hills and the coast). Second, the older resort, Gruissan-Plage, made up of rows of holiday-cabins built on stilts to protect them from the frequent storms and flooding. They look windswept and bizarre, and were the setting for the early scenes of Jean-Jacques Beineix' equally bizarre film *37.2 degrés le matin [Betty Blue]*. Third, across the lagoon, the new 1970s resort of Gruissan, sister to Cap d'Agde and La Grande Motte but smaller and more intimate: its curly-roofed brown houses around the big marina are not unattractive.

Fourth, just north of Gruissan, and in total contrast with the rest of this flat coast, is the wild rocky limestone massif of **La Clape**. You should drive up through it to the remote hilltop chapel of Notre-Dame-des-Auzils (signposted), where memorials to sailors lost at sea, some nineteenth-century, some quite recent, stand either side of a steep pathway. It has all been newly and neatly restored, and is a most appealing spot, amid the gorse, scrub and fragrant pines.

Narbonne-Plage and St-Pierre are two very ugly run-down bathing resorts, just along the coast to the east. An ultra-modern aquarium with 'space-age' exhibits has recently been completed at St-Pierre.

Réserve africaine de Sigean

Ten km south of Narbonne, just off the N9 to Perpignan, is this safari park, one of the biggest in France. The animals live in semi-liberty amid the hills and lagoons. By car you can visit the lions, rhinoceroses and Tibetan bears; on foot you can get close to the antelopes, zebras, alligators and many beautiful birds.

At Portel-des-Corbières, just west of the safari park, the Château de Lastours, tel. 68 48 29 17, is an important centre of Corbières wine production, and is open to visits for tasting and buying.

Abbey of Fontfroide

Over to the south-west of Narbonne, tucked away in a fold of the Corbières foothills, is this lovely eleventh-century abbey, typically Cistercian in its architecture and its setting in this lonely spot. The terraced garden lined with cypresses contrasts with the barren hills behind. You can visit the pretty cloister, and the restored interior with its modern stained glass. Concerts are held from time to time. Various ruined feudal châteaus crown the hilltops all round here, in this wild, impressive landscape.

Carcassonne, the Corbières and Minervois

The mighty medieval fortress of Carcassonne stands above the Aude Valley, north-west of the wild and lovely Corbières hills where there are many interesting, unspoilt villages to explore – notably Lagrasse, with its old abbey, now an unusual religious centre. The vineyards on

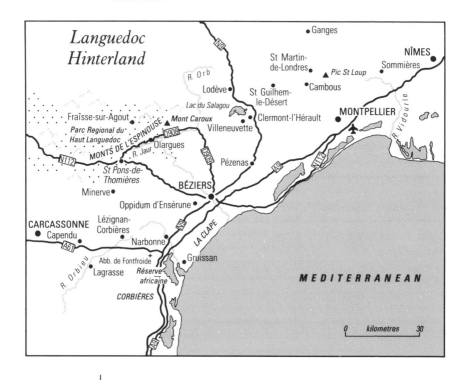

Languiedoc Hinterland

the slopes of the hills produce the fruity red Corbières wines that are excellent value. North of the Aude valley is the Minervois district, also the home of good, inexpensive red wines. Here, astride two gorges, is the strange, remote village of Minerve, whose setting and history never cease to fire my imagination.

Carcassonne
11000

Carcassonne (population 42,450) is in two parts. On a hilltop across the River Aude stands La Cité, Europe's largest medieval fortress and one of the best preserved. It looks spectacular at night, seen from afar, when its great circle of towers and ramparts are floodlit. The newer town down by the river, the Ville Basse, a grid of straight streets, is of no great interest.

History

The town's position in the Aude Valley, between Toulouse and Narbonne, long made it strategic, and its medieval history was stormy. Parts of its walls were built by the Romans, then the Visigoths in the fifth century enlarged it into a fortress (the present line of the towers is theirs), and in the ninth century Charlemagne besieged it for five years. Simon de Montfort and his anti-Cathar Crusaders captured the fortress in the early thirteenth century, and he used it as a base for his murderous forays. Then St Louis (Louis IX) in turn besieged and took La Cité, expelling its population, for whom he built the lower town. His son Philip the Bold strengthened the ramparts, giving the place its present appearance. By then, in the later thirteenth century, the fortress was self-supporting enough to withstand any siege: smiths forged armour, a mill ground wheat, a mint coined money, while a cistern in the Narbonne Tower was capable of holding six months' supply of water. The cathedral was built; also an open-air theatre.

La Cité was a major strongpoint in the seventeenth-century war with Spain: but when, after this, Roussillon was annexed to France, the fortress lost much of its military value and fell gradually into ruin. It was about to be dismantled when in 1844 the State commissioned Viollet-le-Duc to rebuild the ramparts and the cathedral – the world's first restoration on this scale. This controversial architect has since been much criticised, here as in some of his other reconstructions, for being over-thorough and adding too many artificial touches. But time has mellowed his work, which now blends more easily with the original parts. And by restoring the skyline of turrets and towers, he has enhanced La Cité's romantic image.

What to see
La Cité

Park the car outside the ramparts and then walk into La Cité, which measures some 500 m by 250 and is still a real lived-in place, with 500 inhabitants. Its old streets are lined, inevitably, with souvenir shops, plus a few more tasteful craft shops. To take the guided tour or to walk on the ramparts, you must go through the massive gateway of the inner castle, the **Château Comtal**, where it's worth taking a look at the lively museum of fifteenth-century costumes: this is the work of Bermans and Nathans, of London, theatrical costumiers, and includes such figures as an astrologist, monk, fool and troubadour ('the television of the period', says a notice). The guided tour begins with the château, an austere feudal building with a timbered inner courtyard and a wooden balcony from which burning oil was poured on assailants. You are taken up and down steep, narrow stone stairways, and are shown various towers including the **Tour de l'Inquisition** where trials took place (Cathars were tortured here). The outer ramparts have fifty-four towers and measure 1.5 km in circumference: at several points there are good views towards the Pyrenees. The former cathedral of **St-Nazaire**, over-restored in places, has a Romanesque nave and some fine statuary and stained-glass rose windows.

The **Ville Basse** has one or two interesting churches, and an art museum with Dutch, Flemish and French paintings. This museum also contains souvenirs of the family of the great philosophical poet André Chénier (1762–94), who had strong connections with Languedoc. Chénier, a moderate revolutionary, fell victim to the Terror and was guillotined.

What to do
Festivals

In May a ceremony called The Walk of the Donkey takes place below La Cité's west walls. In July operas and plays are performed in the fortress's thirteenth-century open-air theatre, some on medieval themes; there's a big fireworks display there on 14 July.

Where to stay
Top price

Domaine d'Auriac, Route Ste-Hilaire; tel. 68 25 72 22. Three km south of the town, a creeper-covered nineteenth-century mansion with a park and small lake; large rooms (23), pleasant staff, and very good food which is both classic (for example, cassoulet) and innovative, served on the terrace or by a log fire. Closed January, Sunday night.

Medium price

Le Donjon, 2 Rue du Comte Roger; tel. 68 71 08 80. An old building within La Cité, finely converted into a most elegant little hotel (36 rooms): rough stone walls, tiled floors, and a quiet inner garden where meals are served in summer, secluded from the tourist mob. Good local cooking (dinner only).

Montségur, 27 Allée d'Iéna; tel. 68 25 31 41. A useful classic hotel in the Ville Basse; some of the 21 rooms have fine antique furniture. Closed mid-December to mid-January.

Inexpensive

Les Remparts, 3 Place du Grand Puits; tel. 68 71 27 72. A friendly and fairly quiet hotel (18 rooms) in an old building of La Cité. No restaurant.

Cathare, 53 Rue Jean Bringer; tel. 68 25 65 92. Clean, cheerfully decorated; in the heart of the lower town. Goodish inexpensive meals; 17 rooms.

Where to eat
Upper-
medium price

Auberge du Pont-Levis Pautard; tel. 68 25 55 23. Near Porte Narbonnaise, just outside the old city walls. Sound classic cooking, and a view of the old city from the terrace. Closed two weeks October, three weeks February.

Medium price

Le Languedoc, 32 Allée d'Iéna; tel. 68 25 22 17. A serious, comfortable place in the Ville Basse, with a charming garden; classic local cooking. Closed mid-December to mid-January, Monday.

Lagrasse
11220

A road from Carcassonne winds south-east through the wild foothills of the Corbières massif, and after 39 km reaches the old village of Lagrasse, secluded in a lovely valley. Just across the little River Orbieu (note the eleventh-century bridge) stands the **Abbey of Lagrasse** – a most unusual and fascinating place. It dates from the thirteenth century, but was much restored in the eighteenth when the stately château-like main buildings were added. For some time it was empty: but then in 1972 a group of students from Montpellier, led by a monk, took it over and created here a lay religious community, La Théophanie, which is Catholic Melchite and follows a Byzantine liturgy. Their aim, they told me, is to help the Church in the Levant by creating a better understanding of it among Catholics in Western Europe. Some twenty-five adults with thirty-five children live here together, eating communally but remaining financially independent. Some have jobs outside the community; others take part in the making of handicrafts and of apéritifs based on local aromatic plants; and they help to reproduce old icons. All these products, icons included, can be bought in the abbey shop. An artist in the village also makes new icons: if you'd like to purchase one, the abbey will tell you how to contact him.

The abbey's atmosphere is serene, friendly and informal. The church, built on the foundations of an old Carolingian one, has now been decked out in the Melchite manner with icons, carpets and red curtains; soft religious music plays, and incense burns. To one side are some ruined older parts of the abbey, including the eleventh-century south transept and a sixteenth-century tower, which you can climb for a good view. A separate entrance gives access to other old abbey buildings, now municipally owned: the very pretty cloister, much restored, the vaulted refectory, and a chapel with a thirteenth-century ceramic paving.

Concerts and folk-dance shows are held at the abbey in summer.

At **St-Laurent-de-la-Cabrerisse**, 11 km east of Lagrasse, you are in the heart of the Corbières vineyard region. Here the Château de Caraguilhes, tel. 68 43 62 05, is one of the main production centres where you can taste and buy the local wines.

Where to stay
Medium price

Hôtellerie de l'Abbaye; tel. 68 43 12 85. A few nicely-furnished rooms are let out to individuals or groups, and simple meals are offered. Staying here is an attractive way of mixing briefly with the community.

Where to stay
and eat
Upper-medium
Lézignan-
Corbières
11200

Relais du Val d'Orbieu, at Ornaisons, 8 km E of Lezignan; tel. 68 27 10 27. Nicely converted old millhouse, on vine-growing plain. Flowery garden, big pool, warm welcome. 43 rooms.

A small town on the same main road, with an excellent country inn, in the heart of a wine-producing district – Minervois vineyards to the north, Corbières to the south.

Where to stay
and eat
Inexpensive
Minerve
34210

Le Tassigny et restaurant Le Tournedos, Place de Lattre De Tassigny; tel. 68 27 11 51. Another simple, animated auberge; great value both for bed and board; 18 rooms. Closed September.

Minerve, one of the strangest and most evocative places in the South of France, is a tiny remote village up in the *causses* (see p. 273), 45 km north-east of Carcassonne and 33 km from Narbonne. You drive from the south over bare hills, and suddenly there it is below you, stuck on a narrow rocky spur between the twin gorges of the Cesse and Briant – a site both grandiose and austere. It has been inhabited since prehistoric times, as is clear from the many caves and dolmens in the vicinity. The medieval fortress that stood here was the scene of one of the most terrible episodes in the Cathar wars: de Montfort with 7,000 men besieged it for five weeks in 1210, forced its capitulation, then burned alive 140 Cathar *parfaits*, watching the fires 'with great joy' (according to an eye witness). Villagers today still relate this story angrily.

What to see

Park south of the gorge, then walk over the ancient bridge to explore the village. The eleventh-century Romanesque church, newly restored, has fifth- to ninth-century graffiti including an inscription on the altar stone showing that it was consecrated in 456. Nearby is a high keep, last vestige of the Cathars' castle. In the narrow Rue des Martyrs, amid a number of craft shops for tourists, is a museum of prehistory and archaeology, containing remains of a Palaeolithic skeleton dated to 15,000 BC: it was found in 1948 in a local cave. Another small museum has life-size scenes of the Cathar massacre. Just west of the village, accessible by a narrow footpath that leads giddily down the side of the gorge (*not* for those fearful of heights) is yet another unusual curiosity: natural stone bridges in the bed of the gorge, carved by the river in the early part of the Quaternary period.

Where to stay and eat
Inexpensive

Relais Chantovent; tel. 68 91 14 18. Good local cooking served in generous portions, and 5 simple bedrooms, at this pleasant old house above the gorge. Closed January, February.

Languedoc's hilly hinterland

Behind the flat coastal plain of Languedoc lies the undulating *garrigue* country, and behind this again are the southern slopes of the mountainous Cévennes and their south-westerly extension, the Monts de l'Espinouse. This Languedoc hinterland is a wild and lovely region of lakes, forests, ravines and remote unspoilt villages, much of it excellent country for hiking or riding. Alternatively, it can easily be toured by car on day-trips from the coast.

This section traces a route through the hills from west to east, starting with the Monts de l'Espinouse, which form part of the Parc Régional du Haut Languedoc, a recently-created conservation area. Here official efforts are being made to restore old buildings and revive dying handicrafts, as well as to develop leisure centres for canoeing, rock-climbing, potholing and other adventurous sports. Full details can be obtained from the Parc's information centre at 13 Rue du Cloître, St Pons; tel. 67 97 02 10.

St Pons-de-Thomières
34220

This little town in a mountain valley, on the old main road from Béziers to Toulouse, has a museum of local prehistory and a curious cathedral, partly fortified, that dates from the twelfth century and was rebuilt in the eighteenth. Near Corniou, 5 km to the west, on the N112, the **Grotte de la Devèze** has fine filigree-like stalactites and stalagmites, whose ochre colour comes from the cave's iron oxide.

Where to stay
Upper-medium price

Château de Ponderach, Route de Narbonne; tel. 67 97 02 57. This lovely seventeenth-century manor in a vast wooded park has been the home of the Counotte family for 300 years, and they now run it gracefully as a country hotel, with excellent service. The 11 bedrooms offer better value than the meals. Open April to early October.

Medium price

Auberge du Cabaretou; tel. 67 97 02 31. A pleasant inn (10 rooms) in a wild mountain setting 10 km north of St Pons on D907;

Fraîsse-sur-Agout

very good food. Open March to October.

An isolated village in the wooded Agout Valley, 23 km north of St Pons. It contains the **Prat d'Alaric**, a typical old farmhouse of the Espinouse area that has been restored by the Parc Régional as a showpiece of traditional rural architecture; its low roof is thatched with gorse and broom.

Monts de l'Espinouse

This wild rocky range extends for some 25 km, north-east from St Pons. Of the scenic routes that wind through it, one goes from Fraîsse to Olargues, another from Lamalou-les-Bains via Rosis to Murat-sur-Vèbre: if you turn off this road at Rosis to the hamlet of **Douch**, from there you can make a sixty-minute trek to the summit of **Mont Caroux** (1,091 m), where the fantastic view extends as far as the coast and even the Pyrenees. Between Rosis and Lamalou is a forest planted in 1930 in memory of 560 writers who died fighting for France, including Charles Péguy (1873–1914). Many of them, like him, were killed in the First World War.

Olargues

A picturesque village on a promontory above the River Jaur, at the foot of the Espinouse range. To the east, the drive down the Orb Valley to ancient **Roquebrun** is extremely attractive, through a landscape studded with trees of oak and olive, orange and lemon.

Where to stay
Medium price

Domaine de Rieumégé, Route de St Pons; tel. 67 97 73 99. A tastefully converted seventeenth-century house in a peaceful rural setting. Good food; swimming pool and tennis; 12 rooms. Open May to September.

Lodève

A busy market and industrial town (population 8,557) on the N9 highway, 54 km north-west of Montpellier. It dates from Roman times, when Nero had coins minted here; since the thirteenth century it has made textiles, and is now also a centre of uranium mining. Local history is well represented in the **Musée Cardinal de Fleury**; the thirteenth-century part-fortified cathedral of St Fulcran is also worth a visit. The Saturday market is lively, and in May the Fête of St-Fulcran has a colourful procession.

Where to stay

Hôtel de la Paix, 11 Blvd. Montalangue; tel. 67 44 07 46. This hotel makes a useful and inexpensive night's stop; 18 rooms.

Amid wild hills some 20 km to the north-west, in the large converted farmhouse of La Borie-Noble, is the well-known religious community of **L'Arche**, founded by the late Lanzo del Vasco, a Sicilian who was a leading disciple of Mahatma Gandhi. Here a multinational group of over 100 young people practise the simple communal life in an atmosphere of manifest joy and serenity: they pool their money, weave their own clothes, and have no electricity, only candles. Visitors are welcome, so long as they come in the right spirit – and many of them might find L'Arche rather moving.

Villeneuvette

An early example of an industrial estate, this little walled village 3 km south-west of Clermont-l'Hérault was founded in the seventeenth century by Louis XIV as a cloth-weaving centre for the army.

You enter under an arch that bears the words, *'Honneur au Travail'*. On the tiny square are workmen's cottages; nearby you will see factory buildings, and a reservoir once used to wash the cloth. Amazingly, the textile workshops remained in use until as recently as 1955.

Some 5 km to the west is **Mourèze**, a half-ruined village in a fantastic setting of rocks eroded into strange shapes. To the north is the big man-made lake of Salagou, good for bathing and boating.

St Guilhem-le-Désert

St Guilhem is a charming old village with a strange history, tucked away in a ravine of the Hérault gorge, 42 km north-west of Montpellier. Guilhem, a loyal lieutenant of Charlemagne, discovered the site after fighting battles against the Saracens: he founded an abbey here, which still exists, and he gave it a piece of the 'True Cross' (supposedly Christ's) that Charlemagne had received from the Pope. The abbey, tenth-century Romanesque and austerely beautiful inside, is in the tiny main square: only part of its cloister remains, for the rest was bought by an American in 1906 and is now in New York's Metropolitan Museum. The area near the village is quite fertile: *'désert'* refers to the high *garrigue* beyond. The nearby ruined château once belonged to Don Juan, a Saracen who ravaged the region until killed by Guilhem: the latter had the tip of his nose cut off in the fight, and was thus known as *'Court-nez'* [Short-nose].

In the gorge 2 km to the south, by the Pont du Diable, is the remarkable **Grotte de la Clamouse**, a series of caves discovered in 1945 that in places form the bed of the River Hérault. The profusion of stalactites and stalagmites have been eroded into bizarre shapes, today cleverly illuminated. Guided tours are taken all year; there are many steep steps, but all is well lit.

Up in the wild valley of the Buèges, some 20 km to the north, a golf course has recently been built in a superb isolated setting.

St Martin-de-Londres

The name has nothing to do with London, but comes from the old Celtic word *lund* (that is, *lande*, or heath). This particular St Martin-in-the-Fields is an old village in an open rolling landscape, 25 km north of Montpellier on the D986: it has remains of twelfth-century fortifications, and an eleventh-century church gracelessly rebuilt in the 1870s. To the north-east, the pretty village of **Notre-Dame-de-Londres** has an impressive fourteenth-century fortified château. To the east rises the **Pic St Loup**, a high conical limestone hill that dominates the plain of Montpellier: from the hamlet of Cazevieille, to its south-west, you can climb up a path to the summit and be rewarded with magnificent views.

Four km south of St Martin, just off the D32, is the Neolithic site of **Cambous**. Archaeological diggings in the 1960s revealed a village of stone dwellings dated to c. 2000 BC: these can be visited, and are very interesting. The ceramic pots and bronze instruments that were found in them are now displayed in a museum at nearby Viols-le-Fort.

Where to eat

Les Muscardins, 19 Route des Cévennes; tel. 67 55 75 90. A

Upper-medium price

large, comfortable, family-run restaurant: ambitious modern-style variations on regional dishes. Closed February, early November.

Sommières
30250

Here in the Midi that he adores, Lawrence Durrell has chosen to spend his old age in this characterful little town on the edge of the *garrigue*, between Nîmes and Montpellier. It has a Roman bridge across the River Vidourle, a ruined feudal château, fortified gates, and charming arcaded streets and old alleys. In summer there are bullfights, and a lively festival early in August.

The **Paradis des Plantes** is probably the best shop in the south of France for medicinal and culinary herbs, as well as unusual home-made jams, herb-flavoured olive oils, and the like. The owner, herbalist Ludo Chardenon, used to run a herb stall at Arles where he was 'discovered' by Durrell, then seeking a cure for his eczema. Durrell found relief in one of Chardenon's herbs and encouraged him to start his shop in Sommières.

Where to stay
Medium price

Auberge du Pont Romain, 2 Rue Émile-Jamais; tel. 66 80 00 58. A seventeenth-century carpet factory has been converted into an unusual but attractive hotel, with a garden, large bedrooms (14) and delightful staff. The interesting dishes include *'saumon Lawrence Durrell'*, named after one habitué. Closed mid-January to mid-March.

Cévennes (1): from Alès to Mont Aigoual

The Cévennes mountain range is a region of great individual character that has acquired a certain mystique (a bit like the Camargue), due maybe to its distinctive scenery and to the personality and traditions of its hardy inhabitants. Forming the south-east flank of the Massif Central, it is a great block of schist and granite that stretches for 60 km. Its varied scenery, wild in many places, lyrically verdant in others, consists of rolling plateaus that descend gently on the northern side, but to the south are cut by deep and narrow valleys covered with forests of pine and chestnut. You can spend whole weeks hiking, riding or motoring among these lonely hills, where the villages are tiny and the one town, Florac, has a mere 2,000 people. It's an area rich in literary associations (Stevenson, Chamson, Carrière, etc.) and religious ones (don't miss the Protestant museum near Anduze).

Of the sparse population, most are the descendants of Protestants who took refuge in these remote hills after the Reformation and during the Wars of Religion (see p. 15). Today, relations with their Catholic neighbours are almost entirely free of tension: but the past centuries of persecution have left their mark, and the Protestant

The Cévennes and the Causses

Cévenols still honour their martyrs and uphold their old traditions. Their life style is frugal, hardworking, somewhat puritan. Many are peasant farmers, and some of the sheep-breeders even now practise transhumance, taking their flocks to the plateaus for the summer and down to the valleys for winter – the cohorts of sheep on the move through village streets make a picturesque sight. Life in the lone upland farmsteads can be tough in winter: the dour poverty of only forty or so years ago, when chestnut gruel was a staple diet of many families, was vividly depicted by Jean Carrière in his novel *L'Epervier de Maheux*, which won the Prix Goncourt in 1972. Today, the poverty has eased; and since the late 1960s the Cévennes have acquired a new lease of life from the arrival of middle-class immigrant 'drop-outs' from Paris and other cities – students, teachers and others, tired of the urban rat-race, who came to try their hand at rural life, hoping to make a living from pottery, weaving, bee-keeping or goat-rearing. Many soon found that the drudgery and discomfort outweighed the bucolic idyll, and they left. But the serious ones have stayed, have integrated into local life and are respected by the Cévenols. The recent recovery of this depopulating region is due in no small part to them.

It is due also to the patient work of the officials of the Parc National des Cévennes, who encourage the revival of handicrafts and local culture, and promote tourism. They organise many cross-country hikes or guided horseback tours, where you (and your horses) can spend the night in upland hostels. Details can be obtained from the information centre of the Parc National des Cévennes, Château de Florac, 48400 Florac; tel. 66 45 01 75.

This section traces a route from east to west through the southern Cévennes. The next section, Cévennes (2), follows Robert Louis Stevenson's famous journey from north to south through the northern and eastern part of the range.

Alès
30100

Set in a broad valley just east of the Cévennes foothills, Alès (population 44,343) is an old industrial town that has seen better days. Until recently it was a major coal-mining centre, but the seams are now exhausted and the mines closed; and although some new chemical firms have now arrived, it has not been proving easy to attract fresh industry. The local silk trade is also today largely defunct (it was at Alès that Louis Pasteur spent four key years of his early career, from 1865 to 1869, elaborating a remedy for diseases of the silkworm, and a memorial to him now stands near the citadel). For a memorial to the coal industry, visit the old mine 3 km west of the town that has been preserved as a museum of mining, on the spot where Benedictine monks first dug coal from the hillside in the thirteenth century: the visitor is taken on a tour of the underground galleries, and is told about local mining history.

Where to stay
Medium price

Auberge Cévenole, La Favède; tel. 66 34 12 13. In the hamlet of La Favède 15 km north-west of Alès, just west of the former mining town of La Grand-Combe: a traditional auberge in a peaceful wooded setting, with pretty decor, swimming pool, garden, and helpful staff; 16 rooms. Food average. Open mid-March to mid-November.

Where to eat
Medium price

Le Riche, 42 Place Sémard; tel. 66 86 00 33. Alès' best restaurant, with a wide range of menus; 19 adequate bedrooms, too. Closed mid-July to mid-August.

Anduze
30140

The true country of the Cévennes begins at Anduze, a pleasant little riverside town south-west of Alès, at a gap in the hills known as the Porte des Cévennes. It has long been a centre of pottery-making, and was a Protestant stronghold in the sixteenth to eighteenth centuries.

What to see

The Cévennes might seem an unlikely spot for an exotic tropical garden: but 2 km north of Anduze, along the D129, you come to the famous **Bambouseraie de Prafrance**, a huge bamboo-grove founded in 1855 by a local man and since much extended. As well as the dense areas of bamboos, growing to a height of 20 m, there are Californian sequoias and trees imported from the Far East and South America; also Japanese-style water gardens, and Asiatic-style bamboo houses on stilts. The park is immensely popular with visitors, and its shop will sell you bamboo furniture and ornaments of every kind. Prafrance's tropical decor has also been used for location shooting of a number of French feature films, notably Clouzot's *The Wages of Fear* (1953), starring Yves Montand, that was actually set in Central America but was only in part filmed there.

Four km north of Prafrance is the **Mas Soubeyran** with its fascinating **Musée du Désert**, the focal point of Protestant history and tradition in France, and an extraordinarily moving place for any visitor, whatever his or her creed. This *mas* up in the wooded Mialet Valley is a rambling seventeenth-century farmhouse that was the home of the Protestant *Camisard* leader known as 'Rolland', killed in 1704 (see p. 16). You enter down a crumbling prison-like corridor, all eerily secretive, and then visit a series of small rooms full of souvenirs of Protestant persecution – Rolland's Bible, his bedroom just as it was, and the bolthole where he hid from Royalist raiders. Four rooms in a newer wing are now a Memorial to the 'Martyrs du Désert' (that is, the wild Cévennes uplands where the Protestants took refuge during the Wars of Religion). Here there are old bibles and crucifixes, and documents relating to the 2,500 local Protestants condemned for life to the galleys, and others who were killed, imprisoned or exiled. A series of large canvases by Jeanne Lombard graphically depicts the hunted life of the seventeenth- and eighteenth-century Cévenols in their 'desert' – one is of a clandestine baptism, another of a preacher holding a service amid barren rocks. Privately run by a Protestant association, the museum exists mainly as a memorial to past heroism and suffering, and its staff admit readily that times have now changed totally – local Catholics and Protestants today intermarry, and many of the museum's visitors are Catholic. Even so, there is still something rather special about being a Protestant in this part of France. Each first Sunday in September a big open-air rally at the Mas Soubeyran attracts some 15,000 Protestants from all over the country and abroad, and the atmosphere has a true revivalist fervour. They do not forget.

Where to stay
Medium price

Les Trois Barbus; tel. 66 61 72 12. Five km north of Anduze, beside the road to the Musée du Désert, this attractive modern hotel stands dramatically on a steep slope high above the River Gardon: many of its 35 bedrooms enjoy this striking view. Pleasant gardens and swimming pool; good and varied menus; lots of English guests. The 'trois barbus' are the owner's three bearded sons, but only one now works there regularly. Open April to October.

St Jean-du-Gard

Fourteen km from Anduze up the winding Gardon Valley is this old townlet, where Stevenson ended his journey (see p. 270). It has a

Romanesque clocktower, and a thirteenth-century bridge rebuilt after recent flood damage. The Musée des Vallées Cévenoles interestingly depicts the former traditional life of the area, with details of silkworm breeding and of the exploitation of chestnut trees for their wood and their fruit – once the basis of the local economy.

Where to stay and eat Inexpensive

L'Oronge, 103 Grande Rue; tel. 66 85 30 34. Seventeenth-century coaching-house, now a modest and appealing inn. Good local food served on a patio. 36 rooms. Open April to December.

Twelve km to the south, by the D57 from Thoiras to Lasalle, the **Château de Malerargues** is today the home of a most unusual venture – the Roy Hart Theatre Group, London-originated and international, which has carved a niche for itself by presenting plays and providing drama and elocution teaching over a wide local area.

Corniche des Cévennes

This modern scenic road, narrow in places but always passable, winds over the plateau from St Jean-du-Gard to Florac on the north side of the range. There are splendid panoramic views most of the way, notably at the Col de l'Exil and the Col des Fausses. Another good road goes parallel to it, the D983, winding far below in the verdant Vallée Française (so named in the eighteenth century because good Catholics settled here, amid 'alien' Protestant territory). Note that one village on this road is called Barre, another up on the corniche is Le Pompidou, while over on the far side of this Lozère department is the village of Chirac ('We're surrounded by the Right! We're done for!' moaned one local Socialist).

Mont Aigoual

This, the summit of the sprawling Aigoual massif, is the second highest point in the Cévennes (1,567 m). Good roads (closed in snowy weather) wind up to it both from north and south, and on a clear day the views from the top are majestic – as far as the coast, even sometimes to the Alps and Pyrenees. In summer there is often cloud or haze: the best time to go is early morning.

Twenty km west of Mont Aigoual, off the D986, is the remarkable **Abîme du Bramabiau**, an abyss where the happily-named River Bonheur surges roaring out of a cave (the name comes from *'le b/oe/uf qui brame'*, the roaring bull). You must pay to visit the cave area: but when it's closed the torrent can still be seen clearly from the road above. To the south-west, amid a wild landscape, are the impressive gorges of the Dourbie and the Trévezel.

Le Vigan
30120

This pleasant little town amid the southern foothills of the Cévennes (population 4,593) has a fine promenade of tall chestnut trees and a pretty twelfth-century bridge. It also still has one or two active silk-mills, whereas in most other places the Cévennes' silk industry is now dead. The Cévenol novelist André Chamson (1900–83) spent most of his life in the Le Vigan area and described it in many books: *Les Quatre Élements* contains a good account of his boyhood hiking trips to the top of Mont Aigoual.

Where to stay
Medium price

Château du Rey; tel. 67 82 40 06. At Le Rey, 5 km east of Le Vigan, a comfortably converted thirteenth-century mansion in its own big garden, by a river. There are 12 rooms; restaurant. Open April to November.

Ganges

Ganges (population 3,584), 17 km south-east of Le Vigan, began making silk stockings in the time of Louis XIV; some half-dozen little workshops are still functioning though today their stockings are made of nylon, not silk. Seven km to the south-east is the large and beautiful **Grotte des Demoiselles**, discovered in 1770 by local peasants who thought it the home of fairies (*demoiselles*) – hence the name. Several caverns, some vast, are filled with great stalactites and stalagmites of white calcite in strange shapes.

Cirque de Navacelles

Eighteen km south-west of Le Vigan, this huge and very impressive natural crater, 350 m deep, has been formed by a loop in the River Vis which enters and leaves it by narrow gorges on either side; chalk cliffs tower all around. You can drive down into the crater by steep roads with hairpin bends from either side; or, if this would be too giddy-making, you can just admire the view from the top.

The Cévennes (2): Stevenson's route, with some detours

As he recounted in his classic *Travels with a Donkey*, Robert Louis Stevenson trekked on foot through the eastern part of the Cévennes, from north to south, in September 1878 when he was twenty-seven. Today with the aid of this book and a good map it is possible to follow his route exactly on foot (with or without a donkey); and if you are prepared to cheat a little, you can equally do most of it by car, even over the heights of Mont Lozère. The route embraces most of the points of interest in this part of the Cévennes.

Notre-Dame-des-Neiges

Stevenson began his zig-zag journey at Monastier up in the Haute-Loire, south of Le Puy: here for 65 francs he bought the donkey Modestine who was to carry his baggage. At **Langogne** (note the fine Romanesque church) he crossed the old stone bridge over the Allier, now destroyed, and then came up through the pines to the Trappist monastery of **Notre-Dame-des-Neiges**, east of La Bastide. He approached it 'with unaffected terror', so he writes – 'thus it is to have a Protestant education'. But the Presbyterian Scot soon found that these friendly Catholic monks were ready to feed and lodge him, and he judged their community to be happy and sweet-tempered, full of 'holy cheerfulness'. Of those not bound by the Trappist vows of silence, a few did attempt to convert the Protestant intruder to their Catholic faith, but Stevenson retorted amicably and enjoyed the arguments. Today, Notre-Dame is still very much in business. The buildings that Stevenson knew were destroyed by fire in 1912, but the rebuilt white-walled monastery is imposing, in its tranquil and beautiful upland setting. The monks are now fewer, and most are elderly, but they all seem cheerful and welcoming. In summer they sell their home-made wines, foods, artefacts and souvenirs to the hordes of visiting tourists, and they run a hostel for their more religious-minded visitors.

Mont Lozère

Stevenson then struck south-west through the hamlet of L'Estampe, whose narrow street 'stood full of sheep from wall to wall' (transhumance, no doubt) and where a man in a tree with a pruning-hook was 'singing the music of a *bourrée*', the Auvergne dance that can still be seen at festivals. Next the traveller entered the Cévennes proper and hiked up into the wilds of **Mont Lozère**, highest point of the whole range (1,699 m): here on a fine night he slept out under the stars, with no sound save Modestine munching at the sward and 'the indescribable quiet talk of the runnel over the stones'. Today a good scenic road winds over this empty plateau, from Le Bleymard to Le Pont-de-Montvert, and from the Chalet du Mont-Lozère (a hostel) you can hike a three-hour round-trip to the summit of Finiels, for a splendid view of the rolling heights. In winter, Mont Lozère is a popular centre for downhill and cross-country skiing.

Le pont de Montvert

Stevenson next came down into the narrow valley of the upper Tarn, to the old stone village of Le Pont de Montvert, and here at last he entered true Huguenot territory – 'I own I met these Protestants with delight and a sense of coming home . . . In crossing the Lozère I had . . . moved into the territory of a different race.' To this day, the River Tarn is roughly the boundary between the Catholic and Protestant parts of the Cévennes; and it was at Le Pont-de-Montvert in 1702 that the *Camisard* insurrection against Paris began, with the killing of the Abbé du Chayla (see p. 16). Today the village is a busy tourist centre, where the Parc National des Cévennes has created an interesting museum of local history and ecology, the Maison du Mont Lozère. The Abbé du Chayla's house exists no more, and oddly the Protestant temple is now closed: but you can still go for a meal or drink at the old Hôtel des Cévennes beside the rushing river, where Stevenson tried to flirt with the waitress, Clarisse: 'She waited the table with a heavy placid nonchalance like a performing cow; her great grey eyes were steeped in amorous languor.' This old stone auberge with its quaint rustic dining-room seems little changed since his day, although for a good, inexpensive meal I would rather recommend the **Truite Enchantée**.

Stevenson's route from here lay west to Florac. But let us first make a detour east – to **Vialas** and **Villefort**.

Where to stay and eat

Chantoiseau, 48220 Vialas; tel. 66 41 00 02. At Vialas, 19 km east of Le Pont-de-Montvert on the D998 to Alès, this 'singing-bird' is

Villefort
48800

Where to stay
and eat
Inexpensive
Florac

Where to stay
Inexpensive

Cassagnas
to St Jean-
du-Gard

certainly the best place to eat in the Cévennes. The delightful auberge is run in style by patron/chef Patrick Pagès, exuberant poet and raconteur. His regional dishes, using local produce, are superb; his 15 bedrooms are comfortable. However, this remote spot has become touristy: American groups even arrive by helicopter. Open April to October; closed Tuesday night and Wednesday.

On a main road due east of Mont Lozère, in a lovely hilly setting, this old village is a summer resort close to a big lake with plenty of watersports. Along the D906 to the north, it is worth visiting the old fortified village of **La Garde-Guérin**, and the belvedere overlooking the Chassezac gorge.

Balme; tel. 66 46 80 14. A modest village hostelry, clean and friendly, noted for its food. Open February to early November.

Stevenson's path continued west down the Tarn via Cocurès, 'sitting among vineyards and meadows and orchards thick with red apples' – and still as attractive today. The writer's next halt was Florac (population 2,104), chief town of the Cévennes but still quite a sleepy little place. It lies in a lush valley, below the high jagged rocks of the causses to the west. There's a Protestant temple, very spartan inside, and a seventeenth-century château that houses the headquarters of the Parc National. La Cabasse, in the Place Boyer, is a co-operative selling handicrafts made by Cévenols and by the new immigrant 'drop-outs'. Every September Florac is the starting and finishing point of a notable one-day marathon horserace that covers 160 km, including the summits of Monts Lozère and Aigoual. Some sixty riders take part.

Grand Hôtel du Parc; tel. 66 45 03 05. A sizeable (58 rooms) and dignified old hotel, well modernised, in a park on Florac's outskirts. Excellent service and fair cooking. Open mid-March to November.

From Florac, Stevenson struck south-east up the lovely valley of the Mimente, past St Julien-d'Arpaon, which is just below the bare hill where Jean Carrière set *L'Epervier de Maheux* – a far starker vision of the Cévennes than Stevenson's. The Scot came next to **Cassagnas**, 'a cluster of black roofs upon the hillside, in this wild valley, among chestnut gardens': down by the river a simple auberge calls itself *Le Relais Stevenson*, the manager of which swore to me that Stevenson Slept Here – but not according to my reading of the text. The trek then led on south-east, over the heights of Mont Mars, inspiring a fine description: '. . . the wildest view of all my journey. Peak upon peak, chain upon chain of hills ran surging southward, channelled and sculptured by the winter streams, feathered from head to foot with chestnuts, and here and there breaking out into a coronal of cliffs. The sun, which was far from setting, sent a drift of misty gold across the hilltops, but the valleys were already plunged in a profound and quiet shadow.' That scene is unchanged today, but the next village that Stevenson came to, **St Germain-de-Calberte**, has changed: he found it plagued by phylloxera and could get no wine; I, 110 years later, found plenty of local plonk, but was plagued by a rock band called Stress, playing noisily in the tiny square. So much for rural remoteness. After this, Stevenson descended to the edge of the plain at St Jean-du-Gard, and sold the now ailing Modestine. Their 190-km journey had taken them twelve days to complete. In this pleasant Cévenol village, well worth a visit today, his story ends abruptly.

The Causses and the Gorges du Tarn

'Les Causses' is the name given to the vast limestone plateaus that form the south-western part of the Massif Central, west of the Cévennes and south of the River Lot: sheep graze on them, but few people live there. These *causses* are lower and flatter than the high plateaus of the Cévennes, but they are transected by deep gorges, notably those of the Rivers Tarn and Jonte. From Florac, you can drive vertiginously up a narrow switchback road on to the **Causse Méjean**, the most empty and desolate of these plateaus, stretching for 30 km between the gorges of the Jonte and Tarn.

Aven Armand

Near the southern edge of the Causse Méjean is this huge, spectacular underground cavern, discovered in 1987 by a local man, Louis Armand: it is 35 m deep and 100 m long, as large as any cathedral, and is filled with gigantic stalagmites in a variety of strange shapes, giving the impression of a petrified forest.

Four km west, at **Hyelzas**, an old stone farmhouse has been converted into a modest rural museum, to give an idea of life on the *causse* in former times. You can see how the living quarters were heated in winter by the cows in the stable below.

Meyrueis
48150

This big upland village in the upper Jonte Valley has several hotels and makes a good excursion centre for the Tarn/Aigoual area. Eight km west, in the Causse Noir, is the **Grotte de Dargilan**, a huge cavern almost as impressive as Aven Armand: you can make a guided tour (Easter to 1 November) of its various sections, some filled with curious stalagmites.

Where to stay
Upper-
medium price

Château d'Ayres; tel. 66 45 60 10. A converted twelfth-century monastery outside the village, now a comfortable and welcoming hotel (24 rooms); candlelit dinners are served in the lovely floodlit garden, but the food is nothing special. Open April to mid-October.

Medium price

Renaissance; tel. 66 45 60 19. In the village, a charming sixteenth-century manor, with a garden; large rooms (20), courteous service, good regional cooking. Open mid-March to mid-November, New Year.

Inexpensive

Family; tel. 66 45 60 02. In the village, a sympathetic little family-run Logis de France, with good home cooking; 48 rooms. Open mid-March to early November.

Gorges de la Jonte

A good road follows the Jonte through its gorge, from Meyrueis down to Le Rozier where the river joins the Tarn. There are caves in the north cliffside 5 km west of Meyrueis, and further on the river disappears below ground, to re-emerge at Les Douzes (here there's an excellent inexpensive restaurant, called **Les Douzes**). From Le Rozier, sturdy walkers can go on splendid hiking excursions through the high rocky corniches of the Causse Méjean, in the angle between the Jonte and Tarn gorges: you climb first to the ruined hamlet of Capluc with its towering crag, then either hike east to the great rocks of the Vase de Chine and Vase de Sèvres, or north to the toothy peak of Cinglegros. The views over the gorges are great, and the paths are well signposted: but these treks take many hours and are not for the inexperienced or the vertigo-prone. You will need to wear strong climbing shoes, and to take a good local map and some food and water.

Gorges du Tarn

France's most famous gorge is not as vast nor as deep as the Verdon canyon in Provence (see p. 175): but its constantly changing vistas, its many-coloured rocks in strange shapes, and the old castles and quaint villages that line its way, make it even more spectacular and interesting. The gorge was formed by a geological fault separating the Sauveterre and Méjean *causses*, through which the Tarn, rising in Mont Lozère, has thrust its way. The gorge begins at **Ispagnac**, north-west of Florac, and winds for 45 km to Le Rozier: a good tourist road follows its entire length, close to the riverbed, offering dramatic and ever-changing views of the red and ochre cliffs above, over 400 m high at some points, and of the chaos of rocks that have slid into the valley. At some points, including Le Rozier, Les Vignes and Ste Enimie, you can hire canoes or light inflatable boats for trips along parts of the river.

The best views of the gorge are from points above it up on the *causses*, notably the Point Sublime and the Roc des Hourtous (see p. 275), and these you can reach without going down into the gorge. Alternatively, you can drive along its bed, in either direction. If you start at **Le Rozier** and motor upstream, you go first down a fairly broad stretch, below the ruined Castle of Blanquefort and the fierce crag of Cinglegros, like a finger pointing skyward, to reach **Les Vignes**, a village at a crossroads amid vineyards. Here a road winding up the cliffside to the west will take you to the **Point Sublime**, aptly named for its grandiose view over the curving canyon. North from Les Vignes, the road in the gorge leads past the Pas du Souci, where the river almost vanishes beneath a great jumble of rocks, caused by an earthquake in AD 580. (Legend has it that Ste Enimie here chased Satan along the cliff and asked the rocks to prevent his escape. So they provided a landslide, and one big rock, the Sourde, fell on him: but the wily Devil slipped out from beneath and made his way back to Hell.)

Next the gorge widens again into the curving **Cirque des Baumes**, with its tints of blue, grey and black as well as red and yellow. It then narrows into **Les Détroits**, a dramatic defile of high vertical cliffs. At **La Malène**, a steep, narrow side-road loops you up on to the Causse Méjean, where a right turn leads to the **Roc des Hourtous**, maybe the best of all viewpoints over the gorge and its rocky precipices. Upstream from La Malène, St Chély is a pleasant village near to caves and to two *cirques* with high reddish cliffs. Further on the gorge becomes shallower and gentler, reaching **Ste Enimie**, a village set amid terraced orchards of almond and peach; there's an old monastery, and a tiny folklore museum. At **Castelbouc** is a ruined clifftop castle with a strange history, recounted in a *son-et-lumière* in summer. At **Quézac** there's a Gothic bridge – and here the gorge is virtually at an end.

Where to stay
Upper-medium price

Château de la Caze, La Malène, 48210 Ste Enimie; tel. 66 48 51 01. At the foot of the gorge, in a big garden, a finely converted fifteenth-century manor, with modern comforts and authentic antique furnishings; distinguished cooking and good service. The 13 rooms are mostly very large. Open May to mid-October.

Mende
48000

The Lozère department (population 78,000), which includes the Tarn gorges and most of the Cévennes, is the least inhabited in France, with far more sheep than humans – and Mende (12,113 people) is its metropolis. It is on the River Lot, spanned here by a fourteenth-century Gothic bridge. A ring boulevard has replaced the old ramparts, but the fourteenth-century cathedral (much rebuilt after 1600) still stands, amid a network of quaint old alleyways. The Musée Fabre is devoted to local folklore and archaeology, while the Co-opérative des Artisans de la Lozère, 4 Rue de l'Ange, exhibits and sells handicrafts and hand-made furniture from the region. There's a festival in July. La Diva is a disco popular with the young.

Where to stay and eat
Medium price

Lion d'Or, 12 Blvd. Britexte; tel. 66 49 16 46. A solid, well-modernised hostelry with a garden and swimming pool, fine views, friendly service and interesting regional cooking; 40 rooms. Closed January.

Inexpensive

France, 9 Blvd. Arnault; tel. 66 65 00 04. A neat, efficient, well modernised *Logis de France* with 28 rooms; good local food pleasantly served in a beamed dining-room. Closed mid-December to end January.

Marvejols
48100

Lozère's second city (pop. 6,013) is to Mende what Leningrad is to Moscow, or Los Angeles to New York, but that's where the parallel ends: it's a relaxed little place, with paved, traffic-free alleys within ancient fortified gateways, on the N9 that winds over the glorious wide uplands from the Midi to Clermont-Ferrand. You might like to seek out Denis Siorat, who is keeping alive the craft of making old musical instruments such as the *vielle* (hurdy-gurdy) and sometimes has some to sell.

Where to stay

Gare et Rochers, Place de la Gare; tel. 66 32 10 58. Simple and serviceable, with scenic views. Restaurant. 30 rooms. Closed mid-January to mid-March.

Where to eat
Medium price

Viz Club; tel. 66 32 17 69. An elegant place by the N9 going north, with careful country cooking and a garden for summer dining. Closed January.

'Les Loups du Gévaudan'

This open-air zoo full of gentle wolves, by the N9 some 3 km north of Marvejols, is named after a wolf of olden days that was anything but gentle. The area north of Mende used to be known as the Gévaudan, and here in the 1760s a savage creature, the notorious 'Bête du Gévaudan', wrought terrible havoc, devouring some fifty men, women and children in three years. Now a journalist and lupophile from Montpellier, Gérard Manatory, has created this 101-hectare zoo in a lovely wild upland setting, and has filled it with thirty-five friendly, frisky, fluffy wolves from Siberia, Poland, Hungary and Canada. They treat him affectionately, and love playing games with his sheepdog, Roc – and the visitors flock in, attracted in part by the zoo's provocative name with its misleading hint of horror. 'Wolves are never savage or dangerous, that's a false myth,' says Manatory; 'the Loup du Gevaudan was probably a hyena, and probably some homicidal criminal had trained it to attack and devour.' Or are his lovely creatures really sheep in wolves' clothing?

Useful Reading

Non-fiction

Mavis Gallant, *The Affair of Gabrielle Russier* (1971). The true story of a woman teacher in Marseille, persecuted to the point of suicide; sheds grim light on local society in the 1960s. Long, brilliant introduction by Ms Gallant.

Graham Greene, *J'Accuse: The Dark Side of Nice* (1982). This polemical pamphlet is another indictment of local society, in this case the Nice mafia and its hold over senior local politicians.

Patrick Howarth, *When the Riviera was Ours* (1977). A lighter study of the British on the Riviera. Readable, wilfully chauvinistic.

Michael Jacobs, *A Guide to Provence* (1988). A loving portrait mainly of art and history. Erudite, but not always factually accurate.

Emmanuel Le Roy Ladurie, *Montaillou* (1978). Based on a fourteenth-century text, a brilliant and lively portrait of Pyrenéan village life in the time of the Cathars.

Archibald Lyall, *The Companion Guide to the South of France* (1963). An evocative personal view of Provence and Languedoc as they were in the early 1960s. Partially updated in newer editions.

Michelin's *green guides* to Provence, Côte d'Azur, Gorges du Tarn, Pyrénées, Roussillon, and annual *red guide* to French hotels and restaurants. Very detailed; superb maps and town plans.

James Pope-Hennessy, *Aspects of Provence* (1952). A classic travel book, highly personal and vivid, though dated and a bit purple.

Tobias Smollett, *Travels through France and Italy* (1766). The arch-francophobe's truculent diatribe. He stayed mainly in Nice, and is funny and perceptive about his visit. He even liked some aspects of it.

Robert Louis Stevenson, *Travels with a Donkey* (1879). His illuminating account of a hike through the Cévennes.

Laurence Wylie, *Village in the Vaucluse* (1977, 3rd edition). An American sociologist's penetrating study of the village of Roussillon, mainly in the early 1950s, plus some later visits.

Fiction

Michael Arlen, *The Green Hat* (1924). Entertaining picture of the zany life of expatriates on the Riviera.

Henri Bosco, *Le Mas Théotime* (1944). This is the best of his novels of rural life in the Durance Valley.

Jean Carrière, *L'Epervier de Maheux* (1972). A powerful study of peasant poverty in the Cévennes, which won the Prix Goncourt.

André Chamson, *Les Quatre Éléments* and *Les Hommes de la Route* (1927): these are among the best of his novels about the Cévennes, less gloomy and metaphysical than Carrière's, but also less gripping.

Cyril Connolly, *The Rock Pool* (1936), a sardonic portrait of decadent expatriate Bohemian society on the Riviera.

Alphónse Daudet, *Lettres de mon Moulin* (1868) and *Tartarin de Tarascon* (1872): the best known of his satiric portraits of Provençal life and character.

Lawrence Durrell, *Monsieur or the Prince of Darkness* (1974), a typically lurid extravaganza, set mainly in the Avignon area.

F. Scott Fitzgerald, *Tender is the Night* (1934), the best of all novels about the Riviera smart set in the 1920s.

Jean Giono, *Un de Baumugnes* (1929) and *Regain*: among the best of his early lyrical studies of rural Provence; *Le Hussard sur le Toit* (1951) is a harsher book, about the 1848 cholera epidemic.

Frédéric Mistral, *Mirèio (Mireille)* (1859): his epic is available in a bilingual French/Provençal edition, but not in English.

Marcel Pagnol, the *Marius* drama trilogy (1929-36); *Jean de Florette* and *Manon des Sources* (1963): describing life in Marseille, his memoirs, and his studies of rural life near Marseille, these are all worth reading and have been translated.

Index